MW00608367

Tacoma's Dry Goods and Wet Goods: Nineteenth Century Jewish Pioneers

Todah Rabbah — Thank you!

By Deborah K. Freedman

Deb Freedman

Tacoma Historical Society Press
Tacoma, Washington

Copyright © 2016 by Deborah K. Freedman and Tacoma Historical Society

Published by Tacoma Historical Society Press, Tacoma, Washington

ISBN: 978-0-9846234-5-7

Library of Congress Control Number 2016945736

Editing by Dr. Dale Wirsing and Herb Levine

Indexing by Marie Hayden

Printed in Tacoma, Washington by LaserWriting

Cover design by Chris Fiala Erlich

All rights reserved. No part of this publication may be reproduced or transmitted in any form or by any means, electronic or mechanical, including photocopy, recording, or any information storage or retrieval system, without permission in writing from the publisher.

Portions of this material have previously been published in the Washington State Historical Society's *Columbia Magazine*, Tacoma Historical Society's *City of Destiny Newsletter*, and the *Western States Jewish Bulletin*.

Disclaimer: The author has compiled biographies to the best of her ability, using available sources, but most often without the assistance or collaboration of relatives. Errors and omissions are probable. Place names have typically been quoted as they were found in period documentation, and do not reflect modern geo-political changes.

The author, Deborah Freedman, is solely responsible for the research and writing of this publication. The author hereby irrevocably and unconditionally agrees, to the fullest extent permitted by law, to defend, indemnify and hold harmless Tacoma Historical Society, its officers and directors, from and against any and all claims, liabilities, losses and expenses (including reasonable attorney's fees) directly, indirectly, wholly or partially arising from or in connection with any act or omission of the author in supervising and overseeing the execution of this publication.

Preface

This book began as a simple project to computerize the records of the Home of Peace Cemetery, while creating a listing of the tombstone inscriptions. In sifting through maps and cemetery records I determined there were 73 unmarked graves, many known only as a name on a three-by-five card. This represented over ten percent of the cemetery! I began researching those names, locating newspaper obituaries and death records. I am honored to report that Tacoma's Jewish community placed monuments on those graves in October of 2000. The initial book of inscriptions was completed.

As I studied the constitution of the cemetery association, published in 1891, I became curious about the forty original members. I began looking for their names in histories of Tacoma. I was amazed at how little information I found in published sources. Why did history books overlook Tacoma's Jewish pioneers?

As my research progressed and I got a feeling for who these early "Israelites" were, I discovered the vast majority were simple merchants and clerks. They owned a store, partnered with their in-laws, and briefly prospered. The majority came around the time of the railroad boom in the late 1880s, and their wealth grew with the city. Weren't they prominent enough?

Then I realized the primary reason for their exclusion. When Tacoma's economy crashed in 1893, many whose businesses were dependent on the economy left town – most with the bitter taste of bankruptcy. They came, they tried, and they moved on. Even those who stayed in Tacoma another decade almost exclusively chose to retire in San Francisco. Of the forty original members, only sixteen were buried in the cemetery which they helped to create. Four were buried in unmarked graves. None of them have any direct descendants still living in the Tacoma area – not even one. Compounding matters, a surprising number left no descendants at all, no matter where they eventually lived.

I have also struggled to determine who was Jewish, finally deciding to include only those who actively participated in Tacoma's Jewish community. This meant anyone with known membership in a Jewish organization, attendance at a Jewish event, or anyone buried in the Jewish cemetery. This also meant excluding perhaps up to one-third or even one-half of Tacoma's early Jewish citizens who either weren't observant, or weren't mentioned as officers or committee chairs. Excellent minutes were available from the Ladies' Judith Montefiore Society – the forerunner of the Sisterhood, and a few from the *B'nai B'rith,* but original temple membership lists have not been located – in all liklihood sealed in the cornerstone of the second temple building.

Writing about Tacoma's history is very much like assembling a jigsaw puzzle. Through the years authors have worked on parts of the puzzle which interested them. Whether they wrote about the Chinese, Japanese, Germans or Norwegians; union workers, school teachers, firemen, brewers or architects; all have added their pieces, filling in color and bringing details to the overall picture.

This is my attempt to add one more pigment to the picture. I've included the pieces I've found so far, although a great many of them are missing. I've only added the pieces up to 1900, in order to keep the size of the data reasonable. (Hopefully someone else will complete additional volumes.) My primary source has been historical newspapers, an approach which unfortunately creates a distorted view filtered by income and political affiliation. Publicity typically emphasized crime and lawsuits, yet advertising and social mentions provided vital information and insights.

I've also focused on the genealogies of the families, as that is my interest, and I think history is about people and their stories. Perhaps others will add to the total picture. By working together, we will help to create a more complete image of what Tacoma was like in the late 1800s – a colorful community made up of immigrants and natives, dreamers and schemers, power brokers and paupers.

Acknowledgments

Researchers are taught to do interviews first, driven by the realization that "the dead will wait, the living won't." I was fortunate to spend time learning from the following people, *zichronam l'vracha* (may their memories be a blessing) who did not live to see publication of this work: Molly Cone, Jerry Donion, Julia Eulenberg, Sieg Friedman, Caroline Gallacci, Andrew Greendorfer, Lucille Feist Hurst, Stanley Mamlock, Athlyeen Nicholson, Gary Fuller Reese, O. Robert Reichenbach, Simon Rose, Rabbi Richard Rosenthal, Hilde Slotnick, Randy Stehle and Ernest Stiefel.

Editorial team – Dusty Gorman, Rabbi Bruce Kadden, Patricia Miraldi
Northwest Room/Special Collections, Tacoma Public Library
Gaffney Funeral Home (Buckley-King records)
Rally squad – Honorary cousin Harold Friedman, practical friend Debbie Lasko, loving sister Rita Phillips (of blessed memory), mother Adah Fausnaugh and my dedicated and patient Hebrew students.

During my nearly twenty years of research I have corresponded with many, many researchers and relatives who have willingly shared their information. I readily admit I did not keep organized records, never dreaming my project would grow to this extent. Here is my attempt to thank as many as I can. I apologize in advance for the omission of so many others.

Tim Baker (Bellingham)
Ed Ball (Ball)
Jim Bennett (Kempen)
Joyce Berman (Heinemann)
Anita Brew (Elken)
Kathleen Clemence (Davis/Packscher)
Sonia Cook (Packscher)
Joan Curtis (Steilacoom)
Liz & Derek Ernest (Gallewski)
Stephen Falk (Auberbach)
Nancy Ferguson (Ball/Cohn)
Nancy Finken (Davis)
Victoria Fisch (Toklas)
Isabelle Fleuraud (Soulal)
David Flood (Holland)
Gary Flynn (Breweries)
Ann L. Fuller (Jacobs)

Ann Goodsell (D.P. Lewis)
Kay Harris (Loeb)
Carol Olivier (Langert)
Judith Parker Hindin (Winkleman)
Mike Hockett (Eckstein)
Norm Kagan (Alaska)
Patty Koenigsberger (Guatemala)
Bettina Lyons (Donau)
Mike Moyses (Moyses)
Chris Powell (Danziger)
Julie Roberts (Cheim)
Merilyn Rummelsburg (Wallerstein)
Doug Salin (Gross)
Edward Slottow (Hoffman)
Frank Sperling (Imes)
Bill Tivol (Reichenbach)
Patti Winkleman (Winkleman)

Publication and design of this book is made possible by a generous grant from the Tacoma Jewish Community Fund. In addition, more than a dozen individual donations supported printing and free distribution to libraries, archives, and non-profit organizations. Thank you for your generosity and support – financially and personally.

Chuck and Sue Burget
Adria Farber
Harold & Jennifer Friedman
Howard and Alice Greenwood
Jonathan Hurst
Herman and Barbara Kleiner

Pam Mayer
Nancy Powell and Paul Kirschner
Sigrid Elenga and Steve Smyth
Jack and Lilly Warnick

Three anonymous couples

Table of Contents

Biographies

Dedicated to the memory of those whose stories ended too soon.

Tacoma Timeline

Tacoma Events		Jewish Events
Nisqually House established	1833	
	1845	Adolph Friedman?
Fort Steilacoom established	1849	
Puget Sound Indian War	1855	
	1858	Pincus & Packscher
	1863	Heyman Goodtime
Job Carr claim in Old Tacoma	1865	Seraphina Pincus
Commencement City becomes Tacoma	1869	
	1870	"Old" Meyer Kaufman
Terminus of Northern Pacific RR	1873	Louis Wolff
New Tacoma townsite laid out		Levin Brothers
First newspaper	1874	
First church built	1875	
	1878	Gross Brothers
Becomes county seat	1880	
(Population 938)	1882	Holiday dinner, 40?
Old & New Tacoma merged	1884	Wallerstein wedding
Chinese expulsion (Population 5,936)	1885	Weinberg wedding
Switchback over Cascades (County population 11,994)	1887	Magnus wedding
Building era	1888	Cemetery association formed
Statehood	1889	
	1890	J. Montefiore & IOBB Claimed 600 Jewish residents
(Population 35,860)		
	1891	150 at services
(Population 45,789)v	1892	200 at services Harris shooting
National Banking Panic (Population 52,329)	1893	Temple Beth Israel Claimed 100 members
Pacific Avenue paved	1895	Abe Gross suicide
Klondike Gold Rush	1897	Gross brothers split
	1899	Julius Friedman wedding
(Tacoma census 37,000)	1900	Five are confirmed

The history of Tacoma's Jewish community and Tacoma itself are closely intertwined. Throughout the 1860s Pierce County's population lived mostly in Steilacoom, as the future townsite of Tacoma was still mostly covered in trees. Steilacoom's Jewish population was comprised of three families related by marriage – Pincus, Packscher and Goodtime. Altogether they represented about five percent of the population. By 1870 Steilacoom's census included just over 300 names. Washington Territory was under the guidance of a Jewish governor, Edward S. Salomon, who brought a cluster of Jewish families to Olympia.

Tacoma in 1873

When Tacoma sprouted a few shacks and taverns on the waterfront of what is now "Old Tacoma," a few more Jews arrived – Kaufman, Ostheim and Levin. Louis Wolff opened Tacoma's third business – less than a month after the Northern Pacific Railroad announced that Tacoma would be the western terminus of its northern line. As Tacoma grew, so did the Jewish population.

1873 brought a national depression, causing the near-failure of the Northern Pacific Railroad, vital to Tacoma's development. The rest of the nation struggled economically over the next 25 years. Meanwhile, Tacoma was an anomaly, growing in steady spurts and attracting population from all across the country.

Street Names – 1880s and Today

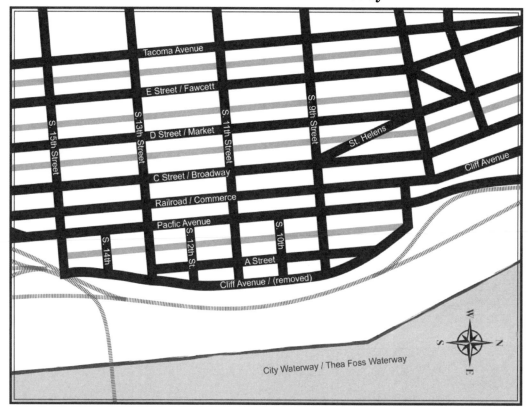

When the streets of "New Tacoma" were first laid out, several Jewish merchants opened shops on what would become the major thoroughfare, Pacific Avenue. Their goods were shipped up from San Francisco, so young men from that city followed the trade north. With the arrival of the railroad came the ability to bring merchandise overland, so still more Jewish merchants followed.

Tacoma was very much a rough-and-tumble man's world in those days, and the stores reflected that. Shops on Pacific sold cigars and tobacco, liquor, shoes and boots, liquor, clothing and liquor. A few barbershops and general stores were scattered in between. The general stores sold "dry goods." Liquor stores sold "wet goods." And the Jewish merchants sold much of it.

In 1884 when the two sections of Tacoma merged, so did the scattered families of Tacoma's Jewish community. Descriptions of Louis and Carrie Wallerstein's wedding reception filled newspaper columns for several days. Families gathered from Olympia, Steilacoom, and Tacoma – both old and new. For the High Holidays it was necessary to rent a hall.

The following year, the Chinese Expulsion brought out the good and bad in everyone. Rabbi Richard Rosenthal once told this author he thought this was the beginning of the decline of Tacoma's reputation. It definitely gained the nation's attention. Even today the "Tacoma Method" is described on a placard in the museum at Ellis Island. Colonel Meyer Kaufman's participation in the Committee of Fifteen was enough to launch his political career, short-lived as it was.

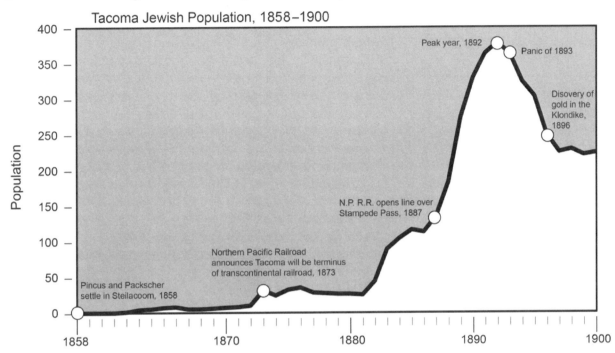

Tacoma Jewish Population, 1858–1900

Along with the growing city, Tacoma's organized Jewish population grew. A cemetery was established in 1888, followed by a religious school in 1890. The women provided charity when needed, the men organized a *B'nai B'rith* chapter, and they all danced at the Harmony Club.

The late 1880s and early '90s in Tacoma were dubbed "the building era." Tacoma's newspaper columns were filled with mentions of new buildings going up at a furious pace. Jews built, too, with some investing in housing and becoming landlords. The ladies formed the Temple Aid Society to raise building funds and Tacoma's first synagogue was dedicated in September of 1893. Several business blocks in Tacoma built around that time carried the names of their Jewish builders – Kaufman, Wolff, Levin, Isaacs and Gross.

But the boom was a false one, built on borrowed East Coast money. As the economy tightened in the East, it failed in the West and a banking panic ensued. During 1893–1894 Tacoma lost half of her population. Jewish merchants, dependent upon the economy, left in droves. Even with a boost from the Klondike, it wasn't until ten years later, when the temple mortgage was burned, that the community again considered hiring a rabbi.

Tacoma's Jewish community also has had its share of political and financial defeats. Meyer Kaufman was the first candidate to be defeated for state treasurer. Adolph Packscher gradually lost his fleet of sailing ships. Isaac Pincus was briefly a millionaire hops merchant. In fact, Tacomans were almost known more for their failures than their successes. Herman Klaber's name, if known at all, was mostly associated with his death on the *Titanic*. His death was noted more in the San Francisco papers than in Tacoma. Most citizens of Tacoma today have never heard of the Gross Brothers' "San Francisco Store," or their free public kindergarten, yet nod their heads in comprehension when told the great store was torn down to build the Pantages Theater.

The vast majority of Tacoma's early Jewish pioneers were German, or of German descent. Some came from German-speaking, Russian-ruled Poland. Others came from areas of Prussia that became part of the German federal state in 1871. Several families were French Alsatians who spoke a Rhenish style of German. A handful of families came from Hungary or Austria, depending on time period and border changes. Many may have spoken Yiddish, but their native tongue was typically German. The vast majority came as young men, often joining a relative or sibling, but leaving their parents and family behind. Some were able to return to Germany – perhaps to visit, perhaps to find a German bride.

Germania Hall,
construction led by Charles Reichenbach
From the collection of the author

Traditionally barred from the professional fields of law and medicine, and prohibited by the guild system from apprenticing as craftsmen, with few exceptions Tacoma's Jewish pioneers came from generations of merchant families. Aided by literacy, Jews had become clerical middle men between Polish and German nobility and common farmers. They also needed careers that were highly mobile. Their ability to sell out their store of merchandise and quickly start over in another city gave them a distinct advantage in the changing economies and opportunities of Europe and the United States.

After emigration to the United States they continued doing what they had been doing in Europe – or what they had wanted to do. The handful who chose military service likely did so because it meant a step up for them.

These Jewish merchants tended to cluster in new and growing areas of the United States, where the community had not yet drawn strict social lines. Typically they were welcomed, not just tolerated, as they brought much-needed retail development, and accompanying advertising dollars. They also tended to join civic organizations and contribute publicly to charities. (Only a generation or two later, in the '20s and '30s with the revival of the Klan, did anti-Semitism gain solid footing.) If anything, Tacoma's early Jewish merchants kept themselves socially separated by hiring Jewish relatives, forming Jewish social and religious groups, and by choosing Jewish spouses. Those who didn't dropped out of the Jewish narrative.

A good number of Tacoma's Jewish merchants were second-generation Americans. They brought with them a wide variety of experiences, typically living in several different states before their arrival in the Northwest. Morris Dobrin's first children were born a few blocks away from Richmond's infamous slave market. Samuel Loeb lived through several yellow fever epidemics in Memphis – his father did not. Archie Ash's father was Rabbi Abraham Joseph Ash, considered to be the nation's first Orthodox rabbi; while Jennie Posner's father, Rabbi Elkan Herzman, was fired twice for his modern views – in Brooklyn in 1866 and in Chicago in 1871.

Merchant families were connected by a vast international communication network of Jewish business and family relationships. On the West Coast those relationships were at first coastal connections – from San Francisco to Portland to Victoria. If suppliers in San Francisco started receiving large orders for merchandise to be shipped to Tacoma, Jewish merchants took note. If a family in Tacoma had several daughters of marriageable age, they made extended social visits to relatives in other coastal cities. In short, everyone knew everyone.

They brought with them to Tacoma their love of music, their knowledge of grains, hops and brewing, and their skills as merchants. They also quickly became used to living without the strict supervision of a rabbi. As Jonathan Sarna wrote in *American Judaism*, Jews came to America seeking freedom *of* religion and freedom *from* religion.

So we begin at the beginning, or at what we think is the beginning...

Steilacoom Was First

There's a saying that when the "first" Jewish settler sailed into port, another Jew was at the dock to meet him. For every documented Jewish pioneer, there were likely several others whose names and stories have been lost to history.

Isaac Pincus stayed in one place long enough to tell his tale himself. In 1908 he gave an interview on the occasion of the 50th anniversary of his arrival in Steilacoom. He told reporters of stepping off his ship onto the wharf on August 10, 1858, after an unsatisfactory trip to the Fraser River gold fields of British Columbia. This came on the heels of a sojourn in Nevada City, California. He and his partner Adolph Packscher unloaded their crates of remaining merchandise in Steilacoom, intending to head overland for the remainder of their journey back to California.

It was perhaps fitting that the pair landed in Steilacoom – a town known today as a town of "firsts." It became the first county seat of Pierce County in 1853 when Washington Territory was separated from Oregon. By 1858 Steilacoom boasted the area's first port, post office, school, jail, court house, Protestant church, and brewery. (Only decades later would Tacoma surpass Steilacoom's prominence.)

But the town needed merchandise. Pincus was able to sell much of his inventory right on the dock. When he was offered $6 for a pair of boots, he knew he had found his new home. Packscher hurried to San Francisco to replenish their stock, while Pincus stayed to rent a storefront and settle down.

Courtesy of Steilacoom Historical Museum Association

Growing towns also needed women, and Jewish men needed Jewish brides. Isaac Pincus married in Victoria, B.C., on Christmas Day of 1864. His bride was Seraphina Packscher, cousin of his partner Adolph. She was living with her divorced uncle A.J. Brunn, as was her younger sister Annie. Both had arrived at a time when Victoria was bringing "bride ships" around the horn, a practice other cities would later imitate.

The following week Seraphina's sister, Annie Packscher, married Jacob W. Davis, a Jewish merchant who was packing freight into the Caribou area. Their son Marcus was born the following year, the first white child born in the area. A decade later, desperately trying to feed a growing family, that same J.W. Davis would ask his supplier, Levi Strauss, to file a patent for him for his invention of a rivet on denim pants.

Pincus and Packscher joined with a non-Jewish third partner, E.A. Light, in operating a lumber mill and building a wharf. With their combined resources they incorporated a woolen mill in 1868, manufacturing woolen items and bartering and selling wool. Isaac Pincus was on his way to becoming a commodities broker. They also began building a fleet of sailing ships, reducing the costs of bringing their merchandise from San Francisco, and sending lumber and other products around the world.

Isaac invested in the community in other ways. He served on juries, as road commissioner, and even took a turn as County Coroner. Pincus and Packscher were both granted U.S. citizenship in May of 1865. In 1871, after the county seat was transferred to Tacoma, Isaac Pincus was elected as the town of Steilacoom's first treasurer. Later he served on the city council in Tacoma.

Doing business anywhere has its challenges, and Steilacoom was no exception. In 1878 Isaac was among seven other defendants who were sued by Allen Weir over the use of the town's printing press. (The matter came to a halt when one of the vital parts of the printing press ended up in the bay.) In 1874 Pincus and Packscher split from Light, and in 1883 Packscher split from Pincus, with both dissolutions sorted out by the courts.

Pincus moved to Tacoma in the early 1880s and began investing in real estate and erecting much-needed town buildings. He also entered heavily into the fields of growing and brokering hops. By some accounts he had to be convinced to leave his beloved Steilacoom. In other accounts he had the business acumen to see the opportunities in Tacoma.

Sarah Packscher   *Adolph Packscher*
Courtesy of Steilacoom Historical Museum Association

Adolph Packscher was not as attached to the Pacific Northwest. When he left Isaac Pincus in Steilacoom in 1858 and headed to San Francisco to purchase merchandise, he started a pattern that he would repeat many times over the next 25 years.

He did more than purchase supplies in San Francisco. On September 14, 1862, Adolph wed Sarah Goodtime. They were married in San Francisco's Temple Emanu-El, by Rabbi Julius Eckman, just before Eckman accepted a rabbinic position in Portland, Oregon. Their son Charley was born in Steilacoom the following August – the first known Jewish child born in Pierce County. Sarah's brother, Heyman Goodtime, soon joined them in Steilacoom.

However, by 1870 Adolph and Sarah had returned to San Francisco, building a large home on Sacramento Street. Unlike Isaac Pincus, who had no known family on the West Coast, Adolph and Sarah had relatives in San Francisco – Packscher and Brunn cousins and Goodtime siblings. Adolph operated a store in San Francisco, again selling a wide variety of merchandise.

The couple returned briefly to Steilacoom in the mid-1870s for the birth of their son Henry Buck Packscher. Henry was named for Adolph's latest sailing acquisition – the bark *Henry Buck*, built in Maine in 1852. Packscher also had an interest in the *Dashing Wave*, the *Two Brothers* and the *Melrose*.

Oil painting of the bark Henry Buck
Courtesy of Steilacoom Historical Museum Association

Adolph's remaining children were born in San Francisco between 1878 and 1888. His eldest son Charley stayed in the Northwest and in the early 1880s operated a store for his father in Tacoma. By 1885 the store was in financial trouble, although the closeout sale continued for over a year.

The fleet of ships deteriorated, gradually going to creditors. The last two were cut up for scrap in the 1890s and used as coal hulks.

SEATTLE, Wash., Dec. 9.—The Oregon Improvement Company's antiquated bark, Henry Buck, around which clusters a memory of forty-three years of navigation in various parts of the world, is to be torn to pieces and its old copper sold to a junk man. For half a dozen years the Henry Buck has been used as a collier, but never venturing upon a sea voyage.

San Francisco Call December 9, 1895

Adolph died in San Francisco in 1899, leaving his wife Sarah with nine living children, ages eleven through thirty-six. None of his three grandchildren left descendants. Their house on Sacramento Street still stands.

Heyman Goodtime also didn't have descendants to share his story, or live to give pioneer interviews. However, he took the unusual step of enlisting in the U.S. Army, 1st Texas Mounted Rifles, in 1852 when he was about 20, surely not realizing he was leaving valuable military records for future researchers. He served for three years on the Mexican/Texas border, and lost his arm in the performance of his frontier duties. His military pension records used the spelling Goethiem, while newspaper articles more accurately used Goetheim.

NOTICE.

THE undersigned, H. Goetheim being about to start for the Crimea, publishes the following, that his friends may know where he is gone to.

Copy.

ARMY OF THE U. S.

TO ALL WHOM IT MAY CONCERN: Know ye, that Heyman Goetheim a private of Captain and Brev't Lieut. Col. B. J. Roberts' company C., of the first Regiment of Mounted Rifles, who was enlisted the eighteenth day of June, one thousand eight hundred and fifty-two, to serve five years, is hereby discharged from the army of the U. S., in consequence of Surgeon's certificate, of disability.

Said Heyman Goetheim was born in Leipsic in the State Poland, is 24 years of age 5 feet 7 inches high, fair complexion, blue eyes, brown hair, and by occupation when enlisted, a glasier.

Given under my hand at Fort McIntosh, Texas, this 9th day of October, in the year of our Lord, 1855.

W. W. LORING,
Lieut. Col. and Brev't Col. U. S. A.
Commanding Post.

CHARACTER.

This soldier lost his arm in the performance of duty. He was a sober, willing soldier, and during three years of hard frontier duty he was faithful. His character is good.

B. J. ROBERTS,
Lt. Col. U. S. A.

Witness:
A. YAGER.

San Antonio Ledger February 9, 1856
University of North Texas Libraries, The Portal to Texas History

In 1853 Heyman married Wilhelmine (Louisa) Sigelmann in Bexar, Texas, near San Antonio, under the anglicized name of Goodtime. The couple made their way to San Francisco a few years later, along with Heyman's sisters Sarah and Emelie (Rosenburg.)

Heyman's sister Sarah Goodtime married Adolph Packscher in San Francisco in September of 1862. A year later Heyman and Louisa turned up in Steilacoom, making several substantial land purchases in the summer of 1863. There they ran a general store and bought and sold real estate, often bearing the mortgages and loans themselves. The majority of the transactions were in Louisa's name. On multiple occasions Heyman sold property and Louisa promptly bought it back. Several California newspaper announcements during 1864 imply that Heyman left debts in San Francisco.

The couple continued buying tracts of land, often dividing them into smaller parcels. In December of 1871 the couple filed the plat for the "Goodtime's Addition," complete with a "Goodtime Plaza." Today that land is just outside the southeast corner of the Steilacoom city limits, partially in the city of Lakewood, partially on Fort Lewis. Shelton and Salomon Streets became 110th and 108th.

Goodtime's Addition to Steilacoom, December 2, 1871

Heyman died of bronchitis on September 2, 1879. He was buried in the Jewish section of the Masonic cemetery in Olympia. His wife Louisa administered his estate.

THE remains of Mr. H. Goodtime, who died at Steilacoom, last Tuesday, were brought here Wednesday, on the steamer *Zephyr*, and interred in the Jewish cemetery. A procession was formed on the wharf, and took in charge the remains as they came from the steamer. Most of the Jewish residents of our city took part in the solemn burial ceremonies, which were conducted at the grave under the direction of the venerable Wolf Schaffer, assisted by prominent Jewish citizens, of this place.

Washington Standard (Olympia) September 5, 1879

Louisa Goodtime
Courtesy of Steilacoom Historical
Museum Association

More is known about Louisa Goodtime, who began life as Wilhelmine Sigelmann and married while in her teens. Local history tells that she introduced Steilacoom's Nathaniel Orr to his future bride by conveniently sending the lady for a pitcher of water at just the right time. The Steilacoom Museum still has the pitcher. Louisa lived just below the Orr wagon shop, and her portrait was found among the Orr family possessions.

Without the responsibilities of children, Louisa became involved in community affairs. In the 1870s Louisa was a key player in what became known as the "Dolly Varden case." Available records of the court case are amazingly complete, including notes of affidavits of witnesses, warrants, and letters. Nineteen women in Steilacoom met in August of 1871 to form a Ladies' Aid Society. Their purpose was to assist in development of the town of Steilacoom. The officers were Miss E. C. Smith, president; Mrs. Ballard, vice president; Mrs. Averill, treasurer; and Miss Mullen, secretary. (Only Louisa was known to be Jewish.) During the winter they, through "balls, festivals, exhibitions & other means, collected near four hundred dollars in gold coin." The exact amount was $396, according to Louisa; $391.65, according to Mrs. Averill.

At their meeting in January of 1872 they voted to use the money to fund a town hall. However, at the February 29 meeting, they disagreed as to the details of what had transpired at the January meeting. President Smith insisted they had voted only to use a portion of the money to buy a lot, and the rest of the money would be a loan for the building. Arguments escalated and the meeting deteriorated. Miss Smith resigned from the group and left without adjourning the meeting.

The group reconvened in Mrs. Ballard's home on March 14th. A new slate of officers was elected. Mrs. Ballard was elected president and Louisa Goodtime was elected treasurer. In an effort to prevent further confusion, a committee was appointed to draft by-laws and a constitution.

The new officers demanded that the previous officers turn over the financial records and the funds raised. Mrs. Averill insisted that she had been elected in August for a one-year term and that she was still treasurer. Both sides dug in their heels and resorted to the courts.

Louisa sued Mrs. Averill in Pierce County civil case #149, cause: "election dispute." The opinion of the court, issued on January 23, 1873, covered several pages. It ruled that as both parties were members of the same society, the property belonged to it in joint ownership. "They have consequently a right to manage, conserve, and dispose of as is at their pleasure." However, the crux of the issue eventually was the by-laws and constitution. Mrs. Averill was ordered to hand over the money and pay court costs. She apparently did, but not promptly. Papers releasing her from the judgment of $391.65 were filed on July 23, 1875 – over two years later.

Throughout the 1870s Louisa routinely bought and sold real estate, in addition to operating the general store in Steilacoom. Frequently she sued to collect promissory notes, so she likely financed many of the transactions. In June of 1876 the *Steilacoom Express* noted that Louisa was the owner of an excellent trotter for which she had refused an offer of $1200. In 1877 Louisa was again charged with sales of liquor to Indians, this time in King County, and was found not guilty. By January of 1879 she had begun to purchase land in "New Tacoma," which was just beginning its boom that would eventually eclipse the town of Steilacoom.

After Heyman's death in the fall of 1879 Louisa continued to run the Steilacoom store herself. She also served as administrator of Heyman's estate, a complex process. Lengthy probate records show that their joint property included 72 acres of woodland and several mortgages and uncollected debts. The only funds not in the common estate were his military pension payments of $18 per month. Affidavits from Adolph Packscher and Isaac Pincus state that on Heyman's deathbed he asked the men to see that each of his sisters received $1000 from his estate. His sisters were named as Sarah Packscher and Emelie/Amelia Rosenburg, both of San Francisco. The final distribution was completed in March of 1882, with all remaining funds going to Louisa. There was not enough in the estate to support payments to his sisters.

Louisa faced other challenges. In June of 1880 the *Washington Standard* carried an article with the headline "Joseph Daniels robs Mrs. Goodtime of Steilacoom of $2500 and is arrested at Puyallup." That was on June 18. By June 25 the headline was "Tried and released." (Her probate records mentioned a nephew Joseph Daniels.)

Her brother-in-law Adolph Packscher took a tough approach. In March of 1882 he applied to have Louisa committed to the Insane Asylum at Steilacoom. Judge Young determined that she was "NOT SO disordered in mind as to endanger… and is NOT unable to manage her own affairs." The judge also ordered that "Adolph Packscher should pay the costs of these proceedings." One can assume the relationship deteriorated after that.

Between 1884 and 1886 local newspapers carried multiple mentions of her travels to visit friends in Olympia and Yelm, so she may not have been operating a store single-handedly at this point.

In June of 1886 Meyer Kaufman's wife Flora died in Tacoma, leaving him with a ten-year-old daughter. Within a year Louisa made the move to Old Tacoma, living with the Kaufman family. Meyer had been a resident for over a decade and was a leader in the growing Jewish community. In 1888 he (and likely Louisa) helped establish a Jewish cemetery, later known as Home of Peace, halfway between Steilacoom and Tacoma. Louisa continued to deal in real estate and offer mortgages.

Louisa Goodtime moved to Elsdorf, Germany, where she died in 1898. Her American estate, which wasn't settled until April of 1903, included her original Steilacoom property in Balch's Lot 3, Block 43.

Another German immigrant who was able to make return trips to his homeland was David Magnus. Coming directly to Washington from his native Berlin in 1868 while just a teenager, David was likely a nephew or relative of Seraphina Packscher, as his mother's maiden name was Brunn. David stayed long enough to become a naturalized citizen in 1873, then promptly applied for a U.S. passport. Over the next decade he apparently made several trips back to Germany. He worked as a clerk in Steilacoom and Olympia, before joining Isaac Pincus in moving to Tacoma in 1884.

June 1, 1880 passport application of David Magnus

In the commotion of the Easter morning fire in April of 1884, the opening of David Magnus' new firm likely went unnoticed. He operated a cigar store in conjunction with the wholesale liquor office of Isaac Pincus. *Tacoma Daily Ledger*, July 11, 1886, "There is a little S shaped tin sign that revolves continually in the wind on Pacific Avenue and attracts no little attention. On one side is the word "Psycho," and before you realize it the other, containing the word "cigar store" is presented. Dave Magnus, who keeps the store, boasts of the quality of the stock he keeps, including the Key West 10c cigar." (At the time the *Ledger* was carrying frequent columns written by George Francis Train, with the word "Psycho" regularly in the headline.)

In 1887 David married Annie Berliner, stepdaughter of Colonel Meyer Kaufman. Both were active in Tacoma's civic affairs until they moved to Seattle around 1895.

Another German adventurer who found his way to Steilacoom via Olympia was Wolf Schafer. After more than a decade in Chicago, Wolf moved to Olympia in 1870, selling tobacco and liquor. His son-in-law, Edward S. Salomon, had become governor of Washington Territory in March. By 1872 Wolf had moved to Steilacoom, where he would live the rest of his life. IRS tax records show that Wolf Schaffer paid $100 as "successor to FA

Sproehnle, Northern Pacific Railroad Brewery." He also paid $25 for taxes as a retail liquor dealer, plus another $5 as a tobacco merchant.

During 1872 and 1873 western Washington was agog over the coming of the Northern Pacific Railroad. Several cities were vying to be the site of the western terminus of the northern route of the transcontinental railroad. In the summer of 1873 Tacoma won the contest, marking the beginning of the end of Steilacoom's prominence in Pierce County.

In 1873 Wolf built a large wooden building on the corner of Pierce and Starling Streets in Steilacoom to house his brewery. His home was a block away on the corner of Pierce and Rainier. He took on a partner for the next five years, William Zoberst, a brewer from California. Zoberst died of consumption in the spring of 1878 at just 28 years of age.

Shafer's Northern Pacific Brewery
Courtesy of Steilacom Historical Society

Wolf's move to Washington territory also came with challenges. Court records show that throughout the early 1870s he was several times a defendant in civil cases involving account collections and mortgage foreclosures. However, during the 1880s he was more often the plaintiff.

In 1879 Wolf officiated at the funeral of his fellow merchant, Heyman Goodtime.

From 1879 to 1889 the brewery firm was known as Schafer and Howard, with Dennis K. Howard as Wolf's partner. Wolf was elected Pierce County treasurer in November of 1878 and served for several years. The county seat was moved from Steilacoom to Tacoma in 1880. That year the firm built a malt mill in Seattle.

Wolf died at his home in Steilacoom on December 9, 1889, at the age of 71. He was buried in Portland's Beth Israel cemetery next to his wife Mina. Their daughter Anna died in 1891, again leaving no descendants. Her probate records include 140 pages of documents, including lists of real estate valued well over $10,000. Curiously, Wolf's will specified that none of his estate should benefit either Edward S. Salomon or Leopold Hirsch, yet Anna's will left token funds for both families. (Both men had married Mina's daughters from her first marriage.) Nearly all of Anna's estate was designated for Jewish charities.

Articles in the Steilacoom Museum Association's newsletter note that the brewery's last entry in the post office was June 29, 1890. The building was later converted to house the Iron Springs Hotel, known for its heated saltwater natatorium. In 1910 the railroad purchased much of Steilacoom's waterfront property, bringing to a close its days as a vacation spot.

Today, in the sleepy little town of Steilacoom, Washington, a short dead-end street bears the name "Isaac Pincus." Local ghost stories include tales of sightings in the old Schafer brewery building. And masters of maritime trivia can trace the brief ownership of several sailing ships to Adolph Packscher. Little else remains to remind residents of a handful of Jewish families, most related by marriage, who were drawn to the Pacific Northwest before the heyday of Tacoma or Seattle, while Washington was yet a young territory and Steilacoom was a town of firsts.

Steilacoom's dominance in Pierce County was quickly usurped by another burgeoning waterfront town, with a little help from the Northern Pacific Railroad...

Tacoma Begins with the Terminus

Often Jewish pioneers sought opportunities in towns with sudden booms in one of two fields – natural resources and transportation. In Tacoma's case, a handful of Jewish merchants established businesses in the early 1870s in what is now "Old Tacoma," hopeful of growth yet to come. They were mostly from "Prussia," and several families were related. They were at the right time, and just a little bit away from the right place. The Northern Pacific Railroad was building a line north from Kalama, but had not yet announced the final terminus of the line.

Meyer Kaufman and his young wife Flora arrived in Tacoma in 1870 from Reno, Nevada, where he was the proprietor of a clothing store. Ahead of the coming crowd, in Tacoma their business was likely a combination tavern and boarding house, optimistically called the Pacific Hotel. Later Meyer operated a large general store.

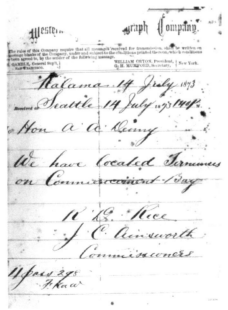

Telegram giving Seattle bad news
Courtesy of Paul Dorpat.com

On July 14, 1873, the Northern Pacific Railroad sent telegrams announcing that the Terminus would be on Commencement Bay. However, the townsite would be farther along Commencement Bay, in an area as yet undeveloped, later called "New Tacoma." Two weeks later Meyer was in trouble for selling liquor along the railroad construction line without a license and for keeping his place of business open on a Sunday. The fine was $50 plus court costs of $4.20. Two years later Meyer's wife Flora gave birth to a daughter Carrie, likely the first Jewish child born in Tacoma, and their only child. All three would live the remainder of their lives in Tacoma, but leave no more descendants.

Meyer Kaufman was joined in the tavern business by two Levin brothers – Philip and Louis. Both had come to Tacoma via Portland, where Philip was active in German and Hebrew schools operated by Rabbi Eckman as early as 1869. Legal notices provide the few records available to modern researchers, as the firm struggled through bankruptcy in Portland in 1871 and sued a steamship line for lost merchandise in 1872. By August of 1873 the *Portland Oregonian* was announcing their unclaimed mail. Their younger brothers, David and Lesser would join them in New Tacoma.

Even in the 1860s the Internal Revenue Service collected taxes and fees from cigar and liquor dealers, leaving breadcrumbs of data for future researchers. Herman Ostheim sold cigars and tobacco in Philadelphia in 1862, and Boise City, Idaho in the late 1860s. He briefly joined his brother Felix in Portland in 1870 before testing the waters of mercantile in Tacoma. Ads for his Pioneer Cigar Store appeared in Tacoma's *Pacific Tribune* as early as May of 1873. He wisely brought gifts of cigars to the newspaper office to celebrate the Jewish New Year that fall. (Even the newspaper had just arrived in Tacoma, moving north from Olympia.)

PIONEER CIGAR STORE,

TACOMA, W. T.,

One door east of Steele's Hotel.

Cigars and Tobacco,

Candies and Nuts,

Pipes, Writing Inks and Stationery,

Always on hand and for sale at reasonable rates.

au9:tf HERMAN OSTHEIM.

Weekly Pacific Tribune August 22, 1873

Local news columns rarely mentioned anyone's departure, unless it was for a short visit or shopping expedition. However, they were quick to note the return of former citizens. *Pacific Tribune,* January 16, 1874, "LOST FLESH. – Our little friend Mr. Ostheim, whose return we chronicled the other day, lost considerable flesh during his absence. When he left Tacoma he was quite rotund and in the best of health; now he is comparatively lean. No place agrees with him so well as our invigorating town, and he is content now to remain."

Apparently he wasn't. *Pacific Tribune,* March 13, "Herman Ostheim is back again, and is again compelled to admit that there is no place equal to Tacoma." He disappeared from Tacoma one more time, likely returning to Germany for several years. His estate was administered in the probate court of King County in 1889, leaving no heirs.

Louis Wolff also leapt at the potential business opportunity. He previously operated a clothing store in Victoria, British Columbia, for more than a decade. Four of his five children were born there and were educated at St. Ann's Convent School and Orphan Asylum, where his three daughters excelled musically and scholastically. Louis was able to make regular buying trips to San Francisco.

In August of 1872 Louis closed his store in Victoria and moved to the emerging town of Tacoma. He built a store building 20 feet by 40 feet on Second Street between Starr and McCarver, (later 2315 North 30th) and in August of 1873 opened the town's third general store. His signature was among the 125 who petitioned the county commissioners for incorporation.

New Store!

HAVING ESTABLISHED MY BUSINESS IN Tacoma, and brought here the finest assortment of merchandise ever opened in the place. I am prepared to sell to the public on as advantageous terms as any of my competitors. My stock consists of

CLOTHING,

The best on Puget Sound ;

Men's, Women's and Children's

BOOTS AND SHOES,

Custom-made and first class ;

HATS AND CAPS,

GENTS' FURNISHIG GOODS,

TRUNKS AND VALISES,

TOBACCO, CIGARS AND PIPES,

YANKEE NOTIONS,

GROCERIES,

&c., &c., &c.

Which will be sold at San Francisco prices. If you don't believe it, you can be convinced by dropping into the store of

L. WOLFF,

Second st., between Starr and McCarver.

au25:tf Tacoma, W. T.

Weekly Pacific Tribune August 22, 1873

Their daughter, Annie, while still a teenager, volunteered as organist at Tacoma's first church, St. Peter's Episcopal. She helped in fundraising events and taught at the school held in the mill company's cookhouse. The family frequently hosted community gatherings and musical evenings at their home, and injured neighbors were occasionally taken there for recuperation.

General Merchandise.

A. FRIEDMAN, Groceries, Tobacco, Dry goods, varieties, and a full line of general merchandise. Second street, First ward.

S. GUTFELD, Gents' furnishing goods, boots and shoes, hats, caps, fancy goods and notions. Our line of groceries will be sold off at cost. Second street First ward.

LOUIS WOLFF, Dry Goods, Hats, Shoes, groceries and general merchandise. Second street, First ward.

A. ZELINSKY, Groceries, Feed, Crockery, glassware and general merchandise. Second street, First ward.

Tacoma Daily Ledger February 11, 1887

In mid-February of 1887 the *Ledger* began printing a directory of local businesses in each edition. Jewish merchants accounted for all four "general merchandise" firms in Old Tacoma, known as the First Ward, based on voting precincts. That fall Louis purchased an additional twelve feet of land adjoining his store for $940, more than twice what he had paid for his entire lot fifteen years before, and the following year built an addition to serve as an office.

Louis Wolff stayed in Tacoma for more than twenty years, maintaining his real estate holdings in Victoria and adding more in Port Townsend. His daughters were active in the general community and his son served on the volunteer fire department.

Within any ethnic group, for every ten or twenty families who are upstanding pillars of the community, there is likely one who causes embarrassment. Morris Dobrin also found his way to Tacoma via Victoria, British Columbia, but under very different circumstances. Victoria *Colonist*, February 8, 1871, "CUT AND RUN – Morris Dobrin, who is mixed up in the Copperman scandal, has cut and run for the American side, whither his family started yesterday to join him. Mrs. Copperman, it will be borne in mind, alleges that Dobrin owes her $1700, and that it was he who induced her to first sign the receipts and then run away so that he might retain the money. Her return to Victoria somewhat marred Morris' praiseworthy plans and, fearing he might be called on to disgorge, he bolted. Why he was allowed to bolt with so serious a charge as subornation to perjury hanging over his head is a mystery. The runaway leaves many creditors who are disconsolate at his untimely departure." Dobrin had lived in Victoria since about 1864, operating the Cheap John Store. His name was frequently in the newspaper, either just ahead of his creditors or fighting with his neighbors. The *Colonist* expressed no love for him. Efforts at extradition failed and Morris Dobrin boldly opened a tailoring business on Main Street in Olympia. At the time the entire population of Pierce County was fewer than 1500 people. He would later move to Tacoma.

MORRIS DOBRIN.

TAILORING AND REPAIRING NEATLY AND promptly done at reasonable charges. Clothing cut and made to order in the latest styles and best manner.
Also Fruits, Confectionery, &c., constantly on hand and for sale cheap. au9:tf

Weekly Pacific Tribune August 22, 1873

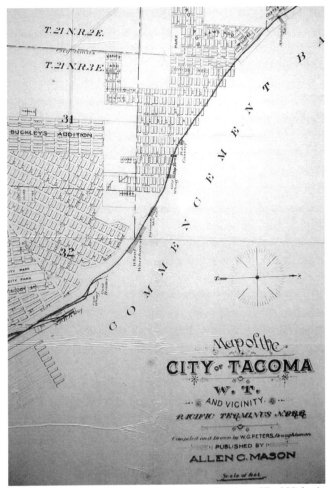

Courtesy of Paul Michaels

Those who stayed in Tacoma – Kaufman, Wolff and Levin – were faced with the hard reality of living a few miles away from where the Northern Pacific Railroad had chosen to build its city. They hung on, and as soon as land was offered for sale, bought all they could in "New Tacoma."

Meyer Kaufman continued running his hotel and store in the First Ward, while steadily buying land. Within a decade he began selling his parcels. In one week alone in December of 1882 he and Flora had the following sales transactions: Dec. 11, 1882, lots 19 & 20 in block 1509, $640 in gold coin. Dec. 14, 1882, lot 17 in section 910, $450 in gold coin. Dec. 14, 1882, lot 18 in block 910, $420 in gold coin.

In 1882 a champagne dinner was served in their home – the first known newspaper mention of a Jewish gathering in Tacoma. (The date was near Yom Kippur.) The following year Meyer started building homes on his lots near Seventh and A Street, as Tacoma was steadily growing and housing was in demand. He obtained a liquor license in New Tacoma, and finally filed for citizenship in November of 1883. He made an

"X" instead of signing, indicating he couldn't read or write English. (This was highly uncommon, as many of Tacoma's Jewish citizens were fluent in several languages.)

On July 24, 1884, fire struck on the west side of Pacific, north of Ninth. (The previous fire on Easter morning was south of Ninth.) Although it was disastrous for the local businesses, the newspaper coverage provided useful details for researchers. *Ledger,* July 25, 1884, "The block burned was the old and original portion of Tacoma, and for several years it has been predicted that it would burn..." Reports of losses and insurance were tallied the following day. Meyer Kaufman, whose building housed the Elite saloon, lost $1,500, of which $1,000 was insured. Meyer Kaufman also owned the building where Leon Hirschberg's wholesale liquor business was located. The liquor stock was a $3,000 loss, the building was valued at $1,000.

That winter the *Ledger* printed several conflicting notices about Mrs. Kaufman's failing health and extended stays in San Francisco. *Ledger* March 15, 1885, "Furniture for sale and house to let, suitable for a sailor's boarding house. Sailors plentiful at this place. Call on Meyer Kaufman, Old Tacoma." A few months later Meyer was narrowly defeated as candidate for councilman. In August he sold his entire stock of groceries and dry goods. His wife Flora died in Tacoma on June 17, 1886, at the age of only 38. Hers was the earliest death date in the Home of Peace Cemetery, and early cemetery records note that she was "re-buried from Olympia."

Meyer kept buying and selling and building. In April of 1888 he and Louis Wolff began construction of twin buildings at 714 and 716 Pacific. The buildings still stand, but the third stories have been removed, along with the names of Kaufman and Wolff.

Meyer finally moved to New Tacoma, renting a home at 1606 Tacoma Avenue in February of 1889. A few years later he moved to one of his homes on A Street. (The site, now part of Fireman's Park, has a spectacular mountain and waterway view.) He continued building, both in Old and New Tacoma.

Meyer's daughter Carrie, now 18, traveled to the Chicago world's fair in 1893, along with Mrs. Sam Andrews. The following spring Carrie was engaged to Frank Miller, a prominent merchant of New York. Parties and receptions continued throughout the year, then suddenly stopped,

714–716 Pacific
From the collection of the author

with no wedding. In 1896 Mrs. Andrews died, and the following year Carrie quietly married Sam, becoming stepmother to his ten-year-old daughter Freda. The couple built a fine home at 10 North E Street, across from what is now called the Rust Mansion. Carrie and Sam never had children together.

Meyer died on March 17, 1900, of Bright's disease.

The Levin brothers made a quicker transition to New Tacoma. Louis had the first saloon and David had the first barbershop. In November of 1879 both were destroyed by fire. Louis lost $1,000, David lost about $200. Philip returned to Germany. Louis went on the road selling cigars, but kept investing in Tacoma real estate. In 1884 Louis married Mary Isaacs and the couple made their home in San Francisco.

David had married May Karnes in 1880. He joined the Tacoma Rifles, Tacoma's first military organization. In 1884 Louis Levin partnered with Meyer Kaufman in building a brick store building on Pacific. David Levin bought the existing wood-frame house on the lot and moved it to A Street. Their younger brother, Lesser, also a barber, was dubbed the "satin barber" for his smooth shaves.

During the first few months of 1888 Tacoma real estate prices spiked again. David and May Levin and Meyer Kaufman bought two lots in February for $2600 and sold them in April for $4000. The following year Louis built two homes on G Street for his wife's brothers, in addition to partnering with them in erecting a large brick building on Pacific. Later numbered 1148 and 1150 Pacific, it was similar to the Kaufman and Wolff double building.

The *Ledger's* columns kept readers informed of Louis Levin's travels on a regular basis. In the summer of 1891 he traveled to Europe to visit his parents, whom he had not seen in twenty-five years. He also visited Paris and London.

By 1892 David and Lesser both worked solely in real estate. But the real estate bubble burst. Lesser moved in with his brother, David, and returned to working as a barber. David was on more solid financial footing. When he ran for city council in 1895 he offered to donate his monthly stipend to charity if elected. He lost, but was elected to the state legislature in November of 1896, and again in 1904.

In 1901 David and his family moved to a substantial home at 306 North J Street. His brother, Lesser, continued working as a barber. David died August 9, 1911, and his wife May on September 10, 1916. Both were buried at Home of Peace Cemetery.

Levin residence, Tacoma, Washington
Courtesy of Elaine Porter

The four Levin brothers were joined in Tacoma by four more brothers who would succeed — and fail — beyond their wildest imaginings...

Dry Goods – When Gross Meant Grandiose

Just as the development of Tacoma's early Jewish community paralleled that of Tacoma itself, the story of the Gross brothers was typical of many Jewish immigrants to the United States – up to a point.

Dave Gross was the first of four brothers to leave their home in Rypin, in Russian-ruled Poland. According to family lore, Dave escaped dressed as a peasant woman wrapped in a shawl. This story has been told among countless Jewish families about young men who left Europe the same way, desperate to avoid lengthy service and cruel treatment in the Russian army. Dave arrived in New York on April 4, 1873, a few months shy of his seventeenth birthday.

A relative helped him outfit a peddler's backpack. Often these peddlers were known as "egg men" because hard-boiled eggs were one of the few kosher foods readily available. Business success meant graduating to a horse and wagon, and eventually a storefront. Dave worked as a peddler for a year, walking and learning English, working his way to Cincinnati, Ohio.

There his brother, Ellis, joined him in the spring of 1874. After two Ohio winters Ellis and Dave traveled to San Francisco and opened a small dry goods store. Following another typical pattern, they partnered with *landsman* William (Wolf) Rudee, a friend from their hometown of Rypin.

However, San Francisco's boom of opportunity had come thirty years earlier. The boys were looking for a place that was just starting to grow. They found it in the Pacific Northwest, where the Northern Pacific Railroad had recently selected Tacoma, Washington, as the western terminus of its northern transcontinental route. Ellis and William headed north, while Dave stayed in San Francisco as a local buyer, in yet another typical pattern.

Just Opened,
NEW STORE,
BY

GROSS & RUDEE

PACIFIC AVENUE,
EEW TACOMA

Dry Goods and Clothing,

BOYS' CLOTHING, GENTS'
FURNISHING GOODS, LADIES'
AND CHILDRENS WEAR,

Boots and Shoes,
OIL CLOTHS, AND NUMEROUS OTHER
ARTICLES,

**Largest Stock ever Opened
in Pierce County.**

All Goods Sold at San Francisco Prices.
je29 d&awtf

Tacoma Herald July 12, 1878

SAN FRANCISCO STORE,
GROSS BROTHERS, - - Proprietors.
PACIFIC AVENUE, NEW TACOMA.

We offer this coming season the LARGEST, CHOICEST and
MOST STYLISH Stock of

Fall & Winter Goods!
—oOo—

We call special attention to our

NOVELTIES in FANCY GOODS,

Choicest variety or Waterproofs, Silks and Satins,

Full Lines of Dress Goods.

Great Inducements in GENTS' BOOST, LADIES' and CHIL-
DREN'S SHOES, a Complete Stock of

Clothing and Furnishing Goods.

Great Bargains in Rubber Goods.

Our Facilities of Buying enables us to UNDERSELL All our
Competitors and to offer our LARGE and WELL SELECTED
STOCK at Prices Never Before heard of in

NEW TACOMA.

Tacoma Herald November 20, 1879

Their first store in Tacoma was a small wooden building on Pacific between Fifth and Seventh Streets, beyond the northern edge of the budding business district. Here they began their lifelong practice of aggressive newspaper advertising, with a prominent ad in the *Tacoma Herald* on July 12, 1878. A month later their ad was on the front page.

Within eight months Ellis and Dave were able to

replace their partner with a third brother, Morris, again following a common pattern. All had apprenticed as tailors, giving them the skills they needed to judge quality in clothing. They called their firm the San Francisco Store, offering quality merchandise at San Francisco prices. They boldly moved into bigger quarters, in the best location and only brick building in the city, 902–904 Pacific. (William Rudee moved to Walla Walla and later to San Francisco.)

Over the next decade the brothers experimented with several expansions. In 1881 Ellis opened a branch store in Port Townsend. Two years later he sold that business and returned to Germany (just across the border from his hometown,) where he served as the brothers' European buyer. He married Johanna Olchevitz in 1884.

Ellis' place in Tacoma was filled by their 15-year-old brother, Abraham, bringing the total to four brothers – again a typical pattern. After attending school in Tacoma for a few months, Abraham took courses in a leading business school in San Francisco before returning to work as bookkeeper for his brothers.

The Gross brothers wisely invested in real estate, purchasing multiple lots on Pacific Avenue. They moved their business to 906–908 Pacific, immediately south of their rented brick. Several years later they announced plans to move the wooden building to their lot on Fifteenth and rebuild in brick at 906–908. Before the wooden building was moved, however, tragedy struck – again a typical pattern. A fire on Easter morning, April 13, 1884, wiped out several blocks on the west side of Pacific. The Gross brothers operated their business out of a temporary building up the hill on the corner of Ninth and C Street (now Broadway) for seven months, selling damaged goods in Tacoma's first fire sale. They fell in love with the site, vowing to return.

The fire spurred a citywide urgency to rebuild in brick. In June of 1884 the Gross brothers signed an agreement with their neighbor on the south to build a shared brick wall. Regular articles in the *Tacoma Daily Ledger* kept readers informed of the construction progress, complete with dimensions and costs. The windows would be the largest on the Sound, 94 by 132 inches. By August workers were laying brick on the

Wooden storefront at 906–908 Pacific c1883
Courtesy of Douglas Salin

second story, which would front on Railroad Street above (now Commerce). The brothers financed some of their $13,000 construction costs by selling their lots on Fifteenth and Pacific for more than double their recent purchase price.

Since their new store building wasn't ready yet, they briefly opened a branch store in nearby Puyallup in the fall. This was just as Native Americans were coming from all over the Pacific Northwest to take jobs picking hops, and would have cash to spend. By October new merchandise was arriving by the ton. A block and tackle was needed to bring the large plate-glass window from the depot, which arrived "broken to fragments." On October 18, 1884, Morris Gross filed an exclusive right to the name "San Francisco Store."

Two days prior he had taken the unusual step of selling the new building and leasing the storefront and two offices back from the purchaser John C. Ainsworth for $200 per month. (Developer Allen C. Mason would rent the other suite of offices.) A series of payments over the next three months would bring $30,000 to the brothers, again quickly doubling their investment.

The store opened on November 3, 1884, even though the replacement glass didn't arrive until the 4th. The grand opening party, complete with music, free cigars, candy, and an evening bonfire, brought an estimated 2,000 people through their doors. They gave a prize of $10 worth of merchandise "to the person guessing the nearest to the number of electoral votes secured by the candidates for the presidency." (Grover Cleveland won the election the next day.) That same day Peritz & Company, a branch of Seattle's Toklas & Singerman, opened on the corner of 13th and Pacific, and the two firms would challenge each other in advertising and incentives over the next seven years.

Just before Thanksgiving Morris Gross spent an entire day canvassing the city for donations for the Fannie C. Paddock Memorial Hospital, again following a typical pattern of philanthropy. Gross Brothers, of course, made the largest donation of ten dollars – a significant amount at the time. On Christmas Eve their former store – a temporary frame building up the hill – collapsed under the weight of a heavy snow. The building had been turned on the lot and used as a skating rink.

Once the Christmas retail season was over Morris Gross made a two-month buying trip to New York City, perhaps checking out the Jewish bridal market – again a typical pattern. Morris

stayed in the East long enough to attend the inauguration of President Cleveland. Dave Gross came to Tacoma to help during Morris' absence, as did his brother-in-law Abraham Friedman, who operated a branch store in Chehalis for several years.

Tacoma Daily Ledger April 15, 1885

Ledger, September 3, 1885, "Yesterday the firm of Gross Bros. received two elegant mirrors for their store. One of these mirrors will be put in the gents' clothing department, and the other will be placed in the ladies' cloak department. The mirrors, which are by far the largest on the Sound, were furnished by the Tacoma Furniture company, who framed them in fine black walnut, and put them up in the store." They were able to face themselves in those mirrors. Throughout October of 1885, while many in the city were working to drive out the Chinese, the Gross Brothers' ad in the Daily *Ledger* was headed by the phrase "Citizens and Strangers Are Invited," a brave statement at the time.

December of 1885 brought another visit from Dave, accompanied by their younger sister Helen, recently arrived from Europe. Within two years she would marry manufacturer William Creger in San Francisco, giving the Gross Brothers the ability to manufacture their own clothing lines. They also began carrying a line of carpets, luxuries for households with rough wooden or even dirt floors.

Ledger, March 19, 1886, "Yesterday a drunken man was strolling leisurely along the avenue, and when in front of the Gross Bros.' store, he reeled against one of the lady figure stands on which there is a long cloak, and the stand tumbled over, and fell upon the sidewalk. The intoxicated fellow very cautiously picked it up, and commenced begging the lady's pardon and offering all kinds of apologies for a moment."

Ledger, March 25, 1886, "Gross Bros. received from Portland yesterday a very handsome circular show case about twenty feet long. This is the largest and only one in the city of its kind." A few months later they purchased land in Napavine to open yet another branch store along the line of the Northern Pacific Railroad. (Similar to today's I-5 corridor.)

The windows continued to cause problems. *Ledger,* December 15, 1886, "Gross Brothers received by steamer from San Francisco a large, new French plate glass, yesterday, which will be placed in their front window in place of the one broken a few days ago." December 16, "The new plate glass was successfully placed in position at Gross Brothers' store yesterday morning by P.A. Paulson, assisted by several others. The largest glass that could be found in San Francisco was purchased for this building and it was found to be several inches too short for the window and had to be patched by a narrow strip at the top."

By February of 1887 the Gross Brothers rented two additional storefronts on Railroad Street (now Commerce) to house their growing wholesale carpet line and a millinery store. On one day alone they received three train cars filled with shoes and 150 dozen hats. Abe Gross's "hard work and abilities" were rewarded on his 21st birthday, April 5, 1887, when he became an equal partner in the firm.

On July 4, 1887, the city of Tacoma celebrated the first train crossing over the Cascades switchback. Thomas Ripley, in his poetic "Green Timber" description of Tacoma, remembered that "Abe Gross, always at the forefront in matters of art, displayed over the door of his brick store an almost full-sized locomotive, puffing an inordinate lot of smoke from its insides."

A FRIENDLY GREETING
——— TO THE ———
Strangers Within Our Gates.
A VISIT TO THE NEW YORK OF THE PACIFIC COAST
Will be incomplete without a visit to its Greatest Store. While we are commemorating our Independence, National as well as Commercial—the first secured by force of arms, and the last by the power of the mighty
DECAPOD ENGINE.
WHICH SCALES THE LOFTY "SWITCHBACK."
Uniting the East and the West in the Bonds of Traffic and good will, keeping pace with the onward march of Tacoma toward renown.
GROSS BROTHERS
Invite all the visitors at our Jubilee to see the unexampled Bargains at the
GREAT SAN FRANCISCO STORE,
Which will be known by its being the most lavishly decorated Business House in the City.
GROSS BROTHERS,
Nos. 906 and 908 Pacific Avenue, Tacoma, W. T.

Tacoma Daily Ledger
July 5, 1887

Ellis Gross returned from Europe in October of 1887 and expressed his surprise at the growth of the city during his five-year absence. "In looking over the broad streets and miles and miles of houses where there used to be only trees and stumps, I am astonished, and were it not for meeting my brothers I wouldn't have believed I was in Tacoma." Within a week of his return he was investing in real estate, building with his brothers eight much-needed residences.

A lengthy "interview" printed in the *Ledger* on Sunday, November 13, 1887, described the growth of the carpet stock from about four pieces rolled out on display, to the current stack of over four hundred. The clothing department occupied an area the size of a full city block, filled with tables piled as tall as a man and bearing men's and boy's suits made by Creger & Gross, clothing manufacturers of San Francisco. *Ledger,* December 4, 1887, "There is always room for others on the ladder, and while we cannot help being at the top we intend to stay there." *Ledger*, December 11, "The clerks are kept as busy as flies in a molasses barrel."

Interior c.1887, probably Morris on left and Abe on right
Courtesy of Douglas Salin

The year ended in style. *Ledger,* Thursday, December 29, 1887, "A Handsome Wagon. It is of a style that is known as the piano box and is highly ornamented...It is the first wagon of the kind to be used for delivery purposes in the territory and its introduction is another example of the enterprise of this firm. For the present it will be in charge of Wm. Siler, the tallest man in the territory, and the two no doubt will be drawing cards." The wagon served as a symbol of the brothers' rapid success, far exceeding that of the average Jewish immigrant. They were about to leap well beyond the ordinary.

On February 5, 1888, the *Ledger* reported the Gross brothers were going to build a new store. "After some difficulty they have succeeded in obtaining one of the finest sites in the city, on which they intend to erect what will be the largest store on the Pacific coast, and may well be called the Wanamaker store of the northwest. The site has frontage of 115 feet on C and Railroad streets and of 100 feet on Ninth Street. It is at the five corners of the city facing the site of the Tacoma Land Company's building and the county court house. No finer site could be found. The building which will be erected will be a landmark in the history of the city." True to their word, they were going back to the site of their temporary location after the 1884 fire. The purchase price was $30,000, subject to a mortgage of only $6,500. Due to existing building leases, they weren't able to begin construction until the following year.

By August of 1888 Morris Gross's East Coast shopping trip brought $100,000 worth of new stock back to their store in Tacoma, along with ideas for the future. *Ledger,* September 1, 1888, "At the Gross Brothers Store...Over in the northern window Ben Harrison and Grover Cleveland are stationed – both are looking for a handsome necktie." (And the presidency.)

During the winter of 1888 the Gross brothers continued to support their community – donating dozens of comforters to the hospital and treating their customers to musical concerts. When an arsonist set fire to the *Ledger* office, Abe and Morris Gross were the first firemen on the scene, "getting out the hose truck No. 1 and rendering excellent service with it."

Before construction could get under way on their new location, their contractor frugally moved the existing buildings. Even today moving large buildings is a challenge, and 1889 was no different.

Ledger, April 6, 1889.
"DOING BUSINESS ON ROLLERS. One Illustration of How Things are Done in Tacoma. One of the novel features characteristic of the rapid development and enterprise displayed in Tacoma may be seen on Railroad Street for the next few days. It is a locomotive loan and real estate office in the shape of the old Nevada saloon building which lately stood on the northeast corner of the lot soon to be the site of the splendid new Gross Bros.' block. The building is being removed south on Railroad Street and the new occupants, who are real estate and loan brokers, still retain their offices and transact business daily, the patrons entering by means of an inclined plank attached to the main entrance with slots nailed to it. This fact also forcibly illustrates the great scarcity of office room as the gentlemen (of which there are two or three different firms) could find no other rooms."

Abraham Gross returned to Europe for an extended visit, not having seen his parents since he was fifteen, and missed the cornerstone ceremony. *Ledger,* May 31, 1889,

"LAYING THE CORNER STONE of the Great Gross Building Yesterday Afternoon. Immediately after the Memorial parade yesterday the corner stone of the palatial block now being erected by the Gross Brothers was laid at the corner of Railroad and Ninth streets. A richly carpeted platform had been erected upon which were arranged the members of the firm and the heads of the different departments of their colossal house. Each individual wore upon the breast a card designating the department to which he or she belonged, and carried some article as insignia of that department, somewhat after the custom of the Masonic fraternity. For example the shoe department was represented by a pair of lady's fine shoes tied with pink ribbon; the bookkeeper had his ledger; the cashier, cash box; underwear department, a lady's robe de nuit, and so forth. Carrying out the idea of patterning after the Masons there was a small white satin bannerette embroidered in gold with the name of the firm. Fastened to the derrick which held the corner stone to be laid was a large drawing of the handsome structure which is to occupy the vast space on Ninth Street between Railroad and C. The usual tin box, containing coin and currency, a record of the building and copies of the *LEDGER* was placed in position, and the stone was duly laid by Morris Gross. In the act of laying the stone instantaneous photographs were taken of the platform. The interesting ceremony was witnessed by an immense concourse of people, principally ladies, who thronged Railroad, Ninth and C streets. Addresses were made by Allen C. Mason, Morris Gross and Rev. Mr. Hosmer...The drawing of the handsome structure which was displayed during the ceremony together with the plans and elevations attracted much attention and evoked considerable comment most flattering to the enterprise and energy of this progressive firm of successful merchants."

On June 8, 1889, Tacoma's *Daily Ledger* described a fire which caused the total desolation of sixty blocks in downtown Seattle. Morris Gross donated $1,500 and offered to sell his merchandise to Seattle merchants at cost until they could rebuild and restock. A fire broke out in his own store the next day, but was quickly extinguished. (That July the city of Ellensburg also suffered a major fire.)

Abraham returned from his six-month stay in Europe, and Morris and Ellis headed to San Francisco in October for a winter break. Abraham kept the news articles coming, sharing construction updates and specific costs on everything from the $800 clock in the tower to the $250 copper ship atop the cupola. The firm would occupy 25,500 square feet of floor space, requiring fifty or sixty clerks. Additional building footage would bring an expected rental income of $20,400 a year, which would, of course, be reflected in lower prices on merchandise.

The Gross brothers continued their civic activities, taking leadership roles in the organization of Tacoma's first Jewish cemetery and congregation, the Northwest Exposition Company, and purchasing box seats in the new Tacoma Theater. Employees of the Gross Brothers' store even marched in the statehood Inauguration Day parade in Olympia, wearing their departmental badges.

As moving day approached the Gross brothers began their clearance, or "removal sale." Their normal *Ledger* ad on page three grew from two columns wide to all seven, bumping the City News to the bottom of the page. By early March Morris was back from his New York shopping trip with a trainload of goods for the new store. A few weeks later special excursion trains, sponsored by the Gross Brothers, would bring customers from neighboring cities and towns for the grand opening.

The event was described by authors Thomas Ripley and Herbert Hunt, and garnered a full-page description in the Sunday *Ledger* on March 23, 1890. Twenty carriages paraded up the hill from the old store to the new, filled with their employees sporting new silk hats and spring bonnets. Atop the building flew a flag with twelve stars – one for each year since the firm had opened in Tacoma. The merchandise was separated into twelve departments with alphabetical labels, likely the first true department store on the West Coast. An elaborate overhead system of baskets and wires carried parcels from the sales floor, through a wrapping room, to the cashier's box, and back to the sales floor. The store even had a baby nursery with a nurse in charge, unheard of at the time. (The policy "No check, no baby" would be strictly enforced.) A few months later the firm completed the ladies' reception room, featuring comfortable furniture, French carpets, and a stained-glass window depicting the Goddess of Justice. (Later that same room would be an ice cream parlor above the candy shop of Charles Muehlenbruch.)

Interior of Muehlenbruch Candy 1916, formerly Gross Brothers' ladies' reception room, with Lady Justice logo in colored glass window
Tacoma Historical Society collection

The brothers continued their prominence in the community and in the local newspaper headlines. *Ledger,* April 18, 1890, "THREE BROTHERS HONORED. An event never before celebrated in the history of Free Masonry took place in this city last night. The three Gross brothers, Ellis, Morris and Abe, were exalted to the august and sublime degree of the Holy Royal Arch in Tacoma chapter No. 4. In conferring this degree no more or no less than three Masons can receive the honor at one time… Never before in the history of the order have three brothers been admitted simultaneously to the degree." Shortly after Morris took his turn visiting their aging parents in Europe.

The new store attracted a transportation hub, as streetcar connections from outlying neighborhoods were completed, beginning and ending at the base of the Gross Brothers' store. Their ads explained to customers how to reach the store with transfers and just one fare.

The happy atmosphere present in Tacoma's business community was suddenly shattered. A competing firm, the Dickson Brothers, distributed a vest pocket memo book. On the back was printed the message: "To the Thinking Public! Do not waste your time and money trying to get the best of the 'Jew' clothing house, but trade at a White American House." The immediate response was testament to the prominence and influence of Tacoma's Jewish community. A lengthy "Open Letter" in the *Ledger* on June 17, 1890, exposed the slur and offered the Dickson brothers an opportunity to explain themselves. "If it is the product of your own brains, why did you dare to shock a thinking public by giving it publicity?" The letter was likely penned by Dave Gross, who was visiting Tacoma at the time.

The next day the Tacoma Ministerial Alliance, through Chaplain R.S. Stubbs, compared the Dickson Brothers' booklet to the corpse of a whale, in that "the sight arouses generous sympathies; but a stranded whale invariably poisons the atmosphere for leagues around and thus awakens feelings only of repugnance. It stinketh. Let its epitaph be an apology to the millions of white Americans for this uncalled for and unjust attack upon our fellow citizens of the Jewish faith." A few days later the Sacramento firm of Weinstock, Lubin and Company sent their own open letter to the *Ledger,* chastising the Dickson Brothers. "You have placed yourselves in rather an embarrassing position. You

have time and again said that whatever success you have attained is due to following the methods we trained you to while in our employ… if so you are following methods taught you by Jews."

The Gross brothers continued giving back to their community. In the summer they opened a suite of reading, writing and lecture rooms on the third floor, offering free use to the clerks of the city and other interested friends. The rooms were furnished with common school education materials and pamphlets.

They also offered the top of their tower as home to the city's new weather instruments, brought to Tacoma by the Chamber of Commerce. Weather reports sent to San Francisco were intended to show the climatic advantages of the state. However, the advantage belonged to the Gross brothers, who included the daily forecasts at the top of their daily newspaper ads, increasing readership and generating "Hurricane Sales" and other weather-related events.

Gross Brothers' Hurricane Sale
Tacoma Public Library BU-12722

September of 1890 featured a three-day fall opening, with yet another novel turn. The store was opened for visitors to view the merchandise and elaborate window displays, but not for purchases. Crowds were ushered in through one entrance, given a souvenir card, led on a carpeted path through the various departments, and escorted out through another entrance, all accompanied by the sounds of an orchestra. Not until September fifth was the merchandise available for sale, "at a great sacrifice." Estimates of attendance exceeded 20,000.

The windows continued to gain publicity, as Morris Gross sent from Vienna a figure of a dancing Spanish girl, whose fan was moved by a clockwork arrangement. She was the centerpiece of an elaborate display of linens and scarves. In order to show the windows to their full advantage, Abe arranged with neighboring merchants to share the expense of installing 25 electric street lights. Gross Brothers paid for four, while the *Ledger* paid for two. By mid-November "King for a Day" featured a fat and dignified turkey on a throne.

December brought the traditional Santa at the mantel, plus a shore scene complete with driftwood, boaters, and mythical swans. The store even opened on Christmas morning to distribute free candy to children. *Ledger,* December 26, "It can be safely estimated that over 5000 children visited the store during the morning… Several of the boys, fearing that they might be refused after the second or third visit, resorted to swapping hats and coats with their companions with a view to changing their appearance and thus secure the favors. The large hallway leading to the elevator was an extemporized dressing room for the purpose, and the antics of the youngsters provoked no little mirth."

The firm of Kaufman and Berliner made the mistake of announcing in a half-page ad that a hurricane had struck their inventory sale, "sweeping and tearing prices to pieces." Gross Brothers responded with a full-page ad and a cyclone sale. *Ledger,* December 28, "During the past sixty days there has been all kinds of sales in the City of Tacoma… We have been quietly watching these wind sales and find they did little other than to concentrate their force into one great cyclone sale that will be let loose by GROSS BROTHERS." Also December 28, "David Gross leaves to-day for New York, where he will meet his brother, Morris Gross, now on his way home from a nine months' sojourn in Europe. Together they will make the spring purchases."

> Abe Gross has the thanks of the LEDGER office for a fine box of cigars he sent last night as a New Year's offering. It is a fact worthy of mention that the weeds are of the same brand that Abe smokes and are therefore in decided contrast to the regulation corncob pipe from which the newspaper man usually draws his inspiration.

Tacoma Daily Ledger January 1, 1891

Abe returned from a quick trip to San Francisco, where he had purchased more goods for their spring opening and first anniversary. Siblings Dave and Helen followed shortly with their families. March 23rd would begin three days of celebration illuminated by 75 electrical lights – inside, outside, in the windows and on the roof. One window held a balcony scene from Romeo and Juliet, complete with ladder and a house

made entirely from handkerchiefs. Another held a "blacksmith shop, completely equipped, fringed and trimmed with lace." The corner window featured a windmill made from napkins and linens, while another duplicated a prize window at the Paris exposition. Early visitors, assuming the promised souvenir of "undressed kids" would be free kid gloves, instead received two miniature dolls, "clad in nature's garb." Attendance figures claimed 10,000 visitors the first night alone.

Gross Brothers' Grand Opening.

Great in advance is this our glorious age;
Rich in ripe record, pure in peaceful page.
Our country free from waste or cloud of war,
Shows Commerce smiling all along our shore.

But a decade ago in sun or shower,
Rose the tall pine where now trade temples tower.
On the steep hills of sunny Puget Sound;
There reigned the stillness of a sleep profound:
How changed the scene where Gross's show case shines,
Emerging from the forest's fallen pines.
Rich in rare fabric that can robe the fair,
Sought beyond seas for womanhood to wear.

Grand was the faith that bid their building rise,
Richer hath none beneath these western skies;
And o'er it all the firm's broad banner flies,
Nothing is wanting that might make it fair,
Doubt not 'twas planned and stocked with studious care.

Our eyes shall see with arch of glittering light,
Pure as the flower that stud the tropic night;
Each flower exotic on their Opening smile,
Nor aught be wanting in the newest style;
I mprove the hour and gaze upon the scene,
N'ere hath Tacoma such an effort seen;
Go search in vain for something poor or mean.

TACOMA, WASH., March 23d, 1891.

Promenade Concert

Monday Evening, March 23, 1891.
SPANISH STUDENTS.
PROGRAMA DEL DOMINGO.

1. "RUMANIA"—March . . . . Granados
2. "A FOU"—Wals . . . . Waldteufel
3. "SIEMPRE TUYA" . . . . Rebagtiati
4. "RIGOLETTO"—Fantasia . . . . Verdi
5. SOLO DE SALTERIO . . . .
   SR. F. MARIN,
   Drill by Mason Zonaves, Capt. E. L. Hills, Commanding.
6. "PALOMA"—Flabanera . . . . Tradier
7. "SERENATA DE" . . . . Schubert
8. "TIPICA"—Polka . . . . Curti
9. "HAIL COLUMBIA" . . . .
10. "SPANISH STUDENTS"—Wals . . . . . . Waldteufel

Tuesday Evening, March 24, 1891.
DE LANGEVIN & GETCHELL'S ORCHESTRA.

1. GRAND MARCH . . . . Saunders
   (Dedicated to Tacoma (first time).
2. OVERTURE—"Home Circle" . . . . . R. Schlepegrell
3. CONCERT WALTZ . . . . Faust
4. SELECTION—Popular Melodies . . . . . .
5. POLKA DE CONCERT . . . . Dalbey
6. SELECTION—Opera, "Beggar Student" . . Millocker
7. PROMENADE—"In Line" . . . . Dalbey
8. WALTZ—"Beautiful Language" . . . . L. O. DeWitt
9. CONCERT GALOP . . . . Trempler
10. FINALE . . . .

1891 Gross Brothers Souvenir Booklet
From the collection of the author

On May 6 of 1891, Tacoma received national attention when President Benjamin Harrison came to visit. The only building big enough to hold the crowds was the Gross Brothers' store. They obligingly cleared the entire first floor of merchandise and turned the second-story balcony into a reviewing stand.

Memorial Day of 1891 was recognized by yet another elaborate window display, created by Gross Brothers' resident designer, F.H. Loring. Inspired by the *Gates Ajar* novel by Elizabeth Stuart Phelps, the window included a graveside broken wheel and broken columns, along with dolls dressed as angels reaching toward white doves. A few weeks later they added a gentlemen's dressing room, complete with seats and mirrors, and lighted with electricity.

Summertime brought baseball games. On several occasions the Gross Brothers' employees played against the clerks from their competitor in Seattle, the firm of Toklas & Singerman. The Sunday games were followed by picnics and store tours, with each taking turns hosting.

That October the Gross brothers exceeded their reputation for philanthropy by opening a free public kindergarten school. They renovated and outfitted a house, hired several teachers, and purchased all supplies necessary to run the school. Thirty children were cared for from 9:30 a.m. to 2 p.m. and given two hot meals daily, entirely at the Gross Brothers' personal expense. Of course Christmas and graduation programs were described in the *Ledger*. Morris gave a speech affirming his beliefs that the rich should help the poor and stressing the need for quality education for all. The kindergarten continued beyond the Gross Brothers' support, eventually evolving into the "Tacoma Free Kindergarten."

FIRST KINDERGARTEN LUNCH.

Twenty-Six Children Sit Down to Enjoy It at Gross Bros.' New School.

Twenty-six innocent children, bright and clean and fresh, and what is more— happy, sat down at the first lunch given at Gross Bros.' free kindergarten, No 2118 G street, yesterday at 11 o'clock

Tacoma Daily Ledger October 24, 1891

Rich, popular, and public-spirited, the Gross brothers made ideal political candidates. When Morris returned in March of 1892 from his annual buying trip to New York, he was asked to be a candidate before the Republican city convention for the nomination for mayor. When questioned by a *Ledger* reporter, Morris deftly avoided answering and turned the interview into a discussion of the spring goods arriving. Although he made a rousing speech at the rally held a week later, he deferred in honor of the incumbent, Mayor H.S. Huson.

Instead, Morris and his brothers put their efforts into preparing the most elaborate spring opening yet. Shoppers overloaded transportation lines and blocked the streets surrounding the store. When the brothers realized there were more people in the streets than in the store, they shifted the orchestra to the outdoor balcony. *Ledger*, March 27, 1892, "The women who success-

fully solved the souvenir cup and saucer problem at Gross Bros.' opening Monday afternoon, gave evidence of patience, perseverance and push, principally push." The first 5,000 were rewarded with painted cups and saucers, created in Germany

Tacoma Daily Ledger March 19, 1892

for the firm. Another 10,000 received erasable celluloid shopping lists. Not bad for a city whose total of registered voters had just reached 8,000.

In April the Gross brothers began yet another novel scheme – Saturday evening exhibitions, held from 7 to 10 p.m., so that ladies could purchase evening wear in evening light. A room was outfitted with special lighting to view silks, velvets and wools by gaslight. More lighting was needed to illuminate the tower clock, finally in place and functioning by mid-November. Their January clearance sale began in 1893 "when the clock in the tower of our establishment strikes eight." The spring opening also promoted their clock, and the "correct time to buy."

"TURN ON, OLD TIME."

"The Clock upbraids me With the waste of Time." —SHAKESPEARE.

"Time conquers all, And we must Time obey." —POPE.

For the last fifteen years our motto has been advance, not with a headlong rush, but constant and steady, with no pause or delay, but like the hands on the clock dial from day to day and from year to year.

During these fifteen years we have had difficulties to contend with, which happens to not a few while engaged in building up a business, but as the poet says:

"Come what come may; Time and the hour runs through the roughest day."

Tacoma Daily Ledger November 6, 1892

Suddenly the competition got interesting. On April fifteenth the firm of Hyams, Pauson & Company took over at 902–904 Pacific, successor to the London and Liverpool Clothing House. With a factory in New York and half a dozen stores on the West Coast, the new folks claimed to be the largest clothing dealers in the world. They appeared to have an advertising budget to match. Gross Brothers responded by tripling the width of their ad, and expanding into the basement of their building on the Railroad Street side. This move took courage. First, it expanded their clothing department into five storefronts that had previously been bringing in steady rental income. Second, it moved the clothing department literally to Hyams, Pauson & Company's back door. The timing couldn't have been worse.

Gross Brothers' Store, c.1894
Courtesy of Douglas Salin

On May 5, 1893, the National Cordage Company failed, and a national banking panic followed. Few at the time understood the devastating impact it would have on the Northwest. Only later was the day dubbed Black Friday. The columns of the *Ledger* rarely hinted that the economy had crashed. Gross Brothers kept running large ads throughout the summer and fall, and kept on keeping up appearances. However, by January of 1894 their ads were a clever parody of the lengthy delinquent taxpayer lists, eye-catching but telling.

Abe Gross c 1889
Courtesy of Douglas Salin

In January of 1894 Abe Gross put his heart and soul into the organization of an Interstate Fair, to be held in Tacoma that fall. Displays and

exhibitors would come from Chicago's world fair, after a Midwinter Fair in San Francisco. Abe believed it would turn around Tacoma's struggling economy. Instead it would be in vain. In March of 1894 the Gross brothers held their annual spring opening, blithely carrying on. Abe made a trip to San Francisco in April to arrange for fair concessionaires. The Tacoma community rallied to clear the 56-acre site, and Abe made the rounds again, collecting donations for construction costs.

1894 Interstate Fair souvenir card
From the collection of the author

The Interstate Fair opened at the end of August. Stores all over town decorated their windows in the fair's colors of blue, yellow, and white. Gross Brothers' elaborate window displays included yards of expensive silks, a hand-carved eagle, and incandescent electric lights alternating in the fair's colors. By September Abe was back in California, rounding up more exhibits. However, the fair was an economic disaster, as few could afford to attend and even fewer could afford to spend. Within weeks the unpaid band members quit.

Abe attempted to boost the lagging holiday season by offering a free light lunch to store shoppers during December. Morris was busy elsewhere. On December 12th he was married to Miss Mollie Bash at the exclusive Delmonico's in New York. (Later her brother Roman would join her in Tacoma.)

History will never know the true reasons, but on Saturday morning, March 30, 1895, Abe Gross was found dead in his bed, a pistol in his hands. The city mourned in disbelief with the family.

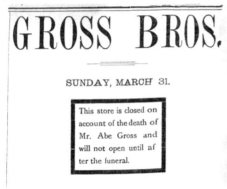

Tacoma Daily Ledger March 31, 1895

The economy continued to decline, with effects rippling upward from the smallest storekeepers to the larger ones. During the fall of 1895 three major Jewish clothing firms went out of business in Tacoma – Solomon Jacoby's Mechanics' Block, Oscar Reichenbach's Hyams, Pauson & Co., and Mentheim Cohn's two clothing stores. All flooded the market with drastic price reductions. To complicate matters, Pacific was impassable due to street construction. All three Gross brothers now had wives and children to support, and Abe's estate to settle. Only 28, he had not left a will.

December brought drastic price reductions, (unheard of before) and hints of impending changes. There was no spring opening in 1896, simply a small ad featuring their fine silks. To complicate matters, the new spring styles for ladies included a new sleeve, greatly increased in size and easily distinguishable from older styles.

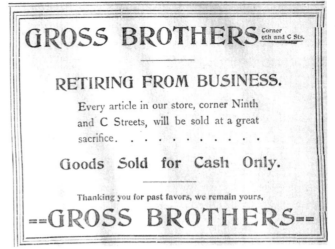

Tacoma Daily Ledger May 24, 1896

Surprisingly, the brothers split up. Herbert Bash, Morris Gross's new father-in-law, bought the business and kept Morris on as manager. Both Dave and Ellis chose to begin business again on their own. Dave incorporated with his wife and her brother, Moses Friedman, selling cloaks from 936 Pacific. Ellis partnered with his best salesman, Morris Summerfield, selling clothing at 944 Pacific.

The Gross Brothers as a firm were no more, but Morris kept the big store running. His ads began with his best features – his location – "Ninth and C" – and his name – "Managed by Morris Gross." He continued on C Street through January of 1897, before returning to the "landmark" store location at 906–908 Pacific. He took advantage of his eastern buying trip in February to confer with his friend Senator John L. Wilson, unsuccessfully offering to rent or sell his mammoth building to the government for use as a customs house and post office building.

Morris needed to sell in a hurry. *Ledger*, February 20, 1897, "The National Home & Loan association yesterday began foreclosure proceedings against the Gross property on Ninth and C streets, this action being based on a note and mortgage for $6000, dated March 11, 1889, due in six years." (The mortgage was two weeks overdue at the time of Abe's suicide. In hindsight, they probably could have covered the balloon payment with what they spent on free souvenirs during 1892 alone.) In late March the weather station was moved to city hall.

The store building was sold in October, and the Standard House Furnishing Company moved into a portion of the premises. Although the word "bankruptcy" was never used, the sum of $22,906.07 from the sale of assets was used to pay all remaining claims at sixteen percent.

In February of 1898 the property known as the Gross block was sold again, this time to William Jones, the Walla Walla wheat king. His purchase price of $51,000 was about one-third of the Gross brothers' investment a decade earlier. Morris and David Gross were not discharged as administrators of Abe's estate until March of 1900.

> The name of the Gross Block, corner of Ninth and C streets has been changed. Hereafter it will be known as the Jones Block.
>
> *Tacoma Daily Ledger August 21, 1898*

In the spring of 1909 Dave was preparing to trade his three parcels on Nineteenth and Pacific for the Star Theater on Ninth and D (now Market.) However, the theater burned down before the trade was completed. The deal was renegotiated, and Dave sold his property on Nineteenth and Pacific for $175,000, plus the theater lot. That fall he leased a prominent business corner in downtown San Francisco and moved his family to that city in February of 1910. At the same time, he continued investing in Tacoma. In 1913 Dave sold his Tacoma store building at 940–942 C Street for $115,000, and the following year built another business block at 1122 C Street.

But he still owned the Star Theater property. In March of 1916 the *Tacoma Times* announced that Dave and Alexander Pantages had reached an agreement, whereby Dave would build an elegant new theater and Pantages would lease it back. Again, the deal didn't go as planned. Just two months later Pantages made the surprise announcement that he would instead build a larger theater at a more prominent location a block away – the corner of Ninth and Broadway. In June demolition began on the Jones block, formerly the Gross Brothers' 1890 giant store. Again, history will never know if the demolition was done in spite, or if Pantages simply needed a larger property.

It took more than a year, but Dave created his own solution for his vacant property. In October of 1917 he arranged for a 50-year lease of the parcel, for a consideration of $275,000. (He was 61 at the time.) In 1918 the Rialto Theater opened on Dave's property, offering moving pictures rather than Pantages' vaudeville theater.

Tacoma's Gross brothers were known for their creative marketing and sound business methods. Many of Tacoma's citizens in 1885 adopted a different method…

The Tacoma Method

November 3, 1885, is now seen as one of the lowest days in Tacoma's history, but many of those who lived through it later celebrated its anniversary. On that day a mob of citizens forced the Chinese population to leave the city. The process later became known as the "Tacoma Solution" or the "Tacoma Method." Those involved were viewed locally as heroes at the time, and many were able to use that fame to launch political careers.

The Anti-Chinese movement had its beginnings in San Francisco. Kearny's Workingman's Party had coined the phrase "The Chinese Must Go," targeting Chinese laborers as a perceived threat to higher-paid whites. Legislation was enacted that was aimed specifically at the Chinese, including a queue ordinance, a cubic air law and

Z. PERITZ.   M. KAUFMAN.   H. BERLINER.

——◦OFFICES:◦——

NEW YORK, 83 Walker Street.   SAN FRANCISCO, 516 & 518 Market Street.

"THE CHINESE MUST GO!"

The mighty magic of far away down prices that has been potent in rolling up the big

majorities in customers and cash at

"THE PEOPLE'S BARGAIN STORE,"

—OF—

PERITZ & COMP'NY

Still works its mighty wonders in Tacoma, towering Himalaya-like over all competitors.

Supreme in the popular heart, we pursue the even tenor of our

way, which leads us to continue our

REDUCTION OF PRICES ON GOODS OF EVERY KIND, CHARACTER AND DESCRIPTION!

We announce to the people of Tacoma and surrounding country that the "El Mahdi"

(of high prices) has been slain by us, and can never again be recalled from

from that grave in which we have forever buried him.

CLOTHING! CLOTHING! CLOTHING! CLOTHING!

As we are not compelled to make up our losses on other goods by our profits on

clothing, we can sell the workingman his suit and overalls cheaper than he can

buy them from any other firm in Tacoma; we can supply the farmer and

and the business man with a suit at a price that will astonish him,

and win for us his gratitude; while we can furnish the

fashion-loving "dude" garments of such

☞ FASHIONABLE CUT AND MAKE! ☜

Tacoma Daily Ledger March 3, 1885

even a national Chinese Exclusion Act in 1882. Coastal cities in the Pacific Northwest had strong ties to the California city and were quick to imitate her in any way.

The movement was fueled by the local press. Just as the pages of the *Tacoma Ledger* had been used to rally support for building in brick rather than wood, and a campaign to close local gambling dens, the paper also freely printed descriptions of public anti-Chinese gatherings. These were combined with lengthy editorials and inflammatory headlines. Even the business ads carried anti-Chinese slogans. Throughout the summer and fall of 1885 the issue was kept in the public eye on a daily basis. While editor Radebaugh was absent, John Comerford carried the campaign to an extreme, which cost him his job upon Radebaugh's return.

On May 24, 1885, the *Ledger*'s description of a meeting of the local anti-Chinese committee mentioned that Meyer Kaufman was among those appointed to solicit funds for the payment of hall rent, printing, etc. It would be his niche. (This is a second Meyer Kaufman, not to be confused with Old Tacoma's Meyer Kaufman, testament that in Tacoma, surnames Kaufman and Wolff were the Jewish equivalent of Johnson and Smith.)

Meyer Kaufman had opened a dry goods and clothing business, Peritz & Co., in Tacoma the previous November. Backed by his wife's complex family network of stores throughout Washington, Meyer was determined to climb to the top of the heap in Tacoma. But he had some catching up to do. He advertised lavishly, openly challenging his well-established competitors – the public-spirited Gross brothers. Meyer also jumped on the bandwagon of the latest craze – the anti-Chinese movement. The Knights of Labor were organized in Tacoma on September 7, 1885, with Meyer as a member. On September

22 Meyer's partner, Zadek Peritz, left the firm to return to Germany, indicating that perhaps the two were not in agreement.

At a statewide congress in Seattle on September 28, Tacoma's Mayor Jacob Weisbach was made president. According to *Hunt,* Volume 1, page 366, the group "adopted resolutions directing the delegates to return to their homes and call local mass meetings October 3 to name committees for the duty of notifying the Chinese to depart November 1." The stage was set.

Many cities tried, their efforts often erupting in violence, but only in Tacoma did events unfold as planned. At the meeting on October third, after a huge torchlight procession, a Committee of Fifteen was appointed, one of whom was Meyer Kaufman. The group included a probate judge, two councilmen, a fire chief and the mayor. Meetings and headlines continued throughout October.

The *Ledger* joyfully printed mentions of employers throughout the Sound who were "releasing" their Chinese workers. (Puyallup released theirs **after** the hop crops were all picked.) About one-third of Tacoma's Chinese population left on their own as a result of the growing intimidation. *Ledger* October 4, "Chinese are leaving in great numbers." October 10, "The Chinese exodus is beginning." October 13, "Going! Going! – Chinese are leaving by carloads." October 15, "Tramp, tramp, tramp the Chinks are marching."

Meyer Kaufman's ad in the *Ledger* proclaimed, "The People's Day – the Chinese are Peaceably Departing." On October 22 Meyer traveled to Puyallup to attend their anti-Chinese mass meeting, where he was chosen secretary. On the 23rd he helped organize steamer transportation for an anti-Chinese excursion to Seattle. As Tacoma prepared for another meeting on October 31st, the *Ledger* noted that M. Kaufman was chairman of the committee of arrangements. The meeting yielded a resolution that on November 3rd the Committee of Fifteen should make a "thorough investigation" to "ascertain how many Chinese remain." Thanks were given for the "indefatigable assistance of Mr. M. Kaufman, the chairman of the committee."

Meanwhile, a secret Committee of Nine had been formed, made up of carpenters and laborers. Each of them recruited another nine and those brought in another nine, again all in secret. These men were determined to actually remove the remaining Chinese, not just count or intimidate them. On November second both committees met and agitated through the night. The smaller group spent the early morning hours canvassing their districts, setting their plan in motion.

The next events are now well-known. On the morning of November third the whistle blew at Lister's Foundry. Heeding the signal, armed men gathered in the streets and methodically raided every Chinese shop and household, ordering all Chinese to leave by 1:30 p.m. *Hunt,* Volume I, page 373, described it as "a mob, but an orderly mob as mobs go." The Chinese were then "escorted" eight miles south to the railroad depot at Lakeview, (today's Lakewood) where they were loaded into boxcars and sent to Portland. The railroad agent extended the Chinese a small courtesy, allowing them to purchase tickets at a group discount rate.

Lorraine Hildebrand, in her book, *Straw Hats, Sandals and Steel: The Chinese in Washington State,* explains that, according to court testimony, "When the whistles blew, Judge Wickersham, a member of the Committee of Fifteen, said he had no knowledge until that minute that the Chinese were to be expelled. He later remembered meeting Meyer Kaufman (a local merchant and fellow Committeeman) who approached him when he saw the mob. Excitedly Kaufman exclaimed, 'My God, Wickersham, there is going to be trouble here today!'… The two stayed together all day. 'Kaufman was exceedingly nervous,' Wickersham recounted." (Judge James Wickersham was appointed to a lucrative position in Alaska in June of 1900, thanks to a friendship with Tacoma's Francis Cushman.)

The *Ledger* headline on November 4, 1885, read simply "Gone." According to the *Ledger,* "No blood has been shed, no one has been hurt; the long agony is at an end and the Chinese have gone."

Not everyone agreed. Newspapers coast to coast cried their outrage. On November tenth twenty-seven citizens were indicted by a U.S. grand jury in session in Vancouver, including Meyer Kaufman. (First identified as Charles Pertz.) Photos of the group were sold to raise funds for their defense. Court records show that case #1878, PRC-1900, conspiracy against the Chinese, was dismissed. Nine men, including Meyer, were re-indicted in October of 1886. That case also failed. Meyer also chaired the finance committee of "late indicted citizens."

1. C. E. King.	8. John Budlong.	15. Geo. D. Lawson.	22. Henry S. Bixler.
2. Geo. R. Epperson.	9. Jacob Ralph.	16. O. J. Anderson.	23. A. W. Cone.
3. E. Von Shrader.	10. D. B. Hannah	17. H. A. Stevens.	24. Louis Stimpson.
4. M. McAtee.	11. A. U. Mills.	18. E. G. Bacon.	25. Wm. Christie.
5. M. Kaufman.	12. B. R. Everett.	19. H. C. Patrick.	26. M. C. Gillis.
6. T. L. Nixon.	13. Mrs. J. A. Comerford and Child.	20. Frank McGill.	27. J. N. Fernandez.
7. A. Redenzel.	14. R. Jacob Weisbach.	21. John Forbes.	28. Jas. Wickersham.

TACOMA'S TWENTY-SEVEN.

Names of the Citizens Indicted for Causing the Chinese Exodus from Tacoma, W. T., November 3d, 1885.

JACKSON, Photographer.

Twenty-Seven Indicted Citizens. Meyer Kaufman seated with legs crossed.
Tacoma Public Library 968-1

Over the next decade or so someone from the group would occasionally resurface for a newspaper quote whenever the Asiatic labor question came up. Chinese merchants were allowed to return in 1895, with the understanding that the common class of laborers were still not welcome. On December fourteenth of that year over 1,000 citizens met in Germania Hall to protest the hiring of two Chinese cooks, which was seen as a violation of that agreement.

Meanwhile, Meyer's committee work moved into the field of politics. On August 18, 1886, the *Ledger* reported that the Democratic Convention had appointed M. Kaufman committee member on Order of Business and as a delegate to the territorial convention from the Third ward. A month later Meyer received ten votes in an election of delegates for the "Anti-Coolie Committee." However, multiple articles over the

next several years also mentioned Meyer's frequent illnesses.

On Sunday, April 10, 1887, the *Ledger* printed a lengthy article describing the appointment of Eugene Semple as Governor of Washington Territory. "The news was first received here yesterday afternoon by M. Kaufman, the Pacific avenue merchant, who had been instrumental along with other democratic citizens of the territory in securing Semple's appointment." In June Meyer arranged for a reception to welcome the new governor. That winter he accompanied the governor to the dedication of the asylum at Steilacoom. *Ledger*, December 17, 1887, "During the time that the electric light was not in working order, and as Gov. Semple was introducing M. Kaufman of Tacoma to Col. Baker and Speaker Clark, the governor asked Mr. Kaufman if he did not want a candle, to be in fashion. 'No, thanks, I don't need it,' was the reply; 'I am an Israel-ite.'"

In April of 1888 Meyer's name was mentioned as a candidate for mayor, but he declined by public card before the nominations began. Meyer also served as Pierce County's delegate to the state Democratic convention. According to the *Ledger* on April 18, "M. Kaufman of Pierce offered a resolution endorsing the administration of Cleveland and his efforts to bring about tariff reform, which was carried amid applause… Mr. Kaufman proved to be the guiding hand of the convention, and with rare political skill succeeded in bringing the delegates to his nominee. He thanked the convention in apt terms that brought down the house."

LAUGHED AT THE WOMEN.

How a Telegram Was Received in the Democratic Convention.

Here is how the democratic territorial convention at Spokane Falls treated the women of the territory:

The following telegram was received by Colonel Kaufman, who read it aloud to the convention:

TACOMA, Sept. 4.—Colonel M. Kaufman, chairman Pierce county delegates, Spokane Falls: On behalf of the women of Washington territory, I ask for an equal rights plank in the platform.

MRS. McCOY,

Vice president for Washington territory of the National Woman's Suffrage association.

The telegram was received with laughter. Colonel Kaufman raised the biggest laugh of the convention when he said: "Gentlemen of the convention, all I have to say concerning this telegram is to repeat my wife's advice. When I left home Sunday morning she said to me: 'Kaufman, nominate a good man; don't fool with the women; leave them alone.'"

Tacoma Daily Ledger September 6, 1888

His friendship with Governor Semple had its rewards. On June 19, 1888, the *Ledger* reported that Governor Semple had appointed the members of his staff under the provisions of the new militia bill. M. Kaufman, of Tacoma, was made Paymaster-General, with the rank of colonel. Meyer was called Colonel Kaufman for the rest of his life, a bit ironic for a former Confederate private. However, it did help to distinguish him from Tacoma's other "Old Meyer" Kaufman.

A year later, as Washington Territory was preparing for statehood, Meyer's political career

peaked. The first elections were to be held on October 1, 1889, in order to have a government ready to go by November. The statewide convention of Democratic delegates would meet in Ellensburg to determine their slate of candidates. On Monday evening, August 12, 1889, a group of 85 prominent men met in the courtroom of Judge Frank Allyn. According to a *Ledger* article the following day, their purpose was to form a club, to elect officials and to "sound the slogan for the coming campaign." The meeting was temporarily chaired by Hugh Wallace. "Nomination for president being in order… Wallace stated that he wished to place in nomination a man who had devoted his life to the good cause of democracy, who, sleeping or awake, was heart, soul and body in advancing the principles of his party, who, even in his last breath would attest his love for Jeffersonian doctrines. He wished, he stated, to place in nomination that honest man of affairs, that sterling democrat, Colonel M. Kaufman." Eugene Semple, now ex-governor, "made an eloquent speech seconding the nomination. Mayor Wheelwright also seconded the nomination. The rules were suspended and Colonel Kaufman's nomination was made unanimous. The motion was carried with an hurrah."

"I will go further than that," said Colonel Kaufman. "On my tombstone I wish the words placed, 'He died as he lived – a democrat.'" An article in the *Tacoma Daily News* on the thirteenth carried the full text of Colonel Kaufman's "remarkable speech," beginning "Gentlemen and democrats – I might as well attempt to gild the sunbeams or paint the lily as to find words to thank you for this honor."

In early September Kaufman traveled by train to Ellensburg. On September tenth the *Tacoma Daily News* reported on page one that the Democratic slate of candidates for the state's first officers had been chosen. "For treasurer, William H. White, of King, nominated Colonel M. Kaufman, of Pierce, declaring that King County was determined to discharge its debt of gratitude, but that it cannot return it in half measure. Hugh Wallace seconded the nomination, eulogizing Mr. Kaufman as a war horse in the democratic cause… Mr. Kaufman's speech of acknowledgment of the honor was the hit of the evening. If the gentlemen of the convention had any money to be taken care of he was ready and was sure the convention would not be ashamed of its nominee for secretary of the treasury. At this the house broke into loud applause." (The "debt of gratitude" was for Tacoma's aid after Seattle's great fire in June.)

During the October first elections Colonel Kaufman "occupied a seat in a neighboring cigar store all day, giving out both tickets and stickers bearing his name." Election returns varied from day to day as officials were replaced and precincts recounted. By October 9 Pierce County's election results were complete, with Kaufman trailing by nearly 800 votes. He was a proud Democrat in a Republican county. October 24 brought final election results – 34,603 votes for A.A. Lindsley; 24,469 for M. Kaufman. Republicans had prevailed statewide.

Colonel Kaufman then returned to the source of his fame. *Ledger*, October 27, 1889, "The committee of fifteen and the citizens who figured in 'the Chinese exclusion act' in 1885, propose to mark the occasion of the fourth anniversary, on November 3, by a banquet." November 1, "The celebration of the fourth anniversary of the eviction of the Chinese from Tacoma will be held on Monday next. There will be public exercises at the Alpha opera house, to be followed by a banquet." The committee continued giving themselves anniversary banquets for many years.

NOTICE.

A meeting of the committee of fifteen and the twenty-seven indicted citizens who had charge of the peaceable exodus of the Chinese from the city of Tacoma November 3, 1885, will meet at the office of Thomas Carroll on Wednesday at 4 p. m. to make arrangements to celebrate the fourth anniversary of the departure of the Chinese.

THOS. L. NIXON,
M. KAUFMAN,
S. B. HANNAH,
JOHN FORBES,
Committee of Arrangements.

Tacoma Daily Ledger October 29, 1889

Meyer's health steadily declined. On November 30, 1889, he signed his will, dividing his personal and real property between his wife and daughter. Colonel Meyer Kaufman died on February 15, 1891, only 46 years old. He was buried in the cemetery he'd helped to create. The stock of his store was sold that fall to satisfy a tangle of creditors and mortgages.

Colonel Kaufman's health failed while he was a relatively young man. Many merchants in the Northwest suffered health problems because of the damp weather and primitive living conditions. Others faced even greater health challenges. . .

Confined to the Asylum

Over a century ago mental health care and treatment typically meant admission to an "insane asylum." Tacoma's Jewish citizens seemed to have more than their share of mental instability. Some lived out their remaining days in confinement. Others did not receive appropriate care and ended their lives tragically. Some may have been institutionalized as the only method of obtaining long-term skilled nursing care.

State Insane Asylum, Fort Steilacoom, near Tacoma, Washington.

Tacoma Historical Society Cristell Collection

As previously noted, in 1882 Louisa Goodtime's brother-in-law applied to have her committed to the asylum in Steilacoom. She was found fit to manage her affairs and he was charged with court costs. Not all were as fortunate.

Joseph Dobrin, son of Olympia's Morris Dobrin, first faced insanity charges in 1879 when he was about 23. Joseph worked as a compositor for the *Daily Olympian*, handling lead type for hours on end. *Tacoma Daily Ledger*, April 8, 1897, "Attendants Johnson and Hunt, yesterday morning took about 30 of the patients with them to the farm, about a mile from the main building, where they were engaged in falling trees and clearing the land. They had one tree cut and wedged, ready to topple over and had placed the patients in a safe place when Dobrin, who was among the number, ran in front of where the tree was expected to fall. He was caught and brought back just as the tree was thrown down, but ran out again, this time being struck by a falling limb and instantly killed. Coroner Hoska fully investigated the case and found the facts as stated. He (Joseph) had been incarcerated in the asylum for the past 17 or 18 years, at different times, his last commitment being in 1888." Joseph Dobrin was buried in Olympia near his father and younger sister.

Henry Harris was a tailor in Tacoma throughout the 1880s. A trustee of the Home of Peace Cemetery, Henry also managed the funds of the Ladies' Judith Montefiore Society. Later testimony revealed that Meyer Kaufman and David Levin had known Harris for twenty years and that "he was subject to insane spells." Henry's wife and son moved to Spokane, and Henry's condition apparently deteriorated. He got the notion that his 25-year-old daughter's reputation had been compromised and feared a scandal, but his actions only made it worse. On August 14, 1892, Henry stabbed and shot his daughter and then shot himself. The murder/suicide became the subject of the *Tacoma News'* first special edition. Father and daughter were both buried in unmarked graves in Home of Peace Cemetery.

EXTRA

KILLS HIS DAUGHTER

KILLS HIMSELF.

Henry Harris, the Tailor, the Murderer and Suicide.

Tacoma Daily News EXTRA
August 14, 1892

Just before Abe Gross's twenty-ninth birthday, as the gavel was being raised on the bankruptcy auction of their nearest competitor, Abe put a revolver in his mouth and pulled the trigger. The *Sunday Ledger* headlines on April 1, 1895 read "DEAD IN HIS BED. Mysterious End of the Most Popular Man in Tacoma. Suicide the Accepted Theory, Though No Cause is Known. A Smith and Wesson Revolver Was Grasped in the Dead Man's Hands." His cause of death was ruled as gunshot by unknown causes. Abe's death remains a mystery.

What little is known of Solomon Zelinsky's wife, Ida, comes from newspaper accounts of his divorce hearing. The couple had been married since 1878. In 1885 she traveled from Germany to New York to join her husband. *Ledger,* November 13, 1887. "He says that he wanted to remain in New York and she would not consent but wanted to go to Germany, so he left her and came to Tacoma. Zelinsky claims that his wife's people in Germany have heard that she was dead, while it was shown that a letter had been received from the superintendent of the insane asylum on Blackwell's Island, New York, stating that the woman was committed to that institution in May, 1886, suffering from chronic dementia. As Mrs. Zelinsky had been nearly crazed by the death of her four children while in route to Tacoma from Germany to join her husband six weeks before the separation in New York, it is not impossible that her mind became unseated by her troubles. It was also proven that more than a year ago Mrs. Zelinsky wrote to her husband's brother in Tacoma asking as to the whereabouts of Mr. Zelinsky, and that the latter requested that a reply be sent that nothing was known about him." The divorce was granted and became final in May of 1888, despite Ida's recovery. (That same year Nellie Bly feigned insanity and spent ten days in Blackwell's Island as an investigative journalist, reporting on the conditions there.) Solomon remarried in July of 1890.

Annie Berliner married David Magnus in Tacoma in 1887. The couple moved to Seattle around 1893. Only one of her four children survived. After David's death in 1923 Annie was moved to the state hospital at Steilacoom for care, where she died in 1934.

Jennie Herzman married Samuel Posner around 1882. The couple moved to Tacoma in the late 1880s and ran a prominent dry goods store through 1906. Sam's clothing store was one of the few that did not go bankrupt during the 1890s. The family moved to Portland in 1907 and ran a clothing store, a fruit business, a grocery, and later a fish market. Sam died in 1911, followed by their daughter Ruth in 1920. A few months after Ruth's death Jennie turned on the gas and climbed into bed with Ruth's two young sons, killing them all. According to a front-page article in the *Oregonian* on May 19, 1920, Jennie had become despondent over her daughter's death and couldn't imagine the boys growing up without their mother.

Abraham Goldsmith moved to Seattle from California with his parents and six siblings sometime before 1880. In 1886 Abraham's sister Belle married Tacoma clothing dealer Henry Isaacs and the various sisters became active in Tacoma's Jewish society. Members of the Goldsmith family lived in Tacoma in 1894 and 1895. Census records included Abe as a patient at Steilacoom in 1900, 1910 and 1920.

Caroline Peyser survived the deaths of her husband, and all but one of her children. Mother and son eked out a living peddling fruit, often receiving loans and assistance from the Jewish community.

Ledger, August 4, 1896:

"William F. Peyser was adjudged insane by Doctors Dewey and Misner in Judge Pritchard's court yesterday afternoon and was ordered committed to Steilacoom for treatment. Peyser is the young man who was examined for alleged insanity before Judge Parker about a month ago and was discharged. For the past few weeks he had worked as a solicitor for the San Francisco Examiner. Recently he became so queer in his actions that the police were compelled to interfere and locked him up as a dangerous character. The examination yesterday developed the fact that the young man was suffering from dementia and believed that enemies were on his track who were bent upon his destruction.

When the medical commission adjudged Peyser insane his mother, who was present, gave way to the emotions that possessed her and fell unconscious in the corridor of the court house. She was carried into the sheriff's office, where she remained insensible for an hour and a half, when she was removed to the city and county hospital. There she was brought out of her unconscious state by the physician in charge and at last accounts last night was getting along all right. It is believed that a short sojourn at Steilacoom will effect a cure in her son's case."

William was released nineteen days later and pronounced cured.

MOTHER AND BOY BOTH MENTALLY DERANGED

Mrs. Pyser Is Held for Examination as to Sanity — Son Sent to Steilacoom Friday.

Tacoma Daily Ledger November 29, 1903

William was again arrested in December of 1900, this time demanding a hearing by a jury and cross-examining witnesses himself. According to the *Ledger* on December 16 he was described as "nutty," with "a weak spot mentally" and "more of an idiot" than insane. "Mrs. P., the defendant's mother, pleaded for her boy. She said that all of her children were dead except this one and that he was a good boy and took care of her. The jury was only five minutes in reaching the conclusion that the defendant was sane." The scenario was repeated in 1903. In July of 1917 William was committed to the Oregon State Hospital for the Insane, but escaped in March of 1918. By 1930 he was again confined, this time at the Connecticut State Hospital for the Insane in Middletown, where he died in 1949.

Solomon Voloshin suffered from alcoholism. Born in Russia and originally trained as a rabbi, he was fluent in many languages. He arrived in Tacoma from Winnipeg around 1897 and worked as a junk peddler. Newspaper mentions of him were found in the police reports – a saloon row on a Saturday afternoon in July of 1897, a knife fight in May of 1899, and a victim of a $6 holdup in December of 1899. He died on March 3, 1902, after "a debauch a week previous." The inquest exonerated Miss Frankie Williams. Solomon's grave was unmarked until 1999.

INQUEST ON DEATH OF JEWISH JUNK DEALER

POST MORTEM EXAMINATION HELD ON SOLOMON VOLOSHIN.

Had Received Severe Injuries About Head Which Caused Concussion of Brain.

The post mortem examination of Solomon Voloshin at Hoska's undertaking quarters last night, preliminary to an inquest which will be held on Saturday, showed that the man was not only in a badly diseased condition, but had received severe injuries a short time previous to his death. He had suffered concussion of the brain and that organ was in a badly inflamed condition along one side. The left eye was also inflamed and bloodshot, but as to whether it had been injured by a weapon or not Coroner Brown is unwilling to state until he has heard the formal report of the physicians. In addition to these injuries the examination showed that the man had been a sufferer from pulmonary weakness and kidney disorder.

Voloshin, who was a Jewish junk peddler, died Monday evening as the result of a debauch a week previous. He had been removed from his quarters on C street to a city hospital. Last week he borrowed a dollar and became so drunk that he remained out in the rain all night. When found he was in a helpless condition,

At the time it was alleged that Frankie Williams, a dance hall habitue, who had formed a strong aversion to the man, had early in the evening stabbed him in the eye with the point of her umbrella, and she was subsequently arrested. Her case

Tacoma Daily Ledger March 5, 1902

Those with means were treated better by the press. The body of Albert Weinberg's new bride, Esther Levy, was found at the bottom of the cliff below the elegant Tacoma Hotel on Thanksgiving morning of 1885. Her death was attributed to sleepwalking. When Archie Ash's despondent 18-year-old daughter Frances put a revolver to her head in 1911, the family assured investigators that she had interrupted a burglar. Fortunately, the bullet merely grazed her forehead. Nearly a decade later Frances "disappeared" while swimming in Waikiki.

Mental health concerns weren't the only problem facing these pioneers. Other perils awaited them...

Perils of Proprietorship

In the horse and buggy days of early Tacoma, the newspapers carried daily descriptions of accidents – riders tossed from their mounts, carriages overturned, and horses running away with their drivers. Tacoma's Jewish merchants, perhaps less experienced horsemen than others, were no exception. Again, those newspaper accounts give modern researchers a detailed look at the challenges faced over a century ago.

The *Olympia Courier* on November 10, 1874, described a serious accident in which a wagon tipped over, killing one of the three occupants. Brewer Wolf Schafer was injured and lucky to lose only several teeth.

Ledger, Tuesday, October 16, 1883, "A runaway occurred yesterday morning near the Tacoma Iron Works. The team, belonging to Wolf Bros., of the New York Bakery, was standing on the side of the avenue, when they became frightened at a log and ran off, but did not succeed in getting far before the driver checked them, but not before the horses had run the wagon into the ditch and broken the spring and several other parts of the wagon, and distributed the pies and bread over the road in a promiscuous manner." Over the next decade the story was repeated nearly every year, typically ending with a description of scattered breads and pastries.

In the fall of 1884 Charles Langert proudly purchased a fine pair of spirited matching bay horses for his wholesale liquor firm. The first runaway in November resulted in the destruction of the firm's delivery wagon and a broken leg for his bookkeeper. The following month, Charles was driving a rented buggy. *Ledger,* December 9, 1884, "C. Langert's handsome bay team took a notion into their heads yesterday afternoon to wake things up on the hill and furnish the newspapers with an item, and to that end inaugurated a disastrous runaway. They began first by trying to kick the dashboard over

Mr. Langert's head. Failing in this, they started down E street at full pace. Mr. L. got frightened, and jumped out and let them have their own way about it. They turned in back of the Catholic Church, where they upset the buggy and broke off the top. The running gears were left in the alley a short distance beyond, and the horses ran to Freeman & Imbrie's stable. The buggy is badly demolished. It belongs to Freeman & Imbrie, and was one of their best. Mr. Langert did not pick for a soft spot when he jumped, and sustained several slight injuries, such as a sprained thumb, bruised shoulder and 'barked shins.' He will be around to-day, but it would be worth a man's life to slap him on the shoulder." By January of 1885 the horses appeared in the classified section, offered for sale.

In March of 1886 hotelkeeper Meyer Kaufman of Old Tacoma was thrown from his horse, catching his foot in the stirrup. He was dragged for over sixty feet, his head striking the ground, before he dropped senseless to the road. Friends came to his rescue and he soon regained consciousness, surprisingly with no serious injury.

Sometimes it was difficult to tell if the newspaper mentions were accident reports or advertisements.

ANOTHER BAD RUNAWAY.

A Scene on Pacific Avenue—A Narrow Escape From Death.

There was another tremendous runaway yesterday afternoon and the serious results that ensued should be a warning lesson to those who have teams to tie their horses. A splendid looking pair of horses became frightened at the wharf at one of the snorting engines of the Northern Pacific railroad, and started up the hill on Pacific avenue toward the headquarters building at a fearful rate of speed. The driver, George Harrison, who had jumped in behind when the horses started and made his way over a lot of boxes to the reins, was powerless to stop the mad animals. When they reached Seventh street the horses gave a wicked spring to the left which wrenched the wagon and the driver was thrown to the ground his head striking on a boulder near the gutter. He was picked up senseless and carried into one of the adjoining stores. Doctor Rafferty, stopping at the hotel Tacoma, was quickly summoned, and pronounced him dead. The horses continued in their mad flight southward and when passing Tenth street Colonel John Holgate, with his usual daring intrepidity rushed into the street and caught one of the animals by the rein near the head. He was thrown against a bulletin board next door to his establishment and doubled up like a boy with the cramps. The horses were not stopped until they reached Colonel Steele's residence near the school section. It was the team of Chapman & Co., the Pacific avenue grocers. Mr. Chapman was quickly notified of the accident and made his way to where the driver was lying. He was not quite dead, and with several bottles of Gordon & Dilworth's blackberry brandy which he took with him and administered to the apparently dying man, he was soon revived. He never ceased drinking until he had stored away twelve bottles of the excellent brandy, and the firm have given him a week's leave of absence to sober up and fully recover from the shock and the palatable liquid. One of the funny incidents of this almost tragic runaway was the manner in which the goods were spilled out of the wagon all along Pacific avenue.

Mr. Rosenbaum went along the line to recover some of them and succeeded in collaring one case of Gordon & Dilworth's preserves, two cases of olives, three cases of tomato catsup, four cases of salad dressing, 7 cases of orange marmalade, 3 cases of capers, 11 cases of Durkee's salad dressing, 2 cases of Sinder's grape sauce, 2 cases of Chili, 3 of spiced lobster, 4 of spiced mussels, 3 of French truffles, 2 of Yarmouth bloaters, 3 cases of Crosse & Blackwell's bologna sausage, 4 cases of midget pickles, 413 boxes of the Franco-American Food company soups.

Mr. Rosenbaum could not find the following goods, which are supposed to have been pilfered by small boys; 10 boxes of French candies, 2 boxes of Autocrat Reisling wine, 1 box each of Zinfandel wine, bock wine, sherry wine, Angelica wine and port wine, 1 case of Richardson & Robbins' plum pudding sauce, 3 cases of plum pudding sauce and 14 cases of potted meats. Last evening the members of the firm were tired, but ready for any emergency.

Tacoma Daily Ledger July 22, 1888

In March of 1892 pawnbroker Archie Ash and his family were about to go for a drive when their horse was startled. It took off running down Thirteenth Street all the way from I Street to Pacific. The wagon finally overturned, throwing the family out of the wagon and against a billboard, breaking their fall. They escaped with cuts, bruises, and broken ribs.

Phœnix Like From the Ashes!

—THE—

Wholesale and Importing House

—FOR—

WINES, LIQUORS AND CIGARS,

—OF—

C. LANGERT

Has survived the recent great fire in Tacoma, and is now temporarily open for business next door to Freeman & Imbrie's livery stable, on

A STREET, BETWEEN 13 & 14,

Tacoma Daily Ledger September 5, 1884

On January 22, 1884, the *Ledger* carried a column headed "Not a Burglar. On Sunday night, as A. Simon, the proprietor of the Terminus boot and shoe store, was walking down Pacific Avenue he noticed a man in front of him, trying all the store doors to see if he could gain admittance. When the fellow reached Simon's store he stopped and peered in at the window and then tried the door. Simon, who was watching him, pulled out a whistle and blew for the police, thinking the fellow intended to burglarize his store. The police were busy just then putting a drunk into the city jail and did not make their appearance for a few minutes, but when they did the man was overhauled and it then became apparent to the guardians of the peace that he was not trying to commit a burglary, but was hunting for a saloon. He had evidently got into the wrong block."

After a fire swept through the heart of the business district on Easter morning of 1884, Abraham Simon had four large wooden boxes built for his merchandise. The boxes were mounted on wheels, so they could be easily moved in case of another disaster. Sure enough, most of Whiskey Row was destroyed by fire in July. Abraham quickly rented a new space and was back in business the next day. However, his system wasn't foolproof. *Ledger* ads throughout the next week read "Missing. Taken or Misplaced, during the late fire, a wagon load of goods, consisting of three boxes boots and shoes, a lot of sole leathers, calf skins and a box of lasts. Any information of the same will be very thankfully received by A. Simon, Pacific Avenue between Fifteenth & Sixteenth Streets." By August he had new merchandise arriving and was selling off his smoke-damaged goods.

Newspaper accounts routinely mentioned fires, broken windows, and other hazards of doing business. Petty thefts and burglaries were common. Often merchants resorted to self-defense.

> The festive burglar has come again. Last week Mr. Joseph Cheim was awakened at 2 a. m. by some one trying to force an entrance to the store through the rear door. Failing in the attempt he tried one of the side windows where, after breaking one of the panes, he had the pleasure of looking down the barrels of two—seven shooters, and into the calm, placid, tranquil face of Mr. C. who quietly informed him that it would be better for him not to call again. He didn't.
>
> *Tacoma Daily Ledger December 30, 1884*

Ledger, August 13, 1887, "He Ought to Buy a Gun. H.W. Bryer was disturbed about 3 o'clock yesterday morning by a burglar trying to force an entrance into his fruit store from the rear of the building, near the room where Mr. Bryer was sleeping. He got out of bed, and the only weapon he could find was a stepladder. With this in hand he made for the door, but the burglar, hearing him, was frightened and hurriedly made his retreat."

Others turned thefts into advertising opportunities. In September of 1888 thieves stole over $1,000 worth of merchandise from the Gross Brothers' store, including rolls of expensive silks. Four young boys from Chicago were quickly caught in Seattle and the goods returned. The store's next ad took advantage of the burglary, encouraging shoppers to come and view the recovered silks and learn the details of the break-in.

Sometimes the supposed-partners were the thieves. *Ledger,* October 18, 1892, "Took His Partner's Tools. Jeweler Adolph Herzog consulted the police yesterday, requesting them to have Van Ness arrested in Spokane for skipping from the city and leaving at least one unpaid debt behind. Van Ness had persuaded Herzog, the lat-ter says, to purchase $40 worth of jeweler's tools and loan him $20 to start out in business with S. Silverman, who had a shop on Pacific Avenue. Silverman, several days since, started out with his pack to peddle his wares in the southern part of the state, and his partner took the opportunity to skip out with the tools. Herzog has telegraphed Silverman to return and learn the amount of his loss."

Later in the same column, "The Peddler Returns. Simon Silverman returned late last evening from the Carbonado mines to look after his partner, Van Ness, who has skipped to Spokane. He was so excited over the affair that he was unable to unlock his safe containing his jewelry, having forgotten the combination. Three years ago he and his partner, Lynch, were robbed of their entire stock of cheap jewelry, and the little peddler was upset over the affair for months afterwards." October 20, "S. Silverman, on his return, found that his safe had been robbed of $300 worth of jewelry by his former partner, L. Van Ness."

In 1894 Henry Krech purposely broke the law by operating his barbershop on a Sunday, so he could challenge the legality of the city's Sunday ordinance. He and his lawyers spent nearly a year working their way through the appeal system, paying fines and court costs until their case was eventually heard in the state Supreme Court. Henry argued that the law was illegal — discriminating against certain businesses, and compelling observance of the Christian religion. The local court ruled that Sunday was merely a day of rest, not of a specific religion, but the Supreme Court overruled the decision.

The following year the city adopted a new Sunday ordinance, and Henry repeated the process, again spending nearly a year in the effort. *Ledger,* September 29, 1896, "Henry Krech, of Tacoma, has won his fight against the city in the matter of Sunday shaving. The Supreme Court has decided that to compel closing of barbershops on Sunday is plainly granting privileges and immunities to one class which did not belong equally to all citizens."

Faced with multiple challenges, many of Tacoma's Jewish merchants formed partnerships — through business, and through marriage...

Partnerships and Unions

Michael Ball and Mentheim Cohn
Courtesy of Ed Ball

Often Jewish merchants operated businesses in partnership – reducing the financial risk and sharing the workload. Typically, the firm carried the name of the two related partners – as in Pincus & Packscher, Kaufman & Berliner, or Feist & Bachrach. These partnerships came through a wide variety of relationships – bringing a brother-in-law into an existing business, marrying a partner's sister or cousin, two partners marrying sisters, or a clerk marrying the boss's daughter.

Other partnerships were made up of brothers or fathers and sons. Additionally, Jewish merchants hired Jewish clerks, preferably a nephew or cousin who would be trustworthy and work long hours for low pay. Study from a genealogical viewpoint reveals that Tacoma's early Jewish merchants were not 165 separate families, but rather clusters of intermarried families, working in similar business fields. The following are just a few examples of the tangles created by those unions.

- Solomon Rogers married Eva Abrams in San Francisco, daughter of the clothing merchant Isaac Abrams. The couple moved to Tacoma and her sisters followed. Lizzie Abrams married Bene Benjamin, Sarah married Joseph Kaufman, and Celia married Dave Shafer. Rogers, Benjamin and Shafer were all Russian/Polish immigrants who operated clothing stores.

- Sisters Jette and Jennie Ascher married Solomon Zelinsky and Julius Rammelsberg. Their brother John worked for Abraham Hockwald, M. Cohn, I. Altman, and later Joseph Cheim.

- One of Mentheim Cohn's stores was managed by Michael Ball. Michael's half-brother George Ball had married Fanny Cohn, Mentheim's sister.

- Louis Wallerstein brought Isaac Cohen into his candy business, then married Isaac's sister Carrie Cohen.

- The dry goods firm of Feist and Bachrach was created when Joseph Bachrach married Theophil Feist's sister Lucy Feist.

- Abraham Goldenson and Samuel Sondheim were partners in the Rochester Clothing Store. First Samuel married Bertha Frank, then Abraham married her sister Rosa Frank.

- Herman Kaufman married Sarah Klaber, sister of Herman Klaber, then managed Herman Klaber's business and estate. (Kaufman's daughter Elsa married Samuel Levinson.)

- Edward Wolff worked for Lewin & Co. in 1888 and in 1889 married Minna Lewin.

- David P. Lewis was the brother of Abe

Simon's wife, Sarah Lewis. David's wife Mollie was the sister of Henry Berliner's wife, Regina Stenger. Later in Portland the barber supply company was Lewis-Stenger, in Seattle it was Berliner-Stenger.

o Samuel Martin partnered with William T. Lewis in the Central Nisqually Land Company and other ventures. William married Sam's sister Lucy Martin. Another sister, Rachel Martin, married pawnbroker Lewis Levy.

o Isaac Pincus had partnered with Adolph Packscher for several years before he married Adolph's cousin, Seraphina. Adolph Packscher married Sarah Goodtime, and her brother Heyman Goodtime joined the families in Steilacoom. Later Joseph Cheim married Seraphina's niece, Rose Davis.

o Solomon Jacoby managed the Tacoma branch of the Prager Brothers store. His sister Frances was married to Hyman Prager. Her son Sidney married Pauline Jacobs, daughter of Moses Jacobs.

o William Eckstein, tailor, married Rebecca Simon, daughter of Abe & Sarah Simon. The firm of R. Eckstein was managed by George Simon, and became Eckstein and Simon.

o Adolph Friedman married his grand-niece, Mascha Stusser, sister of Jennie Stusser.

o Albert Weinberg first married Esther Levy, sister of Hannah Levy, Mrs. William Wolff. After Esther's death he married Mattie Loeb, sister to Sam Loeb, his partner in the brewing industry. Sam Loeb married a daughter of Marcus and Lena Moses, Blanche Moses.

o Wolff sisters created a web of relationships. Fanny married Max Cohn, who worked for Sam Wolff; Paula married Julius Mamlock, Adeline married Amil Zelinsky.

o Rosa Gutfeld married Herman Zelinsky. Her sister Ida married Solomon Ottenheimer.

Inter-marriage didn't automatically assure that the families would get along. *Ledger,* February 11, 1888, "QUARRELING NEIGHBORS. The Wolff-Mamlock Trouble – An Alleged Nuisance. L.H. Wolff and J.B. Mamlock live in adjoining houses on G Street, but have never been able to live peaceably together as good neighbors should. Mamlock once had Mrs. Wolff arrested charged with assault and Mr. Wolff for breaking down a fence. Finally one of them caused a high board fence to be erected between the houses.

Matters have been quiet recently, until yesterday, when Wolff swore out a complaint in Judge Lawrence's court charging Mamlock with maintaining a nuisance in the way of a cow and horse stable." (The charges were dismissed.)

Ledger, Thursday, August 16, 1888, "In Court Again. The case of August Reishal for assaulting Mrs. Sarah Wolff was called yesterday at 2 o'clock before Justice Lawrence. Reishal was found guilty and charged $10 and costs. He gave notice of appeal. Justice Lawrence said after the trial: "This is a hard crowd. Mrs. Wolf and Mrs. Mamlock, who live at the corner of G and Sixth streets; are related, and they are constantly fighting. I am sick and tired of them. There ought to be a special justice elected and stationed up there for their benefit."

And sometimes, when the partnerships dissolved, the former partners turned on each other. *Ledger,* November 15, 1890.

"PARTNERS FALL OUT... The California wine house was established over one year ago by Messrs. Postman and Williams under the firm name of Williams & Co., and it has proven a very successful business venture. Mr. Postman had personal charge of the establishment, and he was generally regarded in business circles as the controlling spirit. Much tact and shrewdness were employed in conducting the house, with the result that it soon became a popular resort for those who are partial to the cheer confined in attractively labeled and cut glass bottles, and in kegs beneath handsomely stained oak bars. A feature of the place, and one that will probably cut quite a figure in the forthcoming legal fight, is a number of paintings in oil, which have been on exhibition from time to time and where were described as the work of celebrated masters. Recently the firm dissolved partnership on the suggestion of an arbitration committee, Mr. Williams continuing the business. An alleged mistake was afterwards discovered, which led to the arrest of Postman on the charge of being an absconding debtor. The case was disposed of by the superior court Thursday in the dismissal of Mr. Postman from custody, and steps were at once taken by the latter to recover damages." Mr. Postman also retaliated by telling the *Ledger* that the paintings by "celebrated masters" were copies done by a local artist, with the frames costing more than the paintings. "I can stand a great deal, but when my business integrity is questioned the matter goes a little too far. I'll make it interesting for somebody before the trouble is settled… The paintings referred to by Mr. Postman were cheap copies of the famous productions known as the "Suicide," "Surprise," "the Renouncement," "Adam and Eve," the "Bath" and several others, the exhibition of which caused a little ripple of excitement in official circles as to their propriety. Mr. Postman has postponed his trip to San Francisco for the present and will go on a keen hunt for Mr. Williams' bank account."

However the most complex web of families was the one woven around Col. Meyer Kaufman's wife. Just before coming to Tacoma in 1884 Meyer had married Minna Auerbach, widow of Isadore Berliner. Her sons, Arthur and Max, were about ten and eleven. Her niece and nephew, Annie and Henry Berliner, joined them in Tacoma. Henry later became a partner in the clothing firm of Kaufman and Berliner. Annie soon married Steilacoom's David Magnus, and Henry married Spokane's Regina Stenger. To complicate relationships, Regina's sister Mollie Stenger married Tacoma's David Lewis in a double wedding.

Meyer Kaufman initially opened his store with Zadek Peritz, supported by the Toklas and Singerman Company. Again, Mina was the connection. Her eldest sister, Henriette Auerbach, was married to Zadek Peritz. Another sister, Jennie, was married to Seattle's Paul Singerman. A fourth sibling, Herman Auerbach, operated the Great Eastern store in Spokane. The extended Auerbach, Stenger, and Berliner families came from Kempen, (now Kepno) Poland.

Another family from Kempen, named Toklas, tangled the web even more, as multiple Toklas siblings entered the mix. Ferdinand Toklas (father of Alice B. Toklas) met Paul Singerman in San Francisco and the two opened a store in Seattle. (The rest of his family used the spelling Singermann.) Ferdinand had married Amilia Levinsky, daughter of developer Louis Levinsky. A decade later Ferdinand's younger brother Nathan Toklas married her younger sister Laura.

Spinning the web further, two Toklas sisters married siblings in Kempen before moving to Washington. Louisa Toklas married Moses Kaufman Gallewski, and Hulda married his brother Nathan. Between the various extended families and their children, they operated stores in more than half a dozen cities in Washington – Seattle, Tacoma, Puyallup, Olympia, Aberdeen, Spokane and Bellingham, plus several in Alaska, under a variety of names. For such a widespread family, they too managed to leave surprisingly few descendants.

But there's one more layer to the web. After Meyer Kaufman died, his stepsons Arthur and Max followed the coffee trade to Quetzaltenango, Guatemala, in the late 1890s, as did many other families from Kempen. They created new lives as Arturo and Maximo – crossing an ocean and learning a new language, as they had already done once before. Their half sister, Martha Kaufman, born in Tacoma in 1885, married Siegfried (Salvador) Koenigsberger. The couple divided their time between New York and Guatemala. Martha's grandson "Skip" shared this photo of their graves in Quetzaltenango.

As we've seen, the partnerships of the men — both business and personal — were extremely complex. The women, however, brought a vast array of experiences to Tacoma, yet often had a great deal in common…

The Fairer Sex

Jeane Jacobs Asher
Courtesy of Ann Fuller

History is often just that – "his" story. It's more difficult to learn about the lives of the women. Census records and passenger lists often abbreviated first names with a single initial. Newspapers rarely mentioned a married woman's given name. Many a genealogist has winced when reading an obituary that ended with the vague statement, "The deceased leaves a wife and two children." Yet still, patterns emerge.

Some women sailed to the United States in the company of close family members. Minna Auerbach Berliner arrived in New York in 1883 with her son, her brother, and his wife. They traveled directly to the Pacific Northwest, where more family members and a potential husband awaited. Occasionally single women traveled alone, as did Seraphina Packscher, who arrived in New York in October of 1862. In spite of the war, or perhaps because of it, from there she got herself to Victoria, British Columbia, to join her uncle.

More typically, married men came ahead, got settled, and then sent for their wives and children. Somehow their wives managed the complexities of travel on their own, often responsible for several young children. Occasionally one of the men got a little too settled, and never sent for his wife. When after nearly a decade Leopold Wolff's wife sent a letter to Tacoma through the German consulate asking about her husband's whereabouts, she learned that he had divorced her for "desertion" and remarried.

Prosperous German merchants were sometimes able to return to visit relatives, as did the Simon Donau family in 1870. However, they took the unusual step of leaving their youngest child in Germany for a decade. More often, women left their parents and family behind, perhaps never to see them again. When Helen Gross married, her brothers commissioned life-sized paintings of their parents as a poignant wedding gift. A year after Belle Reichenbach's arrival in Tacoma she traveled to San Francisco to visit her sister, whom she had not seen for twenty-one years. Two years later, unable to attend her niece's wedding in Philadelphia, Belle hosted an elaborate dinner party in Tacoma in honor of the affair, celebrating vicariously. Several other families in Tacoma hosted similar wedding celebration events.

On the other end of the spectrum, many a young bride brought her mother into the marriage, along with a few unmarried siblings, as Max Broh, Sam Loeb and Archie Ash learned. Those who married sisters shared the duties, including Samuel Sondheim and Abraham Goldenson, who took turns hosting their wives' mother, Emily Frank. In exchange, the in-laws built "double house," or duplexes, for the extended families.

Then, as today, residents typically lived in several states before calling Tacoma home. Vallie Martin lived an extremely nomadic life, as her husband worked as an auctioneer or "huckster." Not only did she give birth to seven children in seven different states before, during and after the Civil War; but when her husband died, she continued the business on her own.

It's impossible to tell if marriages were for love or practicality, by choice or by arrangement. Yet the vast majority of those marriages were permanent, with very few ending in divorce. Women who did divorce could appear in another city calling themselves widows. Before government-issued identity documents, women also had the luxury of rolling their birthdates forward. It was common practice for women – especially unmarried women – to report aging only eight or nine years between each decade of the census.

Tacoma's Jewish women were perhaps most diverse in their financial status. Belle Reichenbach, Amelia Donau and Frieda Cohn topped the social ladder, hosting elegant parties while wearing diamonds and expensive costumes. And all three of them continued their frequent entertaining despite – or maybe contributing to – their husbands' bankruptcies.

Frieda Cohn
Courtesy of Ed Ball

Many brought their own financial resources to their marriage, investing in their husband's business through loans or notes. When those businesses failed, creditors frequently attempted to discredit those debts as fraudulent claims. Bertha Dobrin had to sue to separate her property from her husband's indebtedness, as did Sarah Goodtime Packscher and Carrie Henschel Ball.

On the other extreme, the minutes of the Judith Montefiore Society reflect charity efforts on behalf of struggling widowed women such as Sarah Simon Hirschfield and her children. And after her sister, Rachel Simon Hussey, took the unusual step of fleeing her abusive husband, Rachel had to sue a Portland orphanage for the return of her infant son, even though she was the court-appointed custodial parent.

A good number of Tacoma's Jewish women demonstrated solid business and organizational skills. Augusta Adler filed for three patents in her own name. Tacoma's Jewish women established clubs and organizations, wrote by-laws and elected officers, and fastidiously recorded minutes. Often assisted at home by maids and other servants, they worked in citywide charitable organizations, taught religious school,

and hosted successful fundraising events. And they found time to chaperone visiting nieces and cousins, thinly masking their efforts to find them suitable spouses.

Despite their diverse backgrounds and lifestyles, the vast majority of Tacoma's pioneer women – whether Jewish or not, shared the common experience of loss. A letter might bring word of the death of a parent in Europe weeks or months before. Children succumbed to loosely-diagnosed illnesses such as "summer complaint." Bertha Dobrin lost a daughter to typhoid, suggesting that the family lacked access to clean water. Caroline Peyser buried her 18-year-old son after a failed hip surgery. History will never know of the secret tragedies of miscarriage and the heartbreak of infertility.

As today, parents couldn't always protect their children from accidents and hazards. Pauline Coleman's daughter fell down a stairway and was crippled for life. Lucy Martin's teenage son, Morris Cahen, was thrown from a mule wagon and run over by the wheels. He was fortunate to survive, but at the time a shattered ankle meant loss of the use of his leg. Marie Mamlock died two years before her 18-year-old son, Ludwig, was killed in a creosote explosion. His employer denied any blame. Lottie Winkleman lost her 19-year-old son Gabriel in 1906, and her husband in 1911. Five years later her son Raphael was killed in a warehouse fire in Seattle. Most horrifically, in 1892 Julia Marx lost her toddler son, Berthold, in a freak accident. The couple had no more children.

Little Child Drowned.

SEATTLE (Wash.), Dec. 29.—A thirteen-months-old baby of Mr. and Mrs. Emile Marx was drowned in a slop bowl at the Arlington Hotel last night. The babe was put to sleep in a couch by the mother, who stepped into her sister's room. Returning after midnight, she found the baby dead in the slop bowl. It had awakened, crept off the bed and fallen head first into the bowl containing about two gallons of water.
Sacramento Record Union December 30, 1892

Tracking Tacoma's pioneer Jewish families has been challenging, requiring decades of research. However, in those days, everyone knew the comings and goings of others, because they were printed in the daily paper...

Liberal Use of Printer's Ink

Tacoma Daily Ledger July 22, 1901

In the days before radio, television, and social media, merchants' primary means of advertising was the local newspaper. As Tacoma grew, so did its newspaper. In 1883 the *Ledger* was able to expand from a weekly to a daily. In order to fill the increased number of columns the paper routinely published lists of the names of visitors registered at the three hotels, steamship arrivals, letters waiting to be picked up, and names of drunks sleeping over at the jail. The tone was mostly positive – Tacoma was growing, new people were arriving every day, progress was evident throughout both Tacoma and New Tacoma.

Merchants' ads ran several months without change, likely due to the challenges of setting type by hand. Small communities around the Sound submitted their news. Reporters for the *Ledger* combed the city for information. A regular column called "News Brevities" carried information about the comings and goings of the town's elite, and not-so-elite. Businessmen wisely tucked notices of merchandise available into the "Personal" column. Those who advertised heavily were "noticed" more than others. Although perhaps trivial by today's news standards, the columns provide key details about Tacoma early Jewish merchants and their business dealings.

Here are some examples from the *Ledger*'s first year as a daily:

April 15, 1883, "Gross Brothers intend putting another story on their store room on Pacific Avenue. Credit is due Messrs. Gross Bros. in the opening of a wholesale house. It was very much needed in New Tacoma as they command the most of the trade."

April 26, 1883, "Messrs. McLaren & Wallerstein yesterday shipped from their candy factory a consignment of five cases to Snohomish. This is a prominent instance of New Tacoma wholesale men shipping beyond Seattle."

May 1, 1883, "The new two-story building of A. Zelinsky, on Main Street, Tacoma, in the gale which sprung up on Sunday afternoon, was blown over on its side, and nearly all the lumber was ruined. The building was about 21 x 42 feet in size, sided up and roofed over. The floors were also laid. The wind therefore had a clean sweep, and it was in this manner that the house was blown over. It was partially flattened, and the frame, it is said, is worthless without the lumber being taken off."

May 24, 1883, "A new cigar stand will be opened by Sam Simon, on Saturday next, in the room adjoining that now occupied by Simon's boot and shoe store."

June 3, 1883, "A new auction store has just been started by L. and S. Dobrin in D. B. Hanna's new building on Pacific Avenue."

June 28, 1883, "D. Levin has a beautiful young fawn, only about three or four weeks old, which was recently captured, and which may be noticed occasionally on the streets."

Throughout September Native Americans from all around the Sound canoed to Puyallup, where the hop-picking season was in full swing. Tacoma's merchants were not about to miss this opportunity. In one day's edition, "S. Isaacs & Brother were fined $25 and costs for keeping open their place of business in Puyallup, on Sunday last, in violation of the Territorial law. The fine was paid. Mr. Simon, proprietor of the Terminus boot and shoe store, was also charged with keeping his branch store in Puyallup open on Sunday, and was fined $25 and costs. He refused payment and appealed to the District Court." The case was moved to Tacoma, where it was dismissed after the jury worked until 1 a.m.

January 1, 1884, "Wolf Bros., of the New York Bakery, are fitting up the storeroom on Pacific Avenue, above Ninth Street, lately occupied by Holgate & Robinson, and will open up in a few days a bakery and confectionery store."

On January 3, 1884, the *Ledger* carried a copy of an agreement signed by 23 local merchants, agreeing that between January 2 and April 1, 1884, they would all close their places of business at "8 o'clock p.m. sharp... Saturday evenings excepted, when we shall remain open until the usual hour." (The shorter hours were instituted **after** the Christmas shopping season.) It would become an annual tradition. Over one-fifth of the merchants listed were Jewish, including Gross Brothers of the San Francisco Store, Sam Isaacs and Brothers of the IXL store, A. Simon of the Terminus boot and shoe store, and Adolph Packscher of the Tacoma Bazaar.

January 4, 1884, "The firm of Gottstein, Langert & Co., wholesale liquor dealers of this city, has been dissolved by mutual consent. Mr. C. Langert, one of the members of the late firm, retains control of the business, and will henceforth conduct it under his own name."

January 23, 1884, "There was organized in this city on Monday night a German singing club, known as the Tacoma Harmonics. The object is the cultivation of the voice and the correct speaking of the German language; all conversation and singing being in that tongue...Perfect order is maintained at all meetings." Members included Simon Gutfeld, secretary, and A. Weinberg.

January 31, 1884, "Isaac Pincus & Son have opened up their wholesale and retail liquor store on Pacific Avenue, below Thirteenth Street. They have on hand a large stock of whiskies, wines, etc." Situated directly between Langert's wholesale liquor firm and Leon Hershberg's liquor firm, Isaac was ready to take on the competition.

February 20, 1884, after several weeks of heavy snow, "The awning over Hirshfeld & Coleman's store fell down last night and demolished some of the front windows. The porch in front of the Farmers' and Mechanics' store broke down yesterday from the accumulation of snow upon it." By 7 p.m. the snowfall was recorded as 16 inches.

March 22, 1884, "The family of Isaac Pincus have arrived here from Steilacoom, to make Tacoma their home." March 28, 1884, Olympia, "Mr. James Pincus, of Tacoma, is in this city."

March 28, 1884, "Dennis and Hain, barbers, next door to the Central drugstore, have added three fine bath rooms to their establishment, fitted with combination faucets and shower bath appliances."

TERMINUS

BOOT SHOE & STORE.

Just received, a large stock of the best kind of

WATERPROOF

BOOTS AND SHOES,

Warranted to stand three days in water without wetting the inside. Also a full line of

LADIES' & CHILDREN'S SHOES.

Loging Boots and Shoes

Of the first quality, A full line of **Rubber Goods** always in stock. ☞ Please give me a call and examine stock.☜

A. SIMON, Proprietor.

Tacoma Daily Ledger January 4, 1884

Great Eastern Clothing House.

The finest stock of Winter Clothing for Men, Boys and Children.

Overcoats, $4.50 to $25.

Cashmere Suits, from $4.50 to $25.

Wool Merino UNDERWEAR for Boys

AND GENTS IN TWELVE DIFFERENT QUALITIES

Also Boots and Shoes, Hats and Caps, Rubber Clothing and Trunks.

Pacific Avenue, Near Thirteenth Street.

SAM. GOTTSCHALK.

Tacoma Daily Ledger November 6, 1884

The publicity wasn't always positive, especially for those of the opposite political party. In the late summer of 1885 the Isaacs brothers refused to contribute to a memorial fund after the death of former President Grant. They went a step too far and expressed their contempt for the recently-deceased man. (Grant had gained notoriety within the Jewish community during the Civil War for anti-Semitic orders, quickly rescinded by President Lincoln.) On August 27 the *Ledger* called the fracas a case of a "live ass kicking a dead lion."

In November of 1884 the *Ledger*'s columns began an advertising dance between the established and popular Gross Brothers, and the newly arrived Meyer Kaufman. His Peritz & Company, a branch of Seattle's Toklas & Singerman, opened on the corner of 13th and Pacific – the same day as the Gross Brothers' grand opening of their new building at 906-908 Pacific. Manager Meyer Kaufman began placing large ads in the *Ledger*, often full-length columns. Gross Brothers responded with a four-column ad. Kaufman moved his ad to the front page. Gross Brothers followed suit and for a while the two stores took turns running front-page ads on alternating days.

A boom in business has struck this town and we are the originators of it!

How did it happen? We made up our minds to do a big business this fall and winter, and accordingly purchased an immense stock of the latest styles, patterns and and all the novelties to be had in the market, both in San Francisco and the East.

We are pleased to inform the citizens of Tacoma and surrounding country that **we are not buying off old trash that has laid in a Seattle store for the past ten years and will not sell there,** and bring them to Tacoma and try and make people believe that they are the latest styles of goods.

Remember, we make music and advertise that we have a stock of goods to show which we are not ashamed of.

We advertise what we mean, and we mean what we say. We have marked down prices regardless of profit, to enable us to close out the stock.

A critical inspection will convince the most skeptical that our store is now the bargain-seekers' headquarters. Don't fail to study our prices. We offer a special sale this week of the following goods:

40 pieces Red Twilled Flannel	$0 20
150 Comforters	75
200 pr. Gray Blankets [no horse blankets]	2 00
75 doz. Men's Red Flannel Shirts and Drawers, all wool	75
150 Men's all-wool Pants	2 00
75 Men's Suits	4 00
50 Men's Overcoats	4 00
250 doz. Ladies' all-wool Hose	25
250 doz. Men's all-wool one-half hose	25

Remember the place, and look for the elegant new salesroom of

The Great San Francisco Store!

GROSS BROTHERS,

Pacific Avenue, Tacoma, - - - Washington Territory.

Tacoma Daily Ledger November 26, 1884

Peritz and Kaufman went on the offense, hinting at their competitor's "Gross misrepresentations," of "buying stale goods at auction in San Francisco." Gross Brothers responded by stating they did not sell "trash from Seattle." Anyone in doubt could "ask the freight agents of Tacoma, who gets goods from San Francisco and the East, and who gets them from Seattle." Peritz

and Kaufman began calling the Gross brothers the "Pirates of Penzance" who had "failed to take Tacoma," claiming to be the true "People's Bargain Store." Finally Gross Brothers dropped out of the game by running ads with their best ammunition – simply their good names.

The two were joined be a third contender. Charles Reichenbach arrived in Tacoma from Chicago in February of 1885, following the big fish in a small pond scenario. In March he opened the London and Liverpool Clothing House on the corner at 902 Pacific, Gross Brothers' previous location. His advertising dollars, along with the continued growth spurt of the city, helped the *Ledger* to expand from four pages to eight. His first quarter-page ad was mostly white space, with a small notice in the center – highly unusual at the time.

THE LONDON AND LIVERPOOL

CLOTHING HOUSE

Will open in a few days in the corner store of C. B. Wright's new building on the corner of Ninth Street and Pacific Avenue.

Respectfully,

CHAS. REICHENBACH.

Tacoma Daily Ledger March 3, 1885

Perhaps in part because of their advertising budgets, all three firms' families were mentioned frequently in the local news columns – from business trips to family visits and a whirl of social events – complete with guest lists. Those mentions provide key information about the Jewish community – what they wore, what they ate, and how they were related. For example, in August Charles Reichenbach, his wife Belle, and her niece Gertie Rosenfeld attended a party at the elegant new Tacoma Hotel. *Ledger,* August 15, 1885, Belle wore "black silk, with handsome brocade trimmings, point lace at neck – ornaments, diamonds." Gertie wore "cream lace bunting, trimmed with garnet velvet and lace, ornaments garnets." The menu included spiced oysters, ham décoré, and lobster salad. As Tacoma's German community grew, Charles advertised that German was spoken at his store. His sons excelled in the private German school, taught during the summer months.

The ads of the three competing firms played out the seasons of retail – new spring merchandise, a grand fall opening, holiday specials, and winter clearances. Copy writers filled columns of ad space with flowery descriptions of shopping opportunities. Gross Brothers responded with a large ad which warned against "Talking to Death by our neighbors." *Ledger,* June 4, 1886, after several days of the highest temperatures of the summer, "Gross Bros. have added a fine ice cooler to their store, and now furnish their customers with a free drink of ice cold water." This was just a hint of the shopping incentives yet to come.

Just as the dry goods and clothing stores were settling into an uneasy truce, the candy merchants jumped into the fray. During the summer of 1886 the *Ledger* began running frequent ads for the Pioneer Candy factory tucked in among the news items. June 13, 1886, "The Pioneer Candy factory is being much improved by a summer covering in the shape of a new coat of paint... A really pleasant little parlor to visit with wife, daughter or sweetheart is that of the Pioneer candy factory where ice cream, lemonade and soda water are to be had." July 11, "A great many people, just through the force of habit, drop around to the Pioneer candy factory. It is the headquarters – everybody knows that – for ice cream, soda water, fancy candy and cigars."

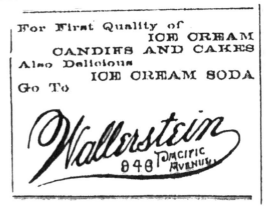

Tacoma Daily Ledger March 3, 1885

Herman Bryer started advertising about the same time. *Ledger,* June 27, 1886, "If a man spends money on cigars, his wife has the same right to eat ice cream, fruit and nuts, and that's the reason men and women take turns in their patronage of the Bon Ton – H.W. Bryer." July 11, 1886, "A convenient, pretty and good variety of goods – fancy candies, fruits and the latest and best brands of cigars and tobaccos – is to be found at W.H. Bryer's Bon Ton."

That summer Meyer Kaufman, now the proprietor of Kaufman and Berliner, was able to move closer to his competitors, although only from 13th to 11th. The "Removal Sale" came with large ads and promises of low prices. All bragged of sidewalks cluttered with arriving merchandise.

The 1886 holiday season stimulated a variety of contests, starting with Harry Lobe. His crockery store at 904 Pacific, the Tacoma Bazaar, was sandwiched between the two clothing giants. *Ledger,* Wednesday, October 27, 1886, "H. Lobe has in his window a large dish of beans, and to those who can guess the nearest to the number in the dish he will present a lady's handsomely embroidered wrapper. The beans will be counted Thanksgiving evening. Several of the female sex have put on their guessing caps already. The men are not allowed to compete." (A wrapper was a lady's robe.)

Gross Brothers brought the game to a new level. *Ledger,* November 28, 1886, "Gross Brothers Prizes. Gross Brothers have displayed in the south window of their establishment $500 worth of prizes which they propose giving to their customers. These include clocks, dressing case, Chinaware, money, etc. A large number of people were attracted to the display and congregated in groups in front of the window yesterday. The list and the plan for distributing the prizes may be seen by reference to the advertising columns." The plan was that "every person who, at any one time, purchases goods of us to the amount of $1.00 or upwards, will receive a numbered ticket which gives them one chance in the drawing for prizes...The drawing will take place at our store on Monday night, Jan. 3, 1887." In January they claimed they had given away 24,000 tickets.

The silver dollars in the large window proved too tempting. On December 5 the *Ledger* reported that a "Bold Burglar" had broken a hole in the glass in order to steal the cash. By the seventh one of the burglars admitted that his buddy had placed molasses on a newspaper and pressed it against the window to deaden the sound of the breaking glass.

Kaufman and Berliner joined the giveaway game. *Ledger,* December 9, 1886, "A Prize of a Splendid Silk Dress. Kaufman and Berliner have an elegant assortment of cloaks and wraps on hand which they offer at special rate on Saturday...To every purchaser of either a cloak or wrap will be given a ticket and on Christmas Eve a drawing will occur for a splendid silk dress."

The contests continued. *Ledger*, January 2, 1887, "Louis Wallerstein & Co. placed a large candy monument in their window several days ago, and for a week or more over 500 persons have been guessing at the weight of the monument." The one coming nearest to the correct weight was to have the candy. The actual weight was 17 pounds 6-7/8 ounces.

In mid-February of 1887 the *Ledger* began printing a directory of local businesses in each edition. Tacoma's Jewish merchants accounted for one of two bakeries, two of five barbers, the only candy merchant, one of three clothing stores, one of four confectionaries, one of two crockery stores, all three dry goods stores, all four general merchandise stores in Old Tacoma, one of 15 groceries, two of eight bakeries, one of 23 saloons, one of seven cigar stores, and both wholesale liquor dealers. The town also boasted 28 law firms and eleven physicians, none of whom were Jewish.

As Tacoma prepared to celebrate the completion of the railroad "switchback" over the Cascades with a gala July Fourth extravaganza, the Jewish community joined in. Contributions, or "subscriptions" for the festivities included $25 from Charles Reichenbach, $20 from Kaufman & Berliner, $15 from C.& Langert, $10 from S. Isaacs & Bro., $2.50 from H. Isaacs and Doc. L. Levin. They decorated their stores, showing their typical competitive spirit. *Ledger*, July 2, 1887, "Gross Brothers have had constructed a large locomotive, which they have placed in front of their business. Upon one side of the locomotive is printed Gross Division, and upon the other, N.P.R.R." Gross Brothers and Kaufman & Berliner both won cash prizes. Meyer Kaufman awarded his to a hard-working clerk. Gross Brothers donated their $25 to the fire department, which was used to start a relief fund.

The *Ledger* was fully aware of the advertising game, and printed this article on September 1, 1887.

A City Editor's Instructions.

"A City Editor's Instructions. Pasted over the desk of the city editor of a Georgia paper are the following instructions: All brides are lovely, beautiful and accomplished, except they be old and tough widows, and then they are amiable and cultivated. All merchants who advertise are enterprising, wide awake and a credit to our city. The names of those who do not advertise must not appear in our paper. All lawyers are able and worthy of a place on the supreme bench. Young lawyers are promising and silvery-tongued. Conductors on passenger trains are gentlemanly and courteous. Doctors are eminent. Farmers are intelligent. Candidates who put their announcements in our paper are gaining ground every day. Those who do not announce are likely to be defeated."

The holiday giveaways of 1887 bordered on the absurd. On October fourth Gross Brothers announced that their second annual gift distribution would include 101 prizes, with the top prize being a "fine young horse and beautiful new phaeton" (buggy).

Kaufman & Berliner took the bait, jumping in the following day. *Ledger*, October 5, 1887, "The splendid Tacoma Hotel not being for sale, W.J. Thompson not being willing to sell the Merchant's Bank Building and Wilkeson & Kandle refusing to dispose of their block we are compelled to do the next best thing by selecting 202 of the most valuable gifts ever offered to the people of Tacoma, valued at $2,500." They placed a Singer sewing machine and a set of mahogany parlor furniture in their display window.

Just in case anyone in Tacoma hadn't noticed, Gross Brothers actually brought the horse into the store. *Ledger*, October 8, 1887, "The Gross Brothers' pretty pony which they will give away as the first prize stood in the front part of their store all day yesterday. It attracted the attention of each passerby who thought it strange to see a live horse in among such a splendid line of dress goods."

Kaufman & Berliner kept trying, offering to give away 25 turkeys on November 22. Winning chances cost just fifty cents. By November 18 the live turkeys were strutting around Pacific Avenue in front of the store. As of the twenty-third only 16 had been claimed.

Charles Reichenbach refused to enter the giveaway game. *Ledger*, October 10, "When You Get Tired and Sick of "Lottery Scheme" Clothes, "Horse and Buggy" Clothes, "Piano" Clothes, "Furniture" Clothes...and would like a beautiful suit....come with confidence to the London & Liverpool Clothing House." And in November, "Do you think you are getting the best of those clothing 'fellars' that give you something to buy a suit or overcoat of them? If you don't PAY for these GIFTS, WHO do you think DOES PAY for them?"

The winners of the Kaufman & Berliner drawing were announced on January 1, 1888. The 202 winning prize numbers filled their entire ad. Apparently the Isaacs brothers had also run a giveaway program, as their 25 winning numbers were published the same day, along with the number of the winner of the diamond ring.

Gross Brothers extended the drama a few days. On January 4 the *Ledger* announced that over 1000 people had crowded into the store to witness the drawing. The following day readers learned that a young farmer from Puyallup had won the horse and buggy. Just three weeks earlier he had purchased his wedding suit from Gross Brothers, receiving forty tickets. "Morris Gross says the moral to this story is: "Young man, get married and buy your wedding suit from Gross Brothers and you will have luck."

As the spring of 1888 brought good weather Tacoma's construction season began in earnest. A real estate boom hit the city, and the *Ledger*'s columns were filled with land transactions. New real estate firms showed up to run full-page ads, giving the dry goods and clothing merchants a chance to travel and replace their merchandise. Radebaugh's *Ledger* also became a decidedly Republican newspaper, and Kaufman & Berliner moved their advertising dollars to the new Democratic newspaper, the *Tacoma Daily News*.

Charles Reichenbach took one more creative step, hiring an illustrator to draw custom cartoon ads for his firm. At the time newspapers didn't have viable methods for printing photographs, and illustrations had to be engraved line by line. The unique drawings were published on the top left corner of the *Ledger*'s first page, with a new ad appearing each Sunday.

WE CARRY THE BIGGEST LINE

of Men's Youths' and Boys' Clothing ever shown and we are matching it by the biggest bid ever made for public favor. Careful purchasers soon find out which side their bread is buttered on, and worn out devices are an old story with them. It is to careful purchasers that we are addressing ourselves now—to purchasers who know just what they are doing, who know what their money ought to bring them every time, and who wisely wait for the chances which clearing-out sales are sure to bring along in January. For such purchasers the opportunity has arrived and here it is with all its force. OUR FIFTEENTH SEMI-ANNUAL CLEARANCE SALE offers a thousand bargains in every department. A crashing mallet pounded the profits out of sight and leaves the entire stock at manufacturers' cost. See our display windows for prices. No goods charged during this sale.

THE LONDON AND LIVERPOOL CLOTHING HOUSE,
Corner Pacific Avenue and Ninth Street.
CHAS. REICHENBACH, - - - - PROPRIETOR.

Tacoma's dry goods and clothing merchants advertised and prospered, as did those who sold other goods. However, the terms used might be unfamiliar to today's readers...

Talk of the Times

The language of 135 years ago was different from today. Newspaper descriptions carried more flourish, speech was more careful. Terms that were in common use then are no longer used to-day. For example, Jews were commonly referred to as "Israelites" or "Hebrews." A rabbi was often called a reverend. A store was run by a proprietor. The word street or avenue was not capitalized. "To-day" required a hyphen. A change of business location required a "removal sale."

Chamber of Commerce Bathing and Shaving Parlors, Pacific avenue, near Twelfth Street, in its new dress is open to the public. Everything in the profession strictly and elegantly attended to. Ladies' and children's hair cutting a specialty. All are cordially solicited to call. D. P. LEWIS, Proprietor. 93-1z

Doc B. Levin's tonsorial establishment; only first-class phrenological and psychological artist in the city. Cranium manipulation and facial improvement a specialty. Prices reasonable. Second barber shop from Ninth street north on Pacific avenue, adjoining Board of Trade billiard hall. Ladies' and children's hair cutting a specialty. *-tf

Tacoma Daily Ledger June 24, 1886

Barbers were "tonsorial artists," and gamblers were "knights of the green cloth." Telephone operators were called "hello girls." Salesmen were "drummers" or "knights of the grip," and "wheelmen" or bicyclists were "knights of the silent steed." Burglars were "knights of the shadow" or "knights of the Jimmy," while butchers were "knights of the cleaver."

Drunks "resigned themselves into the arms of Morpheus" and were "conveyed to the haven of repose so thoughtfully provided for the accommodation of its guests by the City Council" – the city jail. An article about a tombstone monument claimed that it would "ornament the city of the dead." Death was portrayed as a living entity who came to call. "Shoving the queer" meant passing counterfeit money. Rain and wind came on the command of "Jupiter Pluvius." Death by gunshot meant the final chapter of life was "punctuated with a leaden bullet."

Stores were described by the type of merchandise, or "goods" they sold. Dry goods stores sold a variety of merchandise, including fabric. Men's clothing was complicated – collars and cuffs were sold separately as "men's furnishings." Writing was also complicated, and cigar and tobacco stores frequently sold stationery goods, including inks and papers. Shoe stores sold leathers and fastenings. Saloons and liquor stores sold wet goods. Several of these terms have survived, such as sporting goods and white goods. Here are a few of the types of "goods" available more than a century ago.

Case goods – shipped or sold in multiple units.

Consumer goods – used as sold, directly to the consumer.

Dress goods – fabric, notions.

Durable goods – long-lived items such as equipment, furniture.

Dry goods – cloth or fabric.

Ego goods – expensive luxury items.

Functional goods – utilitarian products such as tools.

Gray goods – undyed fabric.

Green goods – counterfeit money, distributed by "green goods gangs."

Hard goods – same as durable goods.

Hedonic goods – art, music, pleasure-oriented items.

Nondurable goods – used in a short time.

Optical goods – glasses, eyewear.

Wet goods – liquor and alcohol.

Tacoma's Jewish merchants were dominant in the early clothing and dry goods fields. They also played prominent roles in another industry — wet goods...

Wet Goods – Taverns,
Sample Rooms, Breweries & Hops

Langert block c.1887
From the collection of the author

Even though Jewish holidays are based on a Hebrew calendar and their exact dates vary from year to year, they still occur near the same season. Some of these holidays seemed to coincide regularly with the liquor industry's cycles. Every spring, as Tacoma's Jewish citizens prepared for Passover, the brewers prepared to release their bock beer. In the fall, as the High Holidays approached, hop growers got ready for the picking season.

Tacoma's Jewish pioneers were involved in every aspect of the liquor business – from the millionaires who traded hops and operated breweries, to the wholesale distributors, proprietors of fine sample rooms and rough taverns, all the way down to the delivery wagon drivers.

In the rough-and-tumble early days of the Pacific Northwest, beer and ale were staples of both diet and economy, and probably safer to drink than the city water. The earliest merchants ran simple saloons or sold liquor through their gen-

eral stores. Due to the ever-changing regulations of the liquor trade, most early mentions of this market are of a legal – or illegal – nature.

In the summer of 1865 Louisa and Heyman Goodtime were arrested in Steilacoom. Their crime, "Liquor, sale to Indians." They eventually paid a $50 fine for selling "two gallons of whiskey to an Indian named Bill." In 1877 Louisa was again arrested on similar charges in King County. This time, however, she was found not guilty.

"In the name of the United States of America you are hereby commanded to take the body of Louisa Goodtime, if to be found in your district, and her safely keep, so that you have her forthwith before the District Court of Pierce County, W. T., now in session at Steilacoom, in the County and Territory aforesaid, then and there to answer on an indictment pending against her for selling liquor to an Indian. Herein fail not, and have you then and there this writ, with your doings endorsed thereon. Witness the Hon. E. P. Oliphant, Associate Justice of Washington Territory, and presiding Judge of the said District Court of Pierce County, W. T., this 19th day of May, A.D. 1865. Chas. Prosch, Clerk."

Wolf Schafer, proprietor of the Northern Pacific Railroad Brewery in Steilacoom, understood the power of the press. On December 26, 1872, the *Puget Sound Dispatch* thanked him for his gift of a keg of "superior lager."

Kaufman & Levin were accused in the summer of 1873 of the "crime of selling spirituous liquors in less quantities than one gallon without obtaining license of the county commissioners as required by law along the line of the N.P.R.R. in said county of Pierce." In those days, men could haul barrels of whiskey out to where the railroad construction crew was working, slap a board over the top of two barrels and declare the bar open for business.

Herbert Hunt (volume II, page 233) tells another story about life in Tacoma in 1873: "One of the characters of Tacoma was 'Potato' Brooks, a man of about fifty, shabby in dress and an utter ne'er-do-well. He was a tin-horn gambler. One night he was gambling in Louis Levin's saloon and was accused by the man across the table of cheating. Safety seeming to lie in flight, 'Potato' dived beneath a billiard table just as the man fired. The bullet struck the table at one corner and shot diagonally across, cutting the green cloth every inch of the way. A man who was playing billiards adopted the old method of stopping further firing by smashing the swinging lamp above the table with a vicious swing of his cue, and in the darkness 'Potato' crawled out and fled. The death of the pool table was mourned by all." Within a year Louis Levin opened the first saloon in "New Tacoma."

Emil Hirschfeld was also in the saloon business in Old Tacoma, managed by his brother-in-law, Hyman Zelinsky. According to cryptic abbreviations in the first Pierce County directory, his saloon was on the south side of 2nd, three blocks west of Starr in Old Tacoma. In 1883 he constructed a public building in "New Tacoma," Hirschfeld Hall, where for many years the town's local politics were decided.

On Friday, January 29, 1886, the *Ledger* carried a lengthy article about an Old Town character named James Lambert.

> "A violent madness came o'er the spirit of his dreams, and the bedlamite took to the warpath on bloody deeds intent, loudly asserting that somebody was seeking to kill him. He first entered Zelinsky's saloon, and at once reached for the proprietor's scalp. He dealt Zelinsky several heavy blows in the face, knocking him down. His foe being prostrate, he looked about for another victim. His eye fell upon the portly form of Meyer Kauffman, and with a yell of rage he started after that gentleman. The latter beholding the madman, turned in an affrighted manner and ran. Lambert ran after him and the latter dashed into the butcher shop, on the corner of Second and Carr streets. Here the crazy man seized a butcher's

cleaver, intending to massacre the object of his vengeance. Several parties arriving at the scene of the conflict, they quickly overpowered the lunatic and conveyed him to the jail. This morning Lambert will be taken before the probate judge, examined on the charge of insanity, and will undoubtedly be committed to the hospital for the insane at Fort Steilacoom."

Tacoma quickly grew in population and transportation options, attracting a wholesale liquor business – or two, or three. In 1882 Leon Hershberg opened a Tacoma branch of his Oakland firm. The Tacoma location was managed by young Albert Weinberg, who had learned the brewing business in Germany from his father. Another location in Portland was managed by Isaac Ryttenberg.

In October of 1885 Albert married Esther Levy, a respected young lady of Portland, and sister of Old Town's Mrs. William Wolff. However, just a month later, early on Thanksgiving morning, Esther drowned after falling from the cliff at the edge of the Tacoma Hotel. Her death was declared an accident, attributed to early-morning sleepwalking. In March of 1886 the liquor firm closed its Tacoma location and the following year the partnership between Hershberg and Weinberg dissolved.

"THE TACOMA"—TACOMA.

Tacoma Hotel
from the collection of the author

Hershberg may have closed because Langert had opened. Charles Langert started a wholesale liquor house in September of 1883 in partnership with Meyer Gottstein, coming from Cheyenne, Wyoming, and Deadwood, Dakota. Four months later the men split up, Gottstein taking the Seattle market and Langert staying in Tacoma. Based on the steady stream of newspaper mentions that appeared in the columns of the *Ledger*, it's quite likely that reporters made a habit of stopping by Langert's store for a cigar and a chat while on their daily rounds. Langert also made a practice of delivering liquid holiday gifts to the newspaper offices on a regular basis.

Tacoma Daily Ledger February 4, 1887

When Isaac Pincus moved from Steilacoom to Tacoma in 1884 he opened yet another competing wholesale liquor business. Pincus and Langert ads appeared on the same newspaper page, and Langert's primary salesman soon went to work for Isaac. Their job was to supply Tacoma's thirty saloons, along with others in the Puget Sound. According to the *Ledger*'s calculation printed on November 9, each saloon paid a liquor license of $500. Fifteen billiards or pool halls each paid a $25 license fee, bringing in an annual city income of $15,000. By estimating Tacoma's population at 7,000, the *Ledger* arrived at a ratio of 1 saloon for every 233 people. By using the same formula, New York City had 1 saloon for every 125 people. Tacoma also claimed a higher ratio of worshipping congregations, and only admitted to "two murders since its existence," as opposed to New York's one murder per day.

In 1886, Tacoma and other cities in Wash-ing-ton Territory had an opportunity to vote on a "local option law," potentially banning liquor sales locally. *Ledger*, June 13, 1886, "The saloon keepers of the city are collecting subscriptions to defray the cost of hiring teams and vehicles to convey voters to the polls on the occasion of the Prohibition election." The saloon keepers prevailed, even though the Temperance folks had a choir of fifty small children, the "Band of Hope" singing in front of the polling places. *Ledger,* June 30, 1886, "Notwithstanding the election on Monday, and the dispensing of free whiskey in the evening of that day," only one case of drunkenness was reported.

1886 also brought increasing notice of the hops industry, a vital ingredient for brewers. Germany's hops crops suffered a major failure, followed by an attack of lice on the hops in New York. The price of remaining bales of hops from Washington's 1885 crop climbed from 15 cents to 25 cents and higher. On August 13, 1886, the *Ledger* reported that hops prices were up to 35 cents. Isaac Pincus began buying local hops by the ton, selling to eastern and European markets. Over the next several decades his opinions of the market fluctuations were printed on a regular basis, often based on telegrams from London. He also developed his own hops ranch in Puyallup, cleverly dubbing the house the "Hop Inn."

Pincus family summer home in Puyallup
Courtesy of Temple Beth El

Playing the market was risky. In the *Ledger* on October 1, 1887, Isaac Pincus said he was shipping hops he had contracted for months ago. He paid 25 cents per pound, but said, "I will gladly give the growers five cents per pound and allow them to keep them."

Most of the hop picking was done by Native Americans, whose wages were quickly targeted. *Ledger,* Friday, September 3, 1886, "During the hop picking season quite a number of Tacoma's business men will open branch stores in Puyallup valley for the purpose of trading with the Indians. Yesterday H.W. Bryer shipped a big load of fruits, cigars & tobacco to Puyallup, where he will open a store."

1887 brought even more growth and optimism to Tacoma, with the completion of the new "switchback" railroad line over the Cascades. (Previously most freight was sent by rail up from the Columbia River, or by ship from San Francisco.) The new line meant Tacoma's markets could receive fresh fruit from Eastern Washington, and Tacoma's wholesalers could ship return merchandise. Charles Langert prepared by securing exclusive rights to popular brands of liquor and cigars from Kentucky and Milwaukee. He also replaced his wooden building on Pacific with a three-story brick. *Ledger,* April 17, 1887, "When completed and furnished with his immense stock now occupying three stores, (it) will be the largest and most complete business concerns of the kind north of San Francisco."

Pacific Avenue 1888
Tacoma Public Library G-61.1-008

Much like modern wine-tasting facilities, some of the more elite saloons operated as "sample rooms." One of the most fabulous was opened in May of 1888 by Albert Weinberg, former manager of Hershberg. The Monogram Sample Rooms, complete with Albert's initials on a special rubber mat in the entrance, boasted a rich bar trimmed in silver, elegant paintings, and an electric bell that sounded five minutes before the curtain went up at the Alpha Opera House next door. A gentlemanly game of cards might be found in the back room.

MONOGRAM SAMPLE ROOM.

The Finest Fitted Up Saloon in the Pacific Northwest to be Opened Tonight.

Nearly every city has a beautiful sample room, surpassing all others in the excellence of the wines and liquors furnished and the appearance of the surroundings. Many of them are filled with works of art, in the shape of fine paintings, engravings, sculpture and bricabrac. There is perhaps no more attractive place in the country of this character than the saloon attached to the Hoffman house in New York, where hangs Cabanel's famous painting of the "Nymphs and Satyr" and other costly paintings. There are many beautiful saloons in San Francisco, but outside of that city the finest on the coast will be opened in Tacoma tonight by A. Weinberg at 1009 Pacific avenue, next door to the Alpha opera house. The sample room is in the rear of the wholesale department, and is unquestionably the finest fitted up room of the kind ever seen here. The bar counter is of solid black walnut neatly polished, trimmed with silver mountings. Back of it are three solid polished walnut sideboards of artistic design, Tennessee marble tops with silver handles and knobs. They are loaded down with fine cut glassware and an array of decanters containing the best unadulterated liquors in the market.

The paper hanging which, is paneled in triangular form, is a marvel of artistic work. Red and gold are the prevailing colors while the beautiful cornice of raised lincrusta work in imitation of brass and copper, resembling forest leaves, is said to be the only border of the kind on the coast. Mr. Cornwall, of Fargo, Dakota, was the artist. This feature of the saloon will attract more attention than any other, as the skylight

Tacoma Daily Ledger May 12, 1888

That same year Lauritz Olsen, whose wife was Jewish, operated the optimistically-named Cosmopolitan Saloon and Hotel on the corner of Eighth and Pacific. It was likely on the east side of the street, aptly nicknamed "Whiskey Row." Olsen's city directory ad claimed he could converse with guests in Norwegian, Swedish, Danish, High and Low German, Dutch, French, Spanish, Portuguese, and Italian. After his wife's shoplifting scandal the family spent a few years in the Yukon, but eventually returned. By 1901 Olsen was back running the Alaska Sample Room at 807 Pacific.

Also that year, a new law required advance payment of the entire $500 annual liquor license fee, rather than allowing quarterly payments. Langert and several brewers quietly advanced the amount of the licenses, in exchange for exclusivity. The cost of a license was then doubled, with the intention of forcing out the shadier saloons. City ordinances attempted to regulate all of the saloons, enforcing Sunday closures and other limitations. By October the *Ledger* launched a major anti-gambling campaign. (Harry Morgan, known for his gambling houses, started the *Morning Globe* newspaper in retaliation.)

The "honest" saloon keepers decided to band together. Twenty-one men, including C. Langert and A. Weinberg, met in the Monogram on October 19 and drafted a petition to the city council to "take necessary steps to secure respect to the law, and to enforce its proper and uniform observance." The existing ordinance was poorly written. One defendant argued that "his door was closed, requiring the lifting of a latch to enter." By November the council recommended the repeal of the current ordinance, and the issuance of a better one. Other petitions urged the council to deny licenses in residential areas, limiting them to establishments on Pacific and the adjoining Railroad Street. (Now Commerce.)

David Hoffman arrived in Tacoma from Leavenworth, Kansas, where he had operated a small candy company. In the summer of 1890 he received a liquor license as manager of the Monogram Saloon. After his marriage the following year to Martha Wolf, sister of Seattle's Rosa Gottstein, David made the transition to wholesale liquor. (His advertising included "Since 1884," perhaps using the date Gottstein split from Langert.) In 1893 David announced his exclusive arrangement as a distributor of Anheuser-Busch beer, practically assuring his success.

He remained in the wholesale business in Tacoma until Prohibition, eventually retiring to San Francisco.

Not all were wealthy owners or wholesalers. Many just eked out a living working as bartenders. Richard Mamlock tended bar from about 1893 until about 1907. Later he retired to a cabin on the side of a gulch, living out the rest of his life as a hermit. Julius Rammelsberg worked as a bartender at several saloons, including the Humboldt House and the Budweiser Saloon. He eventually returned to his earlier career of rolling cigars. His poor widow later tried to make a living selling homemade noodles, purchased more as charity than for their quality.

Julius Mamlock tried several occupations before going into the liquor business. As early as 1885 he sold tobacco and cigars in Tacoma. Later he opened a restaurant, and even made an unsuccessful attempt at turkey farming. Finally he went to work for his cousin, Albert Weinberg, at the Milwaukee Brewing plant. By 1896 he opened the "Smart and Mamlock Liquor Company." A year later Julius kept the business and got rid of the partner. He changed the name of the firm to the "Sun and Moon Bar and Grill," in order to keep the monogram on the window. He sold the grill in 1913 due to ill health.

Joseph Hall and Morris Bloom operated the Kentucky Liquor house, and later the New West Liquor Company. Neither succeeded.

Charles Langert's wholesale liquor firm didn't survive the Panic of 1893 – he simply couldn't collect on his accounts. By the late 1890s the firm was reorganized under the name of his brother Sam. Charles left Tacoma, returning in 1906 to try again. He died of a heart attack during Prohibition, after his morning ritual of calisthenics followed by a brisk cold shower. After his death his family moved to San Francisco, and until recently his grave remained unmarked.

Bernhard Hochstadter came to Tacoma in 1895 from Centralia, where he had operated the Centralia Soda Water and Bottling Works. For ten years he worked as a traveling salesman for Tacoma's Pacific Brewing and Malting Company. Bernhard's reward came in the form of support in opening the Everett Brewery in 1905. (After Prohibition ended he operated the Horluck Brewing Company.) When interviewed about his longevity at age 101, Bernhard gave credit to the beer he had been drinking daily since he was two.

As the smaller saloons and businesses faced challenges, so did the breweries. As previously mentioned, Wolf Schafer operated the NPRR Brewery in Steilacoom from 1872 until his death in 1889. Probate records show that his real estate holdings had more value than his brewery.

Simon Donau incorporated the Donau Brewing Company in Tacoma in August of 1889 with capital stock of $250,000. He served as president, while his sons Alfred and Hugo worked as treasurer and bookkeeper. Simon had come from Denver, via New York and New Jersey, and began building a large brewery complex on the corner of South Twentyfifth and East J Streets. His brewery got off to a rough start when the main brew house collapsed in a windstorm during construction, just as Washington was celebrating its new statehood. *Ledger,* November 18, 1889, "This was a large structure, 121 feet long, 40 feet wide and over 50 feet high. The roof had been finished and the weatherboarding of one end and part of one side already completed. The wind, coming as it did, caught the roof and boarded side like a balloon, and the entire structure was carried from its moorings and fell crashing to the earth…The building would have been a strong one when completed." By the spring of 1890 the plant had progressed enough to begin brewing. Donau's first beer went on the market July 3rd, just in time for holiday celebrations. The brewery was completed by August of 1890, at a cost of about $200,000.

Just two months later the brewery's malt supplier got nervous. Thinking the firm might be operating on slim financing, the supplier filed a writ of attachment to collect a debt of less than $15,000. Feeling wronged, Donau immediately filed a countersuit for $30,000 in damages for loss of production and credit, but the cases took years to settle. By the summer of 1891 the company was in serious financial trouble due to the attachment, with other creditors jumping in. Scholl and Huth, owners of the Puget Sound Brewery, bought the Donau plant. However, due to litigation the plant remained idle for years. Eventually copper thieves took their toll.

BUSINESS WAS RUINED

The Donau Brewing company was given a verdict for damages of $30,000 against Herman Zweig, and William Zinran and August Ludde, his sureties, by a jury yesterday. The brewing company asked that amount of damages for having its business destroyed by the service of a writ of attachment upon its brewery to satisfy a debt of $12,187.25 which was secured by first mortgage bonds. The case was tried before Judge Stallcup. No notice of appeal has been filed, but the attorneys for the defendant announced that one will be filed immediately, and they hope for a reversal of the judgment by the supreme court.

Tacoma Daily Ledger March 3, 1893

Simon Donau attempted to break ground for a new brewery, this time in the name of his son Alfred, but failed. The 1893 banking panic added the final nail to the coffin. The Donau family moved to San Francisco and started over, while Hugo and Alfred worked with their prominent brother-in-law, Albert Steinfeld, in Tucson.

On June 14, 1900, the Ledger described a large meeting of Masons, in which they voted to continue their policy not to admit any men engaged in the liquor trade.

Milwaukee Brewing Company stein c.1891
Courtesy of Gary Flynn

Milwaukee Brewing bottle label
Courtesy of Gary Flynn

MILWAUKEE PLANT.
Tacoma Sunday Ledger July 3, 1898

While Scholl and Huth were trying to figure out what to do with the Donau buildings, along came Samuel Loeb. A young brewer from the Midwest, Loeb had opened the Milwaukee Saloon in Tacoma in 1889. He joined forces with Albert Weinberg to purchase Dietrich Stegmann's United States Brewery in 1891, reorganizing and expanding it as the Milwaukee Brewing Company. (Weinberg had just married Loeb's sister.) Meanwhile, the larger brewers in Tacoma and Seattle formed a combine, buying supplies as a group, and "agreeing" on prices and territories. They didn't bother including the smaller Milwaukee.

Demonstrating the definition of *chutzpah,* Loeb sent his delivery wagons into the streets of Seattle in 1894, offering his beer at one dollar per barrel less than the "agreed" price. The Beer War was on, reaching its peak in the summer of 1897. Seattle powers purchased Loeb's plant mortgage and immediately called it due, but the young brewer was able to scramble to arrange other financing.

Frustrated, that fall Loeb & Weinberg chose to merge their Milwaukee plant with Anton Huth's Puget Sound Brewery. The result was the Pacific Brewing and Malting Company, with several brewing facilities in Tacoma, including the inactive Donau. The merger allowed the combined Tacoma brewers to again reach a settlement with those to the north, renewing their "agreed" price per barrel.

In the spring of 1899 the brewery attempted to ship 200 cases of liquor to Manila aboard the *Glenogle.* After a collision in the harbor the ship broke apart and whiskey and wine washed ashore, to the delight of Old Tacoma beachcombers. Pacific Brewing and Malting kept growing and expanding, holding liquor licenses for over a dozen Tacoma saloons, and donating generously to Tacoma charities. *Ledger,* May 26, 1901, "Pacific Brewing and Malting Company and the Columbia Brewery have signed an eight-hour contract with the brewers and bottlers, and are both now running under union rules."

However, Samuel Loeb wasn't content. In 1902 he sold his Tacoma interests to his partners and moved to Seattle. There he opened his own brewery – appropriately named the Independent Brewing Company. After a disastrous fire he rebuilt the plant, with the help of investor Herman Klaber. Loeb built an elegant home on "Millionaire Row," now a bed and breakfast known as the Shafer-Baillie mansion. His brewery marketed its German lager beer under the slogan "Prosit! Es Giebt Kein Kopfweh," meaning "it doesn't give you a headache." Loeb's Independent Brewing Company operated in Seattle until Washington adopted Prohibition in 1916 – four years before the rest of the nation.

Meanwhile, Isaac Pincus had continued as a large-scale broker of hops. After his wife's death in 1905 he retired, leaving the management of the firm to his sons James, Julius and Harry. As with the trials of Job, one disaster followed another. An early heavy frost ruined their entire Roy crop. $25,000 worth of hops were destroyed in a flooded Oregon warehouse. Just when the firm's cash flow was at an all-time low in 1910, the boys were caught "selling short." They were forced to buy on the open market to fulfill their export commitments to the European brewers. A friend stepped in to buy the remaining hops contracts. Instead of declaring bankruptcy, the Pincus family sold their vast real estate holdings, paying off every single debt dollar for dollar. Although the family never recovered its financial prominence, family members kept their integrity.

Pincus & Sons of Tacoma Are Forced to Suspend After a Half Century in Business.

TACOMA (Wash.), December 13.— Isaac Pincus & Sons, a prominent hop brokerage firm, failed today for $150,-000, with assets about the same. Pincus & Sons are the oldest hop dealers on the Coast. Lately they have suffered heavy losses from frost and a flood recently ruined a store of hops worth $25,00 in an Oregon warehouse. They had contracted to supply from 4300 to 4500 bales of hops to brewers and others, but found this practically impossible, as there are only about 17,000 bales on the Coast, and an attempt to buy, they say, would have forced the prices entirely beyond their ability to pay.

Klaber, Wolff & Netler, the heaviest creditors, expect to ask for a receiver today. The assets consist of an 800-acre farm near Roy and Tacoma real estate. The firm was established fifty years ago.

San Francisco Chronicle December 14, 1910

The friend who stepped in was fellow hops broker Herman Klaber. Klaber came to the Northwest in the early 1890s, partnering with George Rose as a buyer of hops. He worked for many years as an agent of the Uhlmann Company. In addition, he began purchasing land and developing fields of his own. He helped form a hop warehouse and supply firm in Puyallup, while maintaining a residence and an office in Tacoma, next to that of Isaac Pincus on Pacific.

By 1903 Klaber was shipping more than a quarter of a million dollars-worth of hops to London. He was pictured in the newspaper next to his racehorse, Guy. That year he also purchased an 80-acre hop ranch at Boistfort,

near Chehalis, in addition to his 50-acre farm in Lewis County and his holdings in Puyallup. The new ranch developed into a company town known as Klaber, with six large hop drying kilns each sporting a letter of his name. Not to be out-punned by Pincus, he named his summer bungalow the Seldom Inn.

Klaber hop fields
Courtesy of Bart Ripp

As he prospered, Klaber became one of Tacoma's most eligible bachelors. He invested in a variety of enterprises, including an insurance firm and an investment company. He built his own office building on 12th and Pacific. His hops firm had offices in Tacoma, San Francisco and London. In 1906 Herman Klaber married Gertrude Ginsburg, daughter of a prominent San Francisco family. Their daughter Bernice was born in 1910.

In December of 1910 the firm of Klaber, Wolf & Netter sued Pincus & Sons, forcing Pincus into insolvency. (Klaber had advanced nearly $40,000 to Pincus for a hops shipment that sold for only half of that value.) By January of 1911 Klaber had quietly purchased about 10,000 bales of the remaining West Coast crop, successfully "cornering the market" for the first time in the history of the hops trade.

Herman Klaber's international dealings meant regular trips to London. In the spring of 1912 Klaber was scheduled to return aboard the *Olympic*. However, he chose to delay his departure a week so he could sail home on the maiden voyage of the sister ship, the new *RMS Titanic*. His body was among those never recovered.

THE NEW WHITE STAR LINER "OLYMPIC" THE LARGEST VESSEL IN THE WORLD.
45,000 TONS GROSS REGISTER. 66,000 TONS DISPLACEMENT.   LENGTH 882 ft. 6 in. BREADTH 92 ft. 6 in.
ACCOMMODATION 2,500 PASSENGERS. 860 CREW.

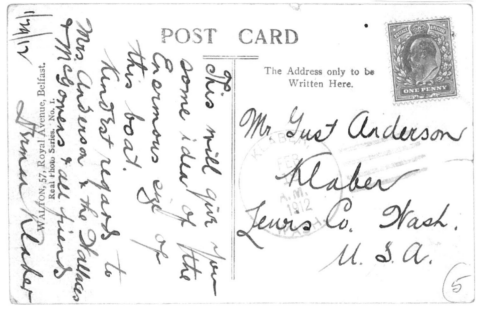

Olympic postcard sent by Herman Klaber
Courtesy of Bart Ripp

Tacoma's liquor industry came to a crashing halt at the end of 1915. On January 1, 1916, a constitutional amendment went into effect, making Washington a "dry" state. An ad in the *Tacoma Daily Ledger* on December 12, 1915, showed an illustration of the Pacific Brewing and Malting Company's new $200,000 plant in San Francisco, built to "retain its California and Export business." The same edition carried a coupon from the Tacoma Bottling Company to arrange delivery of Pacific Beer "to your home, from San Francisco." The new law made it illegal to brew beer in Washington, but with a permit it could still be imported. The rest of the nation adopted Prohibition several years later.

Many merchants in the Wet Goods field survived — or were perhaps even strengthened by — the 1893 banking panic. Those in the Dry Goods field were not as fortunate...

New Suits – Hopelessly Insolvent

Jewish tradition teaches that G-d determines who shall succeed and who shall fail, written in the Book of Life at *Rosh Hashanah* and sealed on *Yom Kippur*. While many Jewish merchants prospered in Tacoma in the 1880s, most in the 1890s ultimately failed – some quite publicly – scrambling to salvage something of their business. Others just left Tacoma for greener pastures, typically assisted by extended family.

Their reasons for coming to Tacoma were varied. Many sought a fresh start after some sort of business debacle, fire, or legal entanglement. Some came barely able to afford the five dollar license fee to sell cigars, while others brought the broad support of investors. Mortgages and ordering merchandise on credit were the norm, as was the temptation to exaggerate financial stability in order to obtain that much-needed credit. Personal loans frequently involved wives and in-laws.

An article in the *Ledger* on December 18, 1898, celebrated the twenty-fifth anniversary of the arrival of the first train in Tacoma. The piece described the young city in 1873, noting that the population then was made up of 48 whites and 175 Chinese. "The same year an Israelite opened a store, 8 by 15, but had to close after running a few months, for want of cash customers." (This could have been Dobrin or Ostheim, but already Kaufman, Levin and Wolff were ignored.) That was the year railroad financier Jay Cooke failed, in the banking panic of 1873. The pattern would be repeated again and again.

Colonel Meyer Kaufman's clothing firm of Kaufman & Berliner had been prominent in the 1880s, advertising heavily. His death in 1891 at the age of forty-six brought on immediate bankruptcy. As most merchandise was purchased on time, there simply was not enough cash flow to supply the demands of the creditors upon his death. Tacoma's newspapers very quickly began informing citizens of the bankruptcy sale. Meyer's loss was offered as a shopper's gain.

> The Bankrupt Sale of Kaufman & Berliner's stock will be closed Monday, October 12th. Tuesday the slaughter of Dry Goods and Clothing will be continued.
>
> P. SINGERMAN, 948 Pacific Avenue.

Tacoma Daily Ledger October 11, 1891

Charles Reichenbach also suffered a very public business failure. From 1885 until 1891 his London & Liverpool Clothing House had been a major advertiser. His ads ran on the best corner of the front page of the *Ledger*, just as his store was on the best corner in town at Ninth and Pacific. His social status peaked in 1892. His son Oscar started the Stag Seven social club, his son Edwin set off for Stanford, his wife entertained frequently and he had a house full of relatives. Charles ventured into real estate development, presenting his wife with a town lot for her birthday. Likely the saturated clothing market in Tacoma couldn't support the family's lifestyle. Reichenbach suddenly moved his ad to the very Democratic *Daily News*, even though he was a staunch Republican. The *Ledger* was happy to inform readers of his fall. Reichenbach sold to Hyams and Pauson, who kept his young son Oscar on as manager. By January of 1893 all 43 blocks of Charles' real estate development, comprising 16 blocks each, were on the lists of delinquent properties.

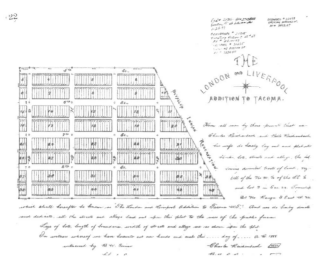

Tacoma's real estate market had skyrocketed. In February of 1893 David Levin asked $37,000 for a lot and store occupied by the City of Paris. Feeling that price too high, the prospective buyers purchased a 25- by 100-foot lot next door for $31,000. The price of $1,240 a front foot was the highest paid for Tacoma real estate up to that time. The *Ledger* reported that the lot had sold in 1873 or 1874 for $200, in 1882 for $1,000, and in 1885 for $6,000.

Some owners claimed they were retiring from business due to health reasons. Harry Frank, of Hirsch and Frank, did just that in April of 1893. The sale lasted for five months before Hirsch bought out his partner, who then set off to go mining in Africa. Jacob Kullman began closing his City of Paris store around the same time, also offering extended Going Out of Business sales. David and Joseph Jacob eventually took on the stock of one and the name of the other.

As previously mentioned, on May 5, 1893, the National Cordage Company failed and a national banking panic followed. The *Ledger* on May 7 accurately predicted that the failure was "only the first act in the tragedy of contraction of loans." However, just as in the 2008 real estate market collapse, those living through it had no way to judge the enormity or predict the duration of the crisis. During June the *Ledger*, without actually admitting there was a problem, began printing a series of paragraphs by prominent citizens giving their viewpoints on how to be happy, though poor. They'd need the advice.

On June 27 the *Ledger* noted that Louis Wallerstein had sold his candy machinery and inventory to Aaron Cohen. The following day brought the first of several lawsuits from creditors. Somehow Wallerstein was able to reopen his factory for wholesale business in mid-September,

but his brother-in-law Aaron Cohen was still in court two years later.

On December 14, 1893, just before the holiday shopping season reached its frenzy, the *Ledger* interviewed "Prominent Business Men of Tacoma." (Definition – highest advertisers.) "All Report a Good Condition of Affairs With Signs of a Steady Improvement." Included were the optimistic beliefs of Manager Jacoby, Morris Gross, Jesse L. Greenbaum and J.Bernhard. All made sure to mention that their stores would be well stocked. All would be in financial trouble within the next few years.

The next to tumble were the Prager Brothers, a Portland firm with a large Tacoma store on Thirteenth and Railroad managed by their brother-in-law, Solomon Jacoby. It would take several years of legal wrangling to finally strangle the business. On January 23, 1894, the *Ledger* announced that the firm's real and personal property had been sold to Archie S. Ash of Tacoma and Henry Ackerman of Portland. Archie began having "trustee sales" to cover the firm's debts of over $230,000. Archie was the treasurer of the recently-completed Temple Beth Israel, Solomon was temple president. By Easter they were selling out at fifty cents on the dollar.

Merchants weren't the only ones in trouble – the entire city treasury was in crisis. During mid-February the city council reduced key city salaries by $68,000. The mayor's reduction was from $3,000 to $2,000 and he lost his clerk. Of course, it took several attempts to get an ordinance passed legally, and the salaries wouldn't actually be paid until over a year later. Further "retrenchment" would take place over the next several years, especially in the school system.

Tacoma Daily Ledger April 3, 1895

Jacob Bernhard toppled next, at 1118 Pacific. On March 27 Miss Cunningham, a milliner who had a shop in his store, announced that the Bernhard attachment had nothing to do with her. The bankruptcy sale began on April second. Bernhard lost his lease, sold from a location on C Street for a week, then was able to sell his inventory to another Tacoma merchant who eventually took over his former location. Before that Julius Basinski had used the site for additional holiday space for his Tacoma Bazaar.

Mentheim Cohn realized that the clothing market was saturated and determined to convert his White Front readymade clothing store to dry goods only. His sales throughout April and May, however, cast even more discounted clothing onto the market. Mentheim at the time was vice president of the congregation and had stores in several cities. He would spend the next several years sorting out the legal tangles.

The summer of 1894 was fairly quiet. By August Charles Langert's liquor company was in trouble. He quickly reorganized and reopened. Solomon Jacoby, Sidney Prager and Archie Ash were able to buy the remaining inventory of the Prager Brothers. They also built a new building on Fifteenth and Pacific and moved their stock there. By January of 1895 they, too, were broke.

Yet, while some businesses failed, others prospered. Meyer Jacob was able to purchase his brother Joseph's shoe inventory from the Snohomish Mercantile Company. Meyer extended his shelving to ceiling-height, doubling the capacity. Over the next several years he frequently purchased large stocks in other cities at auction prices and ran front-page ads in the Sunday papers, often appealing to frugal buyers by offering fire or water-damaged goods. His shoe store was at 1138 Pacific, while his brother Joseph ran the City of Paris at 1136 Pacific.

Tacoma Daily Ledger March 19, 1892

Even the pawnshop industry was at risk. In April of 1894 Sam Andrews sold his interest in the Chicago Pawn to his younger brother Jake. The creditors were after the business in just a few months. In December of 1894 Sam began closing out the remaining merchandise at his other location, Uncle Sam's Pawnshop at 1144 Pacific. Sam was able to continue in the pawn business, eventually becoming a jeweler. (Perhaps assisted by his marriage to Meyer Kaufman's only daughter, Carrie.)

January 8, 1895, brought news of a receiver for the Harris Brothers, commission merchants. Isaac lived in Tacoma, Hyman in North Yakima. By the 11th embezzlement charges were filed against the bookkeeper, Frederick Shepherd, the apparent source of the company's financial woes.

By the end of January the young firm of Jacoby-Ash was also in the hands of a receiver. The receiver objected to the transfer of mortgages to M.S. Jacobs, father-in-law of both Archie Ash and Sidney Prager, but to no avail. In April Moses Jacobs took over the firm. A month later he announced he was quitting Tacoma. The remaining dry goods stock was sold or shipped to Portland, although the sale took most of the year.

On March 3, 1895, C.P. Ferry (The "Duke of Tacoma") wrote an open letter to the editor of the *Ledger*. "Financially Tacoma is busted into ten thousand pieces, and the people are fighting over the fragments, to get material to burn the debris. This is the remark made a few days ago by a gentleman who has loaned considerable money in Tacoma and who wishes he hadn't."

The ups and downs continued. In August Hyams, Pauson and Company, the successor to Charles Reichenbach's London & Liverpool clothing house, suffered major water damage when fires broke out under the wooden sidewalks on two sides of their store. They carried insurance with ten companies, plus had a sale of damaged merchandise. The proceeds allowed them to return to their front-page advertising and purchase new stock – a temporary reprieve.

Tacoma Daily Ledger January 5, 1895

On October 8, 1895, the *Ledger* announced that M. Cohn & Co. had filed chattel mortgages aggregating $35,000, while other debts were about $40,000 more. The firm, made up of Mentheim Cohn and Carrie M. Ball, had two stores in Tacoma and two more in North Yakima and Hoquiam. Mentheim and Carrie were brought into court and questioned about their personal property, including their household possessions and jewelry. During testimony Mentheim had great difficulty remembering exactly how much money he had lost playing poker, and where, but stated he had probably lost over $5,000 just that summer.

Tacoma Daily Ledger November 2, 1895

On October 31st a front-page ad surprised Tacoma's citizens, announcing that Hyams, Pauson & Co. was retiring from business in Tacoma and Seattle. Successor to Charles Reichenbach's London & Liverpool clothing, the firm had the best location in town, in addition to half a dozen other stores on the West Coast. Their merchandise swamped the floundering boat of Tacoma's bankrupt clothing dealers. Unlike others, they took only two months to close out, shipping remaining merchandise to their stores in San Francisco.

More stunning news came on December eighth as the Gross Brothers announced that every item in their store must be sold for cash, as they would have a "change of business" in 90 days. The change was not explained, but the countdown began. They determinedly stuck it out a bit longer, perhaps because their neighbor Hyams Pauson was counting down at the same time, ending on December 29.

Tacoma's government was also in a mess. Lawsuits raged over the purchase of the water company, and the school board couldn't afford to pay its teachers. The ousted city treasurer was sentenced to six months in the penitentiary. By January of 1896 the school district was holding classes on a week-by-week basis, until a special election could raise the district's debt limits. On the sixth of January, city employees were finally paid their October wages – in warrants. The city council approved turning off every other street light. Court cases were delayed because there was no cash on hand to convene a jury. The council considered selling the new city hall and moving into smaller quarters. On March 29 an unsigned letter to the editor wondered "If ten good men could have saved Sodom, desperately wicked as it was, how many will it take to save Tacoma?"

The 1896 Tacoma Polk directory reflected the struggles. Only a dozen dry goods firms were listed; including Gross Brothers, the Jacob brothers' City of Paris, Samuel Posner, and a new firm run by Theo Feist. In contrast the city boasted 96 saloons, over 50 cigar merchants, and 21 dealers in secondhand goods. Tacoma's Jewish merchants accounted for three of five pawnbrokers, five of eleven liquor wholesalers, and one of two breweries. The directory also listed more bicycle dealers than banks.

On Sunday, May 24, 1896, Tacoma's readers opened their morning *Ledger* to learn that the Gross Brothers had decided to retire from business. An interview with Morris revealed the firm had been losing money for three years, a result of many bankrupt stocks on the market, together with the large expense of doing business, particularly in taxes and insurance. "We believe," said Morris Gross, "that for a year or two it is cheaper to be out of business than in it. We… prefer to retire now and keep what we have than to continue losing money."

By July 1st the firm was still contributing $100 to a business fund to pay the city's firemen, unpaid since January. (Not only would the loss of the firemen jeopardize homes in Tacoma, but it would also cause the immediate cancellation of fire insurance policies.) That year the city could not afford to host a July Fourth celebration, so the women sponsored a Rose Festival. Several prominent businesses sponsored large floats – the Gross Brothers did not.

After months of countdown, the stock and fixtures were sold at auction, to one Henry Bash, father-in-law of Morris Gross. Mr. Bash bought the remaining goods for 50 cents on the dollar, plus paid an additional $1,000 for the fixtures. He also kept Morris on as the store's manager. Eventually Morris returned to the firm's old location at 906-908 Pacific.

Prominent Jewish families began leaving in earnest. Pawnbroker Isaac Dornberg moved to Spokane in 1895. Archie Ash and Michael Ball followed in the fall of 1896. Moses Jacobs joined the Prager family in Portland. Mentheim Cohn left for Buffalo in March of 1897 and died suddenly later that year. The Donau family left for San Francisco in 1897. Less-prominent families simply disappeared from the pages of the city directory.

Yet somehow, someone else always seemed willing to step up and fill the void. Theo Feist opened his own firm in 1896 after having worked for Jacob Bernhard since 1889 and witnessing the Bernhard demise firsthand. He was all of twenty-three. He took his brother-in-law as a partner the following year, and Feist & Bachrach was born. As others had done before him, he started on Tacoma Avenue and later moved down to Pacific.

Samuel Posner had been selling clothing on Tacoma Avenue since 1890. In July of 1894 he moved down to 1148 Pacific, vacated by the Isaacs brothers. When Jacob Bloom left to try his luck in Skagway, Samuel moved into his home. In the spring of 1897 Samuel took over Mentheim

Cohn's store space at 1130 Pacific. The following year he moved into a fine home vacated by the Donau family.

The tide finally turned in July, with three major events happening nearly simultaneously. In mid-July word broke of the big gold strike in the Klondike area of the Yukon, immediately boosting the local economy. During the same week the *Ledger*, which had been in the hands of a receiver, was sold. The new management brought renewed optimism and a return to promoting the strengths of the city. Two weeks later President McKinley's promised tariff bill was passed, which would hopefully reopen Eastern mills and factories. For the first time in four years, the future looked bright – golden, shiny bright.

This Is What Was Promised, but I Didn't Think It Would Come So Fast, from All Directions.

Tacoma Daily Ledger August 22, 1897

In June of 1898 thirty-five proprietors of "the larger stores on Pacific" signed an agreement to close in the evenings at 6:30 p.m. Only twelve of the signers were from Tacoma's Jewish community – their former dominance had shrunk to only one-third.

Banking Panic Timeline

1893
January	Charles Reichenbach, London & Liverpool, bankruptcy
April 6	Hirsch & Frank retire, ill health
May 5	Wall Street Black Friday, National Cordage Co failure
May 21	Jacob Kullman, City of Paris, "retires" from business
May 28	Former mayor Sam A. Wheelwright suicide, financial ruin
June 2	Merchants National Bank closes
June 20	Cottage Home Building association receiver appointed
June 27	Donau brewery decision, over $160,000 in foreclosures
June 28	Louis Wallerstein, candy factory sold, then attached
July 22	Traders' Bank closes
July 25	Tacoma National Bank closes, "result of idle gossip"
Aug. 15	Donau Brewery plant sold for $85,000
Aug. 16	Northern Pacific Railway in receivership, still running
Sept. 11	Temple Beth Israel dedicated, *Rosh Hashanah*
Sept. 15	Wallerstein Candy factory reopens
Sept. 21	S. Hirsch buys out H. Frank, continues firm
Oct. 13	Hirsch tailors strike over salary reductions
Dec. 4	Tacoma National Bank reopens
Dec. 31	S. Hirsch stock sold in mortgage sale

1894
Jan. 3	Jacob Kullman moves to San Francisco for health reasons
Jan. 23	Prager Brothers' stock (Sol Jacoby) sold to Archie Ash
Jan. 25	Traders' Bank reopens, Prager Bros. attached
Feb. 18	City salaries reduced
April 2	Jacob Bernhard bankruptcy sale begins
May 12	Simon Hirsch re-opens in Bernhard's store
May 13	Edison Savings Bank receiver, re-opens a week later
May 18	Traders' Bank again closes, liquidates holdings
June 14	*Tacoma News* sold at sheriff's sale
Aug. 16	Officers of Merchants' National Bank acquitted
Aug. 21	Langert's Liquor creditors' meeting
Aug. 22	Public school opening delayed until October 1
Dec. 3	Tacoma National Bank again closes

1895
Jan. 8	Harris Brothers receiver appointed
Mar. 30	Abe Gross commits suicide
April 1	M.S. Jacobs buys Jacoby-Ash stock at auction
April 12	Paul Schulze commits suicide
July 28	Merger of Citizens' National Bank & Pacific National Bank
Sept. 14	Bank of Tacoma receiver appointed
Oct. 8	David Levin receiver for Mentheim Cohn & Carrie Ball
Oct. 17	Commercial Bank closes, city of Tacoma loses funds
Oct. 18	German-American Bank receiver appointed
Oct. 25	Columbia National Bank closed by bank examiner
Oct. 31	Hyams, Pauson & Co. announces retirement from Tacoma
Nov. 12	Isaac Altman buys bankrupt stock of M. Cohn & Co.
Nov. 21	City begs $200 from 150 citizens for interest payments
Dec. 8	Gross Brothers announce final 90 days, then keep going

1896
May 24	Gross Brothers announce retirement from business
July 1	Firemen's salaries paid by merchants
Aug. 29	Henry Bash buys stock of Gross Brothers

1897
January	Gross brothers open individual stores
May 23	New West Liquor assigned receiver
June 29	New West Liquor assets sold
July 16	Word of Klondike gold strike reaches San Francisco
July 18	*Daily Ledger* sold to C.M. Shultz
July 25	Tariff bill passes

As Tacoma's elite Jewish clothing dealers were failing quite publicly, another group of Jewish merchants took a different approach...

From Trash to Treasure – Junk and Pawn

It's been said that during Tacoma's boom years of the 1880s, pennies were rarely used. However, after 1893 their value became more significant. A new market emerged that had been steadily running in the background, operated by junk peddlers and secondhand dealers, some of whom worked as tailors or repaired shoes, often as a home industry.

William Eckstein worked as a tailor in Tacoma as early as 1885, at first sleeping in his boss's store. After his marriage to Rebecca Simon the couple took over her father Abe's former shoe store at 713 Pacific, selling secondhand goods, similar to today's thrift stores. The Ecksteins thriftily re-used the overhead awning by simply flipping the fabric over. Later William partnered with Rebecca's siblings in operating a pawnshop, (holding customers' merchandise as collateral for loans) and living the rest of his life in Tacoma.

713 Pacific Avenue, with reversed
"Shoes, Leathers and Findings" on awning
Courtesy of Mike Hockett

Henry Harris operated a secondhand clothing business in Seattle in the early 1880s, then made his way to Tacoma, where he worked as a tailor. He became active in the formation of the synagogue, but took his own life in 1892.

Auctioneer Samuel Martin came to Tacoma in the late 1880s. Within a few years he also partnered with his brother-in-law, William T. Lewis, in the Central Nisqually Land Company. After the panic Samuel returned to auctioneering, while William sold secondhand furniture. Both families moved to Seattle in 1899, but after a few years the Lewis family returned to Tacoma.

Henry Winkleman moved to Tacoma with his family in 1890, selling junk. By 1900 he'd progressed to scrap iron, adding lumber in 1907. (Decades later other Jewish families in Tacoma would be highly successful in worldwide metal markets – an incredible leap in the course of just one generation.)

Wladyslaw Lubelski and his wife Rachel arrived in Tacoma from Colorado in 1891 with their two married sons. One of the first things they did was host a party on the centennial of the adoption of the constitution of Poland, which assured religious freedom and equal rights to the inhabitants of that country. The extended family operated multiple secondhand furniture locations throughout Tacoma. They were able to purchase estate furniture on a fairly large scale, and attend the 1893 fair in Chicago. After Wladyslaw died in 1894, one son returned to Colorado and another moved to San Francisco.

David L. Kaufman and sons sold secondhand goods in Tacoma from 1892 to 1896, coming from Russia via Minnesota. His son Joseph's ad in Tacoma's 1896 city directory offered "New and Secondhand Furniture, Stoves, Caskets, Crockery and Household Goods." The directory included 21 secondhand firms, a clear sign of Tacoma's descent from boom to bust.

SECOND HAND GOODS.

Abelson Samuel, 1317 Pacific av.
Arnold C H, 1546 South C.
Durie J D, 915 S Tacoma av. (*See p 659*).
Frazier Mrs Adelaide, 1516 South C.
Freeburn James, 941 S Tacoma av.
Fuller T T, 2301 Pacific av.
Geisenheyner J F, 1710 South C.
Hoenigsberger & Co, 1125 South C.
Kaufman D L & Son, 1115-1117 S Tacoma av.
Launder C H, 910-912 S Tacoma av.
Lewis W T, 1326 South C.
Lubelski Henry, 1123 South C.
Martin Jacob, 1210 South I.
Matthews Cyrus, 938 South C.
Onn O P, 306 E 25th.
Philip M T, 1512 Pacific av.
Sam Morris, 2323 Jefferson av.
Singleton James, 1721 Jefferson av.
Sterling 2nd Hand Furniture Co, 934 South C.
Tveter & Anderson, 1110 S Tacoma.
Wallis W J & Sons, 1519-1521 South C. (*See adv below.*)

Tacoma Polk City Directory 1896
Ancestry.com U.S. City Directories

From "South on the Sound" by Murray Morgan

Sam Abelson operated a variety of second-hand and pawnshops in Tacoma from 1893 to 1900, before trying his luck in Skagway, Alaska. Solomon Voloshin sold junk in Tacoma from around 1897 until his death in 1902.

Pawnshops paid an annual license fee of $100, as opposed to the five-dollar cost of a secondhand license. Pawnbrokers also faced strict reporting requirements and ran the risk of arrest for purchasing stolen goods – perhaps unknowingly.

Archie Ash opened a pawn and loan business in Tacoma in 1889. He partnered with his brother-in-law Max Broh, then with Isaac Dornberg. Murray Morgan's book *South on the Sound,* noted that only four of 27 banks survived the financial crash of 1893. Seven of twelve pawnshops survived, including Ash and Dornberg. In 1894 Archie Ash moved into the family home formerly occupied by Charles Reichenbach and purchased the bankrupt stock of the Tacoma branch of Prager Brothers, another related family. After years of legal manipulations, the Ash family moved to Spokane, where they also operated a pawn and loan business.

Hungarians Morris and A. Jacob Bloom also arrived in Tacoma in 1889, first managing the Kentucky Liquor Company. Jacob later sold cigars, then moved to Skagway, Alaska, in 1896, where he lived until his death in 1906. Morris also changed occupations in 1896, entering the pawn business. By 1907 he had progressed from pawnbroker to jeweler. He lived the remainder of his life in Tacoma.

British-born Lewis Levy worked as a pawnbroker in Tacoma for a decade, arriving in 1889 via San Francisco. His marriage to Rachel Martin brought her brothers' auctioneering element to his business. Lewis gained prominence – serving on the park board and investing in mining and transportation. In 1898 he was successful in getting a new pawn ordinance passed that would include the secondhand dealers. Anyone who loaned money on an item, with a provision that the broker could resell the item after a specific time without further legal action, fell under the ordinance. Unfortunately, his Collateral Bank business was one of the first to break the new reporting rules. After repeated arguments with the local police, Lewis Levy moved to Seattle.

NESDAY, SEPTEMBER 7, 1898.

PARK COMMISSIONER LEVY

Heartily Endorses Stuart's Dyspepsia Tablets.

LOUIS LEVY.

Louis Levy, Tacoma's Park Commissioner; one of her most active and successful business men.

Mr. Levy was born in dear old England, forty years ago, amidst the pleasant surroundings of a good home, where he had the advantages of early training and education. Upon reaching early manhood the desire for travel soon possessed him, and it was not long before he was making the trip to the United States, which offered so many inducements for young men. After a few years of varied experiences in different lines of business he left the Eastern States for California.

Mr. Levy's most marked success was in Los Angeles, where he edited the Los Angeles Evening Telegraph for some time. In 1888 he resigned that position to seek a new field in the state of Washington. Since coming to Tacoma Mr. Levy has been very successful in all commercial enterprises undertaken by him. He has large interests in mining properties in this state and Alaska, being a promoter of many new companies. His interest in steamboating in Alaskan waters has added material wealth to his holdings.

He is an active worker in the political field and as a park commissioner has been very successful. Many of the new features as well as many new improvements have been made by his untiring and undivided interest in his new position, which he has held for the past two years.

Mr. Levy has for some time been troubled with dyspepsia and is a firm believer in Stuart's Dyspepsia Tablets. They have done him great good and he conscientiously recommends their use.

Tacoma Daily Ledger September 7, 1898

One of Levy's colleagues in Tacoma was Sam Andrews, who arrived from Chicago in 1890 to operate the Uncle Sam Pawnshop and Chicago Loan. Sam worked with Levy in 1898 to urge the city council to change the secondhand laws, with little initial effect. *Ledger*, February 24, 1898, "Yesterday every gilt ball in the city rattled indignantly." Feeling frustrated, the pawnbrokers threatened to call their businesses secondhand shops, depriving the city of hundreds of dollars of income from annual license fees. The new ordinance quickly passed. When Levy left for Seattle, Sam's pawn business became Andrews Collateral Bank, later evolving into jewelry.

Herman Stusser operated a secondhand business around the turn of the century, then transitioned to jewelry. In 1911 his store was robbed by clever burglars who broke through the floor from the basement below. According to the *Ledger* on March 30th, the stolen goods included "150 revolvers, 500 cartridges, six solid gold watches, 35 watch chains, several trays of bracelets and fancy finger rings and all kinds of odds and ends in good quality trinkets, together with the trays in which they were arranged."

While some businesses succeeded and failed quite publicly, another group of merchants worked — and worshipped — more privately...

Back to Tradition

Tacoma's Jewish community in the 1870s and 1880s was made up mostly of young people from Russian-ruled Poland and Germany, although at the time many would say they were from Prussia. A few were able to travel back and forth, visiting family members and bringing back brides. Another portion were descendants of California's gold rush period – the minors of the "miners of the miners." These Jews prided themselves on being American and for the most part practiced their Judaism in the new Reform way. Stores were kept open on Saturdays by necessity – often until 10 p.m. Pork and seafood were commonly on the menu of Jewish gatherings. Those who needed a more Orthodox way of life simply didn't choose to make their home in the young Pacific Northwest.

By the mid-1890s that began to change. As Russian persecution of Jews increased, a second wave of immigration began. In Tacoma, the vast majority of those were related families from the Courland area of what is now Latvia – Bouska, Riga, Libau, and Sasmakken. Typically the men came first to get established, sending for their wives, children and sisters as soon as possible. Going back was not an option. Not only did they stay in the United States, many stayed in Tacoma.

This group of immigrants practiced a more Orthodox style of Judaism. They were likely shocked at the lack of observance they found in Tacoma. Descendants tell us that the men met daily for morning and evening prayers. Their sons and daughters and cousins intermarried. Eventually the cluster of families grew large enough to form their own congregation, Talmud Torah (1909), and commission their own Torah scroll.

The first of this group to arrive in Tacoma was most likely Adolph Friedman. In 1978 Julius Stusser wrote that his grand-uncle, Adolph Friedman, had come to Tacoma in 1845 with 35 Scandinavian sailors. Then Adolph caught gold fever and went to California, where he lived for nearly forty years before again coming to Tacoma. Based on this recollection, Adolph has been considered to be the first Jewish pioneer in the entire Pacific Northwest.

Adolph sailed from San Francisco to Tacoma aboard the steamer *Mexico* on October 23, 1884, and arrived just as the majority of Tacoma's Jewish population was in Seattle celebrating the 100th birthday of Sir Moses Montefiore, the British Jewish financier and philanthropist. Adolph worked as a clerk for Meyer Kaufman in Old Tacoma, and the following August purchased Kaufman's stock of groceries and dry goods. Business directories in the *Ledger* in February of 1887 included "A. FRIEDMAN, Groceries, tobacco, dry goods, varieties, and a full line of general merchandise. Second Street, First Ward."

Courland Province c 1820
Library of Congress World Digital Library

Adolph also began investing in real estate. In the summer of 1889 the Tacoma and Lake City Railway and Navigation Company began construction of a ten-mile railroad line between Tacoma and American Lake. The lake's popularity as a picnic area skyrocketed. Adolph joined with non-Jewish partners Joseph & Ida Blain and Jonathan & Martha Beardsley in developing a 160-acre tract of lakeside farmland into the town of American Lake Park. (Dr. Beardsley, who died in 1895, was the first physician at the Fannie Paddock Hospital.) The platted area was on the west side of American Lake, just south of the current Veterans Hospital. It contained a beach on the southeast and an open prairie on the west, and enclosed two small lakes. Street names included Friedman, Blaine, Harkness, Prairie, Breeden, Marvin, Beherall, Lowenstein, Kapus, Beardsley, and half a dozen presidents.

A few of the lots were sold, but only one or two houses were built and the venture never prospered. On September 6, 1892, the county commissioners vacated the southern portion containing the beach access. In 1917 the entire area was included in a transaction which established Camp Lewis, now part of Joint Base Lewis McChord. Military conservationists have removed any roads and buildings from the area and returned the land to a natural marshland. Park Lake now appears on maps as Park Marsh.

Hugo, Mascha and Julius Stusser arrived in Tacoma around 1892. They made shoes and clothing, and dyed used clothing – a necessity for keeping up appearances during hard times. Hugo's wife and seven children arrived a year later. Their eldest daughter Augusta Stusser married Julius Friedman in 1899. Hugo found his niche in the secondhand goods and clothing market, although complex reporting requirements caused him one initial legal entanglement.

Birman/Bernhard Yudelson came to Tacoma around 1896, working first for Julius Friedman and then for Hugo Stusser as a tailor. In November of 1901 he was joined by Peter Julius (Pesach Jehuda) Yudelson. (This family wins the award for the most variations of spelling. A page of Home of Peace Cemetery records shows five, as if the author was trying to see which looked right.) PJ was joined the following summer by his wife Bluma. Their five daughters would all marry, helping to establish the next generation of Judaism in Tacoma.

PJ Yudelson Family c.1897
Courtesy of Jim Friedman

On October 21, 1897, the *Ledger* announced the approval of a new "tall hat" ordinance affecting public gatherings. "Tonight all persons attending any theater or public performance must uncover to the gracious god who rules the field of drama and ballet." The actual wording of the ordinance followed, including the provision that "the above prohibition shall not be held to include skull caps, lace coverings or other small and closely-fitting head dress or covering." Clearly Tacoma's Orthodox Jewish community was beginning to make its presence known. A generation later their various extended family members would again dominate the fine clothing stores of Tacoma, with Julius Friedman dubbed the "Grandfather of Pacific Avenue."

Desperate times called for desperate measures. It was time to take a chance...

Ho! To The Klondike!

Tacoma residents had suffered through three long hard years of economic depression. By 1896 jobs were still scarce and wages were low. Many gathered together their few remaining dollars, bought some mining gear and took off, hoping their luck would turn.

Throughout the early 1890s the *Ledger* routinely carried a page in the Sunday edition devoted to mining interests across the Northwest. The page contained news of Cripple Creek in Colorado, as well as other mining areas in Washington, Oregon, Idaho and the far North. Throughout the spring of 1896 steamer after steamer headed to the Yukon with supplies and passengers. Many were looking, it was just a matter of time until someone struck it rich.

By the fall of 1896 mining companies started springing up in earnest. A week's incorporation records from the capital in Olympia might include a dozen mining companies and only a handful of other firms. Those who stayed home invested in other people's efforts. Realtors in Tacoma started including "mining properties" in their ads. The first big Yukon strikes actually came in August of 1896, but it would be almost a year before the gold started rolling into Washington ports, creating a rush.

Olympia's Louisa and Gallewski Kaufman's four eldest sons – Nat, Leo, Sam and Isadore – were ahead of the crowd. Leo and Isadore opened a store in Juneau in 1894. Nat and Sam followed two years later, opening a second store in Skagway. In January of 1897 Leo toured the lower coast cities representing the board of trade of Juneau. He tried to gain support for a congressional delegate from Alaska in order to fight for roads, law enforcement and liquor control. *Ledger*, January 26, 1897, "Mr. Kaufman said last night that Alaska needs a reorganization of the present method of dealing with liquor sellers. The law now forbids with heavy penalties the importa-

tion or selling of any liquor in Alaska, and yet there are 40 saloons in Juneau, a town of 2500 inhabitants. 'A regular army,' says Mr. Kaufman, 'could not enforce the law or prevent the smuggling of liquor across the Canadian border.'" By 1899 Leo was president of the Juneau Chamber of Commerce. The brothers eventually opened a clothing store in Bellingham, in addition to the family's store in Aberdeen, but continued fighting for transportation lines to Alaska.

Several hundred men left Tacoma in the spring of 1897, on their way to the Alaska territory. It would become an annual cycle, "coming out" for the winter and returning after the ice melt. The *Ledger*, always bent on promoting Tacoma, continued to emphasize local mining prospects more than those in the Far North. During April of 1897 much was made of discoveries of copper near Eatonville. During May the *Ledger* claimed that there was gold in the sand of the Narrows.

Finally in mid-July the *Excelsior* steamed into San Francisco with the golden fruits of the miners' labors, and the floodgates to the Klondike were opened. *Ledger*, July 16, 1897, "Millions upon millions of virgin gold, according to the story, await the fortunate miner who has the hardihood and courage to penetrate into the unknown depths of the Yukon district." However, the *Ledger* the next day warned that the claims were "probably much exaggerated." Another gold strike, this time in Gig Harbor, was more prominently featured.

By the eighteenth the story was believed. "Alaska's Golden Sands – Klondike the Richest Spot Known on Earth. Like a Fairy Tale. Gold Washed From Every Pan of Dirt on Bonanza Creek. Millionaires Made in a Day and Miners Crazed With Excitement." Sadly, the bankrupt *Ledger* was itself about to be sold.

Those staying in Tacoma quickly found their niche. By July 20th many ads for sturdy clothing and equipment began "Ho! For Klondike!" Special editions of the *Ledger* were sent east, complete with maps, supply lists and names of Tacoma suppliers. *Ledger,* April 16, 1900, "The state law is explicit in providing that merchants must observe Sunday closing, but by common agreement the law has heretofore been overlooked. This practice began with the Klondike rush, when seven days' work was necessary to handle the crowds."

CITY OF PARIS | CITY OF PARIS

Going to Klondike!

The owner of the City of Paris will go into the Gold Fields early in spring. It is apparent that summer goods and especially Ladies' Straw Sailor Hats will be of little value there. We therefore propose to hold one week's sale on these goods—and what remains goes to auction. So, if you want any of those goods at bona fide factory cost—now is your chance:

We Place on Sale

61 plainly marked 50c Ladies' Sailors, at	30c
73 plainly marked 89c Ladies' Sailors, at	50c
46 plainly marked $1.00 Sailors, at	55c
78 plainly marked $1 25 Sailors, at	75c
86 plainly marked $1.48 Sailors, at	$1.00

54 Ladies' Trimmed Hats—the product of Edson, Keith & Co., Chicago, at **exactly one-half the plainly marked selling price.**
One Case Artificial Flowers, at **one-half the plainly marked selling price.**

800 Ladies' 15c Summer Vests, at	5c
344 Ladies' 25c Summer Vests, at	12c
64 Light Colored Summer Wrappers, plainly marked 89c and $1.25. Closing out price, each	50c
900 yards 10c and 12½c Dimities, Organdies and Light Ducks. Clearance price, per yard	5c
63 Shirt Waists, we have sold from 50c to $1.25. Sale price, each	33c

.... Ho! for New Fall Goods! ....

Before the Gold excitement upset our plans we had bought all our Fall goods. We are compelled to receive them. But will make prices low enough to preclude any possibility of their being in our way when ready to start. While others raise prices to correspond with tariff and rise in wheat—ours will be lower than ever to effect a speedy clearance. Samples of our sincerity may be tested in the following price-list of new Fall goods:

600 yards New 50-inch Black French Alpaca, we bought to sell for 85c.
Sale Price 50c yard

2000 yards New Fancy Figured Black Mohair Dress Goods, we bought to sell for 40c. **Sale Price 25c yard**

1400 yards New Fancy Twill Suitings, we bought to sell for 29c, all desirable shades.
Sale Price 20c yard

1800 yards New Fancy Figured Dress Goods, we bought to sell for 50c.
Sale Price 38c yard

1600 yards Changeable Trimming Silks, in every desirable shade, we bought to sell for 37c.
Sale Price 25c yard

700 pairs Ladies' Fast Black Hose, we never sold a better pair for 20c.
Sale Price 12c a pair

32x22 Pure Linen Napkins, unbleached, a hummer for 25c.
Sale Price 10c each

400 yards Bleached 50c Table Damask, **Sale Price 35c yarp**

180 yards Reversible Table Oil Cloth (red table linen on one side and oil cloth on the other.)
Sale Price 29c a yard

506 Ladies' Steelrod Umbrellas, we bought to sell for $1.10.
Sale Price 75c

120 pairs Cooper's Bicycle Hose, bought to sell for $1.00.
Sale Price 75c

Yard wide Bleached Cotton, worth and sold by us heretofore for 7c.
Sale Price 5c yard

400 Unbleached Turkish Towels—37x19—we bought to sell for 20c each. **Sale Price, 2 for 25c**

300 Pure Linen Glass Towels—30x16—an excellent 12½c value.
Sale Price 6c each

60 Handsome Chenille Table Covers, we bought to sell for 50c.
Sale Price 29c each

44 Young Ladies' Lace-Yokes, marked 89c to $1.50. Sale price one-half the plainly marked selling prices.

CITY OF PARIS 1136 Pac. Ave.

Tacoma Daily Ledger August 15, 1897

While the majority of Tacoma's Jewish merchants were content to stay home and sell to the miners, a handful yielded to temptation, or at least said they were in order to hold a sale. Joseph Jacob, owner of City of Paris, instead stayed in Tacoma and sold "Footwear for the Klondike" with his brother Meyer.

THE KLONDIKE MINER—"CAN'T YOU THINK OF SOMETHING ELSE, MISSUS?"

Tacoma Daily Ledger August 15, 1897

The same edition carried a political cartoon featuring a lady labeled "Dominion of Canada." She was greeting a Klondike miner with a sign stating "I WANT duties on all your provisions and materials, and $15 registration fee; and $100 annual assessment and 10 per cent royalty on claims yielding $500 or less per month, and 20 per cent on claims yielding more..." The Canadian government had been quick to jump in and claim its share. (For the first several weeks the name of the area was spelled Klondyke. On August 22 an article quoted from the *Chicago Tribune* set the record straight. "Since Klondike is the official spelling it must be adopted. Ours is not to reason y.")

The *Ledger* on September first of 1896 noted that J. Bloom was among the passengers headed for Skagway aboard the steamer *City of Seattle.* Jacob and his brother Morris had managed the Kentucky Liquor house in Tacoma for six years. Over the next several years the *Ledger* carried several brief mentions of Jacob in Skagway – returning to Tacoma for the July Fourth celebration in 1899 and another visit in 1903. Depending on the account, he worked either as a wholesale cigar merchant, ran a roadhouse, or operated a saloon. He died in Skagway in June of 1906, and his body was shipped to Tacoma for burial.

Emil Korach had lived with Jacob Bloom in Tacoma, working at the Kentucky and taking over its operation from 1894 to 1898. The *Ledger* on July 31, 1899, in describing Tacomans in the Atlin area, mentioned "Emil Korach, saloon keeper, four claims, one yielding well." Feb. 5, 1903, "J. Bloom, of the firm of Bloom & Korach, left yesterday on the steamer *Dolphin* for a three weeks' business trip to Skagway, where the firm has its largest business house. Mr. Korach, who is there at present, will come down on the return trip of the *Dolphin*, arriving here about the 12th of the month." Emil married Tacoma's Lillie Hain around 1906, and the couple buried an infant child in Skagway.

Several members of Tacoma's Jewish community invested in other ways. Brewer Albert Weinberg and others incorporated the Tacoma and Dyea Trading Company on January 16, 1898, taking lumber to Skagway. Two days later pawnbroker Lewis Levy, clerk John Asher and others formed the Northwest Transportation Company, planning to operate two naphtha launches in Alaska. Within two weeks one of the stockholders was dismissed as manager and the partners took to the courts. An interview with Levy on June 6 revealed that he brought both launches back to Tacoma after only three months on the run between Skagway and Dyea. Levy stated that most people had already moved on to the interior. He also had strong comments about what he felt was corruption in the justice department there.

However, his brother did better. *Ledger,* September 17, 1898 (*Rosh Hashanah*) "FINDS WEALTH ON PINE CREEK. Barney Levy, a Tacoman, Returns With $2,000 to Show for a Few Weeks' Work. Barney Levy, well known in Tacoma, returned from Alaska yesterday with about $2,000 from Pine and Birch Creeks and with two claims yet to draw from. Mr. Levy says nearly a thousand people went to Pine Creek with the rush last month and most are now doing well and many more going in. 'Anyone can find gold,' says Mr. Levy, 'If they take the trouble to hunt for it… The new diggings are about four days from Dyea over a good trail.' Mr. Levy is now on his way to San Francisco to visit his wife and expects to go back in the spring."

The reports continued. *Ledger,* April 9, 1898, "A few former Tacomans are at Skagway, more at Wrangel and the most at Dyea and scattered along the trail here clear over to Lake Linde-

man… 'Jakie' Wolf, well known to the old-time patrons of Dave Hoffman's place, is here and as unique as ever. 'Jakie' is working in a bakery and doing well… I saw David Gross down at Wrangel and at Juneau. He was looking around in a quiet way. He decided not to visit Dyea or Skagway. Mr. Gross is understood to be looking for a location to start a branch store. He likes Juneau and Wrangel, but says rents are too high in Wrangel."

The same article noted "Colonel Charles Reichenbach keeps a cigar store at Main and Third streets." His son Walter had been included in an 1898 census of Jewish residents of Canada. *Ledger,* April 22, 1899, "Colonel Charles Reichenbach of Dawson is in Tacoma for a few days. He was formerly a prominent clothing merchant in Tacoma, and afterward in Everett, but full of the spirit of business venture, seized the opportunity to get into Dawson, where he is engaged in mercantile business and mining. He came out in December, but even at that early date the work in the various diggings was showing up well. Asked as to the probable output of the Klondike this year, he said he would estimate it anywhere from $8,000,000 to $12,000,000. He deemed it best to be conservative. He expects to go into Dawson again in a few weeks, when the river is open."

An article in the *Yukon Sun* on April 22, 1902, described a Passover gathering. Among those present was Colonel Charles Reichenbach. "Mr. Reichenbach was orator of the evening and made a pretty speech or two." An anti-Semitic cartoon on July 9 indicated that not all of his speeches were popular. On Sunday, January 4, 1903, Tacoma's *Daily Ledger* reported that Col. Reichenbach had sacrificed his American citizenship in order to run for mayor of Dawson. By January 28 he had failed to secure the mayoral nomination, so had "put himself up for city councilman instead." He was defeated, 329 votes to 42. By February Charles was in St. Mary's hospital, facing an operation for appendicitis. He returned to his family in San Francisco, where he resumed his American citizenship and collected his military pension.

THE LITTLE GEN
BRIG. GEN
I WISH I WAS A GEN.
THE GEN
FOR VALOR SHOWN ON THE GRAND STAND JEWILE, 4 1902
MEDDLES
GENERAL REACH AN-GO BACH TACOM
BUEL

Yukon Sun July 9, 1902

Along with the influx of travelers headed to the Klondike came a host of scoundrels and cheats, determined to fleece the hopefuls out of their cash. Unfortunately, some of their victims were local. *Ledger*, April 7, 1898, "Simon Silverman is the name of the fleeced and W.M. Cosner and W.C. Miller are the alleged operators. Silverman is a peddler of Hebrew extraction who makes Tacoma his base of operations and sells jewelry. Cosner and Miller are the proprietors of an illusion on lower Pacific avenue where curiosities of various kinds are on exhibition and a more or less correct representation of the Hula Hula dance was to be seen during the early days of the Klondike rush… Silverman dropped into the resort Tuesday evening and wagered a small sum on the game. The game is not known by name to the peddler and is described by the police only as a flim-flam. At any rate there were a number of dice, a table marked off with numbers and a second man who acted as a "capper" on the player's side of the table. The great system of the game appeared to be to double the bet every time a "star" came up and that happened pretty regularly.

Silverman dropped all of his ready money and then went out after more in a desperate effort to get even. The game in the meantime accommodatingly waited for his reappearance.

Twice he secured loans on his stock of goods and yesterday morning he went to Sam Andrews for a further accommodation and after telling his story was advised to go to police headquarters instead. At the station Captain King and two men started with Silverman for the game and after blockading all means of egress captured the whole affair. Cosner had $582 on his person, and Miller $103.50."

Silverman hired an attorney to recover his losses of $600 plus costs, and the Judith Montefiore Society provided temporary financial aid. Finally in December Silverman was awarded a judgement of $250, of which the attorneys claimed $204.

In April of 1899 a fire destroyed over one hundred homes in Dawson – perhaps three-fourths of the town. J.W. Toklas, uncle of the Kaufman boys, was one of three men who trekked out to bring the news – by canoe to Lake Lebarge, then over the ice. *Ledger*, May 22, 1899, "In their trip out the three couriers were forced to every expedient – walking, running with dogs, swimming for life on two occasions and breaking through the ice repeatedly." The town's citizens were reportedly digging through the ashes of the bank hunting for the gold in its vault.

The *Ledger* continued to keep readers informed of the local folks who had gone to try their luck in the Klondike region, even if it was mostly gossip. On July 31st of 1899 an article claimed that so many Tacoma people were there that the list "reads like a city directory… Mrs. Olsen, who, with her mother, Mrs. Fogelbaum, were the star characters in a sensational shop-lifting case in Tacoma two years ago, is also seeking fortune in Atlin." Barbara's brother Jacob Fogelbaum was there also.

Barbara's husband, L.A. Olsen, returned to Tacoma. *Ledger*, January 19, 1901, "Until five years ago I had lived here since 1880, and when I read in the papers that I had been reported lynched at Douglas Island, and again, hanged at Dawson, for misdeeds, I felt there would be those at home who would remember the time when I had never refused to contribute to charity in Tacoma and would not believe the stories." He said he had come south to check on the wife and children of his partner, Oliver Nelson, and would again head north in the spring. Later Mr. Olsen returned to Tacoma to open the Alaska Saloon.

The discovery of gold had definitely given folks something to sing about. Music was an integral part of daily life in Tacoma's early times and the Jewish community was no exception…

On That Note

Today music plays a starring role in Jewish worship services. (One of the nation's most prominent cantors and rabbis is Angela Warnick Buchdahl, raised in Tacoma.) Music also played a key role in the home and social life of Tacoma's Jewish pioneers. Dinner parties often included performances by accomplished young ladies, or a hired string orchestra.

Tacoma's first organist in Tacoma's first church was Annie Wolff, daughter of Louis Wolff. The organ was dedicated at St. Peter's on August 30, 1874. Annie and her sisters were noted musicians, and often entertained for the citizens of what is now "Old Tacoma." (That fall the church received a bell as a gift from St. Peter's church of Philadelphia and placed it atop a tall stump of a fir tree. It became known as the "oldest bell tower in America," due to the age of the tree stump.)

St. Peter's Church July 30, 1890
From the collection of the author

Ledger, July 31, 1887, "L. Wolff, of Old Tacoma, has just purchased a handsome Decker Brothers' parlor grand piano from New York, for which he paid $1,000. The Misses Wolff have this piano at their residence, and it is one of the finest instruments that has ever been brought to Tacoma." All three daughters of Louis Wolff – Annie, Rose and Rachel – had lifelong careers as music teachers.

Many of Tacoma's early Jewish merchants joined German clubs, known for their singing. Tacoma's musical "Harmonie Club" began in 1884 as a chorus of nearly twenty male German voices, including Simon Gutfield, Edward Hains, and Albert Weinberg. Later Charles Reichenbach was an organizer of the Germania Society, whose Sangerbund singing group included Ed Heine and Julius Rammelsberg. Charles Reichenbach's sons frequently performed on violin at social and charity events.

On June 23, 1893, the *Ledger* noted that Professor Pickerill had started a Ladies' Mandolin, Guitar and Banjo club. The club included the Misses Addie Levy and Carrie Kaufman.

When the Gross brothers began hosting grand spring openings in the early 1890s, they arranged for a small string orchestra to play. At one point there were more people in the street waiting to get in than there were in the store, so the orchestra was switched to the balcony and played for the enjoyment of those outside. One of the numbers was the "Gross Brothers March," composed by the local bandleader.

The Hyams Pauson Company followed their lead and printed its own waltz in the *Ledger* instead of their regular Sunday ad. Most likely the page was found on many pianos around town.

Morris Gross had himself married an accomplished musician. During August of 1895 Samuel Clemens, better known as Mark Twain, appeared in Tacoma. (His publisher had gone bankrupt in the panic and Mr. Clemens was obliged to return to the speaking circuit to repair his finances.) The *Ledger*'s society column on Sunday, August 18, 1895, described a reception given by Mrs. Frank Allyn in her apartments at The Tacoma hotel. "A rare treat was enjoyed by about thirty ladies who had been invited to meet Mrs. and Miss Clemens on Monday afternoon… It was an impromptu affair and for that reason perhaps was the more delightful. A most interesting feature of the occasion was the presence of Mr. Clemens, who told some of his well-known and celebrated stories, in his inimitable style." Half a dozen people performed, either giving recitations or doing musical numbers. "Miss Clemens, who was a pupil of Moscowski, played, as did also Mrs. Morris Gross, both numbers being exquisitely rendered and listened to with the closest attention." Mrs. Gross was about six months pregnant at the time.

Not all of Tacoma's music was created by people.

A WEATHER INDICATOR

The North End Whistling Well Is Blowing Hard Again.

A Near Resident Is Convinced That It Is Connected With Mount Tacoma.

Lobo and Others Swear by It as the Best Weather Prophet in the Business.

The whistling well in the Park and Boulevard addition in the North End is again on a musical toot. Night before last and yesterday morning the weird sounds could be heard continuously, and the wind which produced them came out of the mysterious depths of the well in a sinsible gale. The well is 105 feet deep, was dug three years ago the coming June, and according to people near by has been emitting this same whistling noise for about two years past.

Henry Lobe, an expressman, who lives within seventy-five feet of the well, says that it is connected with Mount Tacoma. He says it is the best storm and weather indicator he has ever heard of, and that it kdocks the reports of the weather prophets out entirely. Mr. Lobe told yesterday evening how it had been singing for the gast twenty-four hours, its song indicating that a storm of unusual magnitude was turning things topsy-turvy in some part of the country.

It had predicted the big storms in California recently, as well as the big snow storms in Tacoma during the past winter. In this connection a curious freak about the well has been noticed. In cold weather the well sucks instead of blows. Lobe put a whistle on it a short time ago, but it kept up such a hair-raising screeching that no one could

sleep and he had to ltake it off. The air coming out of the well is sometimes warm and often gaseous, and Mr. Lobe stated that no one had gone in it to investigate for fear of being smothered. The well does not blow all the time, but only at intervals when a storm or some other elemental disturbance of an unusual nature is getting ready for business.

Mr. Lobe says that he takes a weather forecast every morning, and has never yet been caught in the rain without his umbrella. Many of the down-town carmen ask him regularly, when he comes in the morning, what the well has to say, and he never misses it in his predictions.

Ledger May 15, 1893

In the fall of 1898 Tacoma started her first "Philharmonic Orchestra." David Gross' son Leonard played violin in the group, and many members of Tacoma's Jewish community contributed to the organization.

That same year trained vocalist Mrs. Bernard Hochstadter arrived in Tacoma. She immediately became active in the Ladies' Musical Society, performing at many events and fundraisers. Around the turn of the century she started the first choir at Temple Beth Israel. In 1903 she returned to Europe to continue her voice training.

1898 also brought Julius Adler to Tacoma, to take charge of the Tacoma Military Band. He immediately won over the press. Adler composed a march and two-step called "Salute to Tacoma" and donated it to the *Ledger*. Proceeds of the printed music sales were used to raise funds for a memorial to honor the fallen soldiers of the war with Spain. He evidently charmed interviewers, for a description of him on June fourth of 1899 read "Mr. Adler enters his work with genuine pleasure and every wave of his baton shows he is an enthusiast. He is a brilliant conversationalist, a rare raconteur and a mellow Bohemian."

Ledger, June 19, 1899, "Second Concert Tonight… A chorus of 75 voices will sing Professor Adler's new national anthem, 'The Land of Our Fathers' for the first time." By July Fourth Julius was conducting a massive chorus in Wright Park, with the band as accompaniment. The band became known throughout the Pacific Northwest as "Adler's Band." Adler gained more publicity when the following February one of his former band members, E.L. Boyce, killed his wife because she had pawned his trombone. Boyce was executed on August 9, 1901.

Adler's Band July 8, 1899
Tacoma Public Library LOY-001

Grand Band Concert

Given by the Tacoma Military Band

at the Tacoma Theatre

June 12th
ADMISSION
25, 50, 75c
and $1.00.

Monday Evening

The proceeds of this concert will be used to purchase uniforms for the band. Help the good work along by purchasing a ticket.

Tacoma Daily Ledger June 8, 1899

Before coming to Tacoma, Julius Adler gained fame for his opera *The Patriots*, which included the sound of the ringing of the Liberty Bell. In order to get the correct tone, Julius received permission to perform a test, striking the actual Liberty Bell on May 10, 1895, at Philadelphia, and determining the pitch was D flat. (*Atlanta Constitution, Nov. 17, 1895)* The opera premiered in Atlanta in November of 1895 and the libretto was later performed in Boston and Philadelphia.

Philadelphia Times December 15, 1895

As Morris Gross resumed his gala spring openings in March of 1900, he arranged for a pianist to perform at the store each afternoon. The piano was to be raffled for the benefit of the Tacoma Military Band.

On March 19, 1900, the *Ledger* noted that the Tacoma Saengerbund had hosted all of the Western Washington German singing societies. The Tacoma Military Band met the 500 visitors at the wharf and marched them to the Germania Hall. That evening President Ed Heinemann gave the welcoming remarks.

Finally, we have to note that Tacoma's Samuel Sondheim and Joseph Bachrach were distantly related to composers Stephen Sondheim and Burt Bachrach, according to relatives.

We've looked at Jewish social life, as viewed through the very public columns of the city's newspapers. Now let's look at Jewish religious life...

Holidays in a Rented Hall

Today visitors to Tacoma's Temple Beth El step into the rotunda and look up to see a brass rail circling the room. A moveable hand or *yad* points to Hebrew letters above the rail, spelling out the names of 54 weekly Torah readings. Larger letters under the rail spell out Jewish holidays – *Pesach* (Passover), *Rosh Hashanah* (New Year), *Yom Kippur* (Day of Atonement), and more. Guests learn that Jews read from the Torah on a strict weekly schedule, unlike Christians who might choose to discuss a particular theme or book of the Bible. The brass railing and letters serve as a working calendar, a physical reminder that Jews around the world are all reading the exact same holy words each week.

Tacoma's earliest Jewish residents temporarily gave up many of their day-to-day Jewish practices to take advantage of the opportunities in the growing Pacific Northwest. By necessity they kept their stores open on Saturday, (the Jewish Sabbath) ate non-kosher food, and had no synagogue to attend. Yet while they outwardly adapted to the seasons of the pioneer community, they kept an inner Jewish calendar, celebrating Jewish holidays as they could.

Nineteenth century newspapers took note, typically with token articles to educate non-Jewish readers about the different calendar and customs. As the community grew, these articles advised shoppers of major store closures. Jews themselves may have consulted the articles for dates and times of services.

These glimpses of Jewish life are invaluable from a historical standpoint. They provide estimates of the size of the growing Tacoma Jewish population, much larger than previously believed. The reports include details such as who led services in the absence of a rabbi, what languages were used and when the first shofar was sounded. They give hints as to the growing divisions between Reform and more Orthodox worshipers. The explanatory articles imply that several in Tacoma's Jewish community were well-educated. Later mentions describe Jewish practice from an observer's viewpoint, making it clear that a reporter had personally been in attendance. Finally, the articles provide a crucial time line, as a handful of individual Jews evolved into a congregation.

During the 1860s Steilacoom's four Jewish families – Schafer, Pincus, Packscher and Goodtime – most likely gathered at holidays with their counterparts in Olympia – Isaac Harris, Gus Rosenthal and the Bettman brothers – as they would later join in forming a cemetery association in 1872.

Tacoma's *Weekly Pacific Tribune* mentioned the "Hebrew New Year" as early as 1873. In the issue dated September 26, daily columns of the previous week unfolded as follows:

"(From the DAILY of Saturday) HEBREW NEW YEAR. – At 6 o'clock last evening the Jewish New Year began, and has been observed by our fellow citizens of that faith by the closing today of their place of business." The article continued with a description of the holiday of *"Rosh Hashono,"* beginning the Hebrew year 5634, leading up to the Day of Atonement the following Sunday. Six paragraphs later, "A GOOD CUSTOM. – This being the Hebrew New Years, Mr. Herman Ostheim very kindly remembered the *TRIBUNE* office, while making the gifts customary with his people on that day. We have yet to hear from others of that faith in the same pleasant manner."

The ploy worked, and thus was born a long and friendly relationship between Tacoma's Jewish merchants and the local press. "(From the DAILY of Tuesday) THANKS. – Levin & Kaufman, in the good Hebrew manner of friend Ostheim, sent us a bottle of wine, with which to assist them in the proper celebration of their New Years. We only wish these holidays came oftener." This came at a time when the Puget Sound Business Directory noted only four public buildings in the entire Puget Sound area – a wooden capitol building in Olympia, a territorial penitentiary in Steilacoom, a customs house at Port Townsend and a Territorial school in Seattle.

By 1882 the celebration of prominent Jewish families became newsworthy. "All the Jews in Tacoma and vicinity met at the residence of Meyer Kaufman, in Tacoma City, on Tuesday, where a fine champagne dinner was served and a jovial time was spent in celebrating the commencement of their New Year." The dinner may have included nearly forty people. In 1883 the Gross brothers began changing their newspaper ad to reflect the closing of their store. The following year the *Ledger* waxed poetic:

> "To-day is Atonement day among the Hebrews here and the world over. Their stores are closed and business suspended for the nonce. You may scatter these men of commerce; fire and faggot may consume some of them; persecution so severe and shuddering as to make Christians blush for their share in it, may rob and smite them; the Mars of bitter waters may overwhelm them: yet they are always true to tradition and Talmud – to creed and family. Their harps, which were hung by the waters of Babylon, give forth a sad echo, yet it is soothing and tender, and never forgotten. To a certain extent they have made modern civilization a witness to their triumphs."

The summer of 1885 brought a treasure from Europe, sent to Colonel Meyer Kaufman's brother-in-law, Philip Singermann. (The same day's paper carried a description of the formal welcome in New York of Bartholdi's great statue of "Liberty.")

> "A representative of this paper was shown a present much appreciated by the receiver. It was sent from Germany to Mr. P. Singermann, of Seattle, by his aged father. It is a roll of scripture painted in Hebrew characters and covered with a silken mantle. The whole of the Pentateuch is on this scroll. It is called the Torah among the Hebrews, and is retained in their families for generation after generation as a precious heirloom. Mr. Singermann is a

prosperous merchant, and in the cares of business or the successes of life he clings with veneration to the teachings and customs of his ancient creed and people, and with parental foresight inculcates these lessons on his children."

By the fall of 1885 Tacoma's Jewish community had grown enough to support holding services in the new Masonic hall at 952–956 Pacific. Half a dozen lengthy articles were printed over the course of several weeks. Services were led by Mr. W. Wolf, who was described as a rabbi's assistant or "kantor" acting in the absence of a rabbi.

Services continued each fall in the Masonic hall, with regular newspaper mentions. An 1886 article suggested a Reform style of worship. "The event is known as *Rosh Hashanah*, and is observed by the strictly orthodox for two days, but in this country is generally observed for only one day." 1887 notices continued the educational theme. "In the ritual of the Jewish people New Year's day is considered the date upon which everything relating to the destiny of a member is written in the great book. It is believed that all the deeds of the coming year are inscribed in the great ledger by the Almighty, and that it takes ten days, the time between Rosh Hashanah and the Day of Atonement, to remodel the inscribed destiny of the brethren. During these ten days the Jews do penance to appease the wrath of the Almighty…The orthodox and reformed Hebrew alike fast from sunset on the Day of Atonement." Educational articles kept coming during the fall of 1888. "While the five books of Moses are read by orthodox congregations during the period of one year, the advanced congregations read only one-third a year, or the entire Pentateuch in a cycle of three years." The Gross brothers closed their store for the entire day, taking out a large newspaper ad to inform shoppers.

Our store will be closed from 6 o'clock p. m. to-day, Wednesday, September 5, until 6 o'clock p. m. to-morrow, Thursday, September 6.

GROSS BROTHERS

Tacoma Daily Ledger September 5, 1888

A significant article in the fall of 1888 implied that Tacoma's Jewish community had organized in 1885 as a membership congregation, complete with bylaws and officers.

"Three years ago the Jewish population was so small that there were barely enough to organize a prayer meeting, eleven being requisite for that purpose, according to the by-laws of the Hebrew organization. The first meeting was held at that time in Masonic hall, in the Ouimette block, where the society has met ever since. During the first year there were never more than sixteen to eighteen members. During the second year the number had increased to forty, and it now numbers 125."

The article went on to mention the recent formation of the Hebrew Benevolent Association and the election of congregational officers.

"The object of this organization is to make arrangements for erecting a synagogue in Tacoma and for purchasing grounds for a local cemetery... After the regular meeting William Wolff, of the First ward, the reader of the society, was presented with a beautifully chased and ornamented silver pitcher with goblet and drip bowl. The committee who selected the present were Colonel M. Kaufman and Messrs. Morris Gross, A. Weinberg and L. Wallerstein. Colonel Kaufman advanced to the front, bearing the rich and costly gift, and made the following neat presentation speech: 'Mr. Wolff. Allow me, on behalf of the Hebrews of this city, to present to you this silver pitcher and service as a slight token of their appreciation of your services in their behalf, and your worth as a man and friend'... Upon the pitcher is engraved: 'Presented to Mr. Wolff by the members of the Hebrew congregation of Tacoma, W.T., this 15th day of September, 1888.'"

In the summer of 1889 the *Ledger* described the Jewish holiday of "Shevuoth." "The day will be observed in the homes of the orthodox, but business will be transacted as usual." Tucked in several paragraphs later was a hint of things to come. "There is a movement on foot among the Hebrews of Tacoma to build a synagogue here, but the matter has not taken definite shape yet. The Jewish population is constantly on the increase, and is large enough at present to support a rabbi and a synagogue." This was the same day as the great fire in Seattle.

THE JEWISH NEW YEAR.

How It Will Be Celebrated in Tacoma This Year.

The Jewish New Year begins this evening at 6 o'clock and will continue through tomorrow. It is called Rosh-ha-sho-noa, and will be observed by the Israelites of Tacoma. Services will be held in Odd Fellows' hall in the Mason block this evening Rev. L. Eisenbach, of Tacoma, has gone to Seattle to officiate tomorrow, as the services there will be made a special occasion. Messrs. Wolff and Rohr will officiate at the services in this city, they being qualified to act. Most of the Jewish stores in Tacoma will close tomorrow, though some will not celebrate the day to the extent of closing their places of business.

Tacoma Daily News September 25, 1889

By the fall of 1889 the holidays made the front page of the *Tacoma News*. (The fact that many of the paper's prominent advertisers were involved may have been a factor.) "Rev. L. Eisenbach, [Eisbert] of Tacoma, has gone to Seattle to officiate tomorrow, as the services there will be made a special occasion. Messrs. Wolff and Rohr [Broh] will officiate at the services in this city, they being qualified to act... The officers of the Jewish congregation of Tacoma are: President, M. Kaufman; vice president, Charles Reichenbach; secretary, L. Wallerstein; recording secretary, William Wolff; treasurer, H. Berliner; board of trustees, Isaac Pincus, Charles Langert, Henry Harris, Samuel Wolff and M. Kaufman." The *Ledger* carried a similar article.

By 1890 the holidays were again considered front-page news, as the congregation gathered momentum to build. From the *Tacoma Daily Ledger*, "During the new year observances this year a movement will be made to secure a synagogue. It is thought there are Jewish families enough in Tacoma alone to warrant the building of a large synagogue at which members of the faith from all parts of the surrounding country could assemble for worship." From the *Tacoma Daily News*, "Today Pacific Avenue and the other business streets present a somewhat forlorn appearance as in honor of the Jewish New Year all the business houses owned by Hebrews are closed until this evening... The committee on New Year's arrangements is composed of E.H. Gross, L. Wallerstein, and H. Harris, representing the Hebrew Benevolent society; and H. Berliner, Max Broh, M. Germanus and D.P. Davis [Lewis] representing the Independent Order of B'nai B'rith."

The *Tacoma Daily Ledger* continued, "The Jewish new year was fittingly celebrated yesterday in the Turn Hall at 1515 E Street by the 600 Hebrew residents of Tacoma... During the day the people drop in as it suits their convenience, and take part in the exercises. The prayer leaders yesterday were M. Blum, M. Broh and Rabbi Eisbert." Yet another article described the first time the shofar (ram's horn) was blown in Tacoma, in a speech made by president Ellis Gross. He noted that "This is the first *Rosch Haschana* (New Year's day) that we have had the pleasure and opportunity to have and to hear a *Schopher* in this city." He quoted G-d saying to Abraham, "Go from your native country, from the place where you were born, and leave your father's house, and go to a strange place, which I will show you... Let us look back and we will see that everything that happened to Abraham has happened also to us. The most of us left our native country and our father's house and every one of us are strangers in this city."

THE HEBREW HOLIDAYS

Rosh Hoshanah and Yom Kipur at Hand.

WILL BE OBSERVED IN TACOMA.

Feasts and Fasts That Moses Established—What They Are.

According to the Hebrew calendar, Saturday, October 3d, is the first day of the month Tishri of the year 5652. Rosh Hoshanah, as the new year is called in the Hebrew language, will be appropriately observed by all the orthodox Jews in town, and they are not few.

Among those of the faith who have studied the doctrines of the old religion and understand to some extent its mysteries, are Ellis Gross of the firm of Gross Bros, Paul Singerman, who has recently purchased the stock of Kaufman & Berliner, and Mr. Berliner. From these gentlemen yesterday a LEDGER reporter gathered the following facts concerning the holiday:

Tacoma Daily Ledger September 30, 1891

In 1891 the *Daily Ledger* carried a three-column article about the upcoming holidays, including interviews with prominent Jews. "Services will be conducted in Germania hall, which has been leased for the purpose. William Wolff, who is a student of Hebrew theology, will conduct them, performing all parts of the services that a layman may. ...Because of the holiday all the Jewish business houses in the city will be closed. They include all the leading dry goods

stores. Next year it is hoped there will be a more complete celebration of the day, for by that time a congregation may have been formed, and if a synagogue is not built, some room or hall may have been set apart for that purpose."

Several weeks later the *Ledger* described *Yom Kippur* services, led by Rabbi Israel Dantoff of Portland, with about 150 in attendance. Morris Gross' address was the only part of the service read in English, delivering the first of many holiday appeals.

"Ladies and gentlemen and fellow Israelites, I am taking a very unusual step in venturing to speak to you on this atonement day. I feel now like Solomon when he said, "Now, O Lord, my God, thou hast made thy servant king instead of David, my father, and I am but a little child. It is not necessary for me to tell you what duty we have to perform this day, (*Yom Kippor*), as we all know it... When Jacob prayed to God he said (*Hacelini nu miad ochimiad Eisoh*) – "Deliver me from the hands of my brother Esau for I fear him." So it is with us in this country. My friends we don't have to fear, for the people we live with are our friends, and those we ought to fear are those few who are among us and belong to our faith, and to overcome them we must put our hands in our pockets, and shoulder to shoulder, and build synagogues so we can come more together, and we must not be ashamed of our religion and deny our faith in order to make money. Let us take for an example the great English statesman, Disraeli, who, when taunted by noblemen in the House of Commons on his Hebrew origin, sprang to his feet and said: "Yes, I am a Jew." He did not deny it. When such great men as him or Moses, Montefiore, or our great philanthropist and redeemer of the Russian Hebrews, Baron Hirsch, who is our nineteenth century Moses, do not deny our religion, we ought to be proud of our ancestors...My friends, in closing these few remarks I hope that we are and will remain by religious Hebrews, be proud of the name, our nationality shall be that of the land in which we dwell."

In 1892 services were held for the last time in a rented hall, the Unitarian church on Tacoma Avenue and South Third streets. Services were conducted by an undergraduate from the col-

– 81 –

lege in Cincinnati, "Rev. Dr. Fleisher." Professor Meissner conducted a six-person choir.

September 23, "The Hebrews of Tacoma are moving toward having a synagogue, and with that in view have bought from the Tacoma land company two lots at the northeast corner of I and Tenth streets. The land company gave them the lots at half price. Besides buying the lots, subscriptions to the amount of $1000 have been raised for the synagogue. The chief contributors were as follows: Gross Bros., $750; Prager Bros., $150; Isaac Pincus, $150; Mr. Cohen, $100; David Levin, $100; L. Wallerstein, $100; Isaac Harris, $50; A.S. Ash, $50; Simon Hirsch, $50; Charles Langert, $150; M. Ball, $150; S. Jacoby, $50."

An article in the *Ledger* on Saturday, October 1st, 1892, set a pattern for the next seventy years in Tacoma. "*Yom Kippur*, the Jewish feast of the atonement, is being celebrated to-day by the Hebrews with special observances... The orthodox Hebrews are holding their services in Elks' hall, and the reform sect in the Unitarian church." The Jewish community had grown large enough to divide.

Several articles over the next few weeks credited Rabbi Fleisher with rekindling the religious enthusiasm of the city's Hebrews, resulting in plans for a synagogue, to cost over $10,000. "It will be the handsomest synagogue in the northwest, far excelling the new one in Seattle in elegance and interior finish," indicating perhaps a different sort of motivation.

THE NEW SYNAGOGUE.

Tacoma Daily News December 15, 1892

Tacoma Newspaper Mentions of Jewish Holidays

September 26, 1873	*Weekly Pacific Tribune*	Ostheim, Levin, Kaufman – gifts of wine
September 15, 1877	*Tacoma Herald*	Educational, "no business transacted"
September 19, 1879	*Washington Standard*	"We refer our uninitiated readers to their Hebrew neighbors for explanatory details"
September 21, 1882	*Tacoma News*	Meyer Kaufman champagne dinner
October 10, 1883	*Tacoma Daily Ledger*	Most Jewish merchants will close
September 30, 1884	*Tacoma Daily Ledger*	"Business suspended for the nonce"
March 8, 1885	*Tacoma Daily Ledger*	Purim party home of L. Wolff, First ward
June 20, 1885	*Tacoma Daily Ledger*	Torah received by P Singermann of Seattle
September 1885	*Tacoma Daily Ledger*	Masonic Hall, led by W.W. Wolf
September 20, 1885	*Tacoma Daily Ledger*	Dinner to feast after the fast
September 29, 1886	*Tacoma Daily Ledger*	Masonic Hall, led by W.W. Wolf, 1 day only
September 27, 1887	*Tacoma Daily Ledger*	Masonic Hall, description of customs
February 27, 1888	*Tacoma Daily Ledger*	Purim masquerade ball at Germania Society
September 13, 1888	*Tacoma Daily Ledger*	Description of holidays, triennial cycle
September 18, 1888	*Tacoma Daily Ledger*	Congregation growing, gift to Wm. Wolff
June 5, 1889	*Tacoma Daily Ledger*	Feast of *Shavuot*, movement to build
September 25,1889	*Tacoma Daily News, p 1*	Services in Odd Fellows' Hall, Wolff & Broh lead, Rev. Eisenbach gone to Seattle
September 2, 1890	*Tacoma Daily Ledger*	Services will include effort to build
September 15, 1890	*Tacoma Daily News*	Pacific Avenue forlorn, services at Turn Verein Hall, led by Rabbi Eisbert
September 16, 1890	*Tacoma Daily Ledger*	Celebrated yesterday by 600 Hebrews
September 21, 1890	*Tacoma Daily Ledger*	Speech by Ellis Gross, first *Shofar* heard
September 24, 1890	*Tacoma Daily News*	Jewish business at a standstill, city retail deserted, services in Germania Hall
February 8, 1891	*Tacoma Daily Ledger*	Matzos available, Oregon Cracker Company
September 29, 1891	*Tacoma Evening Call*	Services at Germania Hall, tickets Mr. Moses
September 30, 1891	*Tacoma Daily Ledger*	Leading dry goods stores closed
October 12, 1891	*Tacoma Daily Ledger*	Portland's Rabbi Dantoff, Odd Fellows hall 150 present, Morris Gross speech
October 13, 1891	*Tacoma Daily Ledger*	Fast is ended, service in Hebrew and German
September 21, 1892	*Tacoma Daily Ledger*	Unitarian Church, Dr. Fleisher of Cincinnati, 200 people, special choir
September 23, 1892	*Tacoma Daily Ledger*	New Year 5653, purchase of two lots, list of donors
October 1, 1892	*Tacoma Daily Ledger*	Orthodox in Elks, Reform in Unitarian
October 3, 1892	*Tacoma Daily Ledger*	Synagogue to cost $10,000 – will be better than the new one in Seattle, building committee named
October 9, 1892	*Tacoma Daily Ledger*	Farewell parties for Dr. Fleisher, list of guests
April 2, 1893	*Tacoma Daily Ledger*	Passover service 1147 Railroad, W Wolff

*While the Jewish pioneers in the Pacific Northwest
were willing to wait to build a synagogue, death did not wait…*

Clubs & Organizations

Home of Peace Cemetery

13-year-old Celia Dobrin died of typhoid in the summer of 1872. Her family had recently arrived in Olympia from Victoria, British Columbia. It took another two years before the Hebrew Benevolent Society of Puget Sound was formally organized, purchasing three acres of land within the grounds of the Masonic Cemetery in Tumwater. The majority of early burials came from Jewish families in Steilacoom and Tacoma.

June 27, 1872: Celia Dobrin, 13, Olympia, daughter of Morris and Bertha Dobrin
May 9, 1877: Minnie Pincus, 3-month-old daughter of Isaac and Seraphina Pincus, Steilacoom
October 8, 1877: Robert Fischer, 22, Tacoma, brother of Flora Kaufman
September 2, 1879: Hyman Goodtime, 49, Steilacoom, husband of Louisa
June 16, 1882: Eli Coleman, 7 years 11 months, Tacoma, son of Julius and Pauline Coleman
June 27, 1882: Louis Coleman, 6 years, Tacoma, son of Julius and Pauline Coleman
February 28, 1886: Julius Coleman, 44, Tacoma, husband of Pauline
June 17, 1886: Flora Kaufman, 38, Tacoma, wife of Meyer Kaufman
March 31, 1888: 19-day-old son of Ellis & Johanna Gross, Tacoma
July 13, 1888: Milton Mamlock, infant son of Julius and Paula Mamlock, Tacoma
August 2, 1888: Gustave Wolff, 23, Tacoma, son of Louis & Sarah Wolff, brother of William
June 18, 1891: Morris Dobrin, 60, husband of Bertha Dobrin
April 7, 1897: Joseph Dobrin, 41, Tacoma, son of Morris and Bertha Dobrin

Tacoma's *Daily Ledger* on June 18, 1887, mentioned that "Meyer Kaufman of Old Tacoma went to Olympia a few days ago where he had erected a fine monument, costing about $300, to the memory of his deceased wife. Mr. Kaufman was accompanied there by several of his friends from Seattle and Tacoma." Meyer had observed the Jewish custom of waiting a year to "unveil" a tombstone.

By the fall of 1888 several of Tacoma's Jewish leaders had buried family members in Tumwater. Visiting those graves required a full day's travel back and forth by steamer, train, or horse and buggy. (Even today it is a forty-five minute drive, without traffic delays.) Young Gustave Wolff's death following hip surgery was perhaps the final straw. *Tacoma Daily Ledger*, September 18, 1888:

"BENEVOLENT HEBREWS. Organization of a Tacoma Society... At the cele-bration of the Jewish day of atonement last Saturday, a temporary organization of the Hebrew Benevolent association took place...There will be another meeting next Sunday afternoon at 4 o'clock, in Masonic hall, for permanent organization, at which, it is hoped every Hebrew in Tacoma will be present. The object of this organization is to make arrangements for erecting a synagogue in Tacoma and for purchasing grounds for a local cemetery. Heretofore it has been necessary to take the dead to Olympia or Victoria, the nearest places in which were Jewish cemeteries."

The association purchased land southwest of Tacoma, on the Lake City streetcar line between Tacoma and Steilacoom. Young Jennie Mamlock was likely the first burial in September of 1889. The group's first annual meeting was held in October of 1889, immediately after Yom Kippur, at the home of Meyer Kaufman. The organization empowered the trustees to have the society incorporated and the land fenced and platted.

THE HEBREW SOCIETY.

Election of Officers Yesterday and a Projected Synagogue.

The first Hebrew Benevolent Association of Tacoma held its annual election yesterday at the residence of Mr. Meyer Kaufman, 1606 Tacoma avenue, officers being elected as follows: President, Colonel M. Kaufman; vice president, M. Cohn; financial secretary, W. Wolff; corresponding secretary, L. Wallerstein; treasurer, M. Broh; trustees, Isaac Pincus, Meyer Kaufman, Charles Langert, I. Harris and David Levin.

The congregation is in a flourishing condition. It has bought five acres of land southwest of Tacoma for a burial ground, and will fence it in and otherwise improve the land. In the near future the congregation will build a handsome synagogue. The members of the congregation were all pleasantly entertained yesterday by Mr. Meyer Kaufman.

Tacoma Daily News October 14, 1889

Articles of incorporation were filed on April 22, 1891, with $5,000 of company stock. That day was also the first day of Passover. On April 24th the new corporation completed the transactions to purchase 8.01 acres of land from Charles Wright, as president of the Tacoma Land Company, "in consideration of the sum of one dollar, lawful money."

The rules and regulations for the government of the cemetery, *Givos Olom*, were adopted on September 5, 1891. They were signed by "Wm. Wolff, D. Germanus, S. Posner, (Com. on Constitution and By-Laws) and D. Magnus, Sec'y." The society helped organize High Holiday services, held on October 2–3 and 11–12. The constitution was adopted at a special meeting on October 25, 1891. The society had 15 original charter members, with a total of 40 by the fall of their first year. The object of the society was to first minister relief to the distressed, and second to bury the dead – a priority which continues to this day.

Applicants who were accepted for admission were required to pay the sum of twenty-five dollars, plus 50 cents per month as dues. Dues were collected in January and July of each year. Any member who accepted an appointment on a committee and neglected the same was fined one dollar. Any member who refused to come to order when requested by the president was fined "$1 for the first offence, and $2 for the second or any following offence."

Charter Members

William Wolff	Ed. Hain
David Levin	J.B. Mamlok
Henry Berliner	Herman Bryer
Louis Wallerstein	Isaac Harris
E.H. Gross	D. Magnus
D.P. Lewis	J. Bloom
Samuel Langert	Samuel Loeb
Chas. Reichenbach	Amil Zelinsky
Isaac Pincus	A. Friedman
Meyer Kaufman	A.S. Ash
Col. M. Kaufman	A. Simon
(Died Feb. 15, 1891)	Herman Zelinsky
Morris Gross	S.J. Holland
Chas. Langert	M. Moses
Samuel Wolff	Samuel Posner
Albert Weinberg	S. Jacobi
M. Cohn	D. Germanus
M. Ball	Sol. Zelinsky
M. Levin	S. Rodgers
Henry Harris	S. Robinson
	S. Gutfeld

Isaac Pincus and Louis Wallerstein filed the plat of the Home of Peace Cemetery in December of 1891. The cemetery was divided into 128 lots. (In Jewish tradition, drawing lots is a way of letting G-d decide.) As Tacoma's Jewish community grew, so did the cemetery. Additional plots were surveyed in 1910, and in 1921 eight more blocks were added across the back.

On April 11th of 1922, the society's name was officially changed to the "Home of Peace Cemetery Association." However, the name appears on the title page of the first cash ledgers prepared by David Magnus in 1892, and in early photos of the iron gates over the cemetery entrance.

Entrance Gate at Home of Peace Cemetery, September 14, 1926, ordered for Western Iron & Wire Works
Tacoma Public Library A-1712

Adjoining land was purchased in 1914 for a more traditional cemetery. The Chevra Kadisha Cemetery Association was incorporated in 1930. In 1979 the two cemeteries were merged.

Unlike many cemeteries that sell plots, Home of Peace functions today as it began in 1888 – as an association of members. The upkeep of the cemetery is funded through membership dues, investments, burial fees of non-members, and donations from the community.

Home of Peace Cemetery Association Officers and Trustees

Date	President	Vice President	Secretary	Treasurer	Trustees
September 18, 1888 Temporary organization	Col. M. Kaufman	Morris Gross & H. Cohn	Louis Wallerstein	A. Weinberg	William Wolff, Abraham Gross, Isaac Pincus, H. Berliner, S. Gutfeld
October 5, 1888 serve for six months	M. Kaufman	Charles Reichenbach	L. Wallerstein	H. Berliner	Isaac Pincus, Charles Langert, A. Zelinsky, M. Kaufman, W. Harris
October 15, 1889, 1st annual meeting	M. Kaufman	W. Wolff	L. Wallerstein	M. Broh	Isaac Pincus, M. Kaufman, Charles Langert, I. Harris, David Levin
September 30, 1890	Col. M. Kaufman	H. Harris	Wm Wolff, L. Wallerstein	M. Broh	Meyer Kaufman, I. Pincus, D. Levin, M. Moses, I. Posner, M. Cohn
April 23, 1891 Articles of Incorporation	Isaac Pincus				Meyer Kaufman, D. Levin, William Wolff, Louis Wallerstein, Henry Harris, Charles Langert
October 21, 1891 Constitution adopted	Isaac Pincus	S. Posner	William Wolff, D. Magnus	S. Ash	D.P. Lewis, Germanus, S. Jacobi
1896 directory	Julius Basinski	M. Cohn	Samuel Posner	A.S. Ash	Cemetery committee: E.H. Gross, David Levin, Samuel Posner
1899–1900 directories	Albert Weinberg	Meyer Jacob	Sam Posner	Sam Posner	

While Tacoma's Jewish community gathered at the cemetery grounds in sad times, other clubs celebrated the good times. . .

Harmony Club

Tacoma's early newspapers filled their social columns with lengthy descriptions of luncheons, dinner parties and club events. Those newspaper articles describing Jewish club events have tremendous historical value, as they were quite literally a "Who's Who" of the early Jewish community, who clearly felt no need to hide their Jewish identity. Descriptions of gowns and jewelry indicated the prosperity of the members, many of whom most likely took advantage of the latest styles available in their own clothing stores. Attendance lists typically included multiple guests from other cities, possibly with some matchmaking in mind. The mentions also serve as a reminder that these merchants were for the most part young people in their twenties and thirties, quite willing to dance through the early morning hours.

The *Tacoma Daily Ledger* in the summer of 1885 carried descriptions of several picnics hosted between the Jewish people of Tacoma and Seattle. Apparently organizing the picnics called for the formation of a social club. All of the officers happened to be eligible young bachelors, many of whom would marry within the next few years.

Ledger, July 22, 1885, "Last evening a large number of young business men of Tacoma organized "The Standard club" and elected the following officers: Mr. Samuel Gottschalk, president; Mr. H. Isaacs, vice president; Mr. Harry Lobe, secretary; Mr. Dave Magnus, treasurer, and Messrs. Charles Packscher, Ben Einstein and H. Berliner, a committee on constitution and by-laws. This club will give a private picnic at Enell's grove on next Sunday, and expect a large number of their Seattle friends by special steamer. Other festivities will follow this fall and winter, as the club has for its main object social enjoyment." Enell's grove was about a mile north of the wharf in Old Tacoma.

Three years later another group repeated the process. *Ledger*, Friday June 15, 1888, "A number of young men of the Hebrew faith have organized the Phoenix Social club. The object of the club is social advancement. At a meeting last Monday night, E. Oppenheimer was elected president; J. Roedelsheimer, vice president; M. Isaacs, secretary; and Sam Isaacs, treasurer." The following week's picnic included friends from Seattle, and the head of Tacoma's Chamber of Commerce,

who enjoyed himself so much he declared he understood why his hosts were called God's chosen people.

However, the Jewish social club with the most longevity was the Harmony Club, incorporated in March of 1890. (New Orleans had a Harmony Club as early as 1861, for young Jewish men under 30.) The arrival of the Moses and Donau families provided the missing ingredient – female dance partners. The club thrived over the next six years as a gathering place for young Jewish couples, as Tacoma's economy reached its peak for the century. After a year the club secured their own building, with the upper floors providing a home for Jewish bachelors. Each event required committees and sub-committees.

January 4, 1890, *Ledger*, "The first ball to be given by the Harmony club will occur Wednesday evening at the Germania hall. The invitation committee consists of Nathan Todtman, J.E. Willis and Oscar I. Reichenbach." Accounts the following week described costly and elegant costumes, 40 couples in a 10 pm grand march, and dancing until the "wee small hours." The guest list included 32 ladies, about one-half of whom were married. "Committee of arrangements – Al. Weinberg, S.S. Loeb, Ed. Harris. Reception Committee – M. Moses, J. Barnhard, M.G. Meyer, I. Gottstein, M. Ball. Floor committee – H.C. Winslow, H. Frank, W. Jacobs, Ike Harris, S. Hirsch, C. Langert."

The club's 1890 officers were Sam Moyses, President; Simon Hirsch, Vice President; H. J. Green, Secretary; and Isaac Harris, Treasurer. The hall was located at 1137 Railroad. (Now Commerce Street.) The following year's officers included President, D.P. Lewis; vice president, M. Jacobs; secretary, J.G. Meyers; treasurer, I. Harris; trustees, E. Hain, M. Broh and S. Hirsch.

Ledger, Sunday, September 14, 1890, just before *Rosh Hashanah*, "The second annual ball of the Harmony club on Thursday evening was a very pleasant affair. The members turned out in force and the gentlemen in full dress and the ladies in elegant costumes, made Germania hall a bright scene. The ball began at 10 o'clock and for two hours dancing was the chief amusement. At 12 o'clock the guests repaired to the banquet spread below and enjoyed themselves in discussing the dainties of the season. The affair was under the management of the following committees: Arrangements – Mike Jacob, Morris Isaacs, Ed A Hains, M.F. Myers. Invitation – Marcus Moses, C.T. Reese, Sim Hirsch. Reception – Sam S. Loeb, Albert Weinberg, Sam Isaacs, Mike Ball, D.P. Lewis, Jack Stevens, M. Cohn. Floor manager – Harry Frank. Floor committee – Ike Harris, Sam Moyses, Alex Isaacs. The officers of the club are: Sam Moyses, president; Sim Hirsch, vice president; M.G. Meyer, secretary; Ike Harris, treasurer. Board of directors: S.S. Loeb, M. Moses, M. Broh." Among those present were a dozen guests from other cities, about a dozen local couples, yet another dozen local misses and seventeen eligible bachelors.

The club's success continued, warranting a move to their own quarters. *Ledger*, December 18, 1890, "The handsome new apartments of the Harmony club, in the Frazier block, 1149-1/2 C Street, were opened last night with a social party, the first given by the club" With twenty-five members, the space included reception rooms, parlors, a billiards room and a dancing hall. Again the guest list included nine couples, nine young ladies and seventeen bachelors.

The club hosted monthly events throughout 1891 and 1892, receiving regular mentions in the social pages of both of Tacoma's newspapers. Tacoma's 1891 Polk directory showed that Harry C. Frank, Isaac Hirsch and Simon Hirsch lived at the club. The business downstairs at 1149 C was a wholesale wine and liquor firm owned by Sam Holland and S.S. Loeb, with Sam Moyses as manager. By 1892 the club's officers were Isaac Harris, president; J.B. Myers, vice president; and H. Fraley, secretary and treasurer.

In April of 1892 the Harmony Club rooms were used on a regular basis by its members. Seven young gentlemen who called themselves the "Stag Seven" hosted an event. They were Oscar I. Reichenbach, Hugo J. Donau, Sam G. Cohn, Oscar Hoffman, Joseph S. Loeb, Leo Sichel and A. Stein. The following week Mesdames A. Weinberg and S.S. Loeb hosted a party in honor of their brother's wedding in Chicago. Forty-eight guests were present. The dinners and dancing continued throughout the summer.

THE STAG SEVEN.

A Swell Affair at the Rooms of the Harmony Club Last Night.

The Stag Seven, an organization of young gentlemen of the city, gave their inaugural ball at the rooms of the Harmony club on C street last night. The members of the organization, who are well known in Hebrew and Gentile social circles, as well as in business, are as follows: Oscar I. Reichenbach, Hugo J. Donau, Sam G. Cohn, Oscar Hoffman, Joseph S. Loeb, Leo Sichel and A. Stein. It was on the occasion of Mr. Reichenbach's birthday party a short time since that the club was formed, and their initial entertainment last night was a very gratifying success. An entertaining programme had been prepared and the guests enjoyed themselves in the highest degree. Flaskett's orchestra provided the music for dancing, which was continued until a late hour. Refreshments were served throughout the evening and the hosts were generally congratulated on the unqualified success of the first ball.

Tacoma Daily Ledger April 1, 1892

On October 9, 1892 the *Ledger* reported the club had given a farewell reception to Charles Fleisher of Cincinnati, who was acting as a student rabbi for High Holiday services. "The affair was of an informal character, nearly every person of the Jewish congregation being present... Among the number present at the reception were Messrs. and Mesdames Reichenbach, Donau, Posner, Dornberg, Weinberg, Bloom, Cohn, Marks, Ash, Loeb, Fraley, Moses, Chapman, Andrews, A. Isaacs, H. Isaacs, Hirschfeld, Kullman, Hall, S. Isaacs, D. Germanus, Jacobs, Mesdames Loeb, Steinman, Messrs. Abe Gross, Morris Gross, Frank, Barry, Harris, Moyses, Moses, Donau and Hirsch."

By the fall of 1892 Tacoma's economy and Jewish population reached its peak for the decade, with the activities of the Harmony Club reflecting that prosperity.

THE HARMONY CLUB.

The First Ball Given Last Evening With Happy Results.

The winter season of dance was inaugurated last evening by the Harmony club, a popular and successful organization, in possession of handsome apartments at 1149½ C street. The toilets of the ladies were remarkable for their beauty and elegance. A light repast was served the guests, who enjoyed the dance until the morning hours. About fifty couples were present, including members of the Harmony club and their friends. Music was furnished by Miss Galliher and Messrs. Warren and Flaskett.

Tacoma Daily Ledger October 21, 1892

More details followed on October 23rd: "The Harmony club opened for the season its handsomely appointed suite of rooms at No. 1149 1/2 C Street, Thursday evening, with a social ball. It was a delightful affair, attended by prominent members of the club and their lady friends. An informal reception was held in the parlors surrounding the ball room, after which the dance was opened with the double lancers. In the adjoining billiard room a punch bowl filled with nectar refreshed the merry dancers. A buffet supper was served during the evening. Excellent music was furnished by professors Warren and Flaskett and Miss Galliher. The committee on arrangements consisted of Messrs. Frank Harris and Fraley. Messrs. Oscar Reichenbach, Donau and Moses comprised the reception committee. No organization in the city entertains with more éclat than the Harmony club, and all the entertainments given under its auspices are notable for their genuine enjoyment, and also for the rich costumes worn by the attending ladies. On this occasion there were many handsome looking dresses, a few of which are given description:

Mrs. S. Donau – Handsome evening toilette of black lace with bodice of heavy jet and diamond ornaments.

Mrs. S. Posner – Costume of changeable rose and green silk, with trimmings of moss-green velvet.

Mrs. S. Jacoby – Black silk trimmed with silk gimp and natural roses.

Mrs. J. Jacoby – Rose and gray changeable silk with corsage trimmings of point lace.

Mrs. Bernard – Light striped brocade silk and white lace.

Mrs. M. Cohen – Black lace combined with rose silk; diamond ornaments.

Mrs. S. Loeb – Red crepe with embroidered chiffon of the same color, red gloves completing the costume.

Mrs. J. Kullman – Black and white figured silk, trimmed with white lace.

Mrs. A.J. Steinman – Rich black silk and jet; yellow chrysanthemums.

Mrs. H. Fraley – Pale blue silk crepe, finished with blue embroidered chiffon.

Mrs. A. Fort-Louis of Seattle – Black lace, combined with lavender satin.

Mrs. E.L. Mayer of Seattle – Black silk and crepe.

Mrs. Hall – Nile green crepe and gold passamenterie.

Miss Donau – Cream lace gown girdled with gold passamenterie; low corsage filled in with point lace.

Miss Alice Donau – A beautiful pale blue surah gown with a bodice of heavy gold passamenterie. The decolettage was outlined with forget-me-nots, held in place with torquoise jewelry.

Miss Raphael – A becoming empire gown of corn-colored crepe with ornaments of gold passamenterie.

Miss Maud Falk, Chicago – Pale blue costume, relieved with white lace.

Miss Hattie Moses – Black lace; blue crepe and gold passamenterie were prettily combined in the finishing.

Miss Nannie Moses – Red crepe and black lace."

A complete guest list followed, with the vast majority of the names spelled correctly. Monthly mentions continued through the winter of 1892, even as most of the ladies were involved in a fair to raise money for construction of a synagogue building.

Anyone who has spent a winter in Tacoma knows that the days can be damp and gray. Before television and radio, social gatherings provided much-needed entertainment. Creativity was called for. *Ledger,* April 16, 1893, "The Harmony club, a popular Jewish social organization, gave a pretty party in its rooms on C street, last night. The affair was termed a "calico ball," and was greatly enjoyed by two score of prominent people in Hebrew circles. The ladies for the most part wore becoming and appropriate costumes, and the gentlemen were decorated with small bands of calico and lovers' knots of the same material. Music was furnished by Warren's orchestra, and a dainty lunch of sandwiches, cake, ice cream and punch was served. The committee in charge of the affair included Messrs. Rudolph Gross, Hugo J. Donau and Joseph Loeb."

As a result of the Panic of 1893 the *Ledger* greatly reduced its social columns. No mention was made of the Harmony Club for months on end. Tacoma's 1893–94 city directory, published in late October, listed the officers of the Harmony

Club as Abe Gross, president; M.J. Myers, vice president; Oscar I. Reichenbach, secretary; and Simon Hirsch, treasurer.

In early November of 1894 the bankrupt Prager Brothers reached a financial settlement and the *Ledger's* lawsuit against them to collect advertising fees was dropped. News of Tacoma's Jewish community suddenly returned to the *Ledger's* society pages. The Sunday edition on November 4th noted a Tuesday afternoon meeting of the Entre Nous Club, a Thursday afternoon card party at Mrs. Bloom's (probably a Judith Montefiore event), dinner Thursday evening at Mrs. Weinberg's, a Harmony Club party on "Hallow E'en" and the engagement of Morris Gross. Apparently the remaining club members were determined to dance their way through their difficulties.

The November 4th mention included "Messrs. and Mmes. Sidney Prager, S. Isaacs, Archie Ash, Albert Weinberg, A. Isaacs, M. Ball, M. Cohn, S. Posner, J. Meyers; Mrs. Michaels, of Spokane, Mrs. Steinman; Misses Donau, Alice Donau, Rose Prager, Dornberg; Messrs. S. Hirsch, Reichenbach, Greenbaum, Abe Gross, Deautch, Sam Cohn, Moyses and others." Nearly half would fail or relocate in the next two years.

Tacoma's city directory for 1895 was published in February. The Harmony club was served by Abe Gross as president, S.S. Loeb vice president, Oscar I. Reichenbach secretary, and Simon Hirsch treasurer. In March of 1895 Abe Gross took his life. Among his pallbearers were Oscar Reichenbach and Simon Hirsch.

The Harmony Club last appeared in the Tacoma city Polk directory in 1896. Officers were S.S. Loeb, president; Archie Ash, vice president; Oscar I. Reichenbach, secretary; and Simon Hirsch, treasurer. Benjamin Moyses resided at the club. By the end of the year the majority of the club's original members had moved away from Tacoma. The good times were over.

In keeping with the goose and gander saying, since the Jewish men had their own social club, the Jewish ladies began one also...

Entre Nous Club

Beginning in October of 1892, the *Tacoma Daily Ledger* routinely carried society mentions of the "Entres Nous Club." While a Jewish affiliation was never openly mentioned, the names included were exclusively those of women from the Jewish community. The members apparently met weekly for sewing and conversation. ("Entre Nous" literally translates from the French as "Between Us" and means "Confidential.") This group was perhaps a counterpart to Tacoma's "Aloha Club," which despite its welcoming name, didn't happen to have any Jewish members.

Ledger October 9, 1892, "The Entre Nous club was pleasantly entertained, Tuesday afternoon, at the home of Mrs. Emil Marks, No. 608 South I street. Such of the ladies as felt inclined brought their work, and the afternoon was spent in social conversation. A collation was served. The ladies present were: Mrs. Charles Reichenbach, Mrs. S. Donau, Mrs. S.S. Loeb, Mrs. M. Loeb, Mrs. A. Weinberg, Mrs. M. Moses, Mrs. A.H. Steinman, Mrs. Harry Fraley, Mrs. J. Kullman, Miss Donau, Miss Alice Donau, Miss Nannie Moses and Miss Hattie Moses."

Ledger October 16, "The Entre Nous club met Tuesday afternoon for sociability at the residence of Mrs. M. Moses, No. 443 South E Street. A repast was served by the hostess. The ladies of the club are: Mrs. Emil Marx, Mrs. Charles Reichenbach, Mrs. Harry Frailey, Mrs. J. Kullman, Mrs. S. Donau, Mrs. A.H. Steinman, Mrs. Weinberg, Miss Donau, Miss Alice Donau, Miss Moses." October 23, "Mrs. Charles Reichenbach entertained the Entre Nous club Tuesday afternoon."

SEWING FOR THE POOR.

The Entre Nous Club Pleasantly Entertained—More Society.

The Entre Nous club was entertained by Mrs. S. Donau Tuesday afternoon at her home on Tacoma avenue. The ladies of the society meet for social pleasure each week. At the suggestion of Mrs. Donau it was decided, Tuesday, to devote the time to sewing for the poor, and at every future meeting this charitable work will be accomplished.

Tacoma Daily Ledger January 2, 1893

Ledger, January 2, 1893, "SEWING FOR THE POOR. The Entre Nous Club Pleasantly Entertained. The Entre Nous club was entertained by Mrs. S. Donau Tuesday afternoon at her home on Tacoma Avenue. The ladies of the society meet for social pleasure each week. At the suggestion of Mrs. Donau it was decided, Tuesday, to devote the time to sewing for the poor, and at every future meeting this charitable work will be accomplished."

Sunday society, July 16, 1893, "Mrs. Charles Reichenbach entertained the Entre Nous club at her home, No. 301 North J Street, on Tuesday afternoon. The club has given up its literary work for the summer."

The last club mention in the *Ledger* was on November 4, 1894. "Entre Nous Club Meets. The Entre Nous club met Tuesday afternoon at the residence of Miss Moses on South E Street. Mrs. Weinberg, Mrs. Steinman, Mrs. Loeb, Mrs. Michaels, Mrs. Ellis Gross, Miss Moses and the Misses Donau were among those present." The majority of earlier members had moved away from the city.

On December 3, 1899, the *Ledger*'s society page for Olympia noted that an Entre Nous Club had been recently organized in that city. Members included Mrs. Mitchell Harris, Mrs. Gus Harris and Miss Nina Kaufman, among others.

While some clubs were purely social, others were affiliations of national Jewish organizations...

B'nai B'rith

Tacoma's first five years of affiliation with the Independent Order of B'nai B'rith (Sons of the Covenant) were in connection with Seattle. The *Tacoma Daily Ledger* on Friday, October 24, 1884, noted "The Jewish population of the city are in receipt of invitations to attend a grand hop in Seattle next Sunday evening, to be given under the auspices of Seattle lodge No. 342, I.O.B.B., in honor of Sir Moses Montefiore's 100th birthday anniversary. The invitations will generally be accepted." Seattle's B'nai B'rith was established on October 28, 1883, so this was also a celebration of its first anniversary. The Seattle I.O.B.B hosted a Purim party in March of 1885.

During the summers of 1886 and 1887 Rabbi Marcus Levy toured the West Coast as grand president of the I.O.B.B., representing the grand lodge in San Francisco. Both summers he spoke in Tacoma and was optimistic about organizing a local lodge. Membership included a death benefit of $2,000, which was perhaps why Seattle had organized a B'nai B'rith, but not a benevolent society.

Seattle's 1888–89 Polk city directory included a listing of the officers of the Seattle B'nai B'rith. Half were from Tacoma, (albeit with mutilated spellings) including vice president Morris Isaacs, Monitor Sam Simon, Secretary Charles Langert, and OG Amil Zelinsky, indicating a regional organization.

The Tacoma Lodge #406 of the Independent Order of B'nai B'rith was instituted on the evening of June 22, 1890, with forty-five charter members. D.P. Lewis served as the first president, with D. Germanus as vice president. Other officers included H. Berliner, monitor; I. Magnus, secretary [probably David;] D. Lewin [Levin,] treasurer; M. Ball, assistant monitor; W. H. Zelinsky, warden; W. Mambach [Mamlock,] guardian; M. Cohen, S. Jacobs and M. Broh, trustees. An article in the *Tacoma Daily Ledger* the next day described the banquet menu.

"Mountain Trout Sauce, Mayonnaise, Broiled Spring Chicken, Shrimp Salad, Chicken Salad, Cold Tongue, Ham, Russian Caviar, French Sardines, Queen Olives, Fruit, Curacao, Sherbet, Assorted Cake, Café Noir." Tacoma's Jewish men clearly followed the new Reform Judaism, abandoning the practice of eating only kosher foods.

WITH APPROPRIATE CEREMONIES.

Tacoma Lodge, Independent Order of B'nai Brith, Installed Last Night.

Tacoma Lodge of the Independent Order of B'nai Brith, or Sons of the Covenant, was instituted in the city last night by the officers of the grand lodge of the order. This is a Hebrew order and is of a benevolent character, its objects being to aid the poor, take care of the sick, and to provide for the widows and orphans of the deceased members of the order. There are only two lodges of the order in the state. The Seattle lodge was the first lodge instituted and Tacoma the second.

It is an American order, having been founded in the United States about fifty years ago, and has now about 40,000 members. The order has been extended to other countries, and now has lodges in Germany, Roumania, Jerusalem and Jaffa. Six charitable institutions are maintained by the order in different parts of this country and in Germany. One institution for the aged and infirm of all creeds, sects and nationalities is maintained by the order at Yonkers, N. Y. It is divided into nine districts, and each district has a grand lodge which is in authority above all other lodges in the district. District No. 4 consists of California, Oregon, Washington, Montana, Nevada and the territories of Utah and Arizona.

Tacoma lodge was instituted and the officers installed by the officers of the district grand lodge No. 4. The following grand officers of the grand lodge were present at the ceremonies last evening: F. H. Merzbach, grand president; Louis Blank, grand secretary, both of San Francisco, and William Kiershi of Seattle, grand deputy for the northwest.

Following were the officers installed: Monitor, H. Berliner; president, D. P. Lewis; vice-president, D. Germanus; secretary, I. Magnus; treasurer, D. Lewin; assistant monitor, M. Ball; warden, H. Zelinsky; guardian, W. Mamlock; trustees, M. Cohen, S. Jacobs, M. Broh.

After the instituting and installation ceremonies were over, a splendid banquet was served at the Metropole restaurant, corner of Tenth and A streets. During the progress of the banquet many speeches were made. Grand Secretary Louis Blank acted as toast master. The grand president responded eloquently to the "Grand Lodge." Dr. Brodek of Tacoma responded in behalf of Tacoma lodge, the infant of the district. This was one of the best efforts of the evening. Samuel Wolf of Portland followed with the toast of welcome to the new lodge. S. Blake, William Kierzski and others responded to appropriate toasts. It was long after midnight when the banqueters left the table and sought their homes.

The new lodge started off with a membership of forty-five. The visiting grand officers will remain in the city to-day, and to-morrow they will go to Seattle, where they will be banqueted and entertained by the Seattle Sons of the Covenant. Following was the menu last night:

Mountain Trout Sauce
Mayonaise
Broiled Spring Chicken
Shrimp Salad   Chicken Salad
Cold Tongue, Ham
Russian Caviar   French Sardines
Queen Olives
Fruit, Curacao, Sherbet
Assorted Cake
Cafe' Noir.

Tacoma Daily Ledger June 22, 1890

However, they did join with the Hebrew Benevolent Society at *Rosh Hashanah*. *Ledger*, September 15, 1890, "The committee on New Year's arrangements is composed of E.H. Gross, L. Wallerstein, and H. Harris, representing the Hebrew Benevolent society, and H. Berliner, Max Broh, M. Germanus and D.P. Davis [Lewis] representing the Independent Order of B'nai B'rith."

During the next three years newspaper mentions of the order were either notices of the election of officers or descriptions of the Purim Ball. *Ledger*, December 17, 1890, "Tacoma lodge, I.O.B.B., met in regular convention last night and elected the following officers: President, Dave Germanius; vice president, Max Broh; treasurer, H. Berliner; secretary, Dave Magnus; assistant monitor, S. Jacobi; warden, Abe Hockwald; guardian, William Mamlock; trustees, A.S. Ash, Dave Levin and M. Rogers. D.P. Lewis, the retiring president, occupies the position of monitor or past president. H. Berliner is also a delegate to the grand lodge." Another article on January 7, 1891 corrected the names of Dave Germanus and S. Rogers.

Ledger, Tuesday March 8, 1892, "Tacoma lodge No. 406 I.O.B.B. will give a masked ball at Germania hall on Monday night next, which promises to be an unequaled success. The committee of arrangements includes S. Posner, D.P. Lewis, H. Berliner, S. Jacoby, A. Hockwald, D. Germanus, S. Rogers and D. Magnus." Several society articles after the ball mentioned the presence of between 200 and 300 costumed guests, with the most prominent names listed.

On January 16, 1893, the *Ledger* reported on the sixth annual national convention of the I.O.B.B. The assemblage had agreed to repeal a law requiring members to be married by Jewish rites. The headline read, "Gentile Marriages Go," a twist on Tacoma's 1885 phrase "The Chinese Must Go."

Just as the Harmony Club's activities peaked in 1893, so did those of the B'nai B'rith. The last mentions of a Purim party were in February and March of 1893. The reception committee included Jake Bernard [Bernhard,] S. Posner, M. Ball and Charles Langert, along with a floor committee of S.S Loeb, B. Gottell, H.A. Fraley, and Rudolph Gross. After the event social mentions described menus and costumes, with over 100 in attendance.

B'NAI BRITH MASKED BALL.

Handsome Costumes and a Merry Time at Masterson's Hall.

A very pleasant masquerade ball was given by the Independent Order of B'nai Brith at Masterson's hall last night. Gaily attired dancers thronged the room and enjoyed the merry dance until a late hour. The floor was in splendid shape, the music was good and everybody was in excellent spirits. As a result the party was one of the most delightful of the season.

The feature of the affair aside from the costumes, which were unusually elaborate and original, was a group of masquers who were made up as plantation darkies. In each case the costume and demeanor was extremely appropos, and when the octette entertained the gathering with an exhibition of hop picking they elicited loud and approving applause.

Tacoma Daily Ledger March 3, 1893

The Panic of 1893 brought society mentions to a near standstill. Tacoma's *Morning Union* described a visit in August of 1895 by California officials trying to revive interest in the order. Tacoma's 1896 Polk city directory included the I.O.B.B. officers as S. Jacoby, President; M. Cohn, Vice president; S. Posner, Secretary; and M. Ball, Treasurer. That year all but Sam Posner went bankrupt. Mentheim Cohn and Michael Ball both moved away from Tacoma. In October of 1897 Mr. and Mrs. M.P. Stein, of Stockton, stopped in Tacoma while paying an official visit to the western lodges.

JewishEncyclopedia.com quotes a 1905 article on Washington State that includes a brief mention of Tacoma. "A B'nai B'rith lodge formerly existed in the city, but the removal of many members resulted in the return of the charter to the grand lodge." Minute books have been located only from 1912 forward, from the newer IOBB #741.

The brotherhood may have slipped away but the sisterhood would endure...

Lady Judith Montefiore Society

As we have seen, Tacoma's Jewish citizens helped celebrate the 100th birthday of Sir Moses Montefiore in 1884. On July 20, 1884, Julius Mamlock and Paula Wolff named their newborn son Henry Montefiore Mamlock. When Montefiore died a year later, the *Tacoma Daily Ledger* printed an editorial mourning his loss. July 31, 1885, "The death of Sir Moses Montefiore leaves a gap in the ranks of philanthropy... Humanity will not soon be blessed with another so supremely pure, unselfish, faithful and devoted as was Sir Moses Montefiore." Also that day, "The meeting of all the Hebrew citizens will be held at The Tacoma this evening at 8 o'clock to make suitable arrangements for memorial services in honor of the late Sir Moses Montefiore." This was before the first known High Holiday services were held in a rented hall.

Lady Judith Montefiore
Gutenberg Project

While Sir Moses Montefiore was a philanthropist known the world over, his wife Lady Judith was nearly as famous in her own right. She had traveled with her husband, writing and teaching at his side. As Jewish men in many communities formed a Harmony Club and a B'nai B'rith, Jewish women formed their own Lady Judith Montefiore societies. Among Tacoma's early Jewish organizations, this group's minute books are the only ones that have been located. Someone had the foresight to send them to Cincinnati's American Jewish Archives for preservation. The minutes describe a group of women determined to provide a Jewish education for their children, while aiding the sick and the poor. These women also proved to be adept fundraisers and careful accountants, all while fashionably-dressed.

The minutes begin on May 1, 1890, with a copy of the new group's constitution and the election of officers. Lay leader William Wolff was elected president, Mrs. M. Moses vice president, Mrs. Charles Reichenbach treasurer, and Mrs. M. Ball secretary. Monies collected included $37.50 for dues, "and a donation of $20.00 from Mr. Abe Gross and A. Weinberg respectively." The list of original members was signed by Mrs. Jenny Bloom, Mrs. Sol. Jacoby, Mrs. Samuel Posner, Mrs. H. Harris, Mrs. L. Hirschfeld, Mrs. Robert Gans, Mrs. A.S. Ash, Lena Moses, Lena Broh, Mrs. M. Rosenbaum, Mrs. H. Salhinger, Belle E. Reichenbach, Mrs. Green, Mrs. M. Ball, Mrs. Lewis, Mrs. Berliner, Mrs. Magnus, Mrs. A.J. Bloom, Mrs. Ed Wolf, Mrs. M. Cohn, Mrs. Pincus, __ Lewis, Mrs. G. Rosengarden, Mrs. H. Kent, Mrs. M. Liebenthal, Mrs. A. Hockwald, Mrs. C.M. Postman, and Mrs. S.A. Andrews.

At the second meeting, held on May 7, a committee of Mrs. M. Broh, Mrs. A. Ash, and Mrs. Jacoby was appointed "to procure a place of meeting, and to hold Sabbath school." A membership committee was appointed consisting of Mrs. Reichenbach, Mrs. Rosenbaum, and Mrs. Moses. "The majority wished school held on Saturday morning from 10 to 12 a.m. and the Pres. appointed Mrs. M. Rosenbaum, and Ball to teach for the present."

By June 4, 1890, the search for a meeting hall was successfully concluded. "The motion was carried to hold school on Saturday, and organize at once, which opened school Sat. June 7th 90." Mrs. M. Broh, Mrs. R. Ganz, and Mrs. Jacoby were appointed to visit "the school-room previous to school session, in order to see that the room was in complete readiness. Mrs. R. Ganz was also appointed as a teacher. The secretary was authorized to send to Portland for necessary instruction books."

On July 8 the group sponsored a picnic for the children at American Lake, requiring a letter of thanks to Mr. Friedman. (Adolph Friedman had a real estate development there.) At the August meeting it was decided that "A com. of two ladies are to be appointed in alphabetic order as a sick committee." In September the Society met in the Germania Hall, and in October began meeting in the Theosophical Hall. The Misses Mamlock were engaged to teach at a salary of $10 per month. In December the ladies began an annual tradition of holding a "Hanuckah" festival for the children, donating cakes and providing a bag of candy for each child.

In March of 1891 the group agreed to host a Purim Ball in conjunction with the B'nai B'rith. April brought the resignation of Mrs. S. Posner as superintendent of the school. In May the meetings began to take on a more social atmosphere, with a "kaffee klatch" after the meeting, four ladies donating coffee and cake each month. In June of 1891 the meeting place was changed to the Mason Hall on A street, near the elaborate Tacoma Hotel.

June of 1891 brought the first of many strawberry festivals. Coupons were sold for 50 cents, valid for a serving of strawberries. Ice cream and cake could be purchased for 35 cents, beer and sandwiches for a quarter. The event proved to be quite successful as a fundraiser with income of $401.60 and expenses of only $44.75. The *Tacoma Daily Ledger's* description on Friday, June 19, could serve as a template for a modern-day recreation.

> "A society that feels able to meet whatever financial storms may arise is the Ladies' Montefiore society, which last evening invited its friends to a strawberry social in the rooms of the Harmony club on C street. The friends came in large numbers, bringing their purses with them, and most liberally did they purchase the things good for the palate and for the eye which the ladies had for sale. The halls of the Harmony club were packed with a happy crowd. The rooms betokened festivity, for on every wall, across the ceiling, crossing here and there, were streamers of bunting artistically arranged under the direction of Miss C.B. Raphael. Alternating with dances the following programme was carried out: Recitation, Miss Jennie Jacobs. Piano duet, Miss Wolff and Professor Meissner. Vocal solo, Miss Israel. Vocal solo, Mr. Davenport. William Fitzhenry was the auctioneer who disposed of the splendid cakes placed for sale. The fine specimen of the pastry art donated by Wallerstein was sold, donated to the society and resold no less than eight times and the snug sum of $40 was realized from it. It is now in the hands of Mrs. Rose Isaacs, to whom the last gentleman winning donated it. Another cake worthy of especial mention, which by a comfortable sum increased the exchequer of the ladies, was that donated by Miss C.B. Raphael of Portland. Imbedded in it was a silver thimble. The monument of sweetness containing this prize was won by O.E. Nuhn. A pleasant as well as a prominent feature of the evening's entertainment was a skirt dance by Miss Jennie Jacobs of St. Louis, which deservedly received the warm applause of those present. Another interesting event occurring was the auction and sale of Mrs. Bloom. So spirited was the competition for this charming lady that she was finally sold for $100,000. The voting for the most popular lady present created a great deal of merriment. The married lady who was honored by being so designated was Mrs. S.S. Loeb. Colonel Charles Reichenbach was easily decided to be the most popular married man, Miss Hattie Moses the most universally liked young lady, and Sam Moyses received the same honor among the young men. It was in the early hours this morning that the ladies and their friends departed from the hall, and now, after so successful a social, no society is more thankful than this one, both to the Harmony club, which so generously gave their rooms, and to their friends for their liberal patronage."

Sabbath School resumed on September fifth after a summer adjournment, in a hall rented at 903 G for seven dollars per month. The Society began what would be a long history of charitable endeavors, donating a "table cover for our holiday's services," purchased from J Bernhard at a cost of $15.75. In November the initiation fee of $2.50 was set aside for two months, in order to encourage new members. The "Channaka" festival was held at the Oddfellows Hall on A Street in December. Also that month a committee was formed to visit the sick. This would become a key role for the Society. The original wording "to visit any member of this society in good standing" was changed to say "any lady of our faith."

The *Ledger* on Thursday, March 10, 1892, announced the formation of a Jewish congregation. "The ladies of the Montefiore society have already promised the new organization to turn over the Sunday school to them, thus increasing the attendance and prospect of success." In May of 1892 the Society presented the past president, Mr. William Wolf, with a framed letter of thanks. The new officers included president Mrs.

M. Ball, vice president Mrs. S. Jacoby, treasurer Mrs. Chas. Reichenbach, and secretary Mrs. D. Germanus. Their account balance of $250 was drawing interest at 10%.

On Sunday, May 26, 1892, the strawberry festival was described several times in the social columns of the *Ledger*. "The ladies of the Montefiore society succeeded socially and financially at the fete given in Germania hall Wednesday evening. A number of Seattle friends were in attendance. The paper booth in charge of Mrs. Charles Reichenbach, Mrs. Steinman and Mrs. M. Bloom, contained fancy lamps, dolls and fans. All the articles were sold. Mrs. Weinberg had charge of a large booth of cut flowers; Mrs. Alexander Isaacs sold Japanese trinkets; Miss Dornberg delivered letters and Miss Isabel Pincus, express parcels, the candy booth was presided over by Mrs. J. Bloom. Cake, ice creams and lemonade were sold and dancing enjoyed during the evening." That December many of the same ladies would hold a similar sale, on a much grander scale, to raise funds for construction of a temple.

By March of 1893 the ladies began having a "whist" after each meeting. Players likely were charged to play the card game, as each whist resulted in funds for the society. Refreshments were provided by four ladies each month, on an alphabetical schedule. On May 3rd the organization agreed to give $400 to benefit construction of the new Temple. That week a banking panic hit the nation.

In September of 1893, when the new synagogue was dedicated, the Society hosted a reception for the speaker, Dr. Adolph Danziger. The following month the club ladies spent $38 on furniture for the new school room. In December of 1893 another "fancy bazaar & social" was held as a fundraiser, with dramatic entertainment.

The Society continued to support the temple's religious school. In July of 1894 about 40 children were treated to a picnic at Menlo Park, (today's University Place) followed by a streetcar ride to Steilacoom. In December of 1894 the ladies began monthly sewing circles. The February 1895 fundraiser was a masquerade "pink domino," held at the Columbia Hall. Minutes of March 6, 1895, reflect that the Society paid to have the school room cleaned and purchased three new tables.

However, the economy continued to decline and more and more of the members faced bankruptcy, with many leaving Tacoma. In June of 1895 the Society made a loan of $75 to the Beth Israel Congregation at 6% interest and held the annual strawberry festival. In September the number necessary for a quorum was reduced to eight, indicating a decline in attendance. The 1895 Chanukah festival was held at the Harmony Club. Sewing bees and meetings were moved to private homes.

Purim of 1896 was celebrated with a "Progressive Whist Party." Members were charged 25 cents to attend and fined 25 cents if they didn't. Tacoma's *Daily Ledger* on September 20, 1896, carried a lengthy description of the farewell held in honor of Mrs. Ball, the group's president for nearly five years. She received "a very handsome cut glass dish." That generosity wouldn't continue. At the next meeting the ladies decided to draw on the treasury only for charity, not for presents for outgoing members.

Apparently the Sabbath School started and stalled several times over the next few years. In February of 1898 the Society decided to ask Mr. Jacob to teach the children for a Sabbath School. In October of 1898 they again voted to begin a Sunday school, under the supervision of Mrs. J. Jacoby & Mrs. Goldenson. Mrs. S. Isaacs volunteered to act as teacher. In November of 1898 the men of the Temple once more called upon the ladies for financial assistance, asking for $500 to reduce the temple's mortgage interest from eight to six percent.

In January of 1899 the Society's expenditures included "$150 from temple fund" and "$150 borrowed by gentlemen." March 1, 1899, brought approval to arrange for a choir for the "approaching holidays." Mrs. Hockwald agreed to teach the choir. In May it was decided that "each lady should give six glasses of jelly to the society… to be distributed among the different hospitals."

In April of 1900 the Society loaned Temple Beth Israel another $275. The tenth anniversary of the Society was celebrated in May by donating curtains for the temple. Tacoma's 1900 city directory, released in May, noted that Mrs. A. Weinberg was president and Mrs. Alexander Isaacs was vice president. In September the ladies voted to help "the gentlemen" pay the choir, and to hold a *Simcha Torah* Festival. Also that month, "Mr. Jacobs sent word that he was willing to open Sunday school, provided that parents would send their children both regularly and promptly." In December the Society considered joining the Council of Jewish Women, but delayed a vote as many members were out of town.

Over the years the society routinely provided minor charitable donations for local families who were in need of groceries or medical care. Regular contributions were sent to the Hebrew Orphan Asylum in San Francisco, the Denver Hospital for Consumptives, the National Farm School of Philadelphia and other Jewish charities.

The society voted in October of 1916 to join the national Federation of Temple Sisterhoods. With the advent of World War I the Society's charitable efforts were stepped up, supporting the local chapter of the Red Cross and the American Relief Fund for Jewish War Sufferers. In September of 1917 the group chose "to eliminate the serving of refreshments after the meetings, for two months at least, in accordance with the nationwide movement for food conservation." By February of 1918 the society was setting up a surgical dressing unit in the B'nai B'rith Hall and selling "uniongrams." In September they bought two $50 liberty bonds from the sinking fund and encouraged members to donate cakes and cookies to the Soldiers & Sailors club instead of providing refreshments after their meetings.

In May of 1919, the "meeting of the society was ably addressed by our new Rabbi, Dr. Raphael Goldenstein. He explained what his plans for the future were and how we were to assist him. A committee was appointed to write all Jewish women in the city to form a new Temple Sisterhood which is to work in the sole interest of the Temple."

At the March meeting of 1920 the Lady Judith Montefiore Society agreed to "withdraw from the National Federation of Sisterhoods... as a Temple Beth Israel sisterhood was established in Tacoma." That Sisterhood continues to this day as the Sisterhood of Temple Beth El, actively raising funds to support Jewish educational programs.

Pioneer Jewish organizations assisted those in need in Tacoma, but also promoted the welfare of others of the Jewish faith, across the nation and abroad...

Tacoma Relief Society

In early 1891 the mistreatment of Jews in Russia served as impetus for the formation of a social action organization in Tacoma. In keeping with the Jewish value of *tikkun olam* (repairing the world) the group was part of one of several national movements to aid Jewish refugees. While the group itself did not have long-lasting impact, its formation gained attention more publicly than ever before – drawing opinions both positive and negative. The *Ledger*'s treatment of the situation showed considerable respect for those of the "Hebrew" faith, perhaps in part based on their generous newspaper advertising budgets.

TO MEMORIALIZE CONGRESS.

HEBREWS PETITION LEGISLATURE FOR THE RUSSIAN JEWS.

Tacoma Relief Society Organized at a Well-Attended Meeting in the Harmony Club Rooms Yesterday.

A meeting was held yesterday afternoon for the purpose of taking action in regard to the persecution of the Russian Jews. A large number were present, among whom were the following: Abe Gross, Ellis Gross, Martin Rosenbaum, Samuel Moyses, Max Broh, A. Jacobi, D. P. Lewis, George H. Boardman, Albert E. Joab, J. L. Adler, A. Wallerstein, A. Weinberg, S. S. Loeb, M. Germanus, J. B. Meyers, Louis Hirsh, H. Harris, Amile Marx, J. C. Walland, Archie Ash, J. Pincus.

D. P. Lewis was made temporary president and A. Hockwald temporary secretary. A committee on temporary organization being appointed reported the following nominations for officers and they were elected: Abe Gross president, D. Germanus first vice-president, S. S. Loeb second vice-president, J. Pincus treasurer; executive committee, D. P. Lewis, N. Rosenbaum, A. S. Ash, L. Wallerstein and S. Jacobi, The name was adopted of Tacoma Relief society, organized to protest against and relieve the inhumanities perpetrated against Jews in Russia. A committee was appointed to report details of organization at the next meeting, which is called Wednesday night in the same place.

The main business of the meeting appeared when Albert E. Joab presented the following resolution:

To the Honorable, the Senate and the House of Representatives of the State of Washington: We the undersigned, your petitioners, citizens of the state of Washington and of the United States, irrespective of race or creed, respectfully petition your honorable body to memorialize the congress of the United States, at its present session, to take cognizance of the outrages now being perpetrated upon the Jews of the Russian government by that government, and to protest against such outrages in the name of humanity, as contrary to the spirit of the civilization of the Nineteenth century. And for this your petitioners will ever pray. Respectfully submitted.

Tacoma Daily Ledger January 11, 1891

Ledger, January 11, 1891, "A meeting was held yesterday afternoon for the purpose of taking action in regard to the persecution of the Russian Jews. A large number were present, among whom were the following: Abe Gross, Ellis Gross, Martin Rosenbaum, Samuel Moyses, Max Broh, A. Jacobi, D. P. Lewis, George H. Boardman, Albert E. Joab, J. L. Adler, A. Wallerstein, A. Weinberg, S. S. Loeb, M. Germanus, J. B. Meyers, Louis Hirsh, H. Harris, Amile Marx, J.C. Walland, Archie Ash, J. Pincus. D.P. Lewis was made temporary president and A. Hockwald temporary secretary... The name was adopted of Tacoma Relief Society, organized to protest against and relieve the inhumanities perpetrated against Jews in Russia... The main business of the meeting appeared when Albert E. Joab presented the following resolution:

> 'To the Honorable the Senate and the House of Representatives of the State of Washington: We the undersigned, your petitioners, citizens of the state of Washington and of the United States, irrespective of race or creed, respectfully petition your honorable body to memorialize the congress of the United States, at its present session, to take cognizance of the outrages now being perpetrated upon the Jews of the Russian government by that government, and to protect against such outrages in the name of humanity, as contrary to the spirit of the civilization of the Nineteenth century. And for this your petitioners will ever pray. Respectfully submitted.'

The resolutions were adopted by a unanimous vote. The executive committee will open communication with leading sympathizers throughout the United States, urging them to work to the end that the legislatures of the various states adopt memorials to congress. Already the legislatures of Pennsylvania and New York have adopted such memorials. Abe Gross is corresponding secretary of the committee."

The notice was also published in Cincinnati in the *American Israelite* on January 22, 1891. That article concluded, "As far as we know, this is the first organization of its kind, and the Jews of Tacoma are entitled to full credit for having taken the initiative."

The *Ledger* on Monday, January 19, 1891, devoted four columns to the growing movement. The group's officers were from the Jewish community, but several ministers stepped up as speakers and signed the resolution. "A well-attended meeting of the Tacoma Relief society was held yesterday afternoon for the purpose of completing organization for work against the present persecution of Jews in Russia. Organization was completed, with the following officers: Abe Gross, president; D. Germanus, first vice president; S. S. Loeb, second vice president; J. Pincus, treasurer; A. Hockwald, secretary. Executive committee – D. P. Lewis, N. Rosenbaum, A. S. Ash, L. Wallerstein and S. Jacobi… The following resolution was presented and signed as follows: Be it resolved that we hereby pledge ourselves to protest against the barbarities practiced against the Jews in Russia, and further hereby pledge ourselves to aid all in our power to alleviate the suffering resulting from said barbarities, financially and morally, (Signed) R. Stubbs, C. P. Culver, William J. Armstrong, Abe Gross, S. Jacobi, A. Hockwald, Isaac Pincus, Archie S. Ash, Joe Rodeselmer, D. P. Lewis, Max Brox, W. E. Copeland, Martin Rosenbaum, E. H. Gross, Samuel Posner, D. Germanus, Albert Braham, Isaac Harris. During the week a paper will be circulated by Secretary Hockwald to secure subscriptions to meet expenses incurred in prosecuting the work." The complete text of the speeches followed.

On February 7 the *Ledger* carried yet another mention of the persecution of Jews, this time describing an impending banishment from central Asia. "The sole pretext for the demand is that Jews outwit the Russians in trade and are monopolizing the traffic of the Asiatic markets." The *Ledger*, playing on the now-legendary phrase "The Chinese Must Go," captioned the article "The Jews Must Go." Later the headline would be used again with yet another variation, "The Hebrews Must Go."

Abe Gross took his job seriously. An article in the *Ledger* dated February 14, 1891, described some of his fund-raising activities. "The work of securing subscriptions for persecuted Jews in Russia was actively and successfully prosecuted yesterday. D. Luben of the well-known firm of Weinstock, Luben & Co., Sacramento, and Rev. J. L. Levi of the Jewish congregation of the same city, were appointed a committee by the Pacific coast Jewish organization, headquarters at San Francisco to raise money in the northwest yesterday, assisted by Abe Gross and others of the city. They canvassed the city and raised $3000, working until midnight. To-day they will raise this sum to $5000. The scheme is to form a stock company, which shall purchase land in large quantities in California, which shall be sold in ten-acre strips to Russian Jews. Nothing will be given away. Shares are $5, 20 per cent is due in ten days after obligation, 20 per cent in six months, 20 per cent, one year, 20 per cent, 18 months, 20 per cent, two years. The society is to be called the International society for the colonization of Russian Jews. The plan is prospering finely. Mr. Luben himself gave $5000 to it and thirty days' time." This was the same firm of Weinstock, Lubin, & Co. that had come to the aid of Tacoma's Jewish community when the Dickson Brothers printed anti-Semitic advertising.

The views were not all supportive. Apparently a Russian Bishop Vladimir had given a pejorative sermon in San Francisco denying the persecution of the Jews in Russia. The sermon was printed in San Francisco's *Telegraph* and reprinted in the *Ledger*. "It would be just the same fabrication to say that the Chinese and Indians are persecuted by the Americans as to say the Jews are persecuted by the Russians… The Russian Jews are a class of ignorant, money-loving usurpers." The bishop's comments spurred a lengthy editorial and a rebuttal. Sunday, March 1, 1891, his "surprising statements… caused the LEDGER to make inquiry on the subject of one of our own citizens, also a Russian, Dr. Max Axelrood." The doctor promptly contradicted the statements made by Vladimir. The response filled four very long columns.

The *Ledger* continued to speak out against the czar, while supporting the Jewish community. March 12th, 1891, "The czar of all Russias, who has been engaged for a long time in raising something else, is now about to turn his attention to raising cotton. His subjects will hope that the new enterprise will occupy his entire energies."

The ladies of Tacoma also occupied their energies elsewhere…

Temple Aid Society – "A Fair of the Fair"

HEBREWS ORGANIZING

A Very Prosperous Congregation Is Formed by Many of the Faith.

Its Officers Are Already Elected and a Constitution and By-Laws Are Adopted.

A Building Is to Be Erected at Once and First Services Are to Be Held in September.

A very prosperous Hebrew congregation has been organized in Tacoma and plans are now on foot to erect a modest building for its accommodation. Preliminary meetings have been held for some time past and the final arrangements were made on Tuesday night.

The preliminary meeting was held in response to the following call:

MASS MEETING.

Dear Sir: You are respectfully invited to attend a mass meeting to be held at Odd Fellows' hall, Mason block, on Monday, February 15, 1892, at 8 p. m., for the purpose of organizing a Hebrew congregation,

SOL. JACOBY,
ELIAS GROSS,
WILLIAM WOLF,
ARCHIE S. ASH,
Committee.

Tacoma Daily Ledger March 10, 1892

Congregation Beth Israel elected officers and adopted a constitution and by-laws in March of 1892, with incorporation following in July. Several newspaper mentions throughout the year noted the congregation intended to build a synagogue in time for the Jewish New Year in September. However, fundraising apparently took longer than expected and 1892 High Holiday services were held in the Unitarian Church. The ladies stepped in and gave the effort a strong push with a velvet glove.

They planned a fair spanning three days and appealing to Tacoma's population overall – especially the shoppers. Although the event fell during Chanukah, it was really a Christmas bazaar. As capable wives and daughters of businessmen, the ladies formed a benefit organization and elected officers. Advertising began in October and continued on a regular basis throughout the late fall. By naming their organization the "Temple Aid Society," they made sure that their newspaper notices would be placed where they would get the most notice – in the *Ledger*'s Sunday society columns.

A full description was printed in the *Ledger* on Sunday, December 4, 1892.

Christmas Sales.

The new Olympic theater will be opened December 15th, 16th and 17th by the Temple Aid society, who will hold a bazaar, which will be carried out on an extensive scale. The Jewish ladies of the city are energetically working that the entertainment may be successful in order to increase the fund for the erection of a Jewish temple. The merchants of this city and many leading houses in the east have donated with marked generosity, and handsome articles from their establishments will be placed on sale. Furniture, merchandise, jewelry, bric-a-brac and fancy work are among the valuable donations.

The booths are in charge of the following ladies: Dolls, Mrs. Simon Donau; bric-a-brac, Mrs Moses; clothing and dry goods, Mrs. S. Jacoby; cigars, Mrs. Meyers; fancy mats, Mrs. S. Posner; toys, Mrs. Heineman; furniture, Mrs. M. Cohn; flowers, Mrs. Charles Reichenbach; candy, Mrs. A. J. Blum. Miss Alice Donau and Miss Hattie Moses will represent Rebecca at the well, and Miss Jaffa will reveal fortunes. Manager Mark Wilson kindly donates the use of the new theater on this occasion. Each evening there will be music and dancing.

The officers of the Temple Aid society are: President, Miss Florence Donau; vice-president, Mrs. S. Jacoby; recording secretary, Mrs. M. Ball; corresponding secretary, Mrs. A. J. Steinman; treasurer, Mrs. Charles Reichenbach; board of managers, Mesdames Donau, Moses, Loeb, Cohn. Meyers, Ash, Blum, Pincus, Isaacs, Posner.

More details came the following week, then continued daily, with each article describing just a little more about the upcoming event. On the first day of the fair the *Tacoma News* printed a front-page article. "A NEW SYNAGOGUE. Jewish Ladies Will Aid To Build It. THEIR FAIR OPENS TONIGHT. Wit, Beauty and Fashion Enlisted in the Great Cause of Progress." The article included a sketch of the proposed synagogue and again listed the officers of the organization. Mayor Huson would be on hand to open the festivities, which included dancing each evening at 11 p.m. Mrs. A.J. Steinman would be writing and editing a little daily newspaper throughout the fair, from a spaced decorated as a library. On Saturday (Children's Day) every child attending would have a chance to win a magnificent doll. A novel promised feature was a "wonder-rose bush," bearing a profusion of numbered rose buds offered for sale, in one of which was a diamond ring. "The buds are sold and the lucky purchaser of one obtains not only a bud but a dew drop of incalculable and unfading value." Fair admission was just 25 cents.

JEWISH FAIR OPENED

Ladies of the Temple Aid Society Successfully Begin Their Carnival.

Mayor Huson Delivered the Formal Address Before a Large Audience.

Beautiful Costumes Worn by the Ladies Presiding at the Various Attractive Booths.

The auditorium of the New Olympic theater was opened last evening by the ladies of the Temple Aid society, who are holding a three nights' bazaar in aid of the Hebrew synagogue to be erected in this city. A large number of prominent people were in attendance, and the first evening may well be de-

Tacoma Daily Ledger December 15, 1892

Tacoma Daily Ledger, December 16, 1892: "The most noticeable feature of the fair was the number of handsome costumes worn by the ladies in charge:

Miss Donau, president, was beautifully dressed in an evening gown of pale blue crepe, trimmed with chiffon and heavy gold bead passementrie.

Mrs. S. Jacoby, vice president – Grey bedford cord costume, trimmed with grey chiffon.

Mrs. M. Ball, recording secretary – Blue and pink brocaded silk, combined with pink silk.

Mrs. A.J. Steinman, corresponding secretary – Cardinal crepe and satin ribbon; red carnations and diamonds.

Mrs. Charles Reichenbach, treasurer – Black brocaded satin and handsome jet ornaments; diamonds.

Mrs. L. Donau, chairman of the board of managers – Imported dress of black silk, the front being entirely covered with jet; point lace and diamonds.

Mrs. M. Moses – Black satin and jet; diamonds.

Mrs. S.S. Loeb, manager – Cream faille silk with handsome bertha of Duchess lace; pearls and diamonds.

Mrs. M. Cohn – Black silk, trimmed with old rose silk and lace; diamonds.

Mrs. S. Posner, manager – Changeable old rose silk with green velvet garnitures.

Mrs. M. G. Meyers, manager – Tan silk and changeable velvet bodice.

Mrs. Pincus – Black silk and lace.

Mrs. S. Isaacs, manager – Yellow surah silk with overdress of yellow striped gauze; diamonds.

Mrs. M. Bloom, manager – Black lace with gold passementerie; diamond ornaments.

Mrs. Harry Fraley – Pale blue crepe trimmed with embroidered chiffon.

Mrs. Joseph Hall – Nile green crepe with oriental passementerie.

Mrs. J. Jacoby – Old rose changeable silk and point lace.

Mrs. M. Summerfield – Tan evening dress and carnations.

Mrs. A. Isaacs – Red silk empire gown with gold passementerie.

Miss Hain – Yellow crepe and white lace.

Mrs. A. Magnus – Black silk and passementrie.

Mrs. S. Rogers – Black satin, pink silk corsage.

Mrs. Belle Isaacs – Heliotrope China silk, bodice of gold passamenterie; diamonds.

Mrs. E. Marx – Blue-figured India silk, bertha of white lace; diamonds.

Mrs. J. Bernard – Pink Chinasilk, white lace and diamonds.

Mrs. J. Bloom – Black lace and silk, jet trimmings.

Mrs. E. G. Heinemann – Black India silk and jet.

Mrs. Levy – Black brocaded satin and jet; diamond ornaments.

Mrs. L.A. Olsen – Changeable silk bodice with black and white costume.

Mrs. S.A. Andrews – Black brocade with lace overdress; diamond ornaments.

Mrs. A. Weinberg – Blue brocade satin, overdress of embroidered gauze and feather trimming; pearls.

Mrs. M. Liebenthal – Green velvet, combined with nile green moire.

Mrs. Robert Gans – Black satin and roses.

Miss Alice Donau (as Rebecca) wore an oriental costume of blue and tan silk, trimmed with gold spangles.

Miss Jacob – Black silk lace and gold passementerie.

Miss Pincus – Light blue albatross, lace and ribbon; pearls.

Miss Raphael – Pale blue empire gown; diamonds.

Miss Carrie Kaufman – Yellow crepe and chiffon.

Miss Goldsmith – Yellow brocaded China silk with black velvet ribbons.

Miss Levy – White Bedford cord and lace.

Miss Harris – Corn-colored silk and pearl trimming.

Miss Nannie Moses – Pale pink silk, overdress of beaded pink net.

Miss Belle Pincus – Blue albatross, white lace and pearls.

Booths:

Doll's booth: Mrs. Donau, assisted by Mesdames S.S. Loeb, H. Fraley and E. Marks. Draped in pink with sprigs of myrtle. Features three large dolls dressed after little Adele Steinman, Sidney Loeb and Irene Steinfield; dressed and donated by the Jewish ladies of Portland, Philadelphia, New York and Eastern cities.

Bric-a-brac booth: Miss Moses, assisted by Misses Andrews, Weinberg, Rose Isaacs and Hattie Moses. Draped with lemon-colored cloth. Magnificent vase donated by a Philadelphia importing house.

Clothing and dry goods booth: Mrs. Sol Jacobi, aided by Mesdames M. Blum, Liebenthal, J. Jacobi and Miss Gertie Isaacs. Draped in pink and green; offering clothing, furnishing goods and dry goods donated by local merchants.

Flower temple: Mrs. Charles Reichenbach, assisted by Misses Goldsmith, Kaufman, Haines and Isabelle Pincus. Rare exotic plants, cut flowers and boutonnieres.

Fancy bazaar: Mrs. Posner, with Miss Nannie Moses, Miss Gans and Mrs. M. Ball. Needlework and fancy work from ladies of Tacoma, Portland, and many Eastern cities.

Cigar booth: Mrs. Meyer Meyers [Max Myers], assisted by Misses Hall, Kullmann and Belle Isaacs. Draped in orange, offers fragrant Havanas, Key West and homemade cigars.

Refreshment booth, draped in lilac, sells oysters, coffee, cakes, etc.

Toy booth: Mrs. Hirschfield, aided by Mrs. Rogers, Misses Levi, Magnus and Olsen. Draped in dark blue, features toys for Christmas presents.

Furniture booth: Mrs. M. Cohn and Mrs. J. Bernhard, handsome bookcase donated by Holmes & Bull.

Ice cream booth: Mrs. A.J. Blum, aided by Misses Bloom, Heineman and F. Jacobs.

Designed by architect Paul Bergfield, snow mansion with icicle eaves.

Gipsy Tent: Miss Jaffa telling fortunes, reading palms.

Liquid Refreshments: Misses Alice Donau and Alice Moses, two Rebeccas at the well."

Back Row – Virginia Donau Steinman, Bettina Donau Steinfeld. Front Row – Alice and Florence Donau
Courtesy of Bettina Lyons

The *Ledger* on the sixteenth carried a lengthy article about the success of the fair, complete with the text of Mayor Huson's glowing tribute to the untiring energies of the women. Descriptions of the various booths again named the ladies presiding in each, and reminded readers that the bazaar would continue for two more days.

The headline in the *Ledger* on the seventeenth was not quite as elegant and tasteful. It read: "JEWISH LADIES MAKE MONEY. Festivities of the Temple Aid Society Fair Continued With Success." An even larger crowd than the previous evening had helped the ladies dispose of over half of their donations. Follow-up articles on December 18 and 20 continued to increase the amount of the expected profits from the successful fair, estimated from $1,500 to $2,000.

Building could begin...

Temple Beth Israel

Temple Beth Israel
From the collection of the author

On February 15, 1892, a preliminary committee made up of Sol Jacoby, Ellis Gross, William Wolf, and Archie S. Ash called a meeting to organize a Jewish congregation in Tacoma. The meeting was attended by over forty people, who elected a more formal committee to prepare bylaws and a constitution. Serving on that committee were William Wolf, Abe Gross, A. Ash, M. Moses, S. Jacoby, S. Posner, Mr. Loeb and S. Martin.

By March 8 the work of the committee was adopted and officers were elected for the first year, including President, S. Jacoby; vice president, D. Germanus; secretary, D. Magnus; treasurer, A. Ash; trustees M. Moses, M. Cohn and William Wolf.

A special committee was selected to find a suitable location, over which opinions were divided. The congregation planned to spend $10,000 or more on the structure. Services would be in the reform style, with a lecture given in English. Membership had already grown from forty to seventy-five and would continue to grow.

A March 10th article concluded "No steps have yet been taken toward securing a rabbi."

Congregation Beth Israel was incorporated on July 13, 1892. Plans were drawn, but organizers had agreed not to begin construction until all funds were in place. As we've already seen, the ladies stepped in, had one heck of a fundraiser in December of 1892, and building plans could move forward.

On December 20th the *Ledger* reported the site of the synagogue at South Tenth and I Streets was paid for, spanning three lots. Morris Gross took advantage of a business trip to New York to solicit donations, hopefully raising half of the building funds needed. Apparently he didn't quite meet that goal, because on January 15, 1893, John P. Gale granted a $2,500 mortgage to Congregation Beth Israel.

By April 22, 1893 the *Ledger* could report that C.A. Darmer's architectural plans had been selected by the building committee, over several other submissions. The frame structure, 42 x 65 feet, would have a brick foundation. The exterior design, described as "in the Romanesque style, running slightly into the Moorish," featured a main entrance flanked above by two Moorish towers. The building's auditorium would seat 300 and feature windows of colored and leaded glass. The platforms and altar would be finished in white and gold. The full basement would include a children's Sunday school room and committee rooms. The building committee expected to let the contract the following week, with construction completed by August 31st.

On May third the *Ledger* noted that C.A. Darmer received a building permit "for a two-story frame Jewish synagogue, with brick foundations, at South I and Tenth streets, to cost $5500." The timing couldn't have been worse, followed by "Black Friday," on May fifth. Blithely unaware of the coming hard times, the building committee went on with its work.

Ledger, July 9, 1893:

"COMPLETING THE JEWISH TEMPLE. A Rabbi Will Be Engaged in September. The new Jewish Temple at the corner of South I and Tenth streets is nearing completion and will be a monument to the industry and religious faithfulness of the small congregation who have assisted in paying for the structure. The building is 60 x 70 feet, having a basement that will seat about 400 people, and also a kitchen and other small rooms. The auditorium is designed to seat 500 people and is well lighted and nicely arranged. The pulpit is in the east end and raised several feet above the auditorium floor. A pipe organ, costing $3000, will be placed in a rear gallery, where the choir will also sit.

G.L. Freer is the contractor and will finish the work about August 18. His contract price is $6000 and the land on which the building stands is valued at $4000. C.A. Darmer drew the plans for the building, which is frame with stone foundation and has three large, round towers covered with tin, which will be bronzed over.

The church society here is known as Congregation Beth Israel, and has at present about 100 members, which number will be largely increased when a rabbi is engaged to conduct regular services. This will be in September. Connected with the church are three other societies, with memberships ranging from seventy-five to 250 – the Hebrew Benevolent society, the Lady Montefiore society and the Ladies' Harmony society. It is expected that a large number of Hebrews from the surrounding towns will also attend services here after the rabbi is installed."

By August 10 construction was nearly complete, although the cost had increased to $7,000. Dedication would be on the Jewish New Year. *Ledger,* September 8, "The new Jewish temple, which has just been completed, will be formally dedicated next Sunday morning. Dr. Gustave Adolph Danziger, a famous Hebrew author and divine, from San Francisco, has arrived in the city for that purpose. A trained chorus has been practicing for the occasion for some time past." Dates, times, and the musical program followed. Over the next several days, ads noted that Gross Brothers would close all day for the holiday and Prager Brothers would close until 6 p.m.

THE HEBREWS' TEMPLE

It Will Be Dedicated Next Month.

FEAST OF ROSH-HASHANA.

Elaborate Preparations Are Being Made For the Event by the Hebrews.

The Jewish synagogue at the corner of South Tenth and I streets is almost completed and arrangements are now being made for the dedication of the building. The probabilities are that the dedication services will take place on Saturday, September 9, the first day of the Jewish new year.

Rosh-Hashana is the name by which the Jewish new year is known. In the Jewish calender this day will mark the inauguration of the year 5654. According to the solar system of determining a year, the Jewish system gains a day in 216 years. The years differ in the number of days contained in each, some years having as many as 385 days while last year there were only 355 days.

It is the intention to make the dedication services the day before the feast of Rosh-Hashana of more than ordinary solemnity. It is expected that there will be a large attendance of Hebrews from various parts of the State. A rabbi will be engaged shortly to take charge of the temple. The Hebrews in this city form what they call the Congregation Beth Israel. There are about 100 members.

The synagogue or temple is entirely of frame. It is 60x70 feet, having a basement that will seat about 400 people, and also a kitchen and other small rooms. The auditorium is designed to seat 500 people and is well lighted and nicely arranged. The pulpit is in the end and raised several feet above the auditorium floor. A pipe organ, costing $3,000, will be placed in a rear gallery, where the choir will also sit. The building cost $6'000 and the land $4,000.

Tacoma Daily News August 23, 1893

When the new synagogue was ready for the first services in September of 1893, the *Ledger* ran a two-column article describing the dedication of the new temple:

"The services began at 10 o'clock. At that time during an organ prelude by Miss Sarah Beach, a procession composed of the rabbi, officers of the congregation and visiting rabbis, assembled in the vestry room. When they arrived at the inner door they halted and asked for admission, the rabbi saying: "Open unto me the gates of righteousness," which was responded to by the chorus. Then the procession entered, the rabbi first, followed by four little girls dressed in white and bearing bouquets, one of whom carried an embroidered cushion on which lay the key to the holy shrine.

The officers of the church followed, preceded by S. Jacoby, president, who bore the holy scroll. They made a circle of the church twice, keeping time to a processional solo sung by Mr. Andrews. On arriving at the pulpit the second time the rabbi ascended, followed by S. Jacoby and M. Cohn, the little girls taking chairs in front of the rostrum.

President Jacoby, who carried the holy scroll, opened the ark and deposited it within. Dr. Danziger then read Solomon's prayer, after which the key to the ark was presented to Mr. Jacoby. The latter responded, expressing his gratitude and thanks to all who had assisted in building the temple. The lighting of the perpetual lamp was the most impressive of the ceremonies. It was preceded by the reading of nine verses from the first chapter of Genesis with response by the choir. Mr. Jacoby lighted a taper and handed it to the rabbi who slowly climbed three steps to a position and lighted it. The flame dimly shone through the colored glass and everybody knew that the light of Judah burned in Tacoma."

A synopsis of Dr. Danziger's sermon was published in the article, concluding "Now, this temple is pre-eminently an American Jewish house of worship. The very fact that those walls are thin, that those doors are wide open, demonstrates more forcibly than I can explain to you that it is a Jewish temple in America, where walls do not have to be built five or six feet thick and the doors clad with iron to protect the worshipers from the fury of fanaticism. We have no enemy here in free America, but in Europe it is not so..." How prophetic were his words.

There was more the next day, beginning with a lesson on the Jewish calendar and a description of the services. Dr. Danziger addressed a special meeting of the congregation on Thursday, September 14th. His sermon on the eve of Yom Kippur was described in the *Ledger* on Wednesday, September 20, 1893.

AN ELOQUENT SERMON

Impressive Services Held Last Evening at the New Jewish Synagogue.

The Congregation Addressed by Dr. Danziger on "The Purpose of Yom Kippur."

Why To-Day Is Observed With Fasting and Prayer—Regular Services May Be Held.

The annual Yom Kippur services were held last evening at the Jewish synagogue, on the corner of Tenth and I streets. The services consisted of liturgical reading from the prayer book, music and an eloquent sermon delivered by Dr. Danziger, to a large audience. The subject of his sermon was, "The Purpose of Yom Kippur." Dr. Danziger divided the cardinal elements of religion into four phases: First, thought resolving itself into creed and theology. Second, emotion resolving itself into fear or worship. Third, liturgy resolving itself into various forms of expression, as elaborate reading, devotional prayer, music, etc. Fourth, purpose, this being the reconciliation of man to his God, and more especially to man. A synopsis of the sermon is as follows:

The Day of Atonement was intended mainly for the purpose of giving man an opportunity to make good his actions, bad or indifferent, toward his fellow-man. The Talmudic sages, understanding the fact and the main purpose of the Day of Atonement, gave expression to the maxim in these words: "Sins by man against God the Day of Atonement obliterates, but sins by man against his fellow man, the Day of Atonement does not obliterate, unless he speaks to him and asks his pardon. Man's fear of man is often greater than man's fear of God. Just as the purpose of religion is to bring men together into closer relationship and a better understanding of the great love with which the heavenly Father guards His weak children on earth, so that by mutual appreciation of human worth and human love they may glorify God, even so it is the purpose of the Day of Atonement, recurring annually, to bring Israelites together into closer relationship and mutual appreciation. By forgiving only can we hope to be forgiven; by charitableness only can we expect to find grace. No doctrine, no amount of prayers, no promises uttered by lips, can bring us the peace of the soul as readily as the spontaneous giving of our hearts' best love, forbearance and mercy to one another.

The synagogue was crowded last evening to its fullest capacity. The audience contained a liberal sprinkling of Gentiles. The exercises were in part conducted in Hebrew.

To-day is the Day of Atonement and will be observed by prayer and fasting, commencing at 8 a. m. and closing at sundown. Continuous services will be held in the synagogue to-day. The sermon will be preached by Dr. Danziger about noon, and the subject will be: "To Fast or Not to Fast."

Sunday evening will be the beginning of the fast of the tabernacle. Dr. Danziger will not be here to assist in its observance, as he leaves on Sunday for San Francisco.

Arrangements are being perfected to hold regular preaching services, and in the near future it is expected that the synagogue will be opened every Sunday.

Tacoma Daily Ledger September 20, 1893

The search began to hire a rabbi. *Ledger*, October 22, 1893, "May Come Here to Stay. Rev. Dr. Salomon Philo, a Jewish rabbi of Victoria, B.C., is in the city and will lecture before the Jewish congregation of Beth Israel this morning on the subject, 'Science and Religion.' Immediately after the service a meeting of the congregation will be held to decide whether a call shall be extended to Dr. Philo to take charge of the congregation. Dr. Philo lectured to the Hebrews of the city at their temple last Friday evening, taking 'The Temple' for his subject. The reverend gentleman is about 50 years old. He was born in Germany and is a graduate of the Brussels seminary. He came to America twelve years ago and has been visiting various cities of the United States until three years ago, when he settled in Victoria and took charge of the Jewish congregation there. Dr. Philo is a frequent contributor to Jewish periodicals of this country."

Ledger, Monday, October 23, "MAY CALL DR. DANZIGER. A Preliminary Vote Taken Yesterday By Congregation of Beth Israel. It is probable that Dr. Adolph Danziger, the Jewish rabbi of San Francisco, who was here some weeks ago and who dedicated the new Jewish temple, will be called by the congregation of Beth Israel to take charge of the congregation. A preliminary vote was taken yesterday after the services in the temple at I and Tenth streets, which resulted in a majority of the congregation voting to have him called. The calling of Rev. Dr. Salomon Philo of Victoria, who lectured in the temple Friday and preached there yesterday, was also considered." (Rabbi Philo took a job in Vancouver, British Columbia, instead.)

President S. Jacoby appointed a committee consisting of M. Ball, S.S. Loeb, S. Roger and Attorney Gattel. The matter totally dropped from the news columns, so apparently either Dr. Danziger chose not to come or he wasn't offered the position. (A "due diligence" committee would have found that Dr. Danziger was a practicing dentist and later an attorney, not an ordained rabbi.)

אוויזפאקט:

G. A. DANZIGER,
ATTORNEY - AT - LAW.
21 CROCKER BUILDING.

San Francisco Call August 9, 1895

Tacoma's 1893–1894 city directory, released in late October of 1893, noted that services were at 8 p.m. on Friday evening, with Sunday school 10 a.m. and Sabbath school at 10 a.m. on Saturday. No rabbi was mentioned.

By the fall of 1894 the city of Tacoma was feeling even greater economic pressures. Unable to pay teachers, the school district delayed the beginning of the school year until October 1st – *Rosh Hashanah*. On October 11th the *Ledger* ran a *Yom Kippur* article of nearly a full column. The reporter had clearly been in attendance, as he was able to describe the proceedings. "S. Posner, A. Blum and J. Jacobs conducted the services. The whole day is spent in fasting and prayer. In this respect there is a difference between the "Orthodox" and the "Reformed" Jews, as they are termed. While they both observe the day in all its religious solemnity and severity, the reformed Jews do not fast so strictly as their orthodox brethren. Last year services according to both branches were held in the city, but yesterday the members of the faith in Tacoma were united in their devotions, which were held in Temple Beth Israel."

Tacoma's 1895 Polk Directory, released in early February of 1895, again made no mention of a rabbi. Articles in the *Ledger* on March 8 and 11 included J. Jacobs as the reader at the Purim festival. However, help was on the way. The minutes of the Judith Montefiore Society show that on March 6, 1895, a motion was passed to engage Mr. Lincer as a Sabbath school teacher for $10 per month. This was a fairly optimistic move, as the economy had continued its downward spiral.

Martin Lincer apparently served as Tacoma's rabbi for about a year. He was mentioned in the *Ledger*'s columns on March 26, 1895, for a Winkleman circumcision, March 30 for Abe Gross' funeral, and a wedding in August of Joseph Kaufman & Sarah Abrams. *Ledger*, Wednesday, September 18, 1895, "Today Ushers in the Year 5656 of Jewish Chronology… Services will be held in the synagogue, with the orthodox prayer service in Hebrew, Rabbi Lincer officiating, assisted by Mr. Posner, this evening and tomorrow morning." Several articles over the next few weeks described the holiday services, led by Rabbi Lincer. Another circumcision was performed by Rabbi Lincer in January of 1896.

One of the few bar mitzvahs was that of Leonard Gross, eldest son of David Gross. *Ledger*, Thursday, Feb. 27, 1896, "Master Leonard Gross will be *bar mitzva* at the Temple Saturday morning."

Tacoma's 1896 directory included the officers of the temple as Rev. Dr. Martin Lincer, Rabbi; S. Jacoby, President; M. Cohn, Vice president; A. S. Ash, Treasurer; Wm. Jacobs, Secretary. Services were held at 7 pm on Friday and at 10 am on Saturday. Classes were taught Saturday after services and Sunday at 10 am. German and Hebrew school was on Tuesdays and Thursdays at 4 pm. The temple was one of 66 churches in Tacoma. Rabbi Lincer resided at 1917 South E, near the more Orthodox Russian Jews, not near the temple itself. In May of 1896 the Judith Montefiore society ladies provided $25 for the rabbi's departure railroad ticket.

The congregation's newspaper mentions quickly returned to only those of the fall holidays, yet remained friendly. *Ledger*, Thursday, September 17, 1896, "The services were beautiful, alternating with chants, prayers and invocations. *Shachris*, the morning prayer, was opened by A. Bloom, who conducted services until noon. J. Jacob immediately took the lead after Mr. Bloom retired and the service known as *Moosof* was continued until 3 o'clock. S. Posner then took charge and conducted evening prayer, called *Minha*, until 4:30 p.m. J. Jacob again led the flock, concluding the day's observances an hour and a half later with the impressive ritual called *Neele*, which ends with Meyerbeer's beautiful composition, "Yigdal."

By 1897 the rush to the Klondike had spurred the economy. Those Jewish merchants remaining in Tacoma began the process of recovery. On Tuesday, September 28, 1897, the *Ledger* noted that *Rosh Hashanah* services had been led by J. Jacob and Morris Bloom, bringing in the year 5658. "There being no resident rabbi in this city the services were conducted by members of the Hebrew colony of Tacoma." The *Yom Kippur* sermon implied that the congregation's economy had suffered along with its members, bringing an impassioned plea from their lay leader. An article on October 7 carried the full text of Mr. Jacob's speech. He urged those in attendance to examine their lives and make atonement for their sins. "For instance, if you have been neglectful in contributing your mite towards the maintenance of this house of worship, now is your time to reflect... The tenacity and unshaken fidelity with which a handful of Jewish pioneers in Tacoma under the sorest of trials and tribulations maintained this temple will, if ever the history of Tacoma is written, shine forth as one of the most-manly acts on record. You can leave no nobler inheritance to your children than the privilege for them to class you among the pioneer builders and supporters of this house of God. If each one of you will put his shoulder to the wheel at an average of only one penny per day this magnificent temple will continue to be a Beth-El... And so when this evening in concluding our services we declaim the solemn chant of *Shema, Israel*, the Jewish declaration of the Unity of God, let it not be the last sad song of a dying cause in Tacoma."

Tacoma's 1897–98 city directory, released in November of 1897, noted that services were held on Friday at 7 p.m., on Saturday at 10 a.m., with Sabbath School after temple services. The temple also offered Sunday school at 10 a.m. and German and Hebrew on Tuesdays and Thursdays at 4 p.m. Somehow the remaining members had supported their congregation through the worst years of Tacoma's young history.

As war with Spain broke out the *Ledger*'s columns soon filled with news of naval battles, maps of Spanish ports and ads for "Remember the Maine" buttons.

1898 holiday services were again led by a team of lay leaders, including Samuel Posner at the evening service, M. Bloom in the morning, and Ellis Gross and Mr. Bloom in the afternoon, with J. Jacob lecturing on the day's significance.

JEWISH WAR PRAYER FOR USE IN ALL TEMPLES.

Commencing yesterday the following "War Prayer" will be used in all orthodox Jewish temples throughout the country during the existence of the war with Spain:

O, merciful and gracious King, God of Gods and Lord of Lords, in Thy hand is the soul of every living creature and the spirit of every human being, look down from Thy holy dwelling, from heaven, save, we beseech Thee, Thy servants the American nation, who dwell in these United States, who adhere to the teachings of Thy beneficent attributes, to do good to mortal beings, to show compassion to those who are formed by Thy hand, and who risk their lives as they do this day, to shed their blood like water in this war which duty commands, to deliver the Cuban people, who sign and groan beneath the hand of the relentless and cruel Spanish nation, who have thirsted for human blood from days of old.

O, Lord of compassion, we pray Thee, pity and have mercy upon our forces on land and sea, and give them strength and courage to stand before the power of our enemies and to subdue the pride of those who rise against us, that they, our hosts, return not in defeat—O, do Thou avert that!—with head bent downward and faces shamed.

May Thy loving kindness uphold and support us with Thy right hand, to deliver the Cubans who are oppressed and afflicted by their persecutors, and to proclaim freedom for them in order that they may enjoy the glow of enlightenment and freedom which Thou hast apportioned to us, sons of these United States, with Thy full, open, holy, extended hand.

We implore Thee, prosper our ways that no sickness, misfortune, mishaps or evil accidents may befall us. Bring our ships to desired havens and lead us by silent waters. Graciously bestow of thy knowledge, understanding and wisdom upon our authorities, councilors and commanders, that they may succeed in their plans on the lines of love, mercy and humanity, that they may proceed thereon, as now.

Appoint us for salvation and compassion that violence, outbreak and calamity be unheard of in our land, that perfect peace may be accorded to us and to all who dwell in this country, now and forevermore, amen.

Tacoma Daily Ledger May 15, 1898

In 1899 Tacoma's Jewish congregation again turned to the general community for fundraising. *Ledger,* January 28, 1899, "Benefit of the Jewish Temple. Grau's famous opera company has been especially engaged by the most prominent Jewish citizens of Tacoma to appear at the Tacoma Theater for three nights and Saturday matinee commencing Thursday, February 2, for the benefit of their Temple Beth-Israel." On February 3rd the *Ledger* approved of the first evening's performance. "Notwithstanding the intense cold and the icy condition of the streets the Tacoma Theater was well filled with a representative audience." The next evening was not as strong. "The house was not so well filled as at the first performance, but the continuance of the cold weather no doubt was partly to blame." (The other major entertainment offered to Tacoma's citizens that evening was the Poultry show, which featured a night-time program of Dogs vs. Rats. Children were awarded ten cents for any live rat they brought in to be used as bait for the dogs.)

Temple Beth Israel's president in 1899 was Morris Moses. Meyer Jacob was vice president, and Samuel Posner served as secretary and treasurer. According to the city directory Sunday school began at 10 a.m. On Sunday, September 3, 1899, the *Ledger* reported the Jewish New Year would be observed on Monday evening. Lay leaders again included Joseph Jacob and Mr.

Bloom, supported by soloist Mrs. Bernard Hochstatter. Another notice on the same page, under church listings, added "Plenty seats for visitors."

Tacoma's 1900 city directory, released in May, included Temple Beth Israel's officers. Meyer Jacob served as president, S. Winkleman [Henry] as vice president and Samuel Posner as secretary and treasurer. No rabbi was mentioned. Sunday school continued at 10 a.m.

Ledger, Tuesday September 25, 1900, "JEWISH NEW YEAR. Impressive Services Held at the I Street Synagogue Yesterday." Services were conducted by N. Bloom [Morris] and S. Posner. Joseph Jacob gave the address, "The Crucial Hour." A *Yom Kippur* article followed on October 3rd. (The firm of Vaughan and Morrill made the mistake of advertising "Hebrew New Year Cards" on January 1, 1901.)

On Thursday, January 22, 1903, the congregation held a ceremony to celebrate the burning of the mortgage. According to the *Tacoma Evening News,* the event took place at the Masonic hall, with Rabbi Joseph of Seattle as speaker. A banquet began at 10 p.m., indicating the long hours worked by the merchant members. Ellis Gross, president, served as toastmaster at the banquet. "After years of hard work and careful saving the congregation has paid the debt." Other officers included Joseph [Theo] Feist, vice president; Meyer Jacobs, treasurer, and I. [Sam] Posner, secretary.

Work immediately began to procure the services of a rabbi. In March the position was offered to Montague N.A. Cohen, who was currently serving the congregation in Victoria, B.C. He arrived in Tacoma in August of 1903. His one-year contract included a $1,000 salary. (His wife, the former Celia Brash, was a niece of Tacoma's Regina Bell, Mrs. Max G. Myers.)

The congregation barely survived the war years, and many remaining congregants moved to Tacoma's North End. In 1918 the synagogue building was sold to members of the Seventh-day Adventists church for $6500. It served as their church for over 50 years before it was torn down. (The site is currently a parking lot.)

The congregation went back to where it began – holding holiday services in a rented hall. Services were held in Triangle Hall from 1918 until 1922, when the new temple Beth Israel was built on the corner of North 4th and J. The records of the first synagogue were enclosed in the cornerstone of the new building. There they remain. Nearly fifty years later the old building was sold to an Apostolic Faith church.

Temple Beth Israel c 1923
Courtesy of Temple Beth El

A second congregation was begun in Tacoma by Hugo Stusser, Julius Friedman, and a handful of other Ortho- dox Jews, mostly relatives from Latvia. The group incorporated in January of 1909, commissioned a Torah, and purchased a church building on Taco- ma Avenue in 1914. That same year they formed Cemetery Chevra Kadisha.

1529 Tacoma Avenue South
Courtesy of Tacoma Public Library

Julius Friedman served as president for many years and led the building committee in the twenties. In April of 1925 the congregation's members laid the cornerstone of a new building,

Chevra Talmud Torah, on the corner of South 4th & I. Affiliation was switched to Conservative in 1936 and the congregation's name was changed to Sinai Temple.

Talmud Torah Synagogue
Courtesy of Tacoma Public Library D141770-15

In 1960 Rabbi Richard Rosenthal diplomati- cally accomplished a merger of the two congrega- tions. Both temple buildings were sold and a new home, Temple Beth El, was dedicated in May of 1968, as Pierce County's only house of Jewish worship. Although the congregation's official af- filiation was Reform, service schedules and prac- tices maintained a Conservative element.

Demonstrating the repetitive nature of histo- ry, Tacoma's Jewish community was again bifur- cated thirty-five years later when Rabbi Zalman Heber brought a branch of the Chabad-Lubavitch movement to Tacoma. Chabad Jewish Center of Pierce County dedicated a new synagogue build- ing in June of 2010, once again providing a place for Orthodox Jewish worship and practice.

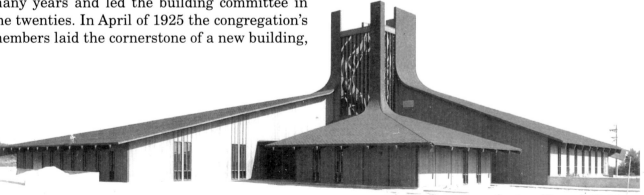

Courtesy of Tacoma Public Library

Tacoma's first temple was built by Congregation Beth Israel, meaning House of Israel. Some of Tacoma's Jewish pioneers also needed a new name...

A Rosen by Any Other Name

Just as Abram became Abraham and Jacob became Israel, Jews have often chosen a name change when starting a new life or going through a personal transformation. Olympia's Jacob Wolff arrived in the U.S. in 1888 on the ship *George Washington* and was so enthralled that he changed his name to George J. Wolff. It was a tale he loved to tell in interviews. However, other name changes have been much more difficult to track down.

Sometimes relatives are aware of the changes. Leta Gross, daughter of Ellis Gross and Johanna Olchevitz, lived to be 101. She explained that her father's family name in Rypin had been Grass. When the brothers learned enough English to realize that "grass" was just the plain green stuff that grew all around, they felt they needed a grander name. In America they hoped their lives would be huge and grandiose, so they chose "Gross," which means "large" or "great" in German. Little did they know the future English slang word would mean "disgusting."

Leta also related that her maternal grandfather, Johanna's father, Wilhelm Olchevitz, had a brother named Julius. Julius was a creative and unusual writer, in a field now called science fiction. Julius married a French girl who was not Jewish. Julius changed his name to the French version of Olche, meaning alder, and created a fictional French lineage, becoming Jules Verne.

Earlier confirmation of Leta's narrative was printed in the *Ledger* on November 17, 1889, after the Germania theatre had presented Jules Verne's *Around the World in Eighty Days*. Abe Gross explained that his sister-in-law, Johanna Olchevitz, wife of his brother Ellis, was directly related to Jules Verne. Abe had personally verified the facts during his recent trip to Europe. He met with Wilhelm Olchevitz, who had been a member of Strasbourg's city council for 24 years. Wilhelm and Jules were brothers, and Wilhelm had regularly sent money to Jules for food and clothing during his early years of struggle. (Verne's descendants denied any Jewish ancestry and his French heritage has become widely accepted.)

Jewish Origin of Jules Verne.

The Jewish World of London states that the various rumors about the Jewish origin of the late Jules Verne, the famous French author, which were recently denied by his son in Le Figaro of Paris, have been confirmed. In the Gazeta Navodowa of Warsaw a correspondence has taken place which shows that Jules Verne was originally called Olszewicz, and was born of Jewish parents in Plock, Russian Poland. His father, according to M. Sokolow, editor of the Hebrew daily Hazephira of Warsaw, was known as "the pious German," on account of his fashionable attire. The son, however, left the country, turned Christian, adopted the name of Verne, and, although he seems to have been a Pole by nationality and by preference, he subsequently became a thorough Frenchman.

New York Times January 15, 1906

– 110 –

relatives waiting to assist him. By the end of February of 1864 Charles, still unemployed and nearly out of funds, crossed over to Trenton and enlisted in the New Jersey Cavalry. He received a $300 enlistment bounty, payable in six month installments. Afraid his family would find out what he had done, Charles enlisted under the name of a childhood friend, Oscar Von Ceder. After the war he simply returned to his real name. Years later an alert letter carrier refused to deliver Oscar's pension checks to Charles. The lengthy investigation that followed was carefully documented in his military pension file, where it silently waited 90 years to be rediscovered.

However, sometimes families chose a common name that is nearly impossible to trace. Olympia's Kaufman family was almost in that category. (Kaufman means merchant.) Toklas and

Pauline Jacobs Prager, Moses Steif Jacobs (seated) and Eddie Jacobs
Courtesy of Ann Fuller

Relatives of Moses S. Jacobs were also able to offer insights. Born Moses Steif, he likely changed his surname to Jacobs to honor a fellow businessman without children. Unfortunately, four of Moses' five children were girls and his son Edward died without marrying, so the Jacobs name was not continued. Moses' brother Hirsch kept the Steif name.

Relatives of Solomon Zelinsky were able to confirm that Sol's son Hugo Zelinsky became Hugo Eidinger. Born in Tacoma in 1892, Hugo also honored someone without children, gaining an inheritance for his effort. Others simply adjusted the spelling. Rel-atives of Tacoma's Winkleman family used Winkelman and Finkelstein, later anglicized even more to Fenton. David Shafer began life in America as David Schofowitch, anglicized from a Cyrilic spelling.

Occasionally research turns up a name change that surprises even family members. Young Charles Reichenbach was sent to New York by his father in December of 1863 in an effort to protect him from German military service. Unlike many immigrants, he had no

Ctf. 1147,928
Chas. Reichenbach,
Alias Oscar Von Ceder,
I, 1 N. J. Cav.

February 7, 1918.

Mr. John P. Hackman,
    National Soldiers' Home,
        Elizabeth City Co., Va.

Sir:

The correct name of the above designated soldier is Charles Reichenbach. He claims to have landed in this country from Germany some time in December 1863, and shortly thereafter went to Newark, N. J., where he remained until February 28, 1864, when he went to Trenton, N. J., and enlisted under the name of Oscar Von Ceder, as a recruit, and was assigned to Co. I, 1st N. J. Cav.

He was about 22 years of age at the time of his enlistment and gave his occupation as clerk, although he says he has not been employed in such occupation after his arrival in this country.

He was forwarded to his regiment from Trenton, N. J., at the same time you were.

Will you please advise this Bureau whether you have any recollection of Oscar Von Ceder as a member of the 1st New Jersey Cavalry, and whether you know what became of him, or furnish the name of any person who is likely to have knowledge of him? Any other information in regard to Von Ceder that you may be able to supply will be appreciated.

Please endorse your reply on the back of this letter and return it in the inclosed envelope without postage.

Respectfully,

AKM/omr

Commissioner.

Pension inquiry letter regarding
Charles Reichenbach, alias Oscar Von Ceder

Goldstein opened in Olympia in 1879. The firm soon became Toklas and Kaufman, with partners Moses G. Kaufman and Nathan G. Kaufman. Moses Kaufman's five children also used the middle initial "G" – unusual for the time period. Ferdinand Toklas, the father of the now-famous Alice B. Toklas, was born in Kempen, (now Kepno) Poland. Birth records from Kempen revealed that the Kaufman brothers had married Ferdinand Toklas's sisters, Louisa and Hulda. Surprisingly, Moses G. Kaufman was born Moses Kaufman Gallewski, brother to Nathan Gallewski. Upon coming to the United States Moses simply switched his middle name and his surname. Moses' brother Nathan also adopted the Kaufman surname. To further confuse matters, the Toklas family opened their Tacoma store in 1884 in partnership with the unrelated, German-born Meyer Kaufman.

Prayer book inscribed to Hulda Gallewski overwritten Kaufman, born Toklas

Other extended Kaufman and Berliner family members moved to Guatemala in the 1890s. There Julius, Arthur and Max became Julio, Arturo and Maximo. German-born Gustave Adolph Danziger returned from a diplomatic appointment in Spain bearing the moniker Adolphe Danziger deCastro.

And of course, Jewish actors and actresses often took anglicized stage names. David Germanus' son Harry performed in vaudeville as Harry J. Parker. Archie Ash's nephew Max Henry Aronson took the name Gilbert M. Anderson and was known as the first film cowboy, Broncho Billy.

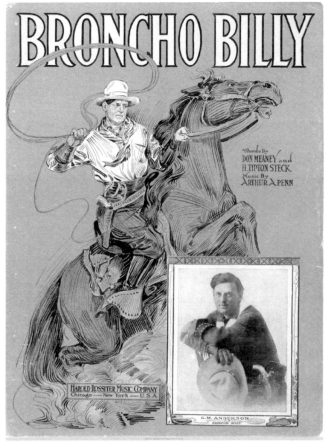

G M Anderson as Broncho Billy c.1914

In summary, the first generation of Tacoma's Jewish pioneers grew with the city of Tacoma – from its infancy in Steilacoom, through its brash and arrogant teenage years as the railroad terminus. They were part of the maturity of the building boom of the 1880s, helping to establish a thriving mercantile district on Pacific Avenue. And Tacoma's Jewish pioneers suffered the sudden retirement caused by the 1893 banking panic. Yet, the organizations they created – a cemetery association, a sisterhood of Jewish women, and a vibrant congregation – continue to the present day.

So now, on to the names...

Abrams Siblings

Isaac Abrams (1835–1913) and his wife Esther (1836–1928) had eight children, the last five in San Francisco. All five of their daughters found their way to Tacoma. Eva married Solomon Rogers in 1886 and started the northward migration. Millie (1868–1918) married Harry Maurice Stary (1850–1944) in Tacoma in 1892. She divorced and married Maurice Marks in Seattle in 1902. Lizzie married Bene Benjamin in 1898. Sarah married Joseph Kaufman in Tacoma in 1895. Celia married David Shafer in Tacoma in 1901. (See spouses' biographies.) Several of their brothers briefly worked in Tacoma and Seattle. Nearly all operated clothing stores. Their parents moved to Seattle around 1897.

Ferdinand and Simon Ackerman

Ferdinand (1862–1940) and Simon (1866–1938) were born in Ligonier, Indiana, the two eldest sons of Isaac and Harriet Ackerman. They operated a saloon in Tacoma from 1890–1892, along with other liquor merchants from Ligonier. (A town once known for its thriving Jewish community, now defunct.) They returned to Indiana and married sisters Belle and Hattie Schloss, in two of many marriages between the Ackerman and Schloss families.

Julius and Augusta Adler

JULIUS ADLER.

Atlanta Constitution December 1895

Julius Adler (1859–1905) was a German composer and band leader who arrived in Tacoma in 1898. For several years he conducted the Tacoma Military Band, frequently composing and donating marches for community fundrais-

ing events. In 1901 the band members voted to change their name to Adler's Band in his honor. The only sources of income for the band (and the conductor's salary of $100 per month) were concert admissions and season subscriptions. By necessity Julius performed and published quite frequently.

His wife Augusta Brown (1874–1956) was one of Philip Brown's thirteen children, from Marysville, California. While in Tacoma Augusta was active in the Jewish ladies' groups and successfully filed for three patents – one for a folding stool to be used at outdoor events. After her husband's 1905 death in San Francisco she married Thomas Murphy. The couple likely had no children.

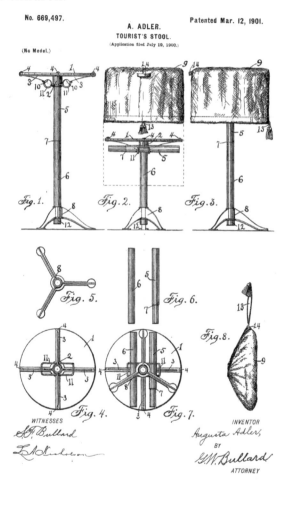

August Adler's 1901 folding stool patent

Samuel Andre Andrews

The eldest of ten children born in Chicago to Andre (1838–1901) and Josephine (1845–1915) Andrews, Sam Andrews (1864–1940) worked in his father's loan and pawn business before coming to Tacoma. (That was conveniently around the time his father was released from Joliet Penitentiary after serving a four-year sentence for receiving stolen property.) Sam operated several stores with his father and younger brother Jake in the early 1890s, including the Chicago Loan, Uncle Sam's Pawn, and the Andrews Collateral Bank. He also invested with Old Town's Meyer Kaufman. Sam survived the 1893 banking panic and was one of several merchants who loaned money to the city to help meet interest payments during 1896. Within a decade he was able to advance his company to mainly jewelry, along with other interests

Sam's first wife Hattie Summerfield (c.1867–1896) was active in Jewish clubs and fundraising events and attended the 1893 fair in Chicago. A year after Hattie's death Sam married Meyer Kaufman's daughter Carrie. She, too was active in Jewish circles, serving several terms as treasurer of the Ladies' Judith Montefiore Society and later as president. In 1909 Sam and Carrie built a two–story brick building at 1109–1111 A Street. One of the bricks on the front of the building still bears their stamped initials – SAA and CKA. Carrie died childless in 1917.

Sam briefly retired, then married Valerie J. Lewitus (1893–1974) in New York. They were married May 15, 1918, at the Hotel Astor by Rabbi Stephen Wise. Sam, Valerie, and her sister Stephanie opened Andrews Women's Apparel in Tacoma in 1920. The store was located for many years at 943 Broadway, and later at the Tacoma Mall, with a second store in Lakewood. Valerie was also active in the Judith Montefiore Society, serving as president in 1920. She gave Sam a son, Sam Andrews, Jr., in 1923. At the time Sam was 59 and Valerie was 29, while Sam's daughter from his first marriage, Freda Andrews Houston (1886–1959) was 37 and had two children.

Andrews Fashions, April 15, 1930
Tacoma Public Library Boland B-22411

During the early 1920s Sam was active in the construction of Tacoma's new synagogue on the corner of North 4th and J, stepping in as chairman of the building committee when David Hoffman resigned. Board meeting minutes indicate that Sam made a large donation to the building fund for two memorial windows in honor of his second wife and her parents. Others followed suit, and eventually nine large stained glass windows were created. Sam survived a broken shoulder, appendicitis, and the loss of two wives, in addition to repeated burglaries and thefts. He helped build not one, but two synagogue buildings in Tacoma. His son Sam Jr. had no surviving children.

John Ascher/Asher

John Ascher/Asher (c.1858–1901) first appeared in Washington in 1887, living in Garfield County in Eastern Washington, along with Abraham Hockwald. Both came to Tacoma around 1888, and John lived in Hockwald's Globe boarding house. John worked as a clerk for a variety of Jewish merchants, boldly facing creditors for Mentheim Cohn in 1893. Later he worked for Isaac Altman and Joseph Cheim. In 1898 John briefly joined with Lewis Levy and others in a Klondike transportation venture. He became ill in the winter of 1900 and died in 1901. Jette Ascher Zelinsky and Jennie Ascher Rammelsberg were likely his sisters.

Archie and Rose Ash

Archie Ash (1863–1940) was the youngest child of noted New York Orthodox Rabbi Abraham Joseph Ash. Rabbi Ash founded Beth Hamidrash Hagadol synagogue in New York in 1859 and prospered selling hoop skirts during the Civil War. Rabbi Ash's 1887 obituary mentioned that all five of his children were in the West.

Archie followed his sister Esther and her husband Henry Aronson to Arkansas, where he married Rose Jacobs (1867–1943) in 1884. (Three years earlier Rose's sister Lena had married Max Broh, also in Arkansas.) Typical of many families at the time, their three daughters were born in three different states – Arkansas in 1885, Missouri in 1887, and Washington in 1893.

Rose Ash and daughters
Courtesy of Ann Fuller

S. Ash is one of the wealthiest men in the city, and owns saloons, pawnshops and brick buildings. He always keeps a lot of diamonds and other jewelry at his home, and it was this the robbers evidently sought and found." Archie diversified, purchasing the Savoy Hotel in Missoula, Montana, then creating positions for his new son-in-law in the Kirkwood Distillery and an insurance agency. Around 1911 the family moved to Medford, Oregon, where they lived until their daughter's death in 1919. As did many Northwest Jewish families, they retired to San Francisco. In 1925 Archie survived a skull fracture he suffered when he was run down by a truck during a visit to Seattle, partially attributed to his deafness. The couple had no grandchildren.

Joseph and Lucy Bachrach

Joseph and Lucie Bachrach, 1920 Passport Application

German-born Joseph Bachrach (1854–1930) got his start in Tacoma working as a clerk for the Gross brothers from 1889 until 1896. In April of 1895 he married Lucy Feist (1872–1961) and in 1897 joined in the clothing business of her brother Theo. Unlike many others, the two men successfully remained in business together in Tacoma the rest of their lives. Lucy Bachrach was active in Jewish groups, serving as treasurer of the Judith Montefiore Society for more than a decade. The Bachrach family made several extended visits to family in Europe, and their daughter, Irma, received musical training in Switzerland. Their son, Herbert, (1895–1981) married Helen Barnett and had a daughter, Ann. Their daughter, Irma, (1898–1985) married Melvin Morris (1893–1966) and had two children – James and Lucie.

Archie initially worked as a pawn and loan broker. After a brief time in Seattle, he arrived in Tacoma in 1889. He partnered with Isaac Dornberg, his brother-in-law Max Broh, and several others. His brother Matthew worked for him as a clerk for several years and sold cigars with Marcus Moses.

Rose and Archie were both active in the Jewish community, serving as officers in the fledgling organizations and attending many social functions. When the congregation was first organized in 1892, Archie's was one of three names attached to the call to meet and served as the first treasurer.

In 1894 Archie became embroiled in the financial manipulations of Portland's Prager Brothers, whose Tacoma store was managed by Solomon Jacoby. Archie was appointed trustee in January and began selling merchandise to cover outstanding debts for the firm. By April the Pragers had worked out their financial difficulties, with the Tacoma firm emerging as Jacoby & Ash. In June Rose's younger sister, Pauline Jacobs, married Sidney Prager. However, in January of 1895 the Portland Prager Brothers failed again. A hasty mortgage to Rose's father, Moses Jacobs, was seen by the receiver as an effort to defraud creditors. At the end of March Mr. Jacobs was able to purchase the entire Tacoma inventory for just $30,000, a fraction of its value.

The following year the Ash family moved to Spokane, partnering with Michael Ball in Ash and Company and the Washington Loan Office. An article in the *Spokane Press,* November 8, 1907, described a burglary of their home. "Archie

Michael and Carrie Ball

Michael Ball
Courtesy of Ed Ball

Michael Ball (1853–1937) was born in Wreschen, Poland, the son of Hyman Ball and his second wife Ernestine Zorek. Michael immigrated as a young man and lived in Warren, Pennsylvania, along with Sol Cohn (brother of Mary Cohn, who had married Michael's half-brother George Ball) in 1880.

In about 1882 in New York Michael married Carrie Henschel, (c.1861–1911) eldest child of Henry and Minnie Henschel. Their son Bertram was born in New York in 1884. Their daughter Mabel was born in Tacoma in May of 1889, exactly nine months after their arrival in Washington. Carrie was a leader in Jewish groups, serving as president of the Montefiore Society for four years, managing the school, and serving in other capacities. She also crossed Jewish lines and participated in other Tacoma women's groups, including the Home Industry Club.

Michael worked as bookkeeper for a third Cohn sibling, Mentheim. Carrie was part owner of the business, as Michael was still sorting out legal entanglements from a prior business failure in Rochester, N.Y. The team operated two locations in Tacoma, in addition to running stores in Hoquiam and North Yakima. They survived several years after the 1893 banking panic, but by November of 1895 the creditors were lining up. Isaac Altman of New York bought the inventory of all four stores for 65 percent of their value, then hired Michael Ball to stay on as manager.

Michael and Carrie moved to Spokane in the fall of 1896. Michael managed a pawnshop for Archie Ash. Over the next decade he prospered, operating several clothing stores in addition to several loan and jewelry firms. Carrie again was an active worker in Jewish circles, serving as president of the Ladies' Jewish Aid Society for 16 years. However, she died in 1911, followed by her daughter in 1913 and her son in 1935, both unmarried.

In 1916 Michael married Carrie's widowed sister, Anna Henschel Erlich (1869–1941). The couple eventually joined Anna's daughter Hazel Erlich Cohn in Youngstown, Ohio.

Rosalie Barlow

Rosalie Quinn Barlow died in Tacoma on June 26, 1892, at the age of 45. A widow, she had operated an 11-room hotel called the Chicago Flats for the previous five years. Half of Rosalie's estate was used to defray the return of her 14-year-old niece Emma Schmidt to the girl's parents in Frankfurt, Germany. Rosalie's nephew, Edward Aldrich, received the remainder of the estate, including a property in Colville, Washington.

Mrs. Barnett

Mrs. Barnett joined the Judith Montefiore Society in March of 1898 and resigned in February of 1899.

Roman Bash

Roman Herbert Bash (1878–1928) lived in Tacoma just one year, from 1898 to 1899. The fourth of five surviving children born to Henry and Eleanora Bash, Roman worked for Morris Gross, who had married his sister Mollie Bash in 1894. Roman returned to New York in 1899 just before the sudden death of his father. He and his wife, Florence, had two children – Emma and Henry.

Julius and Frances Basinski

Julius Basinski (1844–1926) was the only one of Tacoma's early Jewish merchants known to record his adventures, writing several pages of "Reminessences" in December of 1912. Born in

Pakoscz, Germany, in 1844, Julius immigrated to New York in 1866, where he worked for his uncle Benjamin for four years.

Basinski "Reminessences"
Special Collections & University Archives, University of Oregon Libraries

Then he set off to try his luck in the developing territory of Montana. After two years selling cigars, fruit and candy in Radersburg and Keatingville, Julius was joined by his brothers Simon (1850–1933) and Samuel (1853–?). They operated a store in Bozeman, and were among the first to settle near Yellowstone, following military troops into Fort Keogh to open a store in Miles City. In 1882 they built a large brick store in Bozeman, where their safe doubled as an unofficial town bank.

In 1884 Julius married Frances Bruce (1861–1958) while on a buying trip to New York. Her English mother, Isabelle Lyons Bruce (1836–1905) came with the marriage. Frances gave birth to two children while in Montana – Alma in 1885 and Bruce in 1888. Seeking better opportunities for their children, the extended Basinski family headed to Tacoma in January of 1894. They incorporated the Tacoma Bazaar, a business name formerly used by Adolph Packsher and several others.

The Basinskis arrived at a perfect time to fill in the gaps left by the failing economy. First Julius moved into 920 Pacific, a building owned by David Levin and recently vacated by the Isaacs Brothers. When the Gross brothers split up David Gross took the store at 920 Pacific and Julius Basinski moved to 910 Pacific. Then Morris Gross lost his large building on Ninth and C, and the two traded locations, Julius occupying a portion of the massive space.

Samuel briefly operated his own stationery store and Simon sold a variety of items at "The Ark." Both left Tacoma before 1899. Samuel lived most of the rest of his life in Republic, Washington, and Simon moved to New York and married a Lyons relative.

Frances and her mother Isabelle were active in social circles – both Jewish and community. In 1900 Alma was one of five members of Beth Israel's confirmation class, and in 1903 Frances was one of the organizers of the Council of Jewish Women. Isabelle died in 1905 and was buried in Tacoma's Home of Peace Cemetery. Julius and Frances continued as officers of the congregation and Judith Montefiore Society.

In 1909 the Basinskis left Tacoma and tried operating an apple orchard in Wenatchee, the Famous Fruit Orchard. A decade later they retired to Portland, Oregon. Their son Bruce (1888–1970) stayed in Portland with his wife, Vivian Demyrtle (1899–1988). Their daughter Alma (1885–1971) lived in Albany with her husband, Albert Senders (1876–1965).

Zella Belsher

Zella Belsher was noted by historian Herbert Hunt as Tacoma's first woman telephone operator, described as "a dark-haired buxom little Jewish miss."

Bene and Lizzie Benjamin

Bene Benjamin (1867–1959) married Lizzie Abrams (1871–1937) in Seattle in 1898. They soon joined her sisters in Tacoma and operated a clothing store at 809 Pacific, in the heart of Whiskey Row. A brief partnership with Joseph Kaufman, operating the Pacific Bargain House, failed within a few months. Later the Benjamins operated a variety of shoe and clothing stores. Their four sons were born in Tacoma between 1902 and 1910.

Henry and Regina Berliner

Henry Berliner (1859–1921) arrived in Tacoma from Seattle in November of 1884 in company with Meyer Kaufman and Zadik Peritz as part of the firm of Peritz and Company, selling a wide variety of dry goods. (See page 33 for Auerbach connections.) Within a year Peritz returned to Germany and the firm became Kaufman & Berliner. They were located on the corner of 13th and Pacific and called themselves "The People's Bargain Store." Henry was active in the Tacoma Turn Verein and the Germania Club, as well as the volunteer Commencement Hook and Ladder team.

The store's popularity was boosted by Meyer Kaufman's involvement with the Chinese Expulsion in the fall of 1885. By the summer of 1886 Kaufman & Berliner moved to 11th and Pacific, (later identified as 948 Pacific) working their way closer to the center of the business district. Henry's sister Anna Berliner joined him in Tacoma in September, traveling from Germany with the visiting Jennie Auerbach Singerman and family. Within a year Anna married Steilacoom's David Magnus.

J. Bernhard.

SPRING
1892

WEDNESDAY March 16,

WILL SHOW SEVERAL

SHIPMENTS

OF

Imported Novelties

Comprising many new designs, New and Choice Dress Fabrics and Dress Trimmings will be shown and exclusiveness of style assured.

Tacoma Daily Ledger March 19, 1892

ANOTHER LINE BY EXPRESS.

ELEGANT EMBROIDERED ROBES!

In White and Cream.

The latest from New York, now on exhibition at

KAUFMAN & BERLINER'S,

THE PEOPLE'S BARGAIN STORE,

Corner Pacific Avenue and Thirteenth Street, opp. Central Hotel.

Tacoma Daily Ledger June 8, 1886

Henry traveled frequently for the firm, visiting cities all around the Sound. In May of 1888 he became engaged to Miss Regina Stenger (1866–1940) of Spokane. A few months later he helped organize Tacoma's Jewish cemetery, just a few weeks before his October wedding. That same week Regina's sister Mollie married Tacoma's David Philip Lewis and the two young couples moved into a double house. (The Stenger family was from Kempen, as were Auerbach and Peritz.)

In February of 1890 Henry and Regina's four-month-old son Isadore died and was buried at the new cemetery. In May Regina helped form the Ladies' Judith Montefiore Society, and in June Henry was an organizer of Tacoma's lodge of the B'nai B'rith. Both served in leadership roles.

Meyer Kaufman died in February of 1891 and the business began crumbling. The firm had over $70,000 in debts, about one-third of them to Seattle's Paul Singerman. Singerman bought the remaining stock, paid off the creditors at 35 percent, and closed the store. Henry moved to Portland, where he worked as a bookkeeper for his brother-in-law, DP Lewis, a barber, for several years.

By 1897 the Berliners had rejoined the Toklas & Singerman group in Seattle, remaining for a decade. In 1906 Henry moved to Aberdeen and operated a renewed Kaufman and Berliner for two years, this time with Nathan Gallewski Kaufman. Then Henry moved to Seattle and joined in the Stenger and Berliner Barber Supply, an industry his sons Max (1891–1959) and Arthur (1897–1966) would continue.

Max and Arthur Berliner

When Isadore Berliner's widow Minna came to the U.S. in 1883, she brought her sons Max and Arthur with her, aged 8 and 9. Within a year Minna married Meyer Kaufman and moved to Tacoma, along with Isadore's brother, Henry Berliner. The boys grew up in Tacoma, as did their cousin Nathan Peritz, working for the Kaufman & Berliner store and later for Louis Wallerstein. After Meyer Kaufman's death they moved to Seattle with Minna.

However, they soon followed their cousin Nathan in moving to Guatemala – Max in June of 1897 and Arthur in October of 1898. Both Max and Arthur filed WWI draft registrations from Quetzaltenango. Arthur stated he had a wife and three children, and Max had a wife and an 8-year-old child. Their half sister Martha Kaufman Koenigsberger joined them in Guatemala, where they lived as Arturo and Maximo.

Jacob and Fannie Bernhard

Jacob Bernhard (1861–1931) was born in Petaluma, California, just a few years after the town was incorporated. In 1887 he married Fannie Lincoln (1866–1950) in San Francisco. Jacob started in business in Tacoma in August of 1888 at 903 Pacific, opening a branch of Chester Cleary's Seattle dry goods firm. By March of 1889 he was able to move across the street to 934 Pacific. (The dry goods dealers were mostly on the west side, while banks and realtors were on the east side.) In June the Seattle store was destroyed by fire. Losses were first reported at $200,000, later $125,000 with $40,000 insured.

In the fall of 1889 Jacob was joined by his young cousin, Theo Feist. Jacob's brother Joseph also joined him – living with the family and clerking at the store. Fannie joined the Judith Montefiore Society, and the couple attended several social events hosted by Jewish families.

During 1890 the store suffered several floods from broken water pipes on the floor above. Perhaps inspired by the Gross Brothers' elaborate window displays, in December of 1890 the store's windows featured a facsimile of the storefront, created from spool cotton. Jacob bought out Chester Cleary's interest in March of 1891 and the partnership was dissolved. Cleary died suddenly in Seattle on April 17. Probate records show that the value of the Seattle store stock was about $125,000 and the firm employed 35 clerks.

The Bernhard firm gained prominence, evident by increased newspaper ads (next to the Gross Brothers') and mentions of regular buying trips to New York. In the fall of 1891 Jacob received a settlement for damages caused by broken pipes the previous year, then moved up the street to 916–918 Pacific. Part of his space was occupied by Miss Cunningham's new millinery store. (She and her clerk Irma Bachrach had previously worked for the Gross Brothers.)

However, on July 4, 1893, the new store was also flooded by water from overhead. The damage was undetected because of the holiday, and ruined the most expensive velvets and silks. Jacob's younger brother Edward Bernhard (1876–1940) joined the household. In August their home was broken into and their silver was stolen. The thief was arrested and convicted within a week and the silver was returned.

Jacob hosted a grand spring opening in 1894, but by the end of March was bankrupt. He sold merchandise and fixtures to cover $1850 in back rent, then sold the remaining merchandise at auction. As did many other families, he returned to San Francisco where he later sold clothing, real estate and insurance. The couple had three children, Rhea (1892–1967), John Lincoln (1899–1990) and Lincoln Milton (1905–1987). Apparently none of the couple's children married.

Julius and Mina Bilak

Julius Bilak was born in Pleschen, Germany, on November 20, 1871, the son of Herman Bilak and the eldest Auerbach sister, Anna. As a teen Julius came to the U.S. aboard the same ship as the Stenger family. The Stengers went to Spokane, while Julius came directly to Tacoma. He lived with his aunt Minna Auerbach Kaufman and worked at the Kaufman & Berliner store. After Meyer's death in 1891 Julius worked briefly for Jacob Bernhard and became a naturalized citizen in Tacoma in 1893.

Julius then joined Nathan Peritz in Guatemala, although his passport applications over the next several decades continued to list his permanent address as Tacoma. In 1897 Julius (now Julio) married his first cousin, Mina Peritz, sister of Nathan and daughter of Zadik, in the first Jewish wedding celebrated in Guatemala. Their sons Maximoto and Leon were born in Guatemala in 1898 and 1903. Leon became known worldwide as an expert stamp collector, largely through his role as the deputy minister of the Guatemala post office.

Julius operated a stationery store in Guatemala, while maintaining a German exporting branch. He and his family were able to return to Germany regularly, several times traveling with Martha Kaufman Koenigsberger. Frank Bajohr's book on the "Aryanization" of Hamburg includes the firm of Julius Bilak, exporters of food, clothing, haberdashery and paper goods, among the list of Jewish businesses that were liquidated between 1938 and 1939.

Morris and A. Jacob Bloom

A. Jacob Bloom (1853–1906) and his wife Alice (born about 1863) came to the U.S. from Hungary in November of 1886. In the summer of 1889 Jacob applied for a transfer of a liquor license in Tacoma for the Kentucky Liquor Company, along with fellow Hungarian Joseph Hall. The following year Jacob's brother, Morris (1850–1919), and his family joined them in Tacoma, with Morris working as bookkeeper for the firm.

Both Alice and Morris' wife Jennie (1860–1949) were leaders in the Jewish community – serving as officers of the Judith Montefiore Society and hosting numerous social events and gatherings. Morris Bloom frequently led a portion of the holiday services. By 1895 Morris had moved to the business of pawnbroker, adapting to the changing economy, and eventually growing into jewelry. Jacob reorganized the liquor company with Joseph Hall and new partners Joseph and Meyer Jacob, calling the new firm the New West Liquor Company.

In September of 1896 Jacob Bloom set off for Skagway (ahead of the gold rush) where he operated the Monogram Saloon for a decade with Emil Korach until Jacob's death in 1906. Jacob's wife Alice occasionally was mentioned in Tacoma through at least 1903.

Morris had two sons – Nathan and Henry – from his first marriage, and two daughters – Emma and Ella – from his second. In 1903 Nathan opened his own loan business in the new Luzon Building on the corner of 13th and Pacific. In March of 1906 Ella married Samuel G. Kaufman, cousin of Alice B. Toklas, and moved to Aberdeen. Emma married Henry Alexander in 1913 and he continued in the jewelry business. The siblings eventually moved to New York, San Francisco, and Salt Lake City.

Albert Braham

Albert lived in Tacoma in 1891, rooming with Martin Rosenbaum and working for Sol Rogers as a bookkeeper. He attended the organizational meeting of the Tacoma Relief Society.

Max and Lena Broh

Max Broh (1855–1907) emigrated to the U.S. from Prussia around 1870 and in 1876 lived in Prescott, Arkansas. In 1880 Max worked for Thompson and Jacobs in Lewisville, Arkansas, and lived with the Moses Jacobs family. In March of 1881 Max married Moses' daughter Lena (1865–1919). Lena's son Harry was born nine months later. (Lena's sister Rose married Archie Ash in 1884.) The Broh family lived in Magnolia, Arkansas in 1885 and 1887, where Max was active in the Knights of Pythias. Their daughter Sadye was born in Arkansas in March of 1887. (Chicago's Isadore Broh, 1859–1925, also named two children Harry and Sadie and sold wholesale cigars.)

Max Broh   Lena Broh.
Courtesy of Ann Fuller

Max sold dry goods in St. Louis in 1889 before coming to Tacoma. He briefly partnered with Archie Ash in the pawn industry. The following year Max joined with Edward Wolf in selling wholesale cigars. Max and Lena were active in the Judith Montefiore Society, the B'nai B'rith, and regularly attended Harmony Club entertainments. Max assisted Rabbi Eisbert in leading holiday services in the fall of 1890. On April 26, 1891, Tacoma's *Daily Ledger* mentioned the "christening" of Max's youngest son (Byron). It was his last mention in Tacoma for a few years. The couple again lived in Tacoma in 1895 when their son Harry, age 13, was confirmed.

Max Broh and his son Byron
Courtesy of Ann Fuller

Harry stayed in Washington, working in Spokane for his uncle, Archie Ash. His parents and sister lived in Chicago until 1906. Then Max returned to Spokane, again partnering with Archie Ash in the loan business. Max died in Spokane in 1907. His daughter Sadye and her husband Clarence Livingston had a son, Clarence Jr., in Chicago in 1913, but he apparently never married. Lena died in Chicago in 1919.

Sadye's brother Harry married Vera Toklas in Spokane in 1909, daughter of Nathan and first cousin of Alice B. Toklas. Harry died in 1923 and Vera married Albert Menist. She had no children from either marriage. Max and Lena's younger son Byron (1891–1954) also had no children, so the Broh line ended.

Herman W. Bryer

Herman Bryer was born in Hungary April 15, 1847, and immigrated to the U.S. in 1865. From 1869 to 1874 he operated a hoop skirt factory, Miller & Bryer, and dry goods store in Titusville, Pennsylvania. He was naturalized in Pennsylvania in 1871, then lived in Denver, Colorado. He arrived in Tacoma in February of 1885 and opened a cigar and fruit stand at 932 Pacific. Like others, he opened a branch location in Puyallup during the fall hops harvest.

As Tacoma boomed in the 1880s Herman began constructing houses, then selling to merchants including Jacob Bernhard and Isaac Pincus. He joined the Home of Peace Cemetery Association in 1889. He also expanded his fruit business into a candy factory, partnering briefly with David Hoffman. By 1893 his candy factory employed 15 people. However, by 1895 he had returned to selling just cigars and fruit. Herman died in Tacoma in December of 1929 but was not buried in the Jewish cemetery.

Isabelle Lyons Bruce

Born in Manchester, England, Isabelle Lyons (1836–1905) immigrated with her parents Lewis and Fanny in 1846, living in Philadelphia in 1850. She married either Robert or Milton Bruce and had two children in Tennessee just before the outbreak of the Civil War. When her daughter Frances married Julius Basinski in New York in 1884 Isabelle moved to Montana with the young couple. A decade later they all moved to Tacoma, where Isabelle took a leadership role in the Jewish community. She died in Tacoma in 1905.

Cheim Brothers

Joseph Cheim (1857–1933) emigrated from Hungary to California in 1871 when he was just a teenager. He worked for a decade in his uncle Joseph Lask's clothing store in Marysville, California. In 1883 Cheim came to Olympia, working in Sam Gottschalk's clothing store, the White House. (One of San Francisco's most prominent stores at the time was the White House.) The following year Joseph purchased Gottschalk's Olympia interest.

In September of 1887 Joseph Cheim married Rose Davis (1867–1951,) the daughter of Jacob W. Davis and Annie Packscher, and a niece of Seraphina Pincus. (Jacob W. Davis was the inventor of the riveted jeans co-patented with Levi Strauss.) They had five children, but only Elsie survived. The couple moved to Tacoma in 1898, where Joseph operated a clothing store for many years at 1136 Pacific. Elsie married Otto Mayer in 1910, moved to San Francisco, and had a son Joseph in 1913. After Joseph's death in 1933 Rose joined her daughter in San Francisco, where she died in 1951.

After Sam Gottschalk sold his Olympia store to Joseph he briefly moved to Tacoma and opened the Great Eastern clothing store, with Joseph's brother Morris Cheim (1864–1944) as manager. In January of 1886 Louis Lask (also an uncle) purchased Gottschalk's Tacoma interest. By August of 1890 Morris Cheim was able to continue the business on his own. In 1896 Morris married Essie Miller (1873–1927.) She served many years as secretary and president of the Judith Montefiore Society. The couple had two children, Herbert and Natalie. Herbert had a *bar mitzvah* at Beth Israel in 1911 and was a part of Tacoma's Jewish community the rest of his life.

George Cheim (1859–1947) joined his brothers in Olympia in 1885 and came to Tacoma a few years later. He sold men's furnishings in Old Tacoma from 1891 to 1893 and by 1896 had opened a clothing store at 819 Pacific. George returned to Europe in 1897, married Theresa Lecker, moved to Hoquiam, and had three children. They, too, moved to San Francisco. *Utica Daily Press,* February 6, 1947, "For years George Cheim, retired San Francisco shoe merchant, had been an invalid, with his wife Theresa, constantly at his side. When he died, at the age of 87, he and his wife, 73, had been married 48 years. 'God's will be done,' said his widow on learning of his death. 'I'll join him now.' Death came to her within a few hours."

Cohen Siblings

David and Amelia Cohen had five children in San Francisco during the 1850s. The eldest three spent time in Tacoma. Isaac Nathan (1857–1926) worked briefly with Louis Wallerstein as a candy salesman during 1884 and 1885, also investing in real estate. Carrie (1855–1942) married Louis Wallerstein in the fall of 1884. (See Wallerstein biography.) Aaron (1852–1924) lived with the Wallerstein family in 1892 and 1893. When the economy failed in 1893 Aaron spent several years sorting out legal entanglements after Wallerstein transferred accounts to his name. Most of the family returned to San Francisco, where in 1895 Isaac Nathan Cohen and Ben Einstein (nephew of Belle Reichenbach) partnered in a clothing renovating business.

SUDDEN RICHES.

How a Clothes Peddler Brought Wealth to a Capitalist.

Gabriel Karsky rang the bell. His business was that of a second hand clothes dealer, and the bell was that of 10 Liberty street, where David Cohen, a capitalist, resided. Karsky kept a little stuffy shop at 335 Sixth street, and often in the pursuit of his calling he took a turn in the fresh air and gathered up old garments to be furbished up as new. Gabriel had often rang the bell at 10 Liberty street, and when he did so this rainy afternoon, about a month ago, and Mrs. Cohen came to the door, she said, pleasantly, "Nothing to sell to-day, Gabriel."

"I have though," said Karsky, drawing a crumpled paper from his pocket: "I've got a Louisville lottery ticket here, and that is a coupon of ticket 73,947, and I want to sell it." Mrs. Cohen, however, would have nothing to do with the coupon. Karsky insisted, and the argument went on, until Mr. Cohen impatiently shouted from the sitting room, "Give the man a dollar, and let him go." The ticket and Mrs. Cohen's dollar changed places, and Gabriel pocketing the piece, went on his way in the quiet contentment of small profits.

On the 16th of February the list of prizes was published in the *Chronicle*, and Mrs. Cohen, looking over it with mild curiosity, saw with amazement that ticket 73,957 had drawn the first capital prize, and that her coupon was worth $15,000. She collected the money through Wells, Fargo & Co.'s Bank, and, remembering the circumstances of her purchase, sent Karsky $100.

Oakland Tribune March 30, 1887

Max and Fanny Cohn

Max Cohn (1852–1919) was born in Gnesen, Germany, and emigrated in 1872. After living in Texas and San Francisco, Max came to Tacoma in 1888. He worked as a cigar maker for Samuel Wolff, a career he would continue throughout his life. In 1889 Max married Sam's sister Fanny Wolff (1864–1947). They had two sons, Leon (1890–1973) and Irwin (1895–1966). The Cohn family briefly lived in Butte, Montana, in 1900 and Spokane in 1903, but returned to Tacoma. After Max's death in 1919 Fanny and her sons moved to Seattle, nearer to her cousin Albert Weinberg.

Mentheim and Frieda Cohn

Mentheim Cohn
Courtesy of Ed Ball

Mentheim Cohn (1848–1897) was born in Flatow, Prussia, and immigrated to the U.S. around 1866, where he became a naturalized citizen. In January of 1872 he returned to Flatow and married. Prussian authorities felt his citizenship was an attempt to avoid military service. Mentheim applied to the U.S. consulate in Berlin and was issued an American passport. He and his wife Frieda returned to the U.S., living in Buffalo, New York.

Mentheim arrived in Tacoma in the summer of 1888, just as Tacoma was booming. He added an additional clothing store each year, partnering with Michael Ball's wife Carrie. In 1891 Mentheim purchased the bankrupt stock of Louis Moses. Soon he ran four stores in Tacoma plus two in Hoquiam and North Yakima, operating under the names of Globe Clothing, Workingmen's Clothes, New York Clothing House, White Front, and M. Cohn's Famous Clothing.

Mentheim and his wife entertained frequently, with published guest lists often including 25–35 names from Tacoma's growing Jewish community. Both were active organizers of Jewish organizations, typically serving as president or vice president.

The Panic of 1893 flooded the already-saturated luxury clothing market with discounted merchandise. Mentheim lasted until November of 1895. His East Coast creditors claimed he had misrepresented the financial stability of his firm while on his summer buying trip. Several petitioned for the return of their merchandise. David Levin was given the difficult task of serving as court-appointed receiver, but survived with his reputation intact. Mentheim was not as fortunate. His court testimony provided news fodder for weeks on end, including accounts of lavish daily spending and heavy losses at poker games while traveling back east.

In November of 1895 Mentheim's largest creditor (and previous Buffalo employer) Isaac Altman purchased his stock and mortgages, paid off creditors at twenty-five cents on the dollar, and hired Michael Ball to continue the business of selling off the merchandise. Mentheim joined his brother in Pennsylvania in the spring of 1897, but died quite suddenly a few months later. Isaac Altman also failed in Buffalo and died in 1901, leaving his wife Jennie and children "paupers as to property, though millionaires as to debts," (American Bankruptcy Reports, Volume 1) even though at one time his father Jacob's company had employed 800 people.

Samuel G. Cohn

Samuel Cohn was born in New York around 1870 and first appeared in Tacoma's city directories in 1891. He worked as a clerk for the tailoring firm of Hirsch & Frank and later for the Gross Brothers. He was one of seven young men who formed the Stag Seven club in 1892 and lived with several of his friends at the Harmony Club. Around 1900 Sam briefly operated the Oxford Saloon at 1113 Pacific. Over the next several decades he worked as a bartender at various Tacoma locations.

Julius and Pauline Coleman

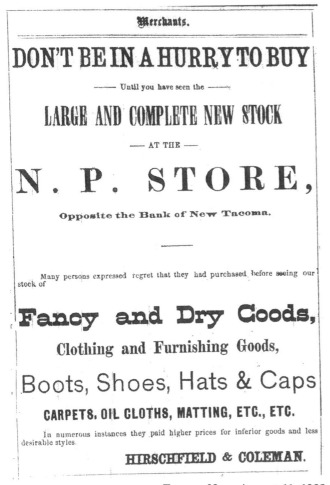

Merchants.

DON'T BE IN A HURRY TO BUY

—— Until you have seen the ——

LARGE AND COMPLETE NEW STOCK

—— AT THE ——

N. P. STORE,

Opposite the Bank of New Tacoma.

Many persons expressed regret that they had purchased before seeing our stock of

Fancy and Dry Goods,

Clothing and Furnishing Goods,

Boots, Shoes, Hats & Caps

CARPETS, OIL CLOTHS, MATTING, ETC., ETC.

In numerous instances they paid higher prices for inferior goods and less desirable styles.

HIRSCHFIELD & COLEMAN.

Tacoma News August 11, 1882

Julius Coleman (1832–1886) was naturalized in San Francisco in 1855. He lived in Calaveras County in 1860 and Amador County in 1870. He married Pauline Gursen (c.1853–1939) around 1872 and had four children by 1880. After a fire in February of 1882 wiped out his store, Julius tried his luck in the Pacific Northwest, partnering with Louis Hirshfeld in operating the N.P. Store in New Tacoma. His prospects only got worse.

His two oldest sons died in June of 1882, and his daughter fell down a flight of stairs and was crippled. The 16 inches of snow that fell in February of 1884 collapsed the front awning of his store, shattering the front glass. By March of 1884 his creditors were nipping at his heels. Hirshfeld moved back to California and Coleman briefly tried running a furniture store in Port Townsend.

Julius and family returned to Tacoma in October of 1885, but his health was failing. He died on February 28, 1886, and was buried in the Jewish cemetery in Olympia near his sons. His widow Pauline scrambled to separate their home and personal possessions from the indebted estate. She moved to San Francisco, where her thirteen-year-old daughter Selma died in 1891. Pauline died in San Francisco in 1939. Her two remaining sons, Arthur and Gustave, stayed in the San Francisco area until their deaths in the 1950s. Gustave was buried in Holy Cross Catholic Cemetery.

Gustave Adolph Danziger (aka Gustavus Adolphe Danziger DeCastro)

Adolph Danziger

In September of 1893 Tacoma's new synagogue was dedicated at *Rosh Hashanah* by Dr. Adolph Danziger, a noted Jewish divine from San Francisco. The *San Francisco Chronicle*, on January 18, 1900, gave a more complete description. "Danziger is a man of varied attainments, having been at various times rabbi, dentist, attorney, teacher in a Mission Sunday-school, physician, musical critic, author, writer and poet. He has also at other times been engaged in pugilistic affrays."

Born in Poland in 1859, Danziger came to the U.S. in the 1880s. The *Oakland Tribune* carried an ad for his new dental firm on September 18, 1886. Within two years he had moved on to the literary field, hiring Ambrose Bierce to edit his stories and improve his newfound English. He began giving public lectures and speaking at the Theosophical Society. He was also active in the Pacific Hebrew Orphan Asylum, a group supported in a small way by Tacoma's Judith Montefiore Society.

In the spring of 1888 Danziger married Bertha Levy (c.1857–1929) and the couple had two children – Beatrice (1891–1974) and Nathan (1894–1965). After his trip to Tacoma in 1893 he served as rabbi in San Jose, where he passed the bar and began working as an attorney. Danziger led holiday services in San Bernardino in 1895 and in Santa Cruz in 1896 and 1897. Much like the *Music Man's* Professor Harold Hill, in both cities he urged the Jewish citizens to work to build a synagogue.

According to his 1915 divorce proceedings, he moved to New York and in 1902 married again, adding bigamist to his list of professions. In 1903 Danziger received a diplomatic appointment from President Roosevelt to serve as Vice-Consul at Madrid, Spain, and took his second "wife" with him. *Oakland Tribune,* April 17, 1903, "The new vice consul is the first Jew to be sent to Spain in the diplomatic capacity since the expulsion of the Hebrews from the Castilian realm in 1492." When he returned to San Francisco in 1915 his wife Bertha filed for divorce, seeking a portion of his pension.

He began using the name Adolphe Danziger de Castro, traveling to Mexico in the 1920s and interviewing Pancho Francisco Villa. He continued actively writing and publishing until his death in Los Angeles in 1959, just eight months before his 100th birthday.

Morris and Bertha Dobrin

Morris Dobrin was born in Zamter, Germany, around 1830. He married Bertha Lichtenstein (c.1832–1912) in the 1850s and joined her relatives in Richmond, Virginia, where he sold dry goods. His store was located near the slave market, and on December 2, 1856, a slave stole clothing from Morris' window. Morris gave chase and ended up in the mud under the Negro, who was promptly sentenced to receive 39 stripes. *(Richmond Dispatch,* December 4 and 9, 1856.)

Their sons Joseph and Mark were born in Richmond in 1856 and 1857, but in 1858 the store's merchandise was sold at auction. Morris worked briefly for his brother-in-law, then moved to California. Three more children were born in the San Francisco area before the couple moved to Victoria, British Columbia, where they had two more children in 1864 and 1865.

Morris was active in the Victoria Jewish community, supervising the baking of Passover *matza* in March of 1869. However, two years later he fled back to the U.S. ahead of creditors and

legal challenges, settling in Olympia, Washington. There he worked as a tailor, mending and repairing clothing. His sons worked as printers and his wife sold fruits and confections. His eldest daughter, Celia, died of typhoid fever the following summer at age 13. Hers was the first burial in the Jewish portion of the cemetery, officially formed two years later.

During the railroad excitement in the summer of 1873, Dobrin briefly opened a store in a canvas building on Second Street in Tacoma before returning to Olympia. His legal challenges continued, as he was repeatedly tried for selling merchandise without proper licenses, overdue debts, and overpricing. His sons' "auction house" was closed as a thinly-disguised gambling house. Dobrin's wife left him, joining her children as they married and moved to California.

Morris spent the last two years of his life in Tacoma, before his death in 1891. His family managed to give the Olympia cemetery association several dollars to cover expenses. However, they did erect two tombstones for him – one in Olympia, and another in California with his wife Bertha. Their seven children provided four grandchildren, but no great-grandchildren.

Simon and Amelia Donau

Simon Donau and Amelia Donau
Courtesy of Bettina Lyons

Simon Donau (1833–1912) was born in Baden, Germany. He was naturalized in Trenton, New Jersey in 1858, where he operated Donau and Kahnweiler, a wine and liquor firm. That same year he married Amelia Sanger (1841–1913). The couple had two children in New Jersey, followed by four more in New York.

In the spring of 1866 Simon Donau, a distiller in New York, was arrested as part of an alleged distillery fraud, along with Jacob Donau, John Frank Kahnweiler, and others. Mentions of the case were carried in several newspapers across the country. The distillery men were accused of "purchasing" a government stamp from an inspector, which was then used to mark barrels as if they had been inspected and the taxes paid. Simon was discharged and not prosecuted.

The Donau family made an extended visit to Germany, where their son Hugo was born in 1870. Hugo stayed with his grandparents in Germany for over a decade, while the Donau family returned to New York. Around 1880 they moved to Denver, Colorado. There Simon ran the Lion Brewing Company, then the Denver Butter Company and later the Swiss Dairy Company. In 1883 their attractive daughter, Bettina, married millionaire Albert Steinfeld of Tucson, Arizona, in what the *Denver Republican* on February 16 described as "one of the most elaborate hymenial occasions ever celebrated in the city."

By the fall of 1889 Simon was living in Tacoma where he incorporated the Donau Brewing Company. The large complex at the head of the bay had a variety of buildings, its own wells and ice house, and initially employed 90 men. His wife and children reigned in the kingdom of Tacoma's social life. Florence, Alice, Alfred and Hugo all participated in Harmony Club events. Hugo was a member of the Stag Seven men's club and the Tacoma Commercial Club. Their daughter Virginia also joined them, after a brief marriage to Adolph Steinman. (See Virginia Steinman biography.) In December of 1892 the Donau women spearheaded the Temple Aid Society with Florence as president, perhaps patterned after a similar fundraiser held during their time in Denver. They regularly entertained in honor of visitors coming and going, while sewing for the poor and assisting in city-wide charity events.

Hugo Donau and Alfred Donau
Courtesy of Bettina Lyons

The Donau family moved to San Francisco in 1897. Hugo and Alfred joined their married sister, Bettina, in Tucson, where Albert Steinfeld had gained a notable prominence in retail, real estate and mining. The 1906 San Francisco earthquake and fire destroyed the Donau house. The family moved to Los Angeles, where Simon died in 1912. Florence never married and Virginia never remarried. Alice married Harold Belcher in Denver in 1906 and became a Hollywood actress, playing in over thirty films as Alice Belcher, most of them silent. She gradually rolled her birth year from 1869 to 1875 to 1882.

Actress Alice Donau Belcher in 1933
www.lordheath.com

Isaac and Mary Dornberg

Isaac Dornberg (1850–1919) was born December 19 in Frankish-Grumbach, Germany, the son of Bernhart Dornberg and Brendell Strauss. He immigrated to the U.S. in August of 1869 and was naturalized in 1882. In the mid-1870s Isaac married Mary Elizabeth Landsperger (1857–1943) and lived in Elden, Pennsylvania. Their sons William and Leo were born there in 1877 and 1880.

In January of 1884 Isaac took out a U.S. passport and traveled back to Germany, returning with his younger sister Dena. She lived with the family for several decades. Isaac operated the Joseph and Dornberg clothing store in Elden, Pennsylvania, one of the leading merchant tailor firms of the county, and then ran the firm alone.

In March of 1889 Dornberg sold his business to his clerk and headed west. He first appeared in Tacoma's city directory in 1890, operating a pawn business with Archie Ash. Over the next several years his Tacoma Loan Office was able to take advantage of the many business failures, often purchasing bankrupt merchandise at tremendous discounts. In December of 1894 Isaac was able to purchase the Hotel Chilberg at public auction.

After a brief venture in Butte, Montana, Isaac moved to Spokane, Washington, as did Archie Ash. Both operated jewelry and loan businesses, as well as investing in other companies. However, Isaac and his wife lived separately in Spokane. In 1905 Isaac renewed his passport, again traveling back to Germany, along with his sister Dena. This time on their return they brought along their niece, Eda Mann. And in October of 1906 Isaac married Nettie Barnhardt (1875–1976) in New York, a woman twenty-five years his junior.

Isaac died in Spokane on February 16, 1919. A week later the *Spokane Chronicle* reported that his wife Nettie would receive a $30,000 payment, his sister Dena $5,000, and his six other siblings would receive $2,000 each. However, his sons Leo and William were left just five dollars each, with no further provision. A few years earlier Leo had married Ethel Levin, daughter of David Levin. (See Levin biography.)

Leo Dornberg
courtesy of Elaine Porter

William and Rebecca Eckstein

William and Rebecca Eckstein
Courtesy of Mike Hockett

William Eckstein (1855–1922) was born in Austria and immigrated around 1880. He arrived in Tacoma a few years later, working as a tailor for a variety of employers, typically sleeping on the premises. In 1893 he married Rebecca Simon, daughter of Abe Simon. (See Simon biography.) She operated a cigar business with her brother George. After the economy declined in the 1890s William sold secondhand clothes, and later ran a pawnshop. Both William and Rebecca lived in Tacoma the rest of their lives and were buried in the Home of Peace Cemetery.

The couple had two sons, Alfred and Carl, but neither were involved in Jewish activities. Alfred (1893–1946) briefly owned and operated the New York Waist House. Later he worked as a salesman for his brother, was a buyer for the Rhodes Brothers department store, and served as a timekeeper for the Todd-Pacific shipyards in Seattle during the war. He married Dora Powers (1893–1955) but the couple had no children.

Carl (1900–1985) lived his entire life in Tacoma. He worked as a sign painter during the 1920s, setting aside enough savings to start his own sign business and keep up his employees' salaries during the Depression. He began creating neon signs, including the marquee for the Cameo Theatre, signs for the old Doric Hotel, and later the Olympia Brewery. His company had several names – Tacoma Neon Products Co., Neon Displays, Inc., Eckstein Neon, and then Coast Neon Displays. Carl married Gladys Huffman Walgraf (1905–1986) in 1930. She had a daughter by a previous marriage, but the couple had no children of their own.

Tacoma's Eckstein family was apparently not related to Seattle's notable Nathan Eckstein, born in Germany in 1873.

Walter and Antonetta Ehrlichman

Walter Ehrlichman (1862–1933) came to the U.S. around 1881. In 1890 he married Antonetta Gruenberg (1873–1947) in Minnesota, where he worked as a police detective and court interpreter. The couple had four children in Minneapolis before moving to Tacoma in the summer of 1900. On July 17, 1900, the *Tacoma Daily Ledger* reported that W. Erlichman's store at 717 Pacific had been burglarized repeatedly since opening three weeks prior. Mrs. Ehrlichman joined the Judith Montefiore Society that fall and served on several committees. In 1903 her stillborn daughter was buried in the Home of Peace cemetery.

The family moved to Seattle, but were separated by 1920. Antonetta became a practitioner of the Christian Science religion. Walter, an ardent Zionist, served as secretary of the Seattle Zionist Branch in 1914. Their youngest son, Rudolph, (1897–1942) married Lillian Danielson in 1923 and returned to Tacoma, where their son John Daniel Erlichman was born on March 20, 1925. Many years later John gained notoriety and prison time for his participation in the Watergate scandal. His mother Lillian died in Tacoma in 1999. Rudolph's brother Ben Ehrlichman was known for his banking genius in helping the city of Seattle in the late 1930s. Ben was named Seattle's First Citizen in 1961, but later failed in his efforts to demolish the historic Pike Place market.

Einstein Siblings – Belle, Bernard, Max and Theresa

Henry Einstein, his wife Henrietta (Lindauer) and their children immigrated to the U.S. in July of 1849 from Jebenhausen, Germany. Four of their children spent time in Tacoma. Belle (1848–1932) married Charles Reichenbach in Philadelphia in June of 1882. (See Reichenbach biography.) Her younger brother Bernard (1854–1940) came to Tacoma with them in the spring of 1885. He worked in Charles' clothing store for nearly five years and was active in Jewish social groups. Around 1890 Bernard moved to California, where he spent the rest of his life selling clothing for a variety of firms. He never married.

In the winter of 1888 Miss Theresa Einstein (c.1843–1896) visited Belle. Theresa opened bank accounts and invested in real estate. She died unmarried in Philadelphia in 1896. Her 1893 will left funds to care for her brother Max and his children, but he died before she did.

Max (1845–1894) married Ella Boate in Philadelphia in September of 1882. They had three children there before coming to Tacoma. Max sold real estate and then clothing. After a brief time in Portland, Oregon, the family returned to Philadelphia. Max's children William and Etta grew up in New Jersey.

Albert and Adeline Elken

Albert Elken
Courtesy of Anita Brew

Albert Elken (1850–1933) was born Abraham Elkan in Zillisheim, France. In 1870 he worked in the crockery store of his uncle Julius Cerf in San Francisco, and lived with the family. Albert married Adeline Rheims (1855–1921) around 1877. The couple had three daughters in the San Francisco area before coming to Tacoma in 1884. Albert worked with his cousins Emile Lobe and Luciene Eger. In January of 1885 Albert brought a rabbi from Portland to officiate at his son's *bris,* or circumcision. Descendants relate that Adeline saw some Native Americans, became frightened, and insisted the family move. They returned to San Francisco in May of 1885, where two more daughters were born. There Albert worked in a variety of occupations – from porter to teamster to drayman to candy maker. He worked many years as a hostler for the police department, handling horses.

Feist Siblings – Irma, Lucy and Theophil

Theophil Feist (1873–1940) was the youngest son of Samuel Feist and Bertha Dreyfus. When Theo came to Tacoma as a teenager in 1889 (just a few months before Washington's statehood) he lived with his cousin Jacob Bernhard, son of his mother's sister, Sarah, and worked at the Chester Cleary store managed by Jacob. In later interviews Theo reflected that he earned no salary for his first year of work, other than room and board. His second year's salary of five dollars per week enabled him to bring his sisters Irma (c.1866–?) and Lucy (1872–1961) to Tacoma from Trimbach in Alsace.

By 1891 Theo had become Jacob's bookkeeper, while Lucy worked as a clerk. Irma became a milliner for the fashionable Miss Cunningham, located within Jacob Bernhard's store. After the

1893 banking panic Jacob lost his business. Lucy and Theo both worked briefly for Bernhard's successor, Sanford, Stone & Fisher. In the spring of 1895 Lucy married Joseph Bachrach, (see Bachrach biography) who had worked for the Gross Brothers for five years.

Tacoma Public Library C8580-1

Theo started his own dry goods store in 1896 at 945 Tacoma Avenue, employing his sister Irma as millinery clerk. The store was in a residential neighborhood, near the school, but several blocks uphill from the main downtown shopping area. When Gross Brothers closed in 1897 Joseph joined with Theo in the new firm of Feist & Bachrach. By November they were able to move downhill to 942 Pacific, with Irma trimming hats. Both Theo and Irma lived with the Bachrach family.

In November of 1900 the team of Feist & Bachrach paid $22,500 to purchase a three-story brick building at 934 Pacific, the exact same building where Theo had worked as a teenager for his cousin. The dry goods and dress goods firm expanded to include 932 Pacific, and Theo started making East Coast shopping trips. In 1908 his artist brother Julien (1867–1909) briefly joined them in Tacoma. In the summer of 1912 Theo traveled to Europe to visit his parents, returning on the *RMS Olympic,* sister ship to the *RMS Titanic.*

In New York in June of 1915 Theo married Jessie Levy, (1887–1976) daughter of Solomon Levy and Lena Metzger. Jessie would later relate to her children that the train ride across the country to Tacoma served as their honeymoon. Jessie recalled stepping off the train, taking a look at the city that would be her home, and bursting into tears.

The following year the firm of Feist & Bachrach moved to 1116–1118 Broadway. Tacoma's shopping patterns had changed, with men's stores located on Pacific and women's stores on Broadway.

Jessie quickly assumed a leadership role in Tacoma's Jewish community, serving as president of the Judith Montefiore Society in 1918 and the Tacoma Chapter of the Council of Jewish Women in 1920. She remained active throughout her life. A nursing scholarship at Tacoma Community College, funded by the Council, bears her name.

The couple had three daughters, Lucille (1916–2010) Doris and Muriel. Although Jessie returned briefly to New York to give birth to her first child, Lucille spent the rest of her life in Tacoma. Educated at Annie Wright, Barnard College and the University of Washington, Lucille married Dr. Cecil Hurst (1914–1954) in 1941. She was an artist, sculptor, activist, and a warrior in the League of Women Voters and the field of civil rights. She held a multitude of board positions, including Faith Home, NAACP, Civic Ballet Board, National Council of Jewish Women, and past president of Temple Beth El, among others. Her children and grandchildren are among only a few direct descendants left in Tacoma's Jewish community from a family dating back to Territorial Washington.

Samuel Finkelstein

Samuel H. Finkelstein worked as a clerk for Charles Langert from 1891 through 1893. He lived at the home of David Magnus. Max Finkelstein was included in the Pierce County Auditor's census in 1892, a clerk aged 26. In April of 1893 Sam participated in Saturday morning services by reading from the Torah.

Fischer Siblings – Flora, Rebecca and Robert

Flora Fischer (c.1849–1886) married Meyer Kaufman (See Kaufman biography). In 1870 her younger sister Rebecca, aged 16, lived with the Kaufman family in Nevada. Their brother Robert Fischer died in Tacoma on October 8, 1877, having recently arrived from San Francisco. He was only 22, born in Exin, Prussia, now Kcynia,

Poland. He was buried in the Jewish cemetery in Olympia.

Fannie Fogelbaum

Fannie Livingstone Fogelbaum, widow of Solomon, lived in Kansas City, Missouri, between 1884 and 1891. Around 1892 she moved to Tacoma with her teenage son Jacob. They joined her daughter Barbara, Mrs. Lauritz Olsen. (See Olsen biography.) Both ladies joined the Judith Montefiore Society, but in 1894 their resignation was not accepted because their dues were in arrears.

In May of 1895 they were arrested in a sensational case of professional shoplifting. Both women were charged with grand larceny, as the stolen coats, fabrics, and dozens of hats found in their possession were valued at over $1500. There was such a crowd at the courthouse to witness the initial proceedings that the crush of people broke a courtroom window. However, the items were eventually returned to their rightful shop owners. In December Fannie pled guilty to a lesser charge of petit larceny, as the items were stolen in small amounts, not all at once. Anxious to return to their holiday trade, the merchants agreed. Fannie was given a suspended sentence, and all charges against Barbara were dropped.

Olsen sold his tavern and the extended families started anew in Skagway, Alaska.

Henry "Harry" & Josephine Fraley

Harry Fraley married Josephine Spiegl (1865–1948) around 1884. Her father Jacob was a wholesale grocer in Portland, Oregon. About 1892 the couple came to Tacoma, where Harry worked as a dry goods clerk for Jacob Kullman. Harry served as secretary/treasurer of the Harmony Club in 1892, and Josephine served on the Temple Aid committee. After the 1893 banking collapse both Kullman and Fraley left Tacoma. The Fraleys lived in Sacramento from at least 1896 until 1902, while Harry managed a store for Weinstock & Lubin. Then the Fraleys joined several Spiegl siblings in Reno, Nevada. Harry operated a cloak and suit store there until his death around 1930.

Emily Ballin Frank

Emily Ballin (1850–1928) married Charles J. Frank (c.1843–1897). Their first daughter, Bertha (1871–1946), was born in New York and later married Samuel Sondheim. (See Sondheim biography.) Their second daughter, Rosa (c.1874–1934), was born in Wisconsin and married Abraham Goldenson in Tacoma in 1898. (See Goldenson biography.) Their third daughter, Else (c.1879–1966), was also likely born in Wisconsin. Else married Milton Weil (1880–1950) in Tacoma in 1903. All were involved in the clothing industry. Emily lived in Milwaukee with her youngest daughter until her husband's death in September of 1897.

Upon her arrival in Tacoma Emily immediately joined the Judith Montefiore Society. She was elected president four different times, but typically resigned within a few months. In 1900 she and her youngest daughter spent several months traveling in Europe. Emily lived in Tacoma through at least 1926, eventually joining her youngest daughter in Seattle.

Harry C. and John J. Frank

HARRY C. FRANK

Tacoma Daily News 1891 annual
Tacoma Historical Society collection

Harry and John Frank were born in Detroit, Michigan, in the 1850s. In 1877 they operated Frank Brothers in San Francisco, selling groceries and liquors, but by 1880 they clerked in Thomas Simon's grocery store. After coming to Tacoma around 1883 their names were frequently mentioned in the columns of the *Ledger*, as they traveled back and forth to San Francisco for health reasons. Both apparently suffered from lung ailments.

John clerked for the Gross Brothers for several years. Harry took a more adventurous route. Gold was discovered in the summer of 1885 in Granite Creek, British Columbia, along the Tulameen River. Harry joined the rush and was able to stake a claim, but by November rode back out on horseback, unable to recover from a bad cold. The following year he again summered in the mines and wintered in San Francisco, but reported that the group of seven had earned only $23, which was split between them.

Harry returned to Tacoma in 1887, as reflected in numerous social mentions. On August 14 the *Ledger* reported that Tacoma's oldest dog, Rover, who had been roaming the streets for 14 years, was nearly impounded by the police. Harry took up a collection and purchased a collar and license for the dog. Both Harry and John worked for Sam Isaacs that year.

Harry spent the summer of 1888 prospecting in the Cascades, and in the fall incorporated the Columbia Consolidated Mining Company. He was also part of the clothing firm of Hirsch and Frank, with Simon Hirsch, for five years. Their specialty was creating men's custom suits, as the majority of Tacoma's clothing dealers offered ready-to-wear.

John Frank died in San Francisco in February of 1889, at the age of 33. A few months later Hirsch and Frank reopened at 1007 Pacific. Harry was active in Harmony Club events over the next several years. At the end of 1891 Hirsch and Frank moved to 948 Pacific, available due to the failure of Kaufman and Berliner. After the 1893 decline Harry sold out to his partner, again citing failing health.

Harry moved briefly to San Francisco, but continued developing mining interests. He was one of the incorporators of the Daphne Gold Mining Company in 1899. He again returned to San Francisco in June of 1905, after a four-year stay in Chihuahua, Mexico. Six weeks later he died of tuberculosis. His will mentioned a sister, Christine Hall, of Washington D.C. His parents were likely Louis and Mary Frank, who died in Detroit in 1874 and 1894, respectively.

Adolf Freiman

Adolf Freiman (1861–1912) was born in Austria and immigrated to the U.S. in 1882. He came fairly quickly to the Northwest, as by 1883 he was sued for account collection in Pierce County. He worked as a clerk for Adolph Packscher between 1884 and 1885 and participated in several Jewish weddings and events. Adolf left Tacoma for San Francisco in 1886. His 1904 naturalization papers stated that he had lived in California, Colorado, and Washington Territory; and had been a resident of New York since 1896. He was likely the same Adolf Freiman who died in New York on April 14, 1912, just before the *Titanic* struck an iceberg.

Benjamin and Rachel Freyd

Benjamin Freyd (c.1865–1934) lived in Seattle from 1893 to 1897, selling clothing. His older brother Harris (1856–1916) sold secondhand goods. In 1894 Benjamin married Rachel Silver (1870–1940), sister of Harry Silver, who ran the Chicago Loan pawn store. Their mother was Sarah Gottstein, a relative of Seattle's Meyer Gottstein.

In April of 1897 Benjamin opened the Chicago Clothing House at 1336 Pacific in Tacoma, supported by loans from his new in-laws. Rachel immediately joined the Judith Montefiore Society. By December the store was in the hands of receivers, with creditors claiming fraudulent misrepresentation of the strength of his assets. The business survived another year with the help of a third brother, Solomon (1878–1943), but Benjamin was again bankrupt in November of 1899.

Both Solomon and Benjamin moved to Seattle. This time Benjamin prospered, and all four of his daughters earned degrees at the University of Washington. Sol married Lena Cohen (1886–1936), daughter of Max Cohen, a junk dealer in Tacoma. Sol lived in Tacoma in the '20s, and operated a clothing store in Bremerton in the '30s, before returning to Seattle. Among them the three brothers had nine children, but only two grandchildren, daughters of Benjamin's eldest daughter Florence Freyd Herzog Arginteanu.

Mitchell and Maude Friedlander

Mitchell Friedlander (1869–1948) was born in Virginia City, Nevada. In 1891 he married Maude Blount (1869–1945) of Tacoma. The couple had three children in Tacoma between 1892 and 1895. The youngest, Kenneth, was circumcised in January of 1896 by Rabbi Lincer. Mitchell worked in Tacoma as a musician for several years.

The family turned up in Chicago in 1910. Mitchell worked as a vaudeville actor, as did his teenage daughters Yvonne and Gretchen, and Mitchell's younger brother Sam. Mitchell, Maude and Sam lived in Chicago the rest of their lives, continuing in the theater business.

Adolph Friedman

Adolph Friedman was born in Bouska, in the Courland region of what is now Latvia. Census records indicate a birthdate ranging from 1831 to 1847, but his age at death yields a birth year of around 1827. Family lore tells that Adolph Friedman first shipped to the U.S. in 1845, landing in Steilacoom and later heading to San Francisco. Passenger lists show that he arrived in Old Tacoma in 1884, purchasing a store from Meyer Kaufman. Later he began developing real estate on the western shore of American Lake. His great-nephew Julius Friedman joined him around 1894, as would many other Friedman relatives.

Adolph continued his general store in Old Town and kept selling real estate. As the market peaked in the spring of 1893 Adolph also served as one of twelve deputy county assessors. After the economy changed in 1895 Adolph began operating a pawnshop. He was absent from Tacoma city directories from 1896 to 1900. Relatives state that Adolph traveled to Victoria, B.C., in the late 1890s and married a relative, Mascha or Marcia Stusser, sister of Jennie Stusser. Adolph was in his seventies at the time, and Mascha was in her thirties.

In September of 1900 Adolph and Mascha lived briefly in the Nicollet House at 728–730 Pacific. An enterprising thief rented the room next door, then broke through the adjoining suite door to steal their trunks of clothing, silverware and personal belongings. The thief was quickly apprehended and the majority of their items returned.

Mrs. A. Friedman joined the Judith Montefiore Society in the fall of 1900. Over the next decade the pair operated a variety of businesses, selling trunks and valises and also operating a pawnshop. Adolph died on March 2, 1911, and was buried in the Home of Peace Cemetery. Mascha then married Joseph Miller, lived in Seattle for a time, and lived out her life in California. She died in San Francisco on March 21, 1950. Adolph Friedman's nephews, great-nephews, and extended relatives became the nucleus of Tacoma's Orthodox Jewish community.

Morris, Harry, Joe and (seated) Nathan Friedman
Courtesy of Jim Friedman

Julius and Augusta Friedman

Julius Friedman
Courtesy of Harold Friedman

Julius Friedman (1872–1937) was the only son of Jacob Friedman and his first wife Rebecca. Julius followed Adolph Friedman to Tacoma in 1894 and immediately purchased half a dozen American Lake lots. Over the next decade Julius would be joined by his four sisters, four half-siblings, his father and stepmother Liebe, and enough aunts, uncles and cousins to give future genealogists migraines.

Julius briefly operated a clothing store with Isaac Moses at 1528 Pacific, then managed on his own, initially selling mostly secondhand items. In the summer of 1899 his younger sister Sarah married Nathan Blasberg. That year Julius also took the matrimonial leap, marrying Hugo Stusser's daughter Augusta (1880–1942) in December. (See Stusser biography.) In 1906 he sold his lot in the Flatiron Block on Fifteenth and Pacific for a significant profit, enabling him to purchase a home and continue bringing relatives from Latvia.

Julius was active in Tacoma's developing Orthodox congregation, serving several terms as president. He and his many extended relatives operated a variety of clothing stores in Tacoma, the majority in close proximity on Pacific. They maintained an unusual closeness throughout their daily routines, sharing New York Yiddish newspapers and morning and evening prayers.

Julius and Augusta had four children. Rebecca (1900–1974) married first Morris Donion and then Otto Miller and had five children. Saul (1902–1976) married Ida Saul and had a daughter Mrs. Bob (Marilyn) Silver. Abedeaux (1905–1954) married Rose Rotman and had two sons, Jules and Harold Friedman. The youngest, Siegfried Friedman, born September 20, 1910, died unmarried on July 21, 2011.

Robert and Celina Gans

Robert Gans (1848–1921) left Hamburg in November of 1866 as a lad of 18. He lived in California in the 1870s and married San Jose's Celina Newman (1854–1920) around 1876. Their daughter Gertrude was born the following year. The family arrived in Tacoma around 1890, where Robert worked as a clerk for Gross Brothers. Celina joined the Judith Montefiore Society and assisted in the 1892 fundraising fair. Their last year in Tacoma was likely 1893, before they returned to San Francisco. Their daughter Gertrude married William J. Hoffman in Stockton in 1897 but the couple had no children.

David and Carrie Germanus

Aaron David Germanus was born in Nyirbator, Hungary around 1850 and came to the U.S. about 1875. In 1880 David was naturalized in Oakland, California, where he worked for Nathan Rosenberg selling cigars. David's younger brother Emil Germanus immigrated in 1882 but settled in Newark, New Jersey.

In February of 1883 in Oakland David married Carrie Mayer (1861–1920), middle child of Leopold and Hannah Mayer. Leopold was an 1858 founder of Portland's congregation Beth Israel and had served as the first temple president.

David and Carrie lost two children in Oakland – a daughter in 1884 and a son in 1886. David worked as a traveling salesman and was in officer in the local B'nai B'rith.

In 1890 David and Carrie moved to Tacoma, where David worked as a traveling agent for liquor dealer Charles Langert. That summer he was one of the organizers of Tacoma's B'nai B'rith chapter, and in the fall was elected president. In the spring of 1892 David was elected vice president of Tacoma's new congregation.

The couple had a son, Harry, in April of 1891. Carrie was active in the Judith Montefiore Society and was elected secretary in 1893. However, the family moved to Portland in the fall of 1893. Harry worked as a bookkeeper for a wholesale liquor company run by Jesse Meyerfeld, who had married Carrie's older sister, Sarah Mayer. Another sister, Rachel, wife of Michael Jacob, had been in Tacoma with them and later moved to Portland. (See Jacob biography.) David's widowed sister Rosa Germanus Crook (1856–1925) also joined them in Portland.

By 1897 David had started his own liquor firm, which lasted about four years. Carrie and her sisters were active in Portland's Jewish community and the Council of Jewish Women. Their son Harry was a talented musician and entertainer. He married Chicago's Violet Anne Bernstein in 1913 and the two performed as Harry J Parker and Anne Butler for Morris Meyerfeld's Orpheum. After a few years she returned to Chicago and resumed her maiden name.

David operated a saloon in Portland until Prohibition, then worked selling insurance. After Carrie died in 1920 and Rosa in 1925, David moved to New Jersey and lived with his nephew, Alex Germanus in 1926. David's death date is unknown. His son Harry died in New York in 1929 and the line ended.

Peter & Minnie Gevurtz

Peter Gevurtz was born in Lublin, Poland, in 1871 and came to the U.S. in 1887. He worked in San Francisco for a few years before coming to Tacoma, where he was naturalized in 1892. He worked as a clerk for Sol Jacoby in a branch of Portland's Prager Brothers clothing. However, in March of 1893 Peter was one of four clerks arrested for stealing trunkloads of merchandise from their workplace. Peter was apprehended at the funeral of his brother Henry in Portland. By April the goods were returned, charges were dropped, and the matter was resolved.

Peter worked in his brother Isaac's furniture store in Portland in 1895, but by 1898 was back in San Francisco, and again arrested for stealing clothing. And again, after a week in jail, charges were dismissed. He returned to Portland, where he married Minnie Cohn (1866–1954) in 1902. They lived briefly in Seattle, selling furniture in 1906 and operating a theater in 1910. By 1912 Peter was able to license a new Ford automobile. The couple moved to California, where Peter worked in motion pictures in San Pedro and Los Angeles. In 1915 he filed a lawsuit against censors who were blocking the showing of a Chaplin film. Peter died sometime between 1928 and 1938, likely in California.

Joseph and Helen Gevurtz (Mrs. David Klegman) arrived in Tacoma twenty years after Peter, and were also from Lublin. Their father was Jacob Gevurtz.

Abraham and Rose Goldenson

Abraham Morris Goldenson (1865–1934) immigrated in 1883 and was naturalized in Pennsylvania in 1887, just before coming to Tacoma to work for Mentheim Cohn. Abe soon joined with Samuel Sondheim and the two opened their own clothing store, later known as Golden Eagle Clothing. As other clothing houses failed, Abe and Sam shifted into their former locations, occupying a variety of storefronts on Pacific Avenue. Reversing the common trend, by 1895 they were able to open a second location in Seattle, called the Rochester Clothing House.

Abe lived in Seattle through 1897, then returned to Tacoma. In the summer of 1898 he married Rose Frank (1874–1934,) whose sister Bertha had married Sam Sondheim the year before. Rose became active in the Judith Montefiore Society and had a son Percival (1899–1970). The firm continued to succeed, and by 1903 the Goldenson family was able to take a three-month extended visit through Arizona and California. In November of 1903 Goldenson and Sondheim opened a second Rochester Clothing branch in Aberdeen, Washington, just after a major fire altered the downtown business landscape.

A second son, Frank Goldenson, was born in Tacoma in 1906. In December of 1908 the family moved to Los Angeles, perhaps following the sunshine they had discovered five years before. Frank died in New York in 1923, but Percival went on to have a career as a musician, copyist, and movie studio librarian. Rose died just four days after Abe in 1934.

(Not to be confused with San Francisco's Abraham Goldenson (1871–1953,) whose brother Aleck was hanged for murder in September of 1888.)

Goldsmith Siblings

Joseph and Dora (Cavo) had seven children in California between 1862 and 1874. By 1879 the entire family lived in King County, later moving farther north to La Conner in Skagit County. In the spring of 1886 their eldest daughter Bella married Henry Isaacs and moved to Tacoma. (See Isaacs biography.) The following year Joseph and Dora's teenaged son Abe was judged insane and sent to the asylum at Steilacoom, where he remained until his death in 1925. Mrs. Goldsmith and her two younger daughters, Sophie and Lillie, often visited Tacoma, assisting in Jewish activities, and lived in Tacoma during the winter of 1894–95. By 1896 all four Goldsmith ladies had moved to Seattle, with Belle apparently separating from her husband. Joseph Goldsmith died in Seattle on February 16, 1901. His wife died exactly five years later.

Heyman and Louisa (Spigelmann) Goodtime/Goetheim (See pages 7–9)

Samuel Gottschalk

Samuel Gottschalk was born in Posen on April 14, 1856. He sailed from Hamburg to New York just before his eighteenth birthday. Sam was naturalized in Salem, Oregon, in 1880. Then he moved to Olympia, Washington, and opened a clothing store called the White House. However, in January of 1884 Sam sold his interest to Joseph Cheim, and the following month filed for a passport and returned to Europe.

After a few months Sam returned, after stopping in New York to order merchandise for a new store – this time in Tacoma. The Great Eastern Clothing House, located on Pacific between Thirteenth and Fourteenth, opened in July. Ads noted that all prices were clearly marked and all sales would be strictly cash – both apparently unusual business methods at the time.

Sam was a popular speaker at Jewish gatherings, and advertised regularly, so his newspaper personal mentions were frequent and flattering. *Ledger,* October 4, 1884, "Two burglars found their way into Gottschalk's clothing house Thursday night, but did not disturb anything. Sam says they looked at the cost marks which were so low they concluded it would be cheaper to buy the goods and have them delivered than to carry them away themselves."

Sam's health began to fail toward the end of 1884. After a severe rheumatic attack he needed the aid of crutches and a few friends just to get to his store occasionally. Just before Christmas Sam left for California to regain his strength. Joseph Cheim's brother Morris came to Tacoma from Olympia to manage the business until Sam returned in late February of 1885. On March 4th the store was connected to new gas lines, and the following week Pacific Avenue was lighted for the first time.

After another health-related trip to California, Sam returned to Tacoma for the summer, serving as first president of the Standard Club of young Jewish men. Before the year was out his business was finished and his creditors sold his merchandise to Louis Lask. In April of 1887 Sam briefly returned to Tacoma, after spending a few months in Olympia, but failed to open a new store.

Sam again went back to Germany, where he renewed his U.S. passport in 1894 and 1896. Each time he stated his intent to return to the U.S. within six months. He likely did not.

(Emil Gottschalk, who started Gottschalk's department stores in California in 1904, was apparently not related.)

Gottstein Cousins – Meyer & Kassell

Cousins "Mike" Meyer (1847–1917) and Kassell (1855–1912) Gottstein were born in Pilviskiai, Poland, now Lithuania. They operated grocery and liquor stores in Deadwood, Dakota Territory, before coming to Tacoma in the summer of 1883. By September the wholesale liquor firm of Gottstein and Langert was open for business. However, in January the partnership was mutually dissolved, with Charles Langert continuing in Tacoma and Gottstein operating in Seattle. In 1889 Meyer Gottstein married Rosa Wolf, daughter of Portland's Simon Wolf. In 1891 her sister Martha married David Hoffman, who later entered the liquor business in Tacoma.

Meyer and Kassell became prominent wholesale liquor dealers in Seattle. Their attorneys spent much of 1915 challenging the validity of the state's new prohibition law. Nearly twenty years later Meyer's only son Joseph would be active in a campaign to legalize horse racing in Washington, and for many years was president of Longacres Race Track.

And apparently unrelated, Isaac Gottstein worked in Tacoma from 1888 to 1890 as a clerk in several clothing stores. He was active in the Harmony Club, then lived in Seattle from 1893 to 1898. He is likely the same Isaac Louis Gottstein who died in the Chicago area in 1915. His will requested that his wife Lena continue supporting his mother Zolatta in Pilwischken.

Green Family

Lena Green lived in Meadville, Pennsylvania, in 1880, along with her daughter Rose. Another daughter, Jennie (1860–1931), lived in nearby Titusville with her husband Lehman Ullman. By 1887 Lena and Rose had moved to Tacoma, where Rose married James Pincus in March. (See Pincus biography.) The Greens lived with H.W. Bryer (see Bryer biography) possibly a relative, as all were born in Hungary. Joseph H. and Herman J. Green joined the household in 1890, and Herman became the first secretary of the Harmony Club. Mrs. Green joined the Judith Montefiore Society in 1890 and resigned in the summer of 1892, joining her widowed daughter Jennie in Youngstown, Ohio. Mrs. Green had two grandchildren, but neither married.

Jesse and Annie Greenbaum

Tacoma Daily Ledger October 18, 1894

Jesse Greenbaum (1868–1930) was the eldest of four children born to Louis and Betsy Greenbaum in Niagara, New York. Jesse came to Tacoma in April of 1893 to manage the clothing store at 902–904 Pacific, formerly owned by Charles Reichenbach, and recently purchased by Hyams, Pauson and Company. The firm had stores in New York, San Francisco, and Seattle. Jesse continued Reichenbach's aggressive newspaper ads for several years, despite the failing economy. In October of 1895 Edward Hyams brought investors to look over the business, hinted they would open two more locations, and instead announced the closure of both the Tacoma and Seattle locations. Jesse worked briefly in Seattle and Fairhaven (near Bellingham,) then moved to San Francisco. He married Annie Sands (c.1870–1938) about 1904, but the couple had no children.

Gross Family (See pages 16–27)

Aaron Grass and Zlota Moses raised at least nine children in Rypin, in Russian-ruled Poland. The eldest four stayed in Europe, including Amalia Grass Lichtenfeld, Toba Grass Schransky, Bila Grass Plenick, and Joseph Grass, who moved to Strasbourg, Germany. The younger five – Ellis, Dave, Morris, Helen and Abraham – each immigrated to the U.S. as they neared adulthood, taking the grand surname of Gross.

Ellis and Johanna Gross

Ellis Gross, Seattle PI December 16, 1915
Courtesy of Seattle Public Library

Ellis Gross (1853–1943) immigrated to the U.S. in 1874, joining his brother Dave. The pair worked in Cincinnati, Ohio, before opening their own store in San Francisco in 1876. Two years later Ellis opened a branch in Tacoma, and in 1881 opened another location in Port Townsend.

Then Ellis returned to Europe, where he married Johanna Olchevitz (1865–1931) in Strasbourg in June of 1884. While in Strasbourg Ellis and Johanna had a daughter Leta, born in March of 1886. Ellis and family returned to Tacoma in May of 1887, purchasing a home at 452 E Street (now Fawcett). They lost a three-week-old son in March of 1888. The couple later had a son, Carl (1890–1945).

During President Benjamin Harrison's visit to Tacoma on May 6, 1891, Ellis' 5-year-old daughter Leta was chosen to present the President with a bouquet of flowers. In the process she burst into tears. In later years she would relate to her grandchildren that he picked her up and kissed her, in an effort to soothe her. *Tacoma Daily Ledger,* Sunday May 10, 1891, social column, "The little daughter of Ellis Gross was a favorite one presidential day. She presented Mr. Harrison with a beautiful bouquet, whereon he lifted her in his arms and kissed her. It is not every girl in Tacoma who can say she has been kissed by the president."

The couple made another trip to Europe in 1892, staying for 18 months, but returning in time for the dedication of the new synagogue in September of 1893. Another daughter, Sylvia, was born in December of 1894. Ellis was an active member of the Jewish community, often serving as an officer.

Johanna, probably more than any other Jewess, was accepted in Tacoma's exclusive social circles. She served as a director of the Children's Home and the Tacoma Free Kindergarten, often hosting fundraisers. In April of 1898 she provided Passover bread, or *matzah,* for an Easter tea.

After the brothers went their separate ways in 1896, Ellis opened a men's clothing store at 944 Pacific, along with his trusted employee Morris Summerfield. In February of 1904 the store's stock and fixtures were sold at auction by a receiver, and purchased by Dave Gross. The following year the family moved to Seattle, where Ellis again operated a clothing store. Leta married Maurice Rhine (1883–1962) there in 1911, and had three children in San Francisco – Cecelia, Leona and Marjorie.

Around 1921 Ellis retired to San Francisco, as did many of Tacoma's merchants, later selling insurance. His daughter, Sylvia (1884–1990) married Michel Gradwohl (1888–1947) in September of 1921. Their daughter Fredrique Gradwohl (1926–2003) married Norton Shafer, (1922–1991) nephew of Tacoma's David Shafer.

Dave and Jennie Gross

Dave Gross
Courtesy of Douglas Salin

Dave Gross (1856–1941) was the first of the Gross siblings to come to the U.S. Arriving in New York in the spring of 1873 and working his way to Cincinnati, Dave and his brother Ellis opened a store in San Francisco in 1876. Dave stayed in San Francisco when his brother opened a branch in Tacoma. For fifteen years Dave served as the firm's buyer, visiting Tacoma for a few weeks each year.

In 1882 Dave married San Francisco native Jennie Friedman (1864–1953). Their three sons were born in California – Leonard in 1883, Mendes in 1886 and Jeffrey in 1889. In February of 1892 the family moved briefly to New York. After the economy collapsed Dave came to Tacoma in June of 1894 to assist in daily operations of the store.

Their children frequently participated in dance and music recitals, with Leonard playing violin. He celebrated his *bar mitzvah* at the new Temple Beth Israel in February of 1895. A month later Dave's brother, Abe, took his life and the brothers divided.

Dave incorporated a new business in January of 1897, with his wife and her brother Moses Friedman. Dave experimented with several lines of dry goods, notions, and ready-made clothing, eventually specializing in fine cloaks. The store was located at 936 Pacific, a building owned by Joseph Goldsmith. Jennie was able to make regular extended visits to San Francisco and Portland.

Dave continued to look for business opportunities, making a trip to Wrangell and Juneau, Alaska, in 1898. Instead he returned to Tacoma and moved his business to the Levin Building, 920 Pacific. In 1903 the *Ledger* reported that Dave had just completed his ninety-eighth trip from the Atlantic to the Pacific. His business prospered, and by 1904 he was able to purchase his bankrupt brother's stock. Instead of continuing to rent, in 1906 Dave built his own store at 940–942 C Street. In 1908 he traveled to Europe for a year, and in February of 1910 returned to San Francisco. Dave and his family stayed in California.

Generations later Mendes' grandson Pete Gross worked in Seattle as a sports broadcaster and became known as the beloved voice of the Seahawks.

Morris and Mollie Gross

Morris Gross
Courtesy of Paul Michaels

Mollie Bash Gross
Tacoma Sunday Ledger August 8, 1897

Morris Gross (1859–1940) came directly to Tacoma in 1879 from his home in Rypin, then Poland, joining his older brother Ellis. Just two years later Ellis left him in charge of the Tacoma store, where he would remain for the next 25 years. By 1889 the firm had 22 clerks and Morris was vice president of the Hebrew Benevolent Society. After the brothers opened their grand store in 1890 Morris returned to Europe, visiting his parents and touring the continent. Thirty-six clerks welcomed him home. Like his brothers, Morris joined civic groups, took a leadership role in the Jewish community, and several times was mentioned as a mayoral candidate. He was able to go back to Europe for nearly a year in 1893, visiting his mother after the death of his father.

Morris returned to find a Tacoma much-changed, with the effects of the declining economy just beginning. In December of 1894 he married Mollie Bash, (1875–1972) daughter of New York's Henry and Eleanora Bash. The wedding took place in New York at the exclusive Delmonico's restaurant. However, just three months later Morris' younger brother Abe ended his life.

In November of 1895 the couple had a baby girl named Amy, likely in remembrance of Abe.

The brothers disbanded in 1896, and the firm's merchandise was sold at auction.

Fortunately for Morris, his father-in-law Henry Bash purchased the stock, paid off the creditors, and kept Morris on as manager. By December of 1896 Morris and Mollie were able to incorporate the Morris Gross Company, moving back to 906–908 Pacific. Mollie's younger brother, Roman, joined them in Tacoma for a few years. However, Mollie's father died in 1899. In 1901 the couple named their newborn son Henry.

Morris continued his business on Pacific Avenue until 1910, when he moved to New York. There he again worked in the clothing industry until his death in 1940. His wife and children all died within thirteen months of each other in 1972 and 1973.

Helen Gross

Helen Gross Creger, April 1887
Courtesy of Douglas Salin

Helen Gross (1863–1958) also came directly to Tacoma. After a brief visit with Morris and Abe she moved to San Francisco with Dave. Fourteen months later she was engaged to William Creger (1853–1920), also a native of Rypin. For her wedding gift in September of 1887 her brothers commissioned life-size paintings of their parents. In 1893 Helen was able to return to Europe to visit her family.

The marriage created new opportunities, including the manufacturing firm of Creger & Gross. The San Francisco clothing factory was located just two blocks from Levi Strauss. The couple had three children – Henry in 1888, Gertrude in 1891, and Arthur in 1894. After the economy crashed William Creger ran a hotel and was in the drug business with his son Henry, a pharmacist.

Abraham Gross

Abraham Gross
Courtesy of Douglas Salin

Abraham Gross (1866–1895) joined his brothers in Tacoma when he was just 15. On his 21st birthday his brothers made him an equal partner in the firm. Abe immediately filed to become a U.S. citizen and was rewarded with a summons for jury duty. He joined a wide variety of fraternal organizations and in 1888, at the age of 22, became an officer in the Hebrew Benevolent Society. The following year he traveled back to Europe, visiting with his parents for six months. During the summer of 1892 Abe made an extended visit to New York, joining his brother Dave.

After the 1893 banking panic Abe worked tirelessly to rebuild Tacoma's economy through the Interstate Fair, which was a disaster. In March of 1895 Abe, just 28 years old, took his life. His death remains a mystery.

ABE GROSS DEAD IN HIS BED

Mysterious End of the Most Popular Man in Tacoma.

Suicide the Accepted Theory.

Tacoma Sunday Ledger March 31, 1895

Sunday Ledger, March 31, 1895, "Mr. Gross was always known as an aggressive, energetic business man and though but 28 years old he had by his enterprise, keen business foresight and untiring industry, attained a prominent position among the leading merchants of the northwest. Several years ago he dealt quite extensively in real estate in which he displayed excellent judgment and acquired considerable property. His admirable social qualities attracted a wide circle of warm friends by whom he was held in the highest esteem.

Like his brothers, Ellis and Morris, he was a thirty-second degree Mason and a member of the Mystic Shrine. He was a member of the Elks and usually attended the social sessions of that order...He belonged to the Eastern Star, the ladies' branch of the Masonic order, and was treasurer of the Masonic lodge of Perfection. He was a prominent member of the Knights of Pythias and a member of the Tacoma Athletic club. He was a prominent member of the Jewish congregation of Beth Israel and contributed toward the erection of the handsome synagogue at the corner of I and Tenth streets. He was at one time president of the Harmony club, a social organization composed of prominent Hebrews, and at the time of his death was president of the Hebrew Benevolent society. He was a member of every organization which had for its object the building up of Tacoma. For a number of years he had belonged to the Chamber of Commerce and two years ago was elected one of the trustees, serving one year. He was a charter member of the Commercial club and one of the trustees of the Interstate Fair association... Many citizens, particularly in the South end, will remember that Gross Bros. established and maintained at their own expense a free kindergarten several years ago. Abe had charge of the arrangements and saw that nothing was lacking to start the kindergarten on a first-class basis... He was a bashful man and naturally inclined to shun the society of ladies."

Rudolph and Rose Gross

Rudolph Gross c.1888
Courtesy of Douglas Salin

Joseph, the eldest Gross brother, stayed in Germany, but his son Rudolph (1873–1945) joined the rest of the family in Tacoma in 1887. Rudolph worked for his uncles and lived with Ellis. In September of 1889 Morris Gross filed a complaint with the police chief that the owner of the Mint saloon had been selling liquor to minors. Rudolph admitted he had been playing cards and billiards there for drinks. The owner was fined $25.

After the brothers went their separate ways Rudolph worked briefly for Joseph Hall and became a U.S. citizen in 1896. The following year he moved to Seattle, where he lived the rest of his life. In 1899 Rudolph married Rose Drosen (1877–1948). Like his uncles, in 1901 and in 1909 he returned to Europe to visit his parents. The couple had no children.

Gutfeld Family

Morris Gutfeld (c.1832–1898) and his wife Rebecca Kicoe (1833–1910) came to the U.S. from Schoensee, Poland, in October of 1891 to join their children in Tacoma. Their youngest daughter Ida traveled with them. They lived in Tacoma until at least 1896, then moved to San Francisco. After Morris' 1898 death Rebecca returned to Tacoma. Morris was buried in the Home of Peace Cemetery in Colma, California, and Rebecca was buried in the Home of Peace Cemetery in Tacoma.

Their eldest daughter Rosa came to the U.S. on her own in July of 1886. Less than two years later she married Herman Zelinsky. (See Zelinsky biography.)

Their eldest son Simon (1863–1934) was likely the first to immigrate, around 1881. He worked as a clerk for the Gross brothers and was responsible for managing a temporary Puyallup branch of the store. In 1885 Simon received a gold match case for his trusted service with the firm. He opened his own gents' furnishings store in Old Tacoma in the fall of 1886, and the following year opened the New England clothing store on Pacific Avenue.

Simon was active in German singing groups, the Germania Society, and the Oddfellows. In 1888 Simon served as financial secretary during the construction of the Germania Hall, and was also an organizer of the Hebrew Benevolent Society.

The following year Simon moved to San Francisco, where he married Rose Klarnet (1870–1957). Their daughter Hildegarde was born there in 1890 and then the couple returned to Tacoma, where Simon briefly operated a bakery with his brother Max. A son Carl was born in Tacoma in 1891, but the family again moved to San Francisco before the birth of Irwin in the fall of 1893. Carl was confirmed in the Geary Street temple in 1904. Simon operated a clothing store with his brothers in both cities, and the moves continued back and forth until he returned to Tacoma in 1908. For several decades Simon worked as a cashier for the streetcar company. His funeral was a Christian Science service.

Charles Gutfeld (1864–1933) joined his older brother Simon in Tacoma around 1883 and in 1885 worked as a clerk for Leon Hershberg. He lived in Fresno, California, from at least 1890 until 1896, then partnered with Simon in San Francisco. Charles returned to Tacoma by 1901, selling men's furnishings until his retirement in 1927.

Max Gutfeld (1866–1923) also came to Tacoma in the early 1880s, working at the New York Bakery in 1885. By 1888 he worked for Herman Zelinsky, his new brother-in-law, who witnessed his naturalization in 1892. Max moved to San Francisco around 1895 and married Emma Lasier (1860–1901). Their two sons, Louis and Arnold, were born there in 1896 and 1898.

By 1900 Max was back in Tacoma, operating the Germany Bakery at 1117 Pacific. After his wife's death he married again in 1903 to Ethel Bloom (1866–1945). The couple spent the next two decades in Skagway, Alaska.

A fourth son, Jacob Gutfeld (1870–1937) lived in Tacoma by 1892. In 1896 he married Helene Loesen (1869–1948) in Tacoma and also worked for Herman Zelinsky. Then he moved to San Francisco, where children Alfred, twins Martha and Selma, and Maurice were born in 1898, 1899 and 1901. Unlike his siblings, he remained in the San Francisco area the rest of his life.

Ida Gutfeld, (c.1875–1950), married Solomon Ottenheimer in Tacoma in 1893. (See Ottenheimer biography.)

Edward and Estelle Hain

Ed Hain (1844–1907) was born in Germany and was naturalized in New York in 1871, where he worked as a barber. His wife Estelle gave birth to Lillian, Gertrude and Abraham in New York between 1869 and 1875. Henry and Sam were born in San Francisco in 1876 and 1878. Estelle, a native of Alsace, died in San Francisco on August 22, 1882, at the age of 38. Ed registered to vote in October of 1882, then headed to Tacoma.

In 1884 Ed operated a barbershop in Tacoma, and in late March installed three bathing rooms with combination faucets. Two weeks later the entire block on the west side of Pacific burned. Ed moved across the street, and the following summer opened the Concordia Beer hall. During 1886 he spent several months in Snohomish, then returned to the barber business, this time on Seventeenth and Pacific.

Ed was active in the German chorus and the Germania Society, serving as secretary in 1888. That year he also briefly worked in real estate. The following year Ed was part of a campaign to obtain a liquor permit for the Germania hall, despite its residential location. He joined the Benevolent Society, and with his daughters was active in the Harmony Club. His daughter Gertrude married Edwin Heineman in Tacoma in September of 1890. (See Heineman biography.)

In October Ed's son Abe, just a teenager, was accused of forging his father's signature on a check. Abe fled to San Francisco, where he again wrote several bad checks – all around $20. He was sentenced to two years in prison for forgery. Abe served in the U.S. Army from 1893–1895, then married Leona Favre (1882–1964) in San Francisco in 1902. They had a daughter Rose (Olney) in 1903.

Ed Hain went missing from Tacoma at the end of May 1893. He turned up in the 1901 Canadian census living in British Columbia. His grave in the Home of Peace Cemetery has a death date of September 11, 1907.

Lillian Hain lived with her sister Gertrude until her 1906 marriage to Emil Korach. (See Korach biography.) Harry Hain (1876–1935) worked at a variety of jobs, from barber to bartender to cigar dealer. He married Jean around 1928 and died in Reno, Nevada.

Sammy Hain outlived all of his siblings. He worked as a quartz miner in Curlew, Washington, in 1900, then mined for gold in Junction City, California. In 1918 he worked at a chrome mine in Eldorado, California. Sammy lived the last fifty years of his life in Goldfield, Nevada, where he died in 1970 at the age of 92.

Joseph and Sarah Hall

Joseph Hall (1862–1914) emigrated from Hungary around 1883. He arrived in Tacoma in time to be included in the 1889 auditor's census, taken in April. That year he applied for a transfer of a liquor license for the Kentucky Liquor House, located at 1019 Pacific. Around 1891 he married Sarah Raphael, the middle of five daughters born to Julius and Helena Raphael of Stockton. Sarah was two years younger than Joseph but used a later birth year. She participated in several Jewish social events and fundraisers.

Joseph operated the Kentucky Liquor House until January of 1895, when Albert Weinberg served as receiver and quickly sorted out the business entanglements. Joseph regrouped, and in July of 1895 incorporated the New West Liquor Company with his wife and Joseph and Meyer Jacob. Joseph operated the firm at 1310 Pacific until May of 1897. That company also failed, but before the accompanying publicity was over Joseph was arrested for contempt of court; accused of removing liquor stock for his own use, of failing to appear in court, and of filing false notes to his wife and mother-in-law. In October his motion for a new trial was denied.

The remaining 21 barrels of liquor were finally sold by the receiver in August of 1898.

Tacoma Sunday Ledger May 23, 1897

Joseph's wife Sarah gave birth to a daughter Bernice in Tacoma on July 13, 1898. (Two earlier children had not survived.) The family spent the next decade in San Francisco with Sarah's family, before returning to Tacoma in 1911. After Joseph's death in 1914 Sarah and her daughter again moved to San Francisco. Bernice (1898–1980) married Arthur J. Philbert around 1927 and had a son Arthur Jr. in 1928 and a daughter Jacqueline in 1938.

Henry and Lena Harris

German-born Henry Harris (c.1842–1892) and his wife Lena had a son Aaron and a daughter, Esther, in New York around 1862 and 1865, and a son Sigmund in California in 1877. From 1880 until 1885 they lived in Seattle. Henry worked as a tailor with his father Isaac, moving to Tacoma in 1888. Henry was one of the first trustees of the Hebrew Benevolent Society, and the family participated in Harmony Club activities. Lena joined the Judith Montefiore Society in 1890 but resigned in June of 1892. Two months later Henry murdered his daughter and took his own life. His son Sigmund married Belle (1885–1968) around 1902 and had a son Leonard about 1906. Sigmund died in San Francisco in October of 1940.

Isaac Harris and Brothers

Tacoma Daily News 1891 annual
Tacoma Historical Society collection

Isaac Harris was the sixth of twelve children born to Marks and Mary (Peiser) Harris between 1856 and 1876. All but the first were born in California, where Marks worked as a clothing dealer. Isaac and his brothers Hyman, Louis and Maurice all found their way to Washington.

In 1889 they incorporated the Yakima-Tacoma Trading and Produce Company, taking advantage of the completion of the railroad over the Cascade Mountains. Hyman served as secretary, living in Yakima. Isaac served as president and lived in Tacoma, with a storefront at 1409 Pacific. He also served as treasurer of the Cle Elum Natural Ice Company, later known as Union Ice, with his friend Simon Hirsch as secretary.

Isaac was one of the first trustees of the Hebrew Benevolent Society, and was active in Harmony Club activities, serving as treasurer in 1891 and president in 1892. For several years he lived at the club, along with several other Jewish men in their mid-twenties.

Tacoma's *Daily Ledger* printed an annual business review in January of 1893. The Yakima-Tacoma Trading Company was included among the wholesale houses, carrying a line of fruits, vegetables, poultry, hay, grain and feed. In April the company was reorganized as Harris Brothers, with Hyman, Isaac and Louis as trustees. The firm moved to larger quarters at 1521–1523 Pacific, occupying four floors in the Sprague block. Harris Brothers also had large warehouses on Dock Street and Puyallup Avenue, with access to railroads and shipping. Union Ice grew to include Union Wood and Coal. Hyman continued to live in Yakima but frequently visited Tacoma.

Isaac was absent during much of 1894, beginning with the death of his mother and continuing due to his illness. In his absence, his bookkeeper embezzled nearly $6,000, putting the firm in financial jeopardy. A court-appointed receiver discovered the theft. The court case and financial settlements continued through April of 1895. That month Isaac served as a pallbearer at the funeral of his friend Abe Gross, then made an extended visit to the East Coast. He never again lived in Tacoma.

His friends and brothers started again, incorporating the Harris-Hirsch Match Company. Louis Harris of Yakima was president and Simon Hirsch and Oscar Reichenbach of Tacoma were trustees. The factory, the former Pacific Match Company on the corner of Twenty-fifth and East G Streets, employed 65 people.

In 1900 Isaac and his brother Michael operated a hotel in Davenport, Washington. Isaac moved to San Francisco, where he operated the Hotel Stanford until just before his death in

1920. His younger brother Maurice Harris died in Tacoma on May 1, 1904, and was interred in the Home of Peace Cemetery.

Edwin and Gertrude Heinemann

Edwin Heinemann (1860–1916) was the fifth of nine children born to Bernhardt and Johanna (Auerbach) Heinemann. The family came to the U.S. from Germany in 1876 and lived in St. Paul, Minnesota.

Edwin came to Tacoma in 1889 and worked as a clothing clerk for a variety of firms. His first employer, Prager Brothers, was succeeded by Jacoby, Ash and Company. Later Edwin worked for Goldenson and Sondheim, and its successor Rochester Clothing. He was active in several German singing groups, serving as president of the Tacoma Saengerbund in 1900.

Edwin married Gertrude Hain, (1869–1932) daughter of Edward Hain, in September of 1890. (See Hain biography.) Their son Bernhardt, born in December of 1891, lived only one week. Their daughter Estelle, born in September of 1893, survived. Gertrude's sister Lillian lived with the Heinemann family until her 1906 marriage to Emil Korach. (See Korach biography.)

Gertrude participated in temple fundraising activities, serving as secretary of the Judith Montefiore Society in 1903 and progressing to president in 1911. Estelle graduated from Stadium High School in 1911.

Edwin ventured into store ownership in 1902, supported by Albert Weinberg. Later he joined forces with Sam Posner to operate a large store at 1352–54–56 Pacific, built by Jacoby, Ash & Prager. In April of 1911 the stock of Edwin's store was sold to creditors. A troubled investment in another city was given as the cause.

Mr. Heinemann and Mr. Posner

—When Mr. Heinemann started to keep store at one end of Pacific Avenue, Mr. Posner was at the other. After a while there was a union of hands, hearts, dollars and stocks. With two stores and two heads getting together there was, from that minute, one good big, growing, lasting store. But the big hive of business at Fifteenth and Pacific tells the story better than ink. There are 65 feet of store front, 85 feet of show windows, 6,500 square feet of floor space, with every foot crowded with merchandise—and it's the kind of a storeful of things that people want, that invites you and me to come. By all means it's not a *shut-in store*, these men who have chosen to storekeep their way through the world seeing to it that they have a *stand-out* store. Their latest move is to make it a sunshine store. Eighteen big sunshine gas arcs are doing the lighting. These big lights get as near sunlight as it is possible to get. They make a bright, steady, cheering light and it makes no difference what kind of a business, *they help pull trade*. The Gas Co. makes no charge for installation.

Tacoma Daily News December 10, 1904

Edwin died in June of 1916 and was buried in the Home of Peace Cemetery near his infant son. His daughter Estelle had just married Isaac Epstein. In 1917 Estelle named her newborn son Edwin Heinemann Epstein. However, in January of 1919 Estelle died of the flu pandemic, while seven months' pregnant. Isaac took his toddler son to his Epstein parents in California. Gertrude moved to Ohio to join her sister Lillian, and died there in 1932.

Leon and Paulina Hershberg

Leon Hershberg (1837–1891) married Paulina Blumberg (1842–1919). They had five children in Prussia between 1859 and 1868, then came to the U.S. around 1870. Two more children were born in Pittsburgh in 1872 and 1877, where Leon operated a wholesale liquor business. The family moved to Oakland, California, around 1878. The couple's eighth child was born in Oakland in 1879. Leon partnered with Isaac Newman and Isaac Ryttenberg.

In the summer of 1883 the firm opened a Tacoma branch, with Albert Weinberg as manager. (See Weinberg biography.) Less than a year later the company's liquor stock, valued at $3,000, was destroyed in a fire that wiped out the entire block. The company tried several other locations on Pacific Avenue, then disbanded in March of 1886, with Hershberg continuing in Oakland. The dissolution of partnership was still in the Tacoma courts in October of 1887. Leon Hershberg died in Oakland in 1891.

Simon Hirsch

Tacoma Daily News 1891 annual
Tacoma Historical Society collection

HIRSCH & FRANK
IMPORTING TAILORS
AND HABERDASHERS

948 PACIFIC AVENUE.

The entire lines for Spring and Summer are now open for inspection.

The largest and most select stock of Merchant Tailoring and Furnishing Goods carried by any one house on the coast.

Also call attention to the change in cutters, having secured the services of Mr. John Leahy, from Chicago, who is considered a cutter second to none in the country.

Tacoma Daily Ledger March 28, 1892

Hirsch and Frank Store, 1007 Pacific
From the collection of the author

Simon Hirsch (1857–1930) was born in Hillesheim, Germany, on April 5, 1857. He immigrated to the U.S. in May of 1873, then lived in Des Moines, Iowa, where he was naturalized in 1879. In the spring of 1889 he opened a men's tailoring store at 1007 Pacific in Tacoma with Harry Frank. Simon also partnered with Isaac Harris in the Cle-Elum Ice Company, and lived with Isaac at the Harmony Club.

In December of 1891 the firm of Hirsch and Frank moved to 948 Pacific, recently vacated by Kaufman & Berliner. During the summer of 1893 they closed out their merchandise, but Simon purchased new stock and continued without his partner. Before year's end his goods were sold at a mortgage sale. He tried again, moving to 918 Pacific in May of 1894, a location vacated by the bankrupt Jacob Bernhard. Within six months Simon sold his fixtures and left the clothing business.

In April of 1895 Simon Hirsch and Oscar Reichenbach became trustees of the Harris-Hirsch Match Company. The company lasted about a year. Both Simon and Oscar headed to Dawson during the Klondike rush in 1898. Simon stayed in Alaska for twenty years, operating the Juneau Liquor Company from 1905 until 1917. He married Henrietta Ridgeway, a woman half his age, and lived the last decade of his life in Portland, Oregon, managing an apartment house.

Hirschfeld Siblings – Louis, Emil, and Rosalie

Louis Hirschfeld emigrated from Hamburg to the U.S. in July of 1862. He became a naturalized citizen in Nashville, Tennessee, in April of 1865. Louis married Clara Nathan (1853–1908) around 1876 and the couple's first daughter, Carrie, was born in Mississippi in 1877. Then they moved to San Francisco, where their daughter Nettie was born in 1879. A third daughter, May, was born in Tacoma in January of 1882.

In Tacoma Louis partnered with Julius Coleman for several years. The clothing store owners satisfied debt collectors in the spring of 1884, but a major fire in January of 1885 ended the business. Louis joined his brother Emil in Traver, California, where sons Leon and Monroe were born. Another fire in Traver in June of 1890 resulted in losses of $25,000 in general merchandise. In 1894 Louis registered to vote in Tulare, California. He died in San Francisco in July of 1902.

Emil Hirschfeld lived in Tacoma in 1883, erecting a public hall in Old Tacoma that was used for dances and receptions. He operated a saloon on the ground floor, renewing his liquor license in 1885. Emil lived in Tulare, California, in 1886. In 1887 he visited his sister, Rosalie Zelinsky, in Tacoma, before making a trip to Europe. Emil was involved in a lawsuit in San Francisco in 1893, and mortgaged property in Fresno and Tulare. In 1902 his name was included among his brother's survivors.

Their sister Rosalie Hirschfeld (1839–1913) married Hyman Zelinsky. (See Zelinsky biography.)

Sigmund and Leah Hirschfeld

Sigmund Hirschfeld (1835–1924) married Leah Levine (1842–1914) in England around 1862. Three children – Bertha, Morris and Clara – were born there in the next three years. Four more children – Rosa, Edith, Minnie and Arthur – were born in California. The family lived in Sacramento and Vallejo.

In 1888 the family moved to Tacoma, around the time Bertha married Henry Krech. (See Krech biography.) Leah joined the Judith Montefiore Society and participated in the 1892 Temple fair. Sigmund's store, Hirschfeld's Bazaar, sold books and stationery – first from 957 Tacoma Avenue and later from several locations on 13th and Pacific. (His brothers Philip and Charles were wholesale stationery dealers in Los Angeles.) Edith married Jacob Stusser in Tacoma in 1897. (See Stusser biography.)

FOR THE 4TH OF JULY 1897

Hirschfeld's Bazaar, 1322 Pac. Ave.

Closing out of Flags at the following low prices:

No.	1—Size 2x3 inches; price dozen	2c
No.	2—Size 2½x4 inches; price per dozen	3c
No.	3—Size 4x6 inches; price per dozen	5c
No.	4—4½x7½ inches; price per dozen	7c
No.	5—Size 6x9 inches; price per dozen	12c
No.	6—Size 8x14 inches; price per dozen	23c
No.	7—Size 12x18 inches; price per dozen	35c
No.	8—Size 18x27 inches; price per dozen	45c
No.	9—Size 20x36 inches; price per dozen	$1.00
No.	10—Size 27x43 inches; price per dozen	1.50
No.	11—Size 30x50 inches; price per dozen	2.00
No.	12—Size 40x66 inches; price per dozen	3.00

Six standard Wool Bunting Flags, size 9x6 feet, full number stars, only 4.50
Fireworks and flags at wholesale.
Bronze paper cap pistols, 35c per

Tacoma Morning Union July 3, 1897

Around 1897 Rosa took over the management of the stationery store, later selling a smaller line of cigars and tobacco through at least 1908. Sigmund and Leah lived in Tacoma the remainder of their lives and were buried in the Home of Peace Cemetery. Their children returned to California. Morris died unmarried in 1896. Clara married Patrick Haley. Minnie married several times, first to Arthur Bob. Her younger brother, Arthur, married Lucille Lancaster.

Harry and Sarah Hirschfeld

Harry Hirschfeld was born in Chicago in 1866, son of Abraham and Bertha Hirschfeld. He married Sarah Simon (1866–1938) in Tacoma in 1895. She was the daughter of Abraham Simon and the sister of Rebecca Simon Eckstein. (See Simon biography.) By the end of 1900 Sarah had given birth to four children – Florence, Alfred, Beno and Harriet. The first three were born in Chicago. Tacoma's 1901 city directory included Sarah as a widow.

Minutes of the Judith Montefiore Society show that in 1902 the group provided financial assistance to Sarah for clothing for the children. In 1904 a committee made arrangements to send the children to the Orphans' Asylum in San Francisco. However, Sarah was included in the 1910 census in Tacoma with all four of her children. The following year she and her son Alfred were in court for a domestic disagreement, accompanied by her trained goose. Alfred had been supporting the family by selling newspapers.

Both of the boys enlisted in the Army, serving just several months at the end of 1918. Then the weddings started – Flora to Leon Vanderbilt in 1919, Harriet to George Paiser in 1923, Alfred to Sybil Sidelsky in 1923, Beno to Lucille Florsheim around 1925, Flora again to Phil Brownstin in 1925, and Harriet again to Harry Jacobs in 1925. Sarah's 1938 obituary mentioned only two of her children as survivors.

Bernhard and Sophie Hochstadter

Bernhard Hochstadter (1866–1969) was born in Munich, Germany, and immigrated to the U.S. in 1884. He married Sophie Drucker (1867–1958) in Vancouver, Washington, on May 28, 1890. The month before he had incorporated the Centralia Soda Water and Bottling Works, manufacturing soft drinks and ciders. In 1895 the couple moved from Centralia to Tacoma, where Bernhard worked as a traveling salesman for the Pacific Brewing & Malting Company. In March of 1898 Bernhard was one of the organizers of the United Order of Commercial Travelers, dubbed by the *Ledger* as "Jolly Knights of the Grip."

Sophie was a trained vocalist and regularly performed with the Ladies' Musical Club, often for charitable benefits. In March of 1899 she agreed to teach the first temple choir. Sophie served as treasurer of the Judith Montefiore Society in 1903, but resigned to travel to Europe for six months, continuing her musical training. Her husband joined her for part of the time.

Upon their return the couple moved to Everett, Washington, where Bernhard was part of a group that started the Everett Brewery. He also operated Grand Leader Dry Goods. The couple again traveled to Europe in 1922. After Prohibition Bernhard returned to the liquor industry, incorporating the Horluck Brewing Company, again with a team of investors. The couple lived in Seattle during the 1930s, then moved to Los Angeles, California. Sophie appeared as a registered voter until her death in 1958 at the age of 91. Remarkably, Bernhard lived until November 14, 1969, his lifetime spanning nearly 103 years.

Morris Hochstetter

Morris Hochstetter (1839–1914) was born in Heinsheim, Baden, and immigrated to the U.S. in 1858. He lived in Niagara, New York, in 1860, as did his older brother Albert. Throughout the 1860s Morris worked for Albert in a dry goods store in Buffalo, New York. Morris made at least two return trips to Germany, in 1876 and 1890.

In 1891 Morris turned up in Tacoma. He lived with Archie Ash and Isaac Dornberg and operated a loan office. An ad in the *Tacoma Daily Ledger* on October 14, 1891, described his business, recently relocated to 1107 Pacific. "Short time loans on good personal security will always receive attention. Also commercial paper bought and sold." In the spring of 1894 Morris briefly operated a branch of the California Vineyard Company of Portland.

Morris spent the spring of 1895 entangled in the receivership of the failed Jacoby, Ash and Company, complete with lawsuits and countersuits. *Ledger,* March 11, 1895,

"The Mortgagee Wants Money. The Creditors Want Money. The Employees Want Money. And the only way out of this trouble is for me to raise money as quick as I can to get out of the receivership so none of these can trouble me again. M. Hochstetter, receiver for Jacoby, Ash & Co." The stock was sold at sheriff's auction on Saturday morning, March 30th, just as Abe Gross's body was found.

In 1896 Morris worked from 1113 Pacific and roomed at the Bostwick Hotel, where several years earlier Rossell G. O'Brien had first proposed a resolution that members of the Loyal Legion always stand and remove their hats during the playing of the national anthem, starting the tradition. Throughout the '90s Morris also speculated in Canadian oil fields, perhaps in conjunction with his wealthy brother Albert and his nephew Ralph.

Morris continued living at the Bostwick and working in real estate and brokering loans well into his seventies. He died unmarried in January of 1914 and was buried in the Home of Peace Cemetery. His brother's children also had no descendants, leaving over twenty million dollars to the University of Buffalo and the University of Rochester.

Abraham and Rosa Hockwald

Although he consistently reported he was born in New York in April of 1853, Abraham Hockwald was likely born in Europe before his father, Israel, immigrated to the U.S. in December of that year. Israel and Mary Hockwald had three children in Austria in the early 1850s, then three more in New York between 1855 and 1863. A seventh sibling was born in Missouri in 1866. The family lived in New Orleans in 1870 and Mary died in Galveston, Texas, in 1874.

Abraham Hockwald registered to vote in San Francisco in the fall of 1875. He worked as a clerk for a decade, and in February of 1886 married Rosa Joseph (1866–1952), daughter of Isaac and Hannah Joseph. Rosa's first daughter, May, was born in Garfield County, Washington Territory, exactly nine months later. The following year the family came to Tacoma, where four more children were born – Elsie, Israel, Lionel and Sigmund. Rosa joined the Judith Montefiore Society in 1890.

For several years Abraham operated the Globe Lodging House in Tacoma. He was active in the B'nai B'rith and the Tacoma Relief Society. During 1892 and 1893 he worked as a commission broker at 1540 Pacific, managing the Northwest Commission Company. An 1893 court case indicated that he had contracted for 150 tons of potatoes at $17 per ton.

After the 1893 banking panic the family returned to San Francisco. Three more children were born there between 1895 and 1901. Abraham found a career selling and manufacturing disinfectant chemicals. The firm began as West Disinfecting and around 1905 became Hockwald Chemical – a name that would survive for over sixty years. Abraham died in San Francisco on December 1, 1917. His sons Lionel and Sigmund continued operating Hockwald Chemical in Sacramento, Los Angeles, Seattle and Hawaii.

David M. and Martha Hoffman

David Hoffman was born in Germany on December 24, 1867. He came to the U.S. around 1884, joining his older brothers Louis and Samuel in Leavenworth, Kansas. After four years working in a candy factory he started his own fruit and candy business, even though he was just 21. It was one of over 30 similar stores in Leavenworth, and located next to his brother's jewelry store. His sister Yetta lived with him, then married Emanuel Waldocks.

David moved to Tacoma, where he managed Albert Weinberg's Monogram Saloon at 1009 Pacific, receiving his own liquor license in May of 1890. Advertising in the *Tacoma Ledger* included the phrase "Established 1884," meaning the Monogram's start date, not David's arrival in Tacoma.

In October of the following year David married Martha Wolf (1867–1948.) She was the daughter of Oregon pioneers Simon Wolf and Regina Riddleheim. Martha's sister Rosa had married Meyer Gottstein in 1889, a Seattle liquor dealer. For the next two decades a steady stream of Gottstein and Wolf relatives paid regular visits to the Hoffman family in Tacoma, with reciprocal visits from Martha to Portland and Seattle. Each visit apparently required hosting a luncheon or reception, with published guest lists reading like a "Who's Who" of Tacoma's Jewish females.

After a brief candy venture with Herman Bryer in 1892, David returned to the liquor business. He managed the Anheuser-Busch Brewing Association, with a large store room at the wharf, plus a saloon at 913 Pacific. (Later 915–917 Pacific.) His exclusive agency for Anheuser-Busch likely helped him survive the tough economy after the 1893 banking panic. The Hoffmans' son, Jacob, was born in Tacoma on December 15, 1893, although the 1892 census included a one-year-old son Willie.

In February of 1897 David moved his business to 1140 Pacific, prompting the city council to propose a new ordinance prohibiting the sale of liquor in buildings on the west side of Pacific Avenue. The east side of Pacific had long been known as Whiskey Row, but the west side (even-numbered) was primarily occupied by retail merchants. David's existing business would be exempt, of course. The firm continued to grow through the end of the decade, advertising heavily.

In the spring of 1898 the Hoffman family made headlines when their 14-year-old maid was arrested, suspected of stealing a pair of diamond earrings valued at $325. The girl's family filed a $2,500 damage suit for false arrest and damage of character. After a lengthy trial, a year later she was awarded $1,000, a decision that was promptly appealed.

Tacoma's chapter of the Council of Jewish Women was organized in February of 1903, with Martha as president. The organization's Seattle visitors included Mrs. Gottstein.

David tried working with several more partners, including F.W. Foulkes and A.J. Wolff, and investing in real estate. Sale of his lot in the Flatiron Block in 1906 brought him $25,000. He briefly retired (aged 39) and took his family on a trip to Jerusalem.

In 1919 David served as president of the congregation, assisting in the choice of a location for a new synagogue. The following year he became chair of the building committee, but by 1922 resigned over differences that were "erased from the minutes." The earliest grave in the *Chevra Kadisha* Cemetery is that of Stewart Hoffman. The headstone says "Dedicated by David M & Martha Hoffman – died *Seventh Shevat*, 1922." Their relationship is unknown.

David and Martha moved briefly to Seattle, then joined their son Jacob in San Francisco, where they died in 1947 and 1948. Jacob (1893–1969) married Esther Roth (1895–1976) but the couple had no children.

David's younger brother Harry died in Tacoma in 1936. He had worked for David as a clerk, then operated Hoffman's Family Liquor House. During Prohibition Harry sold groceries and notions and worked for his nephew, Joseph Weinstein. Harry was buried in Home of Peace Cemetery near his sister, Yetta Waldocks.

Hoffman Family Liquors jug
From the collection of the author

Oscar and Florence Hoffman

Oscar S. Hoffman (1870–1956) was born in San Francisco, son of Simon and Regina Hoffman. He worked as a bookkeeper in San Francisco from 1887 to 1890, then made his way to Tacoma, where he did the same for the Donau Brewing Company. In April of 1892 Oscar joined with Hugo Donau and other young Jewish men in forming the Stag Seven club. He returned to San Francisco and in December of 1900 married Florence Jacobs (1875–1960), daughter of Julius and Sara Jacobs. The couple had no children.

Samuel and Mary Holland

Samuel J. Holland
Courtesy of David Flood

Solomon J. Holland was born in May of 1855 in Brooklyn, New York, the fourth of nine children born to Daniel and Amelia Holland. (Later he used the name Samuel.) He married Mary Scanlan (1856–1910) in Ligonier, Noble County, Indiana on February 21, 1878. Their son Harry was born in Indiana in July 28, 1880. Sam lived in Spokane from about 1884 to 1888. He sold cigars and wholesale liquor, and later operated the Comique Theater.

In 1889 Sam opened a Tacoma branch of the liquor business at 1310 Pacific in partnership with Samuel Loeb, also from Ligonier. The Milwaukee Saloon occupied three stories, with a bar and restaurant on the first floor, and billiards and pool on the upper floors.

Sam joined the cemetery association and Mary joined the Judith Montefiore Society. Their son Leon was born in Tacoma in February of 1890.

By 1892 the family had moved back to Spokane. Sam worked briefly with his brother Isaac, then operated the Washington Liquor Company. The liquor business prospered and Sam's son Harry joined the firm as bookkeeper. Isaac's sons Mose and Julius operated the Kentucky Wine & Liquor company in Ritzville.

In 1901 Sam's son Harry married Clementine Baum, daughter of Portland's Simon Baum and Marjana Bettman. (Marjana's brothers had opened a store in Olympia in 1853, possibly the first Jewish business in that city.) Harry's daughter Harriett (Mrs. Charles Hassmann) was born in Spokane in July of 1907. A month later Sam Holland died in Sandpoint, Idaho, while on a business trip. Apparently he slipped on the wet tracks while crossing from his hotel to the depot and was struck by a train. Mary died in Spokane in 1910.

Adele Joseph Strasburger Imes

Adele Joseph Imes Family
Courtesy of Frank Sperling

Adele Joseph was born in New York in 1859, daughter of Ellis and Rosetta Joseph. While still in her teens she married Morris Louis Strasburger, who with his brother Isadore operated the Colorado Store in Virginia City, Montana. The couple had three children in Montana – Nathaniel, Herman and Leah – between 1877 and 1884. (The children later used the name Strasburg.) Morris died in 1884.

In May of 1885 Adele married attorney William A. Imes (1856–1920) in Bozeman, Montana. Their daughter Clara was born there the following summer. In the summer of 1893 the family arrived in Tacoma, and William filed his Montana bar certificate in Pierce County in November.

In February of 1894 William was one of the incorporators of the Tacoma Bazaar company, along with Julius, Simon and Samuel Basinski – all recently arrived from Montana. (See Basinski biography.) Adele was elected secretary of the Judith Montefiore Society in May of 1894, but resigned the following week. William continued practicing law in Tacoma through 1895, with no other affiliation with Tacoma's Jewish community.

The family moved to San Francisco. However, Adele filed for divorce in October of 1903. William died in 1920 and was buried with his brother James. Adele lived briefly with her brother Philip in Michigan, then returned to San Francisco, where she died in 1935. Her obituary mentioned a fifth child, Frank Cutter, of New York.

NEW FIRM !
NEW GOODS !

IXL STORE
Mann's Block,
— DEALERS IN —
GENERAL MERCHANDISE
BOOTS, SHOES,
CLOTHING
DRY GOODS,
GENTS' FURNISHING GOODS
S. ISAACS & BRO.,
Mann's Block, second door from Bank.
Tacoma News September 14, 1882

Isaacs Siblings

Michael Isaacs and Johanna Michaels had at least ten children. The birthplaces of their offspring indicate the journeys of the family – the first two born in Nakel, Prussia, in 1851 and 1852; the third in New York around 1854; and the remainder in San Francisco between 1857 and 1874. Michael worked as a tailor and operated clothing and furniture stores.

The eldest son, Isador, married Jennie Wertheimer around 1878 and moved with her family to Portland, Oregon. Henry, Alexander and Samuel operated a clothing store together in San Francisco between 1878 and 1880, then opened a store in Tacoma in 1882. In 1883 they registered a trademark for the IXL Dry Goods Store, causing confusion with Abe Simon's IXL Boot and Shoe Store. Abe changed his to Terminus Boot & Shoe, while the brothers added their name to their firm.

That summer Samuel Isaacs and Louis Levin purchased land on Pacific Avenue and built a two-story brick building. Younger brother Morris joined the firm in the spring of 1884, arriving just two days before a major fire wiped out the entire block. Their father came from San Francisco to sort out insurance, the brothers regrouped, and Louis Levin rebuilt.

In October of 1884 Louis Levin married Mary Isaacs, starting a string of annual weddings. (See Levin biography.) Henry made Bella Goldsmith his bride in 1886, (see Goldsmith biography,) Lena married Aaron Yehl in 1887, (see Yehl biography,) and Samuel married Gertrude Jaffe in 1888. (See Jaffe biography.) Alexander followed suit in 1889, marrying Rose Martin. (See Martin biography.) Morris waited until 1893 to marry Anna Isaacs, perhaps distracted by his musical training. The siblings built homes and business buildings, and extended family members made regular visits between San Francisco and Tacoma. The wives frequently wintered in San Francisco.

Isaacs siblings were actively involved in Jewish social groups, including the Harmony Club and the Judith Montefiore Society. In December of 1892 they brought additional family members to Tacoma to assist in the Temple Aid Society events. They survived the 1893 banking panic and continued to be active in the Jewish community for another decade.

Samuel and Alexander stayed in Tacoma through 1902, but were jailed in 1904 for their inability to pay creditors. Morris found work as a liquor salesman and lasted a few more years before joining family in San Francisco.

Jacob Siblings

Five children born to Pauline (Wormser) and Alexander Jacob in Schalbach, Lorraine, made their way to California and then to Tacoma. Their uncle, David Jacob (1838–1898), came first. He was followed by Abraham (1858–1900) and Michael (1862–1912), who operated Jacob Brothers' boot and shoe store in Oakland, California, in 1879. A few years later the arrival of Meyer (1872–1935) gave them the opportunity to add a second location. After a brief venture in San Diego the brothers opened a store in Tacoma, around 1888.

The Chicago Shoe company, first located on 10th near Pacific, opened at 1017 Pacific in March of 1890. A.J. Jacob served as proprietor, and Michael and Meyer worked as clerks. The brothers moved to 1140 Pacific in 1892, and by fall the company was in David's name.

Sister Florestine (1859–1936) arrived around 1892, immediately participating in Jewish social activities and working at the Temple fair. Florestine didn't marry, but most of her brothers did. Abraham married Sarah Lippmann (1865–1945) in 1887. Their first daughter, Pearl, was born in California in 1888 before the family came to Tacoma. They returned to California and lived in San Diego, where another daughter, Ruby, was born in 1896. Abraham died in June of 1900. His sister Melanie (1870–?) lived with the family.

Michael married in 1891, to Miss Rachel Mayer (1864–1925) of San Francisco. She was the daughter of Hannah and Leopold Mayer, first president and an 1858 founder of Portland's congregation Beth Israel. Rachel's sister Carrie had married David Germanus in San Francisco in 1882. (See Germanus biography.) Michael and Rachel had a son Edwin in Tacoma in the spring of 1892, and a daughter Hortense in San Francisco in 1895, before moving to Portland, Oregon, around 1898. Both Michael and Rachel died in Portland.

Meyer emerged as the proprietor of David Jacob & Co. He advertised regularly, emphasizing bargains and offering creative sales promotions. Meyer was able to turn the 1893 banking panic into opportunity. He frequently purchased bankrupt stock at auction in other cities, then passed the savings on to Tacoma's shoppers.

In the summer of 1894 Meyer purchased the stock and shelving of the Snohomish Mercantile Company, right around the time his brother Joseph (1865–1929) moved to Tacoma from Snohomish. Meyer shifted one door north to 1138 Pacific, while Joseph sold dry goods at 1136 Pacific. Joseph started with the bankrupt clothing stock from Simon Hirsch's inventory, and the City of Paris name from Jacob Kullman. In the fall of 1894 Joseph gave the sermon at *Rosh Hashana* and was a lay leader during *Yom Kippur* services, starting an annual tradition.

WE WANTED TO GET OUR SHOES INTO ALL THE LADIES' HEADS.

There may be a few who don't know that we carry a complete line of Ladies' Shoes. To these few ladies who have not heard of it, we now extend a cordial invitation to come and see the largest and best assorted stock of Ladies', as well as Men's and Children's Shoes in the State. In every case the prices are guaranteed lower than similar goods elsewhere. Here are two samples of many good values for today and to-morrow:

Ladies' Tan Oxfords, needle and narrow square toe, from AA to EE, sizes 2½ to 8. Sold elsewhere $2.00. Our Price .... **$ .98**

Ladies' Tan Juliets and Prince Alberts, all styles of toe and last. Value $3.00. Our Special **1.48**

CHICAGO SHOE STORE,
Sign of the Big Silver Boot Over Entrance.　　1138 Pacific Ave.

Tacoma Daily Ledger June 7, 1895

Joseph and Meyer kept expanding, and in August of 1895 incorporated the New West Liquor Company with Joseph Hall. The venture lasted just two years, as Hall got behind on his license fees and lacked cash to pay the resulting fines. Ads for Chicago Shoe and City of Paris dry goods firm kept growing and growing, with no mention of the Jacob name. The Jacob brothers understood that Tacoma's shoppers couldn't afford top-quality merchandise. Sales typically included merchandise slightly damaged by fire or flood.

In February of 1898 Meyer Jacob married Jennie Marks, (1871–1945) eldest daughter of Stockton's Moses and Carrie Marks. Both Joseph and Meyer transferred their business interests to David Jacob. David then gave a large chattel mortage to his mother-in-law, Caroline Boris, which caught the attention of creditors and brought five garnishment suits. A month later, before the problem was resolved, David suffered a fatal heart attack.

Meyer cut short his wedding trip and returned to Tacoma. Two months later the creditors settled for twenty cents on the dollar and Meyer and Joseph were back in business. Jennie

and Florestine became active in the Judith Montefiore Society, and Joseph taught the religious school students. Meyer began a lengthy term as temple president.

May brought yet another death, that of their maternal uncle, Michael Wormser, "Don Miguel." However this time, each of the Jacob siblings inherited a portion of their uncle's half-million dollar Phoenix estate, consisting of over 10,000 acres of land. The following year, after the land was sold, Joseph traveled to Europe. On his return he married David's daughter, Helene Jacob (1877–1940). Their daughter Madeleine was born in California about 1903. Then the family moved to Aberdeen, Washington, where Joseph sold shoes, was active in the small Jewish community, and taught language classes. They returned to San Francisco in the '20s.

Meyer and Jennie also had children. Their three-year-old son Armand Wormser Jacob died in 1905. Daughters Margaret (1906–1983) and Clemence (1909–1999) survived. When Dave Gross left Tacoma in 1910, Meyer bought his interest in the Lou Johnson Company, a ladies' clothing store. Meyer and Jennie lived another decade in Tacoma, then retired to California. Throughout their thirty-plus years in Tacoma their name was consistently misspelled in newspaper mentions, typically Jacobs rather than Jacob.

Their daughter Margaret married Walter Kaplan, known for introducing the charge card to the West Coast. Clemence married three times; to Philip Selig, A. Samuel Glikbarg, and Rollin Wheeler. Meyer's sister, Florestine Jacob, stayed in Tacoma and died in 1936.

Moses Steif and Anna Jacobs

Moses Steif Jacobs and daughters circa 1915
Courtesy of Ann Fuller

Moses Steif (1841–1920) and Anna Wendum (1844–1899) had two daughters in Austro-Hungary (now Drohobycz, Ukraine) before coming to the U.S. Shortly after their arrival they took the surname Jacobs. Their next three children were born in New York, Arkansas and Missouri. They returned to Arkansas, where two of their daughters became brides. Lena married Max Broh in 1881, and Rose married Archie Ash in 1884. (See Ash and Broh biographies.)

The Jacobs family lived in St. Louis, Missouri, from about 1889 to 1893. Then they joined their married daughters in Tacoma. In 1894 their third daughter, Pauline, married Portland's Sidney Prager, son of Hyman Prager and Frances Jacoby. (See Prager biography.)

Moses Jacobs was one of the charter trustees of Temple Beth Israel during its formation in 1893. He served as the second temple president, following Solomon Jacoby. During 1894 and 1895 the intermarried families of Ash, Jacobs, Jacoby and Prager went through a series of complex financial maneuvers trying to salvage the large dry goods firms in both Tacoma and Portland. By 1896 all had moved from Tacoma.

The Jacobs family settled in Portland, where Anna died in 1899. Their fourth child, Edward (1875–1913), operated the Peoples Store clothing firm and lived with Pauline. Their youngest daughter, Jeane (1878–1961), married Albert Asher around 1903. Following Edward's death the majority of the remaining family members moved to San Francisco, where Moses died in 1920.

Solomon and Bertha Jacoby

Solomon and Jacob (James) Jacoby
Courtesy of Bob Jacoby

Solomon Jacoby (1853–1934) and Bertha Mayer (1857–1943) were married in Germany in April of 1879. Their son Julius (1880–1949) was born in New York the following summer, followed by Mollie (1885–1958). In 1886 the family moved to Portland, Oregon, joining Sol's sister Frances, Mrs. Hyman Prager. Hyman operated a large clothing store in Portland, along with his brother, Louis, and a third brother, William, in New York. Sol worked for Prager Brothers in Portland for several years, then opened a Tacoma branch.

The team signed a lengthy lease and built a three-story brick on the corner of Fifteenth and Railroad, now the site of the convention center on Commerce. The $34,000 store opened in October of 1889 as the Farmer's and Mechanic's Store, offering one clearly-marked price to all. Within three years the firm boasted growth from eight employees to 32 and made a large addition to the building.

Tacoma Daily Ledger February 9, 1892

In 1890 Bertha helped organize the Judith Montefiore Society and served several terms as vice president. Sol was a charter officer of the *B'nai B'rith*. The following year Sol served as a trustee of the Hebrew Benevolent Society. He went on to chair the synagogue organizing committee and served as first temple president. During the 1893 building dedication Sol had the honor of carrying in the Torah scroll and lighting the flame for the *Ner Tamid* (Eternal Light).

On an 1892 East Coast buying trip Sol met his younger brother Jacob (James) and family on their arrival from Germany to help run the store. Descendants relate the family traveled across the country in a private railroad car. (James was married to Sophie Meyer, sister of Sol's wife Bertha.) James moved to Seattle around 1899 and died there in 1906. Several of his six children moved to Los Angeles, and the rest went to Vancouver, British Columbia.

Prager Brothers, and its successor Jacoby-Ash, did not survive the effects of the 1893 banking panic. Goldenson and Sondheim (later Rochester) took over the store location, keeping Sol on as a clerk. Mollie Jacoby was confirmed in 1900 and in 1903 Bertha was elected treasurer of the newly-organized Council of Jewish Women.

In 1906 the family returned to Portland, where Mollie married Milton Freiberg and had two children – Bernice and Jerome. Around 1909 they all moved to Spokane, where Sol and Bertha were again active in the Jewish community and lived the remainder of their lives. Julius married Elsa Guettel in December of 1909 and moved to Providence, Rhode Island, but had no children. Mollie and Milton Freiberg moved to Seattle. Their daughter Bernice married Phillip Soth, and their son Jerome married Adelyne Raban.

Hannah Kant

Miss Hannah Kant, born in Germany around 1861, lived in Tacoma from about 1887 to 1892. She attended Jewish social events and joined the Judith Montefiore Society. Hannah operated a lunch business and built her own home. A three-week hospital stay in the fall of 1890 cost $36, which Hannah borrowed from the Society and repaid in installments.

Marcus B. Katze

Marcus Benjamin Katze was born in San Andreas, California, in 1862, son of Benjamin and Virginia Katze. He lived in Tacoma as Mark Katz between 1890 and 1893, working for the Harris Brothers in their Yakima-Tacoma Trading Company. Marcus worked as a salesman in San Francisco from 1896 to 1900, before moving to Mexico City, Mexico. He married first Amelia Cohn in 1890, then Leah Nichols in 1902. Leah had two children in Mexico City – Wallace in 1903 and Mark in 1906. After several decades in Mexico, Marcus moved to Los Angeles, where he died in 1931.

David L. and Sarah Kaufman & Sons

David L. Kaufman (1852–1931) and his wife Sarah Topper (1857–1943) had four sons in Kippen, Russia, before coming to Minneapolis, via Montreal – Joseph, Jacob, Charles and Samuel. In Minnesota they had another son and a daughter, Philip and Annie.

David and his older sons sold secondhand furniture and household goods in Tacoma from 1892 to 1896, while their younger sons sold newspapers. Their store was on the east side of Tacoma Avenue just south of 11th. Mrs. D.L. Kaufman joined the Judith Montefiore Society briefly in 1893. David and most of the family moved to Spokane and later Los Angeles.

D. L. KAUFMAN & SON,
DEALERS IN
New and Second-hand Furniture,
Carpets, Stoves, Etc.
Crockery and Queensware.
1131 Tacoma Avenue,
TACOMA, WASH.

Tacoma City Directory 1893–1894

David's eldest son Joseph married Sarah Abrams in 1895. (See Abrams biography.) Their daughters Lillian and Ruth were born in Tacoma in 1896 and 1898. Mrs. Joseph Kaufman was a member of the Judith Montefiore Society from 1901 to 1908. Around 1911 the couple joined Sarah's Abrams relatives in Seattle.

About 1930 they followed the rest of the Kaufman family to Los Angeles. Joseph and his mother lived together the remainder of their lives, while their spouses lived separately. Both of Joseph's daughters died unmarried in Los Angeles in the 1970s.

Colonel Meyer and Minna Kaufman

Col. Meyer Kaufman
Courtesy of Tcoma Public Library

Meyer Kaufman was born in Dramsfeld, Germany in 1844. A week after his seventeenth birthday he enlisted in the Army of the Confederacy, serving as a private in the Eighth Georgia Infantry. His pension records indicate that during two enlistments spanning four years he suffered three flesh wounds, in addition to frequent epileptic seizures. Little is known of the next two decades of his life.

His future bride, Minna Auerbach Berliner (born 1857), arrived in the U.S. in November of 1883 with her two sons, Max and Arthur, along with her brother Hyman Auerbach and extended family. Within a year Minna and Meyer were married and ready to open a store in Tacoma, along with Minna's brother-in-law, Zadek Peritz. The store was a branch of Toklas & Singerman, of Seattle, made up of a complex network of Auerbach and Toklas relatives.

Peritz & Co. opened in November of 1884, selling dry goods, clothing, hats and caps, boots and shoes from the corner of Thirteenth and Pacific. A bit off the beaten retail path, the firm compensated with rigorous newspaper advertising, which was rewarded with numerous social mentions. Meyer and Minnie's daughter Martha was born in Tacoma on August 18, 1885.

A month later Zadek returned to Europe and Meyer continued the firm with Henry Berliner, another brother-in-law of Minna's.

Meyer also jumped on the bandwagon of anti-Chinese sentiment, serving on several prominent committees. After the November 3rd riots and expulsion, Meyer was one of 27 people indicted for conspiracy against the Chinese and later acquitted. With his newfound popularity, Meyer was able to move the store to 948 Pacific the following year, and to launch a brief but prominent political career supporting the Democratic Party. By the fall of 1887 the name Kaufman & Berliner was so well-known that their ads could simply begin with a large block-style "K. & B." Meyer's political work was rewarded in June of 1888 when Governor Semple appointed him to his staff as Paymaster-General, with the rank of colonel.

Meyer, now Colonel Kaufman, was also active in the Jewish community. He served as the first president of the Hebrew Benevolent Society and helped organize the first congregation.

Minna joined the Judith Montefiore Society but was absent from most of the meetings.

Their Toklas and Singerman relatives lost heavily in the 1889 Seattle fire. Kaufman & Berliner started cutting back, closing out lines of clothing and shoes. When Meyer died in February of 1891 the firm was dissolved. Creditors were happy to get 35 cents on the dollar. Minna, her daughter Martha, and her sons Arthur and Max Berliner, moved to Seattle. The boys followed Peritz and Bilak relatives to Quezaltenango, Guatemala.

Martha Kaufman (1885–1965) joined her half-brothers in Guatemala and married Siegfried Koenigsberger (1870–1947). Siegfried and his brothers were in the export/import business and traveled frequently. In December of 1899 he and his brother Gustave tried unsuccessfully to "export" $2,300 in silver coin from Guatemala, and were fortunate to secure release after only one night in jail. Siegfried and Martha's only child, a son Milton John, was born in Guatemala City in 1904.

"Old" Meyer and Flora Kaufman

Meyer Kaufman was born around 1833 in Gallantsch, Prussia, or Golinch, Germany, now Golancz, Poland. He arrived in New York in August of 1857, and in 1860 lived in San Francisco. Around 1869 Meyer married Flora Fischer and in 1870 the couple lived in Reno, Nevada.

Then they made their way to Tacoma, where Meyer operated a store and saloon/hotel. Their daughter Carrie was born in Tacoma on June 24, 1875, possibly the first Jewish child born in Tacoma. Carrie later married her father's business partner, Sam Andrews. (See Andrews biography.) Meyer wisely invested in real estate, which he began selling in the 1880s. By 1883 he was able to purchase a prime lot on 2nd Street, now the corner of North 30th and McCarver, for $5,000. He also built homes on A Street and several large business buildings on Pacific Avenue.

After another Meyer Kaufman moved to Tacoma in 1884, newspaper mentions began describing Old Town's Meyer as "Old Meyer." He continued selling property and a grocery business as his wife's health declined. Flora died in Tacoma on June 17, 1886, at the age of only 38. She was buried in the Tumwater cemetery near Olympia. In February of 1887 Meyer filed to become his minor daughter's legal guardian. For the next decade he had to request permission of the courts every time he wished to buy, sell, or mortgage any of Carrie's real estate holdings.

The following year the widowed Louisa Goodtime came to help run the household, moving from Steilacoom. During 1889 they moved to New Tacoma, into a home located at 1606 Tacoma Avenue. In October Meyer hosted a meeting in his home to form a cemetery association. At some point Flora's grave was moved to Tacoma.

As a teenager his daughter Carrie assisted in fundraising events for the Temple Aid Society, and joined the citywide Ladies' Mandolin

Club. In March of 1894 she was briefly engaged to Frank Miller, of New York. However, in 1897 Carrie married Tacoma's widowed Sam Andrews. (See Andrews biography.) The couple had no children and the Kaufman line ended.

Meyer Kaufman died in Tacoma on March 17, 1900, of "Bright's Disease" at the age of 67. His obituary, published in Tacoma and Seattle, described him as a large property owner, a generous giver to charities, and a promoter of public enterprises. However, nearly every date and number in the obituary was inaccurate – including his age, his date of death, his daughter's name, and even the spelling of his own name.

Herman Klaber

Herman Klaber (1870–1912) was the second of three children born in San Francisco to George and Bertha Klaber. His younger brother Selig died in 1877. His older sister, Sarah (1868–1904), married first Louis Danhauser, giving birth to a daughter, Dorothy, in 1890. Louis died in 1891. Sarah later married Herman Kaufman (1865–1926), bearing a daughter, Elsa in 1901. George Klaber died in 1893 and Herman's relatives followed him to the Northwest. Sarah died in Tacoma in 1904, as did her mother Bertha in 1911. Both participated in Jewish social circles.

As mentioned, Herman was in business throughout Washington as a grower and broker of hops, with offices in San Francisco and London. In 1906 he married Gertrude Ginsberg, (1885–1961), daughter of Samuel Ginsberg and Bertha Rosenzweig. Herman and Gertrude's daughter, Bernice, was born in Portland in 1910. (Bertha's sister Lillian married Marcus Netter in 1901, part of Herman's brokerage firm.) The Klaber family lived in Portland and summered at their "bungalow" at Klaber, cleverly titled the "Seldom Inn."

Herman traveled to Europe in 1912, returning on the ill-fated maiden voyage of the *RMS Titanic*. The *Tacoma Times* on Monday, April 15, erroneously printed an early report stating that all 1300 passengers had been rescued. Herman did not survive. His brother-in-law Herman Kaufman managed his estate and continued the business.

S. S. TITANIC WRECKED

(By United Press Leased Wire.) HALIFAAX, N. S., April 15.— With its 1,300 passengers safely transferred to another vessel, the White Star liner Titanic is slowly approaching this port. Passengers were taken aboard the White Star liner Olympic, then transferred to the Baltic, now steaming for New York.

The fact that the Titanic is the world's biggest vessel is probably the only thing that prevented great losses of life. It is not believed that any other craft afloat could have withstood the shock.

"Water Tights" Saved It.

The Titanic's prow was shattered but the water tight compartments automatically closed, and with the pumps working well the crew managed to keep the vessel afloat.

MONTREAL, April 15.—Crashing into an iceberg while running in a dense fog, the steamer Titanic, Captain Smith, White Star line, carrying 2,075 souls and diamonds and bonds worth $5,-000,000 900 miles east of New York, began calling for help at 10:25 last night.

Gracie, Benjamin Guggenheim, Henry B. Harris, theater magnate, and wife, C. M. Hays, president of the Grand Trunk railway; Imlay J. Bruce, chairman of the White Star line, Col. Washington Roebling, who with his father designed the Brooklyn bridge; Countess Rothes, F. D. Millett, president of the American academy of Rome.

Mrs. Jack Cudahy In Trouble

Tacoma Times April 15, 1912

Herman's niece Dorothy Danhauser, daughter of Sarah and her first husband, Louis, stayed in Tacoma. A popular vocalist, she was active in the Judith Montefiore Society. Three days after she inherited her share of her uncle's estate ($25,000) in 1914 she married Sidney Lee Johnson, whose father managed the *Tacoma Times*. A week later, while on her San Francisco wedding trip, Dorothy was murdered by a former suitor. He immediately attempted suicide, but survived. Dorothy's half sister, Elsa, married Samuel Levinson and lived in Seattle, where she was active in the formation of the Washington State Jewish Historical Society.

Herman Klaber family
Courtesy of Ruth Levinson

Herman's widow Gertrude died in 1961. Her daughter Bernice married Samuel I. Jacobs and had a daughter, Laurice. Gertrude's 1962 obituary described her as an active worker for the Camp Fire Girls.

Gertrude's niece married Charles Wallace Rummelsberg, son of Emily Wallerstein, and grandson of Louis and Carrie Wallerstein. (See Wallerstein biography.)

Emil and Lillian Korach

Emil Korach (1868–1926) was the youngest of seven children born in Hungary to Haskell and Lena (Klein) Korach. Emil immigrated to the U.S. in 1886 as a teenager, and worked as a clerk in a liquor store in St. Paul, Minnesota, in 1888.

Then he moved to Tacoma, where he lived with fellow Hungarian Jacob Bloom, who operated the Kentucky Liquor House. Emil was naturalized in Tacoma in 1892. After the 1893 banking panic Emil emerged as manager of the Kentucky Liquor House, located at 1019 Pacific.

He stayed in Tacoma through 1898, then joined Jacob Bloom in selling liquor in Skagway, Alaska. In July of 1901 the renewal of their yearly liquor license cost the pair $1500.

Emil Korach returned to Tacoma to marry Lillian Hain in March of 1906. (See Hain biography.) Jacob Bloom died in Skagway in June of 1906. Emil and Lillian's infant son died in Skagway in August of 1907. Emil continued operating the Monogram Liquor House in Skagway through 1912, although their son Edward was born in New York in 1910.

Then the Korach family moved to Akron, Ohio. They were joined by Lillian's widowed sister Gertrude Heinemann. Emil died in Akron in 1926, followed by Gertrude in 1932 and Lillian in 1957. Their son Edward died in Los Angeles in 1967 and the line ended.

Moses and Gusta Kornbloom

Moses Kornblum (1859–1916) and his wife, Gusta Greenbaum (1863–1950), arrived in New York from Austria in May of 1888 with their two children, Ada and Abraham. They were enumerated in Pierce County in April of 1892. Moses worked as a tailor from 713 St. Helens. In April of 1893 he helped lead Passover services. After the 1893 banking panic the family left Tacoma, moving eventually to Los Angeles.

Moses (now Morris) was naturalized there in 1896, and the following year built a home. He operated a small dyeing business that grew, and in 1905 incorporated the Berlin Dye Works, with his family members as officers. Later he bought and sold real estate.

In the fall of 1906 Morris was one of the organizers of conservative Sinai Congregation in Los Angeles, donating a Torah Scroll on his twenty-fifth wedding anniversary. The synagogue building was dedicated in 1909. Around that time Morris and Gusta built an elegant home on Wilshire Boulevard which they soon re-sold, tripling their investment.

Their daughter, Ada Edith (1882–1967), married Gustave N. Floersheim and had three children – Julius, Beatrice, and Sydney. Their son, Abraham (1884–1956), married Mae Ellen and had two children – Sherman and Bernice. All remained in Los Angeles.

Henry and Bertha Krech

Henry Krech (1859–1933) was born in Frankfurt, Germany and immigrated around 1885. He opened a barbershop in 1887, and in June of the following year traveled to San Francisco to apply for naturalization. The next day he married Bertha Hirschfeld (1863–1927) eldest daughter of Sigmund and Leah Hirschfeld. (See Hirschfeld biography.) The pair attended several Harmony Club events, then moved briefly to Steilacoom in 1891. Their only child, a daughter Eunice, was born in August.

Henry's business grew, and within a few years he operated one of the city's largest barbershops. Located at 748 Pacific in the Fife Hotel, the shop employed three assistant barbers. After spending much of 1894–1896 challenging the Sunday closure laws, Henry moved into his own storefront at 952 Pacific in September of 1897. The new shop included modern hydraulic revolving chairs.

At Home
In Our
New Quarters
952 Pacific Avenue.

Henry Krech Co.

We desire to thank the citizens of Tacoma for their very liberal patronage in the past, which has enabled us to add all the latest improvements and fit up the finest barber shop in the city. Every department is now complete. We have just installed new hydraulic revolving chairs, of the most modern design, and in all other respects we are abreast of the times. Ours is the only shop in the Northwest which occupies an entire store. Customers can secure a shave and a shine at the same time without any inconvenience.

REMEMBER

a bath in one of our porcelain tubs is a luxury, and it costs but 15 cents. Our barbers are better paid than any others in the city, and we have always found that good salaries and first-class artists are inseparable. We invite the public generally to call. First-class work and courteous treatment guaranteed.

Henry Krech Co.,
952 Pacific Avenue.

Three doors North of Eleventh Street.

Tacoma Daily Ledger September 18, 1897

In the summer of 1898 diphtheria struck over twenty children at the Children's Home. Henry responded with an ad for his steam bath rooms, equipped with the most improved sterilizers, claiming "Steam Will Kill Anything."

During February of 1899, when Henry was briefly out of business, the remaining local barbers mutually agreed to close on Sunday. A month later Henry re-opened in the O.K. Baths, next to Chilberg's hotel, "where his patrons will find their cups and receive first-class work."

That summer the family moved to Okanogan, Washington, returning to Tacoma after a few years.

Henry and family then relocated to Spirit Lake, Idaho, opening the first store there in 1907. Later he converted the store into the Cozy Theater, then moved to San Diego and operated the Liberty Theater. After Bertha's death in 1927 Henry went back to Idaho, where he died in 1933, unfortunately after successfully committing suicide on his third attempt.

Their daughter Eunice (1891–1965) worked as a music teacher and musician and moved to Los Angeles. In 1920 she took the adventurous step of driving from California to Idaho with a girlfriend, camping in the car as they traveled. Two years later she married Jacob Hauskins (1881–1968.) While the couple lived in New Mexico Eunice wrote a book *Folk Dances of the Spanish Colonials*. They had no children.

Jacob and Emma Kullman

Jacob Kullman (1864–1945) was born in Stockton, California, in 1864, eldest son of Hermann and Amelia (Stein) Kullman. In 1888 he married Emma Sichel (1865–1935), daughter of pioneer dentist Max Sichel. The following year Jacob opened the City of Paris dry goods store in Tacoma, in partnership with Abraham Lippman of San Diego. (City of Paris was a major department store in San Francisco for many decades.)

In March of 1891 Jacob bought out his partner, and in May moved just three doors south to 1118 Pacific. Showing steady growth, he was able to heavily advertise his spring opening in 1892, and by fall hosted a large dinner party. The following week his store was burglarized. Emma assisted in the Temple Aid Society fair in December, and the couple took a two-month trip east to purchase merchandise.

However, in April of 1893, just before the banking panic, Jacob announced that he was retiring from business due to ill health. Perhaps due to the failing economy, the close-out sale lasted until year-end. (In August of 1894 City of Paris reopened at 1136 Pacific, with Joseph Jacob as proprietor.)

The Kullmans moved to California, but went their separate ways. Emma returned to her parents' household and later married Emanuel Stolz. Jacob entered his family's tanning business in Benecia, with his brother-in-law Edward Salz. In 1902 Jacob married Jean McGregor (1880–1962) and in 1903 the couple had a daughter Helen, but divorced in 1911. Jacob married a third time in 1920, to Jane Creeden Roberts (1890–1931). Jacob's daughter Helen Jones VanMarter died less than a year after her mother in 1962.

Charles and Miriam Langert

Charles Langert was born in Germany about 1856 and declared his intention to become a U.S. citizen in November of 1878. He lived in Laramie, Wyoming in 1880, working for his cousin Max Colman as a clerk in a wholesale liquor firm. In 1883 Charles opened a liquor business in Tacoma, and soon bought out the interest of his partner, Meyer Gottstein. Arriving in Tacoma ahead of the boom, he wisely bought real estate and advertised heavily. His merchandise, valued at $3,000, was totally destroyed in a major fire in 1884, despite his role as foreman of the Commencement Hook & Ladder fire company.

His firm sold wholesale liquor and cigars across the territory. In November of 1884 Charles received 100,000 cigars in one shipment, the largest in Tacoma's short history. The following year he received the first carload of beer ever shipped to the city – as sole agent for the Schlitz Brewing Company of Milwaukee. Frequent newspaper reports of his purchases indicated steady growth. In 1887 his brother Samuel (c.1868–1954) arrived to help, and Charles was able to make an East Coast buying trip, securing exclusive arrangements with several major companies. In March of 1888 he moved into the ground floor of a large brick building occupying 710–712 Pacific. That year his sales topped $200,000.

Charles was active in Tacoma's Jewish community, serving as a trustee of the Hebrew Benevolent Society and attending Harmony Club events.

Charles consistently struggled to collect on accounts due, frequently having to sue to collect overdue payments from taverns and real estate mortgages. By August of 1894 he was unable to make payments to his own creditors. The firm briefly operated under Samuel's name, and in July of 1895 Charles opened the Charles Langert Company at 1307 Pacific. A year later he was again in financial trouble and lost his company.

After several years in bankruptcy courts Charles took a job in King County. He married Miriam Goodman (1876–1953) in 1906 and their daughter Frances was born there in 1907. Then the family returned to Tacoma, where daughter Edith was born in 1910. Langert Liquors operated from 1115 Pacific.

Charles Langert family
Courtesy of Carol Olivier

His brother Samuel moved to Spokane and in 1904 married Netta Kellner (1880–1974), living with her parents for several decades. The couple had no children. When Washington State became "dry" on January 1, 1916, both Langerts were out of work. Charles died in 1921 and his wife and children joined relatives in California. Frances married Frank Canatala and Edith married Louis Fox.

Asa F. Leopold

Tacoma's 1895 directory, published in February, included Asa F. Leopold living at 1220 South I. That same month Mr. Leopold was among the guests at a "pink domino" held by the Judith Montefiore Society ladies.

Levin Brothers – Philip, Louis, David, Lesser

Abraham and Dora Levin had at least four sons and a daughter in Kolmar, Germany. The eldest known son, Philip, was born about 1847. He lived in Portland from 1869 to 1872, then came to Tacoma and ran a saloon in Old Tacoma with Meyer Kaufman. He stayed in Tacoma through at least 1878, then returned to Germany, where he was living at the time of his brother's 1911 obituary. A sister, Rose Flanders, also stayed in Germany.

Louis (1849–1932) lived with Philip in Portland and later Tacoma. In 1884 Louis married Mary Isaacs (c.1863–1936) of San Francisco, and moved in with her parents. (See Isaacs biography.) Louis took a job selling cigars, traveling routinely across the Pacific Northwest. He frequently sent letters to the *Ledger*, informing readers of conditions and progress throughout the area. Louis also visited Tacoma regularly, staying with his brother David and checking on his real estate holdings.

After the birth of his first son, Harold, in 1888, his wife began spending summers in Tacoma. Their second son, born in August of 1890, lived only one week. A third son, Daniel, was born in 1892. The family remained in the San Francisco area. Their grandson, Daniel Levin, Jr., later sold wholesale jewelry.

David Levin (1852–1911) joined his brothers in the Northwest, where in 1873 he added his signature to the official petition asking the county commissioners to incorporate the city of Tacoma. The following year his barbershop was among the first businesses in New Tacoma, on Ninth and Pacific.

On October 23, 1880, David married May Karnes (1862–1916), daughter of Thomas and May Karnes. Together the couple wisely invested in Tacoma's fledgling real estate market, while living at 810 A Street. In 1887 they built a one-story brick building at 1118 Pacific, at a cost of $1,500. David rented the store to D.P. Lewis for a barber supply shop, causing immediate name and spelling confusion.

David joined the Hebrew Benevolent Society and served as one of the first trustees, and was the first treasurer of the B'nai B'rith. He retired from active barbering and continued in real estate. Their daughter Ethel was born in 1891 and in 1892 May assisted in the Temple Aid Society fundraiser.

David and May Levin with their daughter, Ethel, c.1896.
Courtesy of Elaine Porter

The couple attended several social events at the home of Mentheim Cohn, who rented a store from Louis. When Mentheim's business failed

David was appointed receiver, a position that caused David nothing but trouble and occupied much of his time during 1895.

The following year David jumped headfirst into political waters. In the fall of 1896 he was elected to the Washington State legislature. He immediately introduced a bill requiring property owners to pay their tax assessments within 90 days, rather than the current 18 months. He served on several standing committees, including one governing hospitals. As the session was drawing to a close, the *Ledger* reported on March 14, "When the proposition to cut down appropriations for the maintenance of insane asylums was under consideration, Levin protested, and said in substance: 'I think these appropriations ought to be increased. After the adjournment of this body everybody is likely to go crazy and these institutions must be maintained.'"

Representative Levin Introduces New Measure In the House.

OLYMPIA, Jan. 26.—Representative David Levin of Tacoma has introduced a bill in the house relating to savings banks, loan associations and other institutions in which deposits are made and on which interest is paid. The object of the bill is to compel such institutions to make a sworn statement of deposits on hand in the name of depositors who have not made a deposit or withdrawn any funds from such bank for a period of ten years or more.

Evening Statesman (Walla Walla) January 26, 1905

David was again elected to the state legislature in the fall of 1904. He died in 1911, just two days before his daughter Ethel's 20th birthday. In 1915 Ethel married jeweler Leo Dornberg, son of Isaac Dornberg. (See Dornberg biography.) May Levin died in Tacoma in 1916, five weeks after the birth of her granddaughter Vivian in Spokane. Ethel and Leo later moved to Los Angeles, where their son Leo was born in 1928, but lived just a few months.

David's young brother Lesser (1854–1929) known as Doc Levin, opened the Central barbershop in Tacoma in October of 1884, near the Central hotel. Two years later he moved to a building north of the Alpha Opera House. In 1887, in anticipation of the future Northern Pacific headquarters building, he moved to 709 Pacific.

In June of 1889 Doc also built a building, on Tacoma Avenue near Tenth. A three-story

Colonial-style with a basement, it had 26 rooms and two stores. In 1892 he enjoyed a brief period as a "capitalist." However, the following spring his mortgage of nearly $16,000 was foreclosed. Doc lost his building and moved in with his brother David. A year later he was evicted from a barbershop on D Street, owing $32.50 in back rent. Over the next two decades he worked for a variety of employers. After David's death Doc moved to San Francisco, where he died in 1929.

Marquis Levin

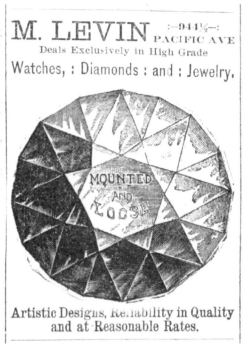

Tacoma Daily Ledger January 2, 1891

Marquis Levin was born in Russia about 1851. He worked as a watchmaker and jeweler in Tacoma from about 1887 to 1893. Marquis operated a small stand within other stores, often moving on an annual basis. In 1888 he traveled along the line of the Northern Pacific Railroad, synchronizing timepieces. Marquis joined the Hebrew Benevolent Society in 1889 and was naturalized in Tacoma in December of 1892.

Levy Siblings – Hannah, Abraham and Esther

Isaac (c.1816–1879) and Henrietta (1836–1901) Levy lived in California when their first four children were born – Hannah, Joseph, Abraham and David. A fifth, Esther, was born in British Columbia around 1863. Their son Louis was born in Oregon about 1868. All of their sons worked as barbers. At least three of their children later lived in Tacoma. Hannah Levy married William Wolff in 1872. (See Wolff biog-

raphy.) Esther Levy married Albert Weinberg in the fall of 1885. (See Weinberg biography.)

Abraham Levy (1857–1912) married Briley/Bertha (1859–1909) in about 1886, and their son Irvin was born in Oregon in November of 1887. In 1889 they lived in Tacoma, where Abraham worked as a barber. After both of his parents died in California, Irvin returned to Oregon. He married Irene Hefter and had a daughter Barbara (Robison).

Isaac and Hannah Levy

Isaac Levy (1836–1927) and Hannah Jewell (1839–1918) had four children – Lewis, Charlotte, Bernard and Elias – in London, England, between 1858 and 1867. A fifth child, Adelaide, was born in San Francisco in October of 1869. Isaac sold wholesale clothing and his son Lewis sold boots and shoes. Charlotte married Simon Jacobs in about 1877, and in 1880 Lewis briefly married Pauline Bloch. Most of the family moved to Tacoma in 1889.

Isaac and his son Lewis (1858–1938) worked as pawnbrokers, with locations at 819 and 1121 Pacific. Their names were frequently mentioned in the newspapers columns as victims of theft or fraud, and occasionally as receivers of stolen property. In the summer of 1892 Lewis married Rachael Martin (1873–1948), daughter of Vallie Martin. (See Martin biography.) Isaac and Lewis advanced to running the Collateral Bank at 1119 Pacific, and Bernard sold cigars. Lewis also worked as an auctioneer with his Martin relatives.

In June of 1896 newly-elected Mayor Fawcett appointed Lewis as one of five Park Commissioners. In October the election results were reversed and Mayor Orr resumed office, appointing new officials, but Lewis stayed on, awaiting legal opinions. Eight months later Fawcett was back in office. Rachael Levy joined the Judith Montefiore Society in December of 1897.

During the Klondike excitement Lewis briefly attempted to develop a transportation line between Tacoma and Alaska. His brother Bernard (1864–1943) met with some success in mining in Dyea, then moved back to San Francisco. In 1899 the Levy and Martin families moved to Seattle.

Lewis and Rachael had three daughters. Victoria, born in 1893, died in Seattle in 1900. Vivian (1900–1990) married Tommy Kearns. Lucille (1901–1991) married Max Lachman. Lewis died in Seattle in 1938, followed by Rachael a decade later. His parents, Isaac and Hannah, returned to San Francisco to join their married daughters, Charlotte Jacobs Chaney (1860–1935), and Adelaide Peironnet (1869–1932).

William H. Levy

William H. Levy, a native of Wales, declared his intention to become a citizen in January of 1889 in Tacoma. He sold secondhand goods from a variety of locations over the next three years. His wife briefly joined the Judith Montefiore Society, but resigned in 1891.

He was possibly the same William Levy, aged 46, who died in a cave-in January 10, 1901, at Hunker Creek in the Klondike, near Dawson. He left a widow Annie, a resident of Penrhiwcaiber, Glamorgan County, in Wales.

Emanuel and Lilly Lewinstein

Emanuel Wendel Lewinstein (1867–1921) was the middle of three children born to Bernard (later Bennett) Lewinstein (1828–1911) and Hannah Wendel (1832–1911). Emanuel was born in Detroit, and worked with his family selling clothing in Bay City, Michigan, from 1883 to 1895.

In 1898 Emanuel and his father Bernard operated the Columbia Clothing company in Tacoma, moving from 744 Pacific to 936 Pacific. (Recently vacated by Dave Gross.) In February of 1899 Emanuel married Lillian "Lilly" Goldsmith (1874–1953) in Seattle. (See Goldsmith biography.) Her sister Belle Goldsmith Isaacs was a witness. That fall Lilly joined the Judith Montefiore Society.

Tacoma Daily Ledger June 3, 1899

Over the next several years Emanuel hosted a variety of close-out and auction sales. His father Bernard returned to Michigan around 1900. In 1901 Emanuel moved from his prime location to 1508 Pacific, suggesting to his shoppers that "Low store rent means low prices." After his father-in-law, Joseph Goldsmith, died in February, Emanuel's merchandise was immediately sold in an "Executor's Sale," implying Joseph had been a financial partner.

The couple moved to Seattle, where Lilly's mother died in 1906. Emanuel wrote his will in Chicago in 1916 and died there in 1921. Lilly joined her remaining siblings in California and died in Los Angeles in 1953. The couple had no children.

David and Mollie Lewis

Sarah Lewis Simon, wife of Abe Simon, came to Tacoma from California with her husband and family around 1883. Two years later her brother David P. Lewis followed her. (See Simon biography.) Born in Thorn, Germany in 1858, David immigrated to the U.S. when he was only ten years old. He was naturalized in Essex County, New Jersey, just after his 21st birthday.

David arrived in Tacoma in July of 1885 from Elmira, New York. He opened the Chamber of Commerce Barbershop in the new Chamber of Commerce building on Twelfth and Pacific.

The following year he added bathing rooms in the back, complete with hot and cold water. After several brief partnerships with other barbers, David started a barber supply business in 1887 in David Levin's new building, 1118 Pacific. Later he added a line of knives and cutlery, and a steam-powered grinding and sharpening service.

On October 18, 1888, David married Mollie Stenger (1868–1926) at her mother's home in Spokane. It was a double wedding. Mollie's sister Regina Stenger married Henry Berliner on the same day, and the two couples shared a home in Tacoma. (See Berliner biography.) Mollie's brother, George Stenger, also lived with them and worked for David. (See Stenger biography.) Mollie joined the Judith Montefiore Society, David was the first president of the B'nai B'rith, and the couple attended Harmony Club events.

In the fall of 1889, as statehood approached, David became prominent in the Democratic Party, frequently attending conventions and serving on committees. His activities were often praised in the *Ledger*, an openly Republican newspaper. In 1891 David moved his barber supply firm to yet another new building, the Wallace Block on 12th and A Street.

Wostenholm Cutlery,

RAZORS,

Looking Glasses,

TOILET GOODS,

Hair Brushes,

Clothes Brushes,

ETC., ETC., ETC.,

—AT THE—

Northwestern Barbers' Supply House,

D. P. LEWIS, Proprietor.

Tacoma Daily News October 7, 1889

David and Mollie had two children. Their son Adolph (Dolph) Grover Lewis was born in 1889, exactly nine months after their wedding. Their daughter Ruth was born two years later, weighing in at 11 pounds.

Then the extended household of Lewis/Stenger/Berliner families moved to Portland, Oregon. George Stenger worked as a salesman for the barber supply company and Henry Berliner served as bookkeeper. Mollie's mother Cecelia joined them in Portland, moving from Spokane, as did Mollie's brother Albert.

Around 1903 George Stenger became a partner under the company name of Lewis-Stenger Barber Supply. Within five years the firm had expanded to Seattle, under the guidance of Henry Berliner and his sons.

David's sister Sarah Simon died in Tacoma in 1904, and Mollie's mother Cecelia died in Portland in 1905. During the war years George took over the barber supply and David served as vice president of the American Ship Building Company.

Both children married. Dolph (1889–1973) married Georgia Loveland (1889–1964) in 1912 and lived in British Columbia until 1919. Dolph sold cutlery and later lived in Seattle importing leathers.

Ruth Lewis (1891–1980) married Isaac Neuberger (1883–1973). During the twenties David ran the Bohemian restaurant and bakery with his son-in-law. David died in 1924, followed by Mollie in 1926. Their grandson Richard Neuberger (1912–1960), served in the state legislature and for six years as a U.S. Senator. After Richard's death his widow, Maurine Brown (1906–2000), also served in the Senate. Richard's sister, author Jane Neuberger Goodsell (1921–1988), married James W. Goodsell, editor of the *Oregon Labor Press*.

William T. and Lucy Lewis

Ruth Comber Jacobs, Sarah Lewis Tone and Jenny Lewis Comber
Courtesy of Al Tone

William T. Lewis (c.1849–1926) married Lucy Martin (c.1853–1917) sometime in the early 1880s. She was the eldest of nine children born to Mordecai and Welcome "Vallie" Martin. (See Martin biography.) Lucy had previously married Sol Cahen, and had a son Mordecai (Morris) Cahen, in Arkansas in January of 1873. William and Lucy had a daughter Jennie in Louisiana in 1885, a son Edward in Mississippi in 1887, and a son Samuel in Louisiana in 1888. Their daughter Vallie was born in Tacoma on July 12th of 1890. They lost an infant son Gustave in 1892, and another daughter, Sarah, was born in 1894.

Lucy's brother Sam had come to Tacoma as early as 1888, and another brother Joseph partnered briefly with William in a restaurant. In February of 1891 the family incorporated the Central Nisqually Land Company, with William as secretary and treasurer and Samuel Martin as president. Lucy's mother joined the Lewis household, along with several other Martin siblings.

After the 1893 banking panic William ran a secondhand store, often from a different location each year. Most of the Martin family moved on to Seattle. William and Lucy stayed in Tacoma, selling junk, and later furniture. As their children grew they found employment within Tacoma's Jewish community, but only two found spouses. Jennie (1885–1971) married Bernard Comber (1884–1947) and had two daughters, Ruth and Vivian. Sarah (1894–1975) married Robert Tone (1894–1949) and had two sons – Al and Bill. Lucy's son Morris Cahen died in Santa Clara in 1956.

Max and Dora Liebenthal

Max Liebenthal was born in Germany June 20, 1851, son of Moses and Laura Liebenthal. The family lived in Philadelphia in 1870 and in Columbus, Ohio, in 1880. In the spring of 1884 Max applied for a U.S. passport from Williams County, Ohio. He apparently made a summer trip back to Germany, as he arrived in New York from Bremen in August.

Max married Dora Stern, born around 1859 in Williams County, Ohio, daughter of Emanuel and Henrietta Stern. Their daughter Estrella was born in Ohio in November of 1885.

The family moved to Tacoma, where Max sold cigars with a variety of partners from 1890 until 1893. His last partner was Dora's brother, Abraham Stern.

Dora joined the Judith Montefiore Society, and the couple attended Harmony Club events. In December of 1892 Dora participated in the Temple Aid Society fair. In August she attended the Chicago World's Fair with her brother Abraham.

Max and Dora moved to Syracuse, New York, before 1900, joining Dora's widowed mother. Max worked at a variety of jobs, from auctioneering to manufacturing mica, before returning to selling cigars. The family lived in Manhattan in 1920. Estrella, single at 33, worked as a millinery clerk.

Rabbi Martin Lincer

Martin Lincer served as Tacoma's rabbi from March of 1895 through May of 1896, living at 1917 South E Street. (Now Fawcett.) During that time he officiated at least two circumcisions, one wedding and one *bar mitzvah*. The Judith Montefiore Society paid him a salary of ten dollars per month to teach Sabbath School, then paid $25 for his railroad ticket.

Henry and Mae Lobe

Simon Lobe and Caroline Dennery had two children (Anatole & Leon) in France around 1844 and 1846. Their next two children (Gustave and Emile) were born in New York around 1848 and 1850. Their remaining three children (Louise, Henry and Nannette) were born in California around 1855, 1858 and 1859.

Tacoma Daily Ledger July 22, 1883

In the spring of 1880 Anatole opened a crockery store in Portland. Brothers Leon, Emile, and Henry followed him to the Northwest. In 1883 cousins Emile Lobe, Luciene Eger and Albert Elken opened a crockery store in Tacoma. In the fall of 1885 they moved to 904 Pacific, tucked in between the clothing stores of Charles Reichenbach and the Gross Brothers. Only Henry stayed in Tacoma, operating the store under the name of H. Lobe and Company, and the Golden Rule Bazaar. (His brothers had similar stores in Seattle and Bellingham.) Henry joined the Standard Club and several German clubs. By 1887 Henry's crockery business was bankrupt.

In December of 1886 Henry married Mae Elsie Hyatt (1869–1938). Their daughter Pearl was born in Tacoma in October of 1889. The couple joined in North End neighborhood groups, but Mae apparently did not participate in any Jewish activities. Henry's sister Louisa Lobe married Julius Bornstein, and his sister Nannette married Samuel Frank.

After the 1893 banking panic Henry found work with the Harris brothers, and after a few years moved to Seattle. However, his marriage ended and Mae married jeweler Henry Abrams and moved to California. Henry Lobe celebrated his 80th birthday at Seattle's Kline Galland Home in 1938, and passed away in 1941.

Samuel and Blanche Loeb and Family

Samuel Loeb (1862–1947) was the third of five children born to Simon and Mariana (Goldsmith) Loeb. The first three – Tillie, Louis and Samuel – were born in Ligonier, in Noble County, Indiana. The last two – Mattie and Joseph – were born in Memphis, Tennessee. Simon died in the yellow fever epidemic and Mariana returned to Ligonier as a widow.

Samuel lived with Adolph Loeb, (likely his uncle) in Chicago in 1885, before coming to Tacoma around 1889. He worked in the liquor business with Sam Holland, also with Ligonier connections. Samuel joined the cemetery association and the Harmony Club. He and his younger brother, Joseph, both lived at the club. His fellow club member, Albert Weinberg, traveled to Ligonier in 1890 to marry Samuel's younger sister, Mattie. (See Weinberg biography.) That winter Samuel married Blanche Moses, daughter of Morris Moses. (See Moses biography.) Guests at the elaborate wedding included his mother from Ligonier, his brother Louis from Duluth, and his brother Joseph. The Loebs lived at 802 South G, with the Weinbergs next door at 804.

Shortly after the wedding Samuel sold a saloon and theater for nearly $18,000. Then he partnered with Albert Weinberg to purchase the United States Brewery, growing it into the Milwaukee Brewing Company. In addition to his interest in the Holland Liquor Company, Samuel also was president of the Perfect Collodion Paper Company. Samuel's brother, Joseph, lived with Samuel, worked as his bookkeeper, and joined the Stag Seven.

Blanche gave birth to a son Sidney in November of 1891. The following spring the Loebs and Weinbergs hosted a large party in honor of Louis Loeb's wedding in Chicago to Cecelia Keller. In December of 1892 Blanche was an active participant in the Temple Aid Society fair.

After several years Joseph Loeb moved to Duluth, working in the wholesale liquor business of his brother Louis. Joseph caught pneumonia and died suddenly in December of 1896.

His obituary in the *Ledger* on December 16 described him as "of large and heavy build," and just 26 years old. "He had always intended to return to Puget Sound to live, for he much disliked the rigid winters of the east. He still called Tacoma his home and stated frequently that he would rather be a poor man here than a rich man in the East."

In 1897 Samuel ended the Beer War by combining his brewery with the Puget Sound to form the Pacific Brewing and Malting Company. A year later his brother-in-law, no longer an officer but still a stockholder, sued the firm to gain access to inspect the accounting books.

In 1902 Samuel and Blanche moved to Seattle, where Samuel opened the Independent Brewing Company. Their daughter Lucille, born in Tacoma in 1898, died in Seattle in 1908. Sam's mother, Mariana Loeb, was buried next to her in December of 1915.

Sam Loeb cartoon
Frank Calvert, 1911

After Prohibition was enacted in Washington, the Loeb family moved to San Francisco, where for several years Samuel was president of the Old German Lager Brewing Company. With the outbreak of World War One the name was shortened to Old Lager Brewing Company. After national Prohibition went into effect in 1920 Samuel sold near-beer for a few years, then retired to Los Angeles to sell real estate. They all died in the Los Angeles area – Blanche in 1944, Samuel in 1947, and Sidney in 1986.

Lubelski Family

Wladyslaw Lubelski was born in Warsaw in 1827. His Hebrew name was Wolf, his American name was William. He married Rachel Cohen, born about 1840 in Posen. Their son Henry was born in 1862, followed by Antone (Tony) around 1869. Three other children did not survive.

The family ran a boarding house in Leadville, Colorado, in 1880, then sold secondhand goods in Aspen, Colorado. Henry married Anna Edith Spears (1869–1916) in November of 1885 and their daughter Frankie was born in Colorado in 1887. On October 30, 1886, the *Rocky Mountain Sun* dubbed Tony the "enterprising young mayor of Frying Pan," Colorado. Tony married Julia Schmidt about 1890, and their daughter Rita was born in San Francisco June 19, 1890.

Henry and his parents moved briefly to Seattle, where each family member operated a secondhand store, then came to Tacoma. Henry's daughter Sara was born in Tacoma in June of 1891. In 1892 Henry operated the Tacoma Secondhand Store at 1719 Jefferson, Anton sold secondhand goods from 1310 C (now Broadway) and their father, William, ran a variety store at 809 Pacific. Henry also offered furnished rooms.

LOST.

On SEATTLE TRAIN OR IN CITY, RED leather pocketbook, containing 300 shares Golden Star mining stock; 100 shares Crown Point, twenty shares Building and loan association of Seattle, three deeds to Frying Pan lots in Colorado. All papers assigned to W. and R Lubelski. Papers of no use to anyone but owner. Finder will be liberally rewarded for returning same to W. Lubelski, 809 Pacific avenue.   790

Tacoma Daily Ledger March 6, 1892

On May 8, 1892, Henry and Rachel celebrated their silver wedding anniversary, bringing Rabbi Genss from Seattle to re-do their son's marriage ceremony, which had previously been performed by a justice of the peace. Three months later the parents set off on a year-long tour of Europe.

Henry moved to 1344 Pacific in 1893, but the store was badly damaged by a fire in August. The following year he won the soda water and lemonade concession at the interstate fair, but was barely able to pay his vendor fees.

Henry's father, Wladyslaw, died on October 25, 1894, and was buried in the Home of Peace Cemetery – his only known affiliation with Tacoma's Jewish community. His newspaper obituary described him as one of the oldest residents of the city, aged 68. The following year Antone lived at 1310 C, Henry at 1112 C, and Rachel at 1536 Pacific. All sold secondhand goods.

Henry and his wife and mother returned to Colorado, living in Cripple Creek in 1900. Henry sold cigars, then managed a theater. He moved to Seattle, where he operated the Lyric Theater. His wife Edith died in Seattle in 1916, followed by Henry in 1930.

Tony returned to San Francisco, registering to vote in June of 1896. Then he followed the Klondike rush, opening a tent store in Skagway

in 1897 and living in Dawson in 1899. His son Kenneth was born in San Francisco in 1901. Tony later operated the Novelty Theater and several others. He gained enough prominence that he was robbed several times of diamonds and cash. His wife Julia died in 1914 and Tony died in 1938.

David and Annie Magnus

David Magnus was born in Berlin in 1851 to Jacob Magnus and Pauline Brunn. He immigrated to the U.S. as a teenager, joining the Pincus and Packscher families in Steilacoom. In 1884 David moved to Tacoma and sold cigars in a liquor store run by Isaac Pincus. He joined the Turn Verein, the Standard Club of young Jewish men, and for years held offices in the Odd Fellows.

David married Annie Berliner in May of 1887, in an elaborate wedding at the home of her step-father, Colonel Meyer Kaufman. She gave birth to a daughter Amalie one year later. David went to work for Kaufman & Berliner, but Kaufman died in 1891 and the store was closed in bankruptcy.

Annie joined the Judith Montefiore Society and was active in the 1892 Temple Aid Society. David served as treasurer of the new Temple Beth El, and of the Hebrew Benevolent Society. He recorded the death of his son Max in the cemetery records, but failed to note the date. The couple also lost two other children.

The family moved to Seattle around 1895, where David worked in a variety of clerking positions. In 1901 he served as secretary/treasurer of the Toklas and Singerman Company. Their daughter Amalie married Otis Wood in August of 1911. Amalie had a daughter Alice in 1912 and a son David Sherman Wood in 1914.

David Magnus died in 1923, having worked most recently as cashier of Seattle's Hub Clothing Company. His widow, Annie, lived out the remainder of her life as an inmate of the Western State Hospital in Steilacoom. She died there in 1934. Her daughter Amalie Wood died in Seattle in 1982. Amalie's children stayed in Seattle.

Mamlock Siblings – Julius, Jacob and Richard

Meyer Mamlok and Rosalie Fuchs had at least seven children in Koschmin, Posen. All three of their sons eventually lived in Tacoma.

According to family history, as a teen Julius Mamlock (1854–1914) came to the U.S. as a stowaway, nearly drowning in the hold of the ship during a particularly rough storm. He met his future wife, Paula Wolff, (1858–1944) in California in 1880. Paula was the daughter of Henry Irwin Wolff and Ernestine Cohn. After a brief period working in a mining smelter in Butte, Julius returned to San Francisco and his sweetheart.

They were married in July of 1883 and left for Tacoma the same day, joining Paula's sister Adeline, who had married Amil Zelinsky. (See Wolff and Zelinsky biographies.) Paula's son Henry Montefiore Mamlock was born in Tacoma the following year, the centennial of the birth of Sir Moses Montefiore.

Julius, or J.B., operated a cigar store on Pacific Avenue, in a block that was destroyed by fire four days after the birth of his son. He reopened farther south on Pacific, on the corner of Jefferson, selling cigars and tobacco, confectionery and notions. In 1886 Julius opened the California Chop House and Bakery at 821 Pacific, specializing in 15-cent meals. Their daughter Stella was born that November.

A son Milton, born in 1888, lived only six months and was buried in the Olympia cemetery. That fall the family built a home at 708 North Sixth, on the corner of G, but were burglarized in January of 1889. In June Julius sold his restaurant and briefly moved to Roy to raise turkeys. Their thirteen-month-old son, Melvin, died in 1890 and was buried in the new Home of Peace Cemetery. Julius moved back to Tacoma in 1892, and worked for a variety of liquor firms, one of the few stable industries in Tacoma after the 1893 banking panic. In 1906 he opened his own store, Smart and Mamlock, converted the following year into a bar and grill. Later the couple again ran a restaurant and bakery.

Julius died in 1914 and was buried in the Home of Peace Cemetery. A few years later Paula briefly married his widowed brother, Jacob. Then she lived with her cousin Albert Weinberg in Seattle, where she died in 1944.

Paula's son Henry (1884–1954) married Gertrude Zelinsky (1894–1947). They had four children: Earl, Stanley, Stella and Virginia. Paula's daughter Stella (1886–1921) married Archibald Isham Button and had two sons: Arch Isham, Jr., and Julian Mamlock Button.

Jacob Mamlock, San Quentin ID
Ancestry.com California Prison Records

Jacob Mamlock (1861–1929) and his wife Marie Wreschinski, had five children in Koschmin in the 1890s. Marie died in 1911 and Jacob came to Tacoma, bringing two of his sons. Ludwig, just 18, was killed in an explosion of creosote in 1913. After his marriage to Julius' widow ended in 1919, Jacob moved to San Francisco. In 1923 he was convicted of killing his landlady and sent to San Quentin Prison. Jacob was released in 1928 and died in 1929. His four remaining children all died in the San Francisco area: Max in 1958, Reinhold in 1983, Lucy Verber in 1967, and Ruth Koltun in 1987.

Julius and Jacob's older brother, Richard (1852–1930), also came to the U.S. as a teen. After working as a miner in Colorado, Richard came to Tacoma around 1890. He worked as a bartender, tried ranching with Julius, and for many years ran a saloon at 805 Pacific.

William and Henrietta Mamlock

William M. Mamlock (1822–1903) married Henrietta F. Wolfstein (1821–1905) in Germany about 1850. Like many newlyweds, they immigrated to the U.S. shortly after. Their daughter Rachael was born in New York about 1852, then the family moved to San Francisco, where William worked as an upholsterer. They had at least five more daughters there – Jane, Sarah, Bertha, Jennie and Henrietta.

In the 1880s the family moved to Tacoma, joining Julius Mamlock, probably William's nephew. Their daughter Jennie died in September of 1889 at the age of 23, likely the first burial in the Home of Peace Cemetery. The following year her sisters taught Sabbath school and Bertha served as secretary of the Judith Montefiore Society. William continued working as an upholsterer and his wife worked as a dressmaker.

Around 1895 the family returned to California, where William died in 1903, followed by Henrietta in 1905. Only three of their daughters survived. Rachel (1852–1926) married Christian Thede. Bertha (1866–1942) married Maurice David. The youngest, Henrietta (1870–1939) died unmarried.

Mordecai and Welcome (Vallie) Martin

English-born Mordecai and Welcome Martin had perhaps 14 children, of whom nine have been identified. The first, Lucy, was born around 1854 in New York, while her parents were still teenagers. Mordecai worked as a peddler, auctioneer or "huckster," and their first seven children were born in seven different states. Samuel was born in Wisconsin about 1856, followed by Joseph in Illinois around 1858. David was born in Kentucky about 1859, and the family was enumerated in St. Louis, Missouri, in 1860. Deborah was born in Tennessee in March of 1863, followed by Isaac in Ohio around 1866. Jacob was born in Missouri about 1868 and Ida in Missouri in August of 1869. In 1870 the family lived in Little Rock, Arkansas. Their youngest daughter Rachael was born in Arkansas in September of 1873. Welcome was widowed by 1880 and continued working as a "huckster" to support her large family.

Her eldest daughter, Lucy, followed in her footsteps – marrying Sol Cahen and giving birth to a son Mordecai Cahen in January of 1873, while still in her teens. A decade later Lucy married William T. Lewis and had children in Louisiana and Mississippi, before joining her family in Tacoma. (See Lewis biography.)

Lucy's brother Samuel lived in Tacoma in 1888, working as a clerk in Louis Henschel's pawnshop. He frequently held animal auctions in the street on the corner of 11th and Pacific. The following year Samuel was able to open his own auctioneering firm and later moved to 1330 Railroad.

S. MARTIN,

1330 Railroad Street.

AUCTION, LIVERY,

Sale and Feed Stable.

Best place in the city to buy or sell

HORSES, WAGONS

AND HARNESS.

Prompt attention given to the sale of

Stock, Furniture and Real Estate.

AUCTIONEERS

Furnished for Country Sales. P. O. Box 63. Telephone 338.

Tacoma Daily News October 12, 1889

Samuel's extended family members joined him in Tacoma around 1890, attending Harmony Club events and assisting in temple fundraisers. Samuel's mother used the name Vallie instead of Welcome. In February Samuel incorporated the Central Nisqually Land Company with his brother-in-law, William Lewis, frequently selling lots for ten dollars each. In July of 1892 Sam's youngest sister, Rachel, married Lewis Levy. (See Levy biography.)

Joseph Martin married Flora Lewis, daughter of Abraham and Dora Lewis. Their son Morris was born in 1893. In the fall of 1899 the various Martin and Levy families moved to Seattle, where their mother Vallie died in 1918. Joseph died in Seattle in 1927, followed by Flora in 1935. Joseph's sister Deborah died unmarried in Seattle in 1932.

Jacob Martin also worked as an auctioneer, then sold secondhand goods. He stayed in Tacoma with his sister Lucy through at least 1900, then moved to San Francisco. Jacob died in Santa Clara in 1934.

Samuel Martin moved to Milwaukee, Wisconsin. Around 1895 he married Norwegian Margaret Westine. Their three children – Vallie, Raymond and Morris – were born in 1896, 1898, and 1904. Samuel was active in the Elks, helping to form a chapter in Sheboygan. His daughter Vallie used the stage name Vallie Belasco Martin, drawing on the fame of her father's cousin,

David Belasco. (David's mother Reyna Martin was likely the sister of Mordecai Martin.)

Emile (Julia) and Louis Marx

Marx brothers Emile and Louis were born in Goennersdorf, Germany, (formerly Alsace) in 1866 and 1867, sons of Lazare Marx. Emile worked in Portland in 1886 and 1887 as a traveling sales agent for the wholesale liquor firm of Daniel Marx, likely a relative. The following year Emile worked for Charles Langert in Tacoma in the same capacity.

Emile traveled to San Francisco, where in 1890 he married Julia Goldsmith, daughter of Simon Goldsmith and Pauline Weil. He then partnered with Charles Helm in the wholesale liquor and cigar firm of Helm and Marx, located at 1545 Dock Street. As agents for the Pabst Brewing Company, they purchased beer in casks directly from the brewer and bottled it locally.

Around 1892 Emile and his brother Louis (now Leon) changed occupations, working for the Northwest Commission Company selling wholesale produce for Abraham Hockwald. They lived at 608 South I. That fall Julia hosted the Entre Nous club in her home, and in mid-December assisted in the Temple Aid Society fair. At the end of the month Julia visited her sister, Delphine Pickard, in Seattle. On the night of December 28 Julia's 13-month-old son Berthold fell from a folding bed into a large slop jar full of water and drowned. The couple had no more children.

After the 1893 banking panic Emile returned to Portland and the liquor industry. Over the next decade he frequently visited Tacoma while on his sales travels, often giving updates on conditions around the Northwest. (Another Louis Marx, born in Germany about 1848, operated a restaurant in Tacoma for several decades.)

Around 1904 Emile and Louis moved to Seattle, working as manufacturing agents for wholesale clothing companies such as the Unity Hosiery Mills. In 1914 Louis returned to Germany, where he lived for several years before moving to Zurich, Switzerland, for health reasons. His 1917 passport renewal application described him as an invalid unable to travel, complete with a description of his symptoms and diagnosis.

Julia died in Seattle in 1936, followed by Emile in 1949. They were survived by Julia's nephews, Jerome and Paul Pickard.

Isaac Moses

Isaac Moses was born in the early 1870s in what is now Latvia. He came to the U.S. in December of 1888, and by 1892 was working for Henry Winkleman, sorting junk. Isaac briefly sold clothing with Julius Friedman in 1895, then returned to working for the Winklemans selling junk, and later running the Tacoma branch of their burlap bag company. Isaac lived in Tacoma through 1933, then died in Portland in 1934. Minnie Winkleman handled his estate.

Morris and Lena Moses

Morris Moses was born in Forbach, Lorraine, in 1837. He married Lena Hoffstadt, born around 1842. Their six children were born in Ohio between 1862 and 1873 – Nannie, Marcus, Hattie, Blanche, Fannie and David. At least the last three were born in Gallipolis, Ohio – a town that later lost its Jewish community. Morris sold clothing.

The Moses family arrived in Tacoma in the winter of 1889, bringing six eligible young adults to the growing Jewish community. M. Moses and Company, later the Bouquet Cigar Store, was located at 944 Pacific. Morris joined the Hebrew Benevolent Society and the Harmony Club, and all the women participated in the dances, flashing feathers and diamonds. Lena joined the Judith Montefiore Society and served as the first vice president, but resigned in the fall due to ill health. Their fourth child, Blanche, was the first to wed, marrying Samuel Loeb in November of 1890. (See Loeb biography.)

Morris helped arrange for High Holiday tickets in the fall of 1891, and in February of 1892 served on the temple building committee. He was elected one of the first trustees and in July of 1892 was named as one of the incorporators of Congregation Beth Israel. In December of 1892 the entire family devoted their energies to the Temple Aid Society events.

After the 1893 banking panic Marcus partnered briefly with Matthew Ash, selling cigars from 1340 and then 1140 Pacific. David operated a separate store at 1309 Railroad, with his father as manager. The entire family lived with Samuel Loeb at 443 South E.

Lena Moses, aged 52, died in Tacoma in August of 1894. The following year Morris petitioned for citizenship. David (1873–1923) married Jean Franklin in 1898 and moved to San Francisco. (Their son Leslie likely never married.) The rest of the family stayed in Tacoma through 1902, then moved to Seattle, still living with Samuel Loeb. In 1910 Hattie Moses (1865–1947) married David Kaufman, of Anaconda, Montana, but he died two years later. Morris Moses died in Seattle in May of 1917 and was buried in the Moses/Loeb family plot in the Hills of Eternity Cemetery.

Marcus (1863–1946) married Mary Schooley (1878–1919) in Everett in 1914, then moved to California. Nannie (1862–1943) joined her siblings in Los Angeles and died unmarried.

Moyses Family

Grocer Benjamin Moyses, Sr. (1822–1862) and his wife Caroline Rosenthal (1829–1903) had at least six children in Wabash, Indiana, between 1855 and 1863: Matilda, Emanuel, Gertrude, Catherine, Samuel and Benjamin. The youngest was born after his father's death. Rodef Sholem Cemetery in Wabash is the final resting place of Ben and his wife Caroline, their daughters Gertrude and Matilda, and their son Ben.

Emanuel Moyses (1856–1924) married Carrie Brunswick (1864–1925) in Chicago in 1883 and later moved to New York. (Carrie's father Joseph founded the Brunswick billiard and bowling company.)

In 1889 Sam Moyses (1860–1923) managed a wholesale wine and liquor business in Tacoma owned by Sam Holland and Sam Loeb – both of Ligonier, Indiana, not far from Wabash. In 1890 he served as president of the Harmony Club, then moved to Portland, Oregon. In 1894 he married Flora Zeiner in Chicago and lived there until about 1915. (Flora was Carrie Brunswick's niece, daughter of Carrie's sister Julia.) After a few years in Butte, Montana, Sam returned to Portland, where he died in 1923. His daughter Berenice (1896–1985) married Henry Feldman in 1916, while staying with her uncle Emanuel in New York.

Sam was replaced in Tacoma by his younger brother Ben, who had previously worked in Indiana and Mississippi. In 1892 Ben lived with Sam Loeb, and early the following year Ben traveled to St. Louis to purchase large equipment for the new Milwaukee Brewing Company facility. After the 1893 banking panic Ben had the difficult task of working as an account collector for the brewery.

A bachelor, he lived with Albert Weinberg, then moved into the Harmony Club. Ben began extending his interests, partnering with Albert in 1895 to incorporate the Tampa Cigar Company, and later the Pacific Pulley Manufacturing Company. He continued working as a salesman for the Milwaukee Brewing Company, later part of the Pacific Brewing and Malting Company. In 1900 Ben joined with others in securing mining claims in eastern Kittitas County, forming the Mount Alta Mining Company. He also considered opening a brewery in Stockton, California, and worked as a hop merchant with Herman Klaber. (In 1912 Herman would write to his friend Ben from London, describing his eagerness to be coming home soon aboard the new R.M.S. Titanic.)

In 1902 Ben Moyses and Sam Loeb moved to Seattle, where Ben partnered with Sam in forming the Independent Brewing Company, serving as secretary and treasurer. Both sold their interests in Tacoma's Pacific Brewing and Malting Company in 1906. Ben went on to invest with others in an irrigation project in Mountain Home, Idaho, purchasing 100,000 acres of land, including a race track and most of the townsite. Ben continued with the Independent Brewing Company until the enactment of Prohibition in Washington. He died in Chicago in April of 1916 following an operation. He likely never married.

Max and Johanna Myers

German-born Max G. Myers (c.1851–1915) and Johanna Ball (1857–1938) were married in January of 1885. In 1889 and 1890 their Tacoma cigar store at 1336 Pacific was in the name of Johanna, with Max as manager. They lived at their store. The couple attended Harmony Club events and Max served several terms as secretary. Around 1891 they moved to 609 I Street. The following year Johanna ran her cigar store from her home with Sol Ottenheimer as clerk, while Max managed a cigar store for A.I. Weiler. In December of 1892 Johanna ran the cigar booth at the Temple Aid Society's fair. Later the couple lived at 710 I and Max managed the Havana Cigar Company at 902 Railroad.

In 1894 Johanna's niece, Miss Eda Brash, visited from Victoria, along with her sister from Seattle, Mrs. James Coleman. (Eda Brash's sister Celia Brash later married Rabbi Montague N.A. Cohen in Victoria in 1903. Rabbi Cohen served several times as rabbi in Tacoma.)

After the 1893 banking panic Max worked as a salesman for Joseph Hall's New West Liquor Company. In January of 1897 the couple moved to St. Joseph, Missouri, for a few years, then settled in Portland, Oregon, joining Johanna's Ball siblings. Max died in Portland in 1915 and was buried in the Orthodox Ahavai Sholom Cemetery. Johanna worked for Jewish social services well into her sixties. She died in Portland in 1938.

Barbara Fogelbaum Olsen

German-born Barbara Fogelbaum (1862–1913) was the daughter of Solomon and Fannie (Livingstone) Fogelbaum. She married Norwegian Lauritz Arndt Olsen around 1882. Their children – Louis, Sadie and Fred – were born in Texas, Wisconsin and Missouri in 1883, 1885 and 1887. In 1888 Lauritz worked as a bartender in Tacoma at the Cosmopolitan Hotel at 801 Pacific. Several years later he ran the saloon and hotel himself.

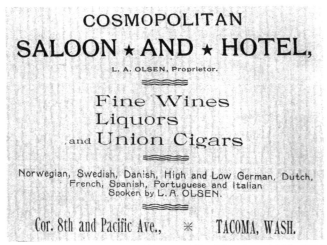

Tacoma City Directory 1893–1894

In December of 1892 Barbara assisted in the toy booth during the Temple Aid Society's fair. Several times over the next several years she was not allowed to resign from the Judith Montefiore Society because her dues were in arrears. In 1895 the Olsen family lived at 609 South I, formerly the home of Max and Johanna Myers. That year Barbara and her mother were arrested, charged with professional shoplifting. (See Fogelbaum biography.) Most of the merchandise was returned and the charges against Barbara were dropped.

The families headed to the Klondike for a few years, then returned to Tacoma. In 1901 Lauritz operated the Alaska Sample Room at 807 Pacific. Several years later he made improvements to an old park in Spanaway, including pedestrian and bicycle paths along the lake shore. Other activities required a saloon license. Barbara died in Tacoma in 1913 and was buried in the Tacoma Mausoleum. Lauritz died in Aberdeen in 1923, where his sons Fred and Louis lived.

Herman Ostheim

Herman Ostheim was born in Germany around 1840. After living in Philadelphia and Boise, he joined his older brother Felix in Portland about 1870. Both sold cigars and stationery. Portland's 1872 directory listed Mrs. H. Ostheim as vice president of the Hebrew Ladies' Benevolent Society. In April the *Oregonian* noted that Felix Ostheim was returning permanently to his Fatherland.

Herman then moved to Tacoma, operating the Pioneer Cigar Store. After a few years he apparently joined his brother in Germany, but in 1881 returned to the United States. Herman's estate was administered in Seattle in 1889.

Sol and Ida Ottenheimer

Sol Ottenheimer was the fourth of eight children born within ten years to Reike Fleischer and Moses Ottenheimer in Jebenhausen, Germany. Born in 1868, Sol came to the U.S. as a teen and worked as a clerk in San Francisco in the late 1880s.

In 1890 Sol worked in Tacoma for John Rainey's billiard hall at 906–908 Pacific, recently vacated by the Gross Brothers. He lived at the same boarding house as Arthur and Max Berliner and Sam Holland. Later Sol worked in a cigar store run by Johanna Myers.

In February of 1893 Sol married Ida Gutfeld, (1875–1950), sister of Charles, Simon and Jacob Gutfeld. (See Gutfeld biography.) Their wedding was witnessed by D. Magnus and Herman Zelinsky. (Herman was married to Ida's sister Rosa.)

Sol found work in the liquor industry, as a salesman or "city solicitor" for Charles Langert's liquor company, which failed in 1896. Then he worked for the New West Liquor Company, which also failed. Around 1898 he found stable work as a delivery driver or "expressman" for the Eagle Bottling Works.

The couple lived at several locations in the vicinity of East 26th and East D, in a cluster of Zelinsky and Gutfeld families. They buried an infant in February of 1895, and a three-month-old daughter in 1896. Their son, Maurice (1898–1901) died of meningitis. Ida did not join the Judith Montefiore Society until 1902. She had two more sons, Albert in 1904 and Eldon in 1909. She was hospitalized in 1906.

Sol continued working as a driver for the Eagle Bottling Works, first delivering liquor and later bottled sodas. He died in 1921, but apparently was not buried near his infant children in the Home of Peace Cemetery. Ida lived in Tacoma until her death in 1950. Her obituary described her as a member of the Scientist First Church of Christ.

Their son Albert (1904–1980), graduated from the University of Washington in 1927 and helped found the Seattle Repertory Playhouse. He served as their press agent, producer, and starred in over 150 productions. Albert was convicted by the Canwell Committee in 1949 for refusing to answer whether he was or ever had been a member of the Communist party. Only decades later was Albert able to revive his acting career, playing a small part in Annie Hall in 1971. He likely never married.

Their son Eldon (1909–1993) began working for the *Tacoma Ledger* as a teenager. In March of 1937, just before the *Ledger* ceased publication, Eldon accepted a position with The Associated Press in San Francisco. That December Eldon returned to Tacoma to marry Pearl Anderson (1911–1993). The couple had two children in San Francisco. Eldon worked for AP there for 35 years, publishing many articles during the 1940s in his role as war editor. Eldon and his wife Pearl both died in Nevada in 1993.

Adolph and Sarah Packscher

The Packscher family in San Francisco
Courtesy of Steilacoom Historical Museum Association

Adolph Packscher was born in 1838 in Grandenz, West Prussia, now Grudziadz, Poland. When he arrived in Steilacoom with Isaac Pincus, after trying his mercantile luck in Nevada City, California, and in the gold fields of the Fraser River in British Columbia, he was just twenty years old. At 24 he married Sarah Goetheim, (anglicized to Goodtime) in San Francisco and began what would be a family of twelve children. The birthplaces of his children indicate the couple's moves back and forth between the two cit-

ies – Charley and Caroline in Steilacoom in 1863 and 1865; Malvina and her twin in 1867 and Tessie in 1873 in San Francisco; Maurice and Henry in Steilacoom in 1875 and 1876; and the remaining five in San Francisco between 1877 and 1888 – Samuel, Cherof, Leon, Albert, and Hazel. Three died in childhood.

Adolph spent time in Washington during the 1880s – attempting to have his sister-in-law declared insane in 1882, running a store in downtown Tacoma in 1884 and 1885, and suing his partner of thirty years in 1888. He was also a heavy taxpayer in Pierce County, indicating he had taken advantage of his early arrival by investing in real estate. His eldest son Charley likely ran the Tacoma store, and joined in Jewish activities and served on the fire department.

Adolph Packscher died in San Francisco on August 16, 1899, at the age of 63. His children lived with Sarah (1844–1927) and were slow to marry, if at all. Tessie (1873–1923) married Leon Hart in 1910 and had a son Alvin in 1912. Henry (1876–1936) married Ruth Bock and had a son Henry, Jr. in 1917. Samuel (1877–1938) married Verna Smith and had a daughter Gertrude in 1919. Albert (1885–1959) married Esther Hayes but had no children. The remaining five did not marry – Charley (1863–1914), Malvina (1867–1955), Maurice (1875–1939), Leon (1880–1944), and Hazel (1888–1965). None of the three grandchildren had children.

Sarah and Adolph's youngest child, Hazel, worked as the librarian of the Voorsanger Memorial Library in San Francisco's Temple Emanu-El during the 1940s and 1950s. She compiled lists of confirmation classes for reunions, and helped prepare congregational documents for the Judah L. Magnes Museum in Berkeley, including her parents' 1862 wedding record.

Zadek and Henrietta Peritz

READ! READ! READ!
AND VISIT
PERITZ & CO.
"THE PEOPLE'S BARGAIN STORE."
Tacoma Daily Ledger December 30, 1884

Zadek Peritz was born in Kempen (now Kepno, Poland) in 1832, son of Schmul Peritz and Hawe Grum. He lived in the U.S. from 1860 until about 1870, then returned to the Kempen/Ostrowo area to marry Henrietta Auerbach. The couple had at least six children – Leon, Nathan,

Mina, Richard, Martha and Hedwig – in the late 1870s and early 1880s. Zadek came to the U.S. a second time, arriving in Tacoma in 1884. He brought his two eldest sons with him, while the rest of the family stayed in Europe.

In Tacoma Zadek partnered with Meyer Kaufman and Henry Berliner, operating a branch of Seattle's Toklas and Singerman. In September of 1885, after less than one year in Tacoma, Zadek sold his interests in the firm and rejoined his family in Prussia. In 1888 Zadek again arrived in New York with his sons Leon and Nathan. Leon worked in Seattle selling newspapers in 1889.

The entire Peritz family moved to Guatemala, as did others from Kempen, following the booming coffee trade. Various passport applications over the next decade indicated that their permanent residence was Tacoma, if perhaps only on paper. The family lived in Champerico in 1892 and in Quezaltenango in 1894, regularly returning to Europe. In 1897 Zadek's daughter Mina married Julius Bilak in Los Altos, Guatemala. (See Bilak biography.) Nathan Peritz died in Austin, Texas, in 1906, while en route to New York from Guatemala.

Caroline Nelson Peyser Family

Caroline Nelson was born in Boston on May 16, 1847, daughter of Samuel and Rachel. On January 31, 1866, she married Simon Peyser in Boston, son of Nathan and Hannah. Their son Samuel was born in November of 1867. Then the family moved to Cambridge, Massachusetts, where their daughter Anna was born in December of 1869, followed by a son William F. in February of 1872. The couple lived in Providence, Rhode Island, in February of 1876 when their son Marcus was born.

They were likely the same family that lived in Portland, Oregon, from 1879–1881, where Simon worked as a tailor. He was probably the Simon Peyser who was shot in Oregon in 1882 and died in Sacramento.

By the time Caroline arrived in Tacoma in the 1890s she was widowed and had only three children left – sons Samuel, William and Marcus. Samuel died in March of 1892, and Marcus died in 1894 following a hip operation. Both graves in the Home of Peace Cemetery were unmarked, as was a third, described only as "Doc Peiser."

William worked initially as a clerk for the Harris Brothers, but suffered from bouts of dementia. He was sent to the asylum at Steilacoom several times in 1896. William and his mother lived in Puyallup in 1903, and moved to Oregon about 1906. Carolyn died there in 1907 and was buried in the Beth Israel Cemetery. William was again institutionalized in Oregon in 1917 and later in Connecticut, where he died in 1949.

Isaac and Seraphina Pincus

Isaac Pincus was born May 4, 1833, in Grodno, Poland, now Horodno, Belarus. His father Selig died about 1845, just as the family was preparing to emigrate. Isaac eventually set off on his own, living briefly in Nashville and New Orleans before coming to San Francisco in 1853. After a few years in Nevada City, California, and then following the stampede to the Fraser River in British Columbia in 1857, Isaac landed in Steilacoom in 1858.

Isaac operated a general store in Steilacoom with Adolph Packscher, who served as the San Francisco buyer. In the winter of 1864 Isaac traveled to Victoria to marry Adolph's cousin, Seraphina Packscher. (See Packscher biography.) Over the next 13 years they had seven children. The youngest, Minnie, lived only a few months in 1877. During his time in Steilacoom Isaac supported the community by serving as road supervisor, treasurer, and even took a turn as coroner.

In the 1880s Pincus and Packscher opened a branch store in Tacoma, built the National Theater building and ran a liquor business. Later Isaac branched out into the hops field, buying and selling on an international scale. In the spring of 1884 the Pincus family moved to Tacoma. That June Isaac's 15-year-old daughter Isabelle graduated from high school with the highest grades ever awarded.

In March of 1887 Isaac's oldest son, James (1865–1917), married Rose Green (1865–1936). Their daughter, Minnie, was born that winter. All of the ladies of the Pincus family assisted in the 1892 Temple Aid fundraiser, and Isaac served as an officer of the congregation.

Isaac Pincus and his daughters in their hop garden
Courtesy of Temple Beth El

In April of 1893 Isaac was elected to a two-year term on the city council, a month before the 1893 banking panic began. He served on the fire and water committee, responsible for purchasing Mason's water and light plant. His wife Seraphina died in 1905, and Isaac retired from active business. However, when his sons' hops company failed in 1910, Isaac sold his real estate holdings to cover their debts. He died in Tacoma on January 14, 1920.

In February of 1911 Isaac's unmarried son Harry died of meningitis. Another son, Marcus (1867–1940), married Laura Nell in 1913 and Margaret Harris in 1922, but had no children from either marriage. Isaac's son Julius (1870–1922) married Mary White in 1907 and then Louise Taylor. Their son, Julius I. Pincus, was born in Portland in 1918 and later moved to Salem, where he died in 1989.

Isaac's daughters never married. Bessie (1871–1939) died in Portland. Isabelle, born in 1869, died in Tacoma two months before her nineth-ninth birthday. (Lucille Feist Hurst, who remembered Isabelle, reported that Isabelle simply never met a man equal to her intelligence.)

Pincus family visiting Paradise August 22, 1918
Courtesy of Temple Beth El

Samuel and Jennie Posner

Jennie Herzman was born in New York in 1865, although her headstone says 1867. She was the second of at least five children born to Rosa and Rabbi Elkan Herzman. Shortly after her birth her father was fired from his position in Brooklyn, and successfully sued the congregation for $800. He was again fired from his Chicago congregation in 1871 for eating ice cream on a fast day, even though he felt he had explained his modern views at the time of his hiring. The family moved on to Council Bluffs, Iowa, and then Fargo, North Dakota.

Jennie married Samuel Posner (1851–1911), and their daughter Sara was born in North Dakota Territory in October of 1883. A few years later Jennie's sister, Lottie, married Elias Posner, and named her first son Samuel.

Sam and Jennie came to Tacoma around 1889, and likely lost a child in the summer of 1890. Jennie joined the Judith Montefiore Society, and in December of 1890 stepped in as vice president. Sam served as an officer of the Hebrew Benevolent Society and in 1892 served on the temple building committee. Jennie participated in the 1892 Temple Aid Society. The couple also attended Harmony Club events. Their daughter, Ruth, was born in January of 1892.

Sam's store at 943 Tacoma Avenue sold ladies and men's clothing and dress goods. In May of 1893 Sam moved south two blocks to 1107 Tacoma Avenue. The store often advertised special prices for underwear and hosiery.

He rode out the banking panic, and in 1894 was able to move into Louis Levin's building at 1148 Pacific. On July 8 the *Ledger* noted that Sam's would be one of only two dry goods firms on Pacific between the Northern Pacific wharf and Thirty-fifth Street. He frequently gave away dolls or other toys as holiday shopping incentives. In the spring of 1897 he moved up to 1130 Pacific, and the following year to 946 Pacific.

POSNER, 946 Pacific Avenue.

Summer Underwear

Ladies' Sleeveless Vest at 25c, 15c, 10c	**5c**
Ladies' Long Sleeve Vest in blue, pink and cream, at 19c and	**15c**
Ladies' Long Sleeve, at 25c and	**19c**
Ladies' Fancy Hosiery, polka dot and stripes, at 50c, 25c and	**19c**
Ladies' Lisle Drop-stitch Hose, 69c and	**50c**
Summer Corsets—A good, durable Corset for summer wear, at 50c and	**25c**
Children's Trimmed Hats, at $1.25, $1.00, 89c, 75c and	**59c**
New Wash Fabrics, just in, at 25c, 15c, 10c and..	**7c**

POSNER,

946 Pacific Avenue.

Tacoma Daily Ledger May 3, 1900

Jennie frequently hosted birthday parties for her children. Sara was confirmed in Beth Israel in 1900, and Sam served as secretary-treasurer of the congregation. After Sara turned 18 she was regularly shipped off for extended visits to other cities, increasing her opportunities to meet eligible Jewish bachelors. She also volunteered as the temple's organist.

Sam's business continued to prosper. In March of 1903 he was able to purchase Albert Weinberg's interest in Edwin Heinemann's dry goods store. The new firm of Heinemann & Pos-

ner occupied all of 1352–4–6 Pacific. The family moved to 513 North E, and their previous home was converted for use as a private sanitarium. In 1906 Samuel was president of congregation Beth Israel.

That winter the family moved to Portland, where Samuel continued selling clothing and mens' furnishings. Later he and Jennie sold fruit. Their daughter Sara (1883–1974) married Dr. Samuel Gellert and had three daughters – Virginia, Mary Jane and Betty. Sam, born 1851, died in Portland in June of 1911. A year later their youngest daughter, Ruth, married Edward Kramer and together the families ran a fish market. Ruth's sons Sam and Frederick Kramer were born around 1914 and 1916.

Ruth died in Portland in February of 1920. Her death was attributed to the flu epidemic. After her passing Jennie became despondent, and in May killed herself and her two grandsons. The Gellert family remained in Portland.

Charles and Frances Postman

Charles Postman was born in Germany around 1860, and in 1883 served in the California National Guard. He attended business school and sold dry goods in San Francisco through 1885, then worked in St. Paul, Minnesota, selling California wines.

In San Francisco on May 1, 1890, Charles Postman of Tacoma married Frances Rosenfeld, only daughter of Solomon and Rosa. A few weeks later Charles filed a timber claim in Albany, Oregon, giving his residence as Tacoma.

In Tacoma Charles managed the California Wine House, in partnership with Frederick Williams. Frances joined the Judith Montefiore Society and the couple attended Harmony Club dances. In November of 1890 the Williams/Postman partnership dissolved.

The Postman family moved to Portland and operated the California Wine House with partner C. H. Soltz. Their daughter Rita was born in Portland in January of 1891. Frances' father died in 1892 and the couple returned to San Francisco. Charles began making trips to Colon, Panama. Another daughter, Felice, was born in San Francisco in March of 1900. In March of 1912 Charles died in Barbados, West Indies. Frances continued living in San Francisco with her three unmarried brothers, where she died in 1947. Her daughter Rita (1891–1924) married Harry W. Friedman, and her daughter Felice (1900–1978) married Fred Hammer.

A Model Business House of the City of Tacoma, Washington.

THE MECHANICS' BLOCK IN 1889.

THE MECHANICS' BLOCK IN 1890.

THE MECHANICS' BLOCK IN 1893.

Tacoma Daily Ledger May 2, 1893

Sidney and Pauline Prager

Sidney Prager was born in Portland around 1876, the third child born to Hyman Prager and Frances Jacoby. His father and his uncle, Louis Prager, operated Harris and Prager in Portland as early as 1873. They started the Farmers' and Mechanics' Store in 1877, with a third brother,

William, serving as New York buyer. In 1889 the Prager brothers built a Tacoma store, managed by Solomon Jacoby, brother of Frances. (See Jacoby biography.) Still a teenager, Sidney lived with his uncle in Tacoma in 1890 and worked at the store as a bookkeeper, then returned to his parents in Portland. By 1893 Sidney was managing the large Portland store.

The Tacoma branch did well at first, expanding rapidly and advertising heavily. But the 1893 banking panic took its toll on even the largest firms. In January of 1894 the Prager brothers executed a deed of trust, transferring their Portland property to Henry Ackerman and their Tacoma property to Archie Ash. The claims of creditors totaled over a quarter of a million dollars. By April they were briefly back on their feet, and Sidney performed a violin solo at the celebration party.

A month later Sidney and his uncle Solomon announced they would build their own store in Tacoma, not part of Prager Brothers. And in June Sidney Prager married Pauline Jacobs, daughter of Moses Jacobs, and sister of Archie Ash's wife Rose. (See Jacobs biography). The new firm emerged as Jacoby, Ash, and Company, with Sidney as the "and company." During construction they were accused of violating the building ordinance because only three walls were of brick, but were ultimately acquitted.

Pauline joined the Judith Montefiore Society, and frequently entertained Portland guests. She gave birth to a daughter, Rita, in May of 1895. However, the new firm was still caught in a legal tangle with Prager Brothers in Portland. Pauline's father came to the rescue, then closed the Tacoma firm.

Sidney and Pauline moved to Portland when their daughter was just two months old. Another daughter, Eleanor, was born in March of 1896. The marriage ended and each returned to their parents' households in Portland. Later Pauline lived in San Francisco, where she died in 1942. Apparently neither daughter married. Rita Jean Prager died on July 3, 1948, followed by Eleanor Amy Prager on January 18, 1952.

Sidney moved to Spokane with his parents, who both died there in 1922. Sidney sold clothing and died in Spokane in 1947 at the age of 73.

Julius and Jennie Rammelsberg

Julius Rammelsberg (1860–1931) was the eldest of at least ten children born to Moses and Henrietta Rammelsberg – the first four in Prussia, the last six in Cincinnati. Moses worked as a tailor, but Julius learned the trade of making cigars, earning a listing in the city directory when he was just 17. Julius stayed in Cincinnati through at least 1885.

Julius was occupied as a cigar maker in Tacoma in 1889, then worked for a decade as a bartender. For several years he was the proprietor of the Budweiser Saloon at 1207 Pacific. He was also known for his excellent tenor voice – participating in a special choir at *Rosh Hashana* services in 1892, and frequently singing in Tacoma Sangerbund concerts at Germania Hall.

In June of 1893 Julius married Jennie Ascher (1868–1944), who's sister Jette had married Sol Zelinsky. (See Zelinsky biography.) According to the *Ledger* on June 11th, the wedding party was held in the Pioneer building at Old Town, and included "a large number of the prominent Hebrews of the city." The couple would have no children.

Around 1900 Julius returned to making cigars, working for a variety of employers and from his home at 739 Tacoma Avenue. Julius was active in the Tacoma Trades Council, serving as president in 1902–1904. In January of 1903 the cigar makers' union formed a "blue label league, to discriminate in favor of American-made cigars."

Julius died in Tacoma in 1931, followed by Jennie in 1944. Their graves in the Home of Peace Cemetery were unmarked until a community project in 1999 righted that wrong.

Charles and Belle Reichenbach

Charles Reichenbach
From the collection of the author

Charles Reichenbach was born in Breslau, Germany, (now Wroclaw, Poland) in 1842. He was one of at least four sons of Isaac and Rosalie, and his mother died at the time of his birth. Arriving in New York in 1863, Charles served in the Union Army, then worked for Louis and Marcus Stein in Milwaukee, Wisconsin.

In 1870 he married their sister, Julia Stein. Julia gave him three sons – Oscar and Edwin, born in Menominee, Wisconsin, and Walter, born in Chicago. Julia died in 1880 and Charles married Belle Einstein (1848–1932) in Philadelphia in 1882. Their daughter Eda was born in Chicago in 1883. In February of 1885 the family arrived in Tacoma.

Charles immediately rented the best retail location in town – a new brick building on the corner of Ninth and Pacific. He aggressively advertised his London and Liverpool Clothing Store, going head to head with his respected neighbors – the Gross Brothers.

The following year Charles expanded his business, opening a summer branch store in Chehalis, managed by his fifteen-year-old son, Oscar, and his nephew, Ben Einstein. His family also expanded, with the birth of Katherine Teresa, known as Tessie. Or, as the *Ledger* put it on June 9, 1886, "Born... to the wife of Charles Reichenbach, a female voter." (Charles was active in the Lincoln Republican Club.) He made regular buying trips to the East Coast and continued advertising heavily. In August of 1887 Charles expanded into the adjoining store, occupying 902 and now 904 Pacific.

As Tacoma's real estate market boomed, anyone who could raise cash invested in land. Charles and his Stein in-laws bought 40 acres and created the London and Liverpool Addition, divided into 43 blocks with 16 lots each. The addition spanned South 56th and 60th, between East R and East N, encompassing what is now Portland Avenue. Charles gave his wife five lots for her birthday.

Charles was active in the Germania Society and sent his sons to a private German school. In 1888 Charles chaired the Germania Society's committee to build a new hall. Located on 13th and E, (now Fawcett) the building was dedicated in February of 1889 and had a seating capacity of 1500. The hall was often rented for High Holiday services and other Jewish gatherings. The following year Charles helped incorporate the German Benevolent Society and served as its first president.

His interests kept growing. Charles was vice president and later treasurer of the Puget Sound Dressed Beef company, a director of the Phoenix Fire and Marine Insurance Company, and ran unsuccessfully for school board and council positions. With the arrival of another nephew, Max Stein, Charles was able to open the Star Clothing House at 1306 Pacific in November of 1889.

As if that wasn't enough, he also invested in the "Round the World Publishing Company," hoping to profit from George Francis Train's whirlwind trip. Charles was able to accompany Train on the initial and final legs of his 67-day journey, and helped finance Sam Wall's book about the trip. Charles' political efforts were rewarded in May of 1890 when he was selected as an aide-de-camp on Governor Ferry's staff, a position carrying the honorary rank of lieutenant-colonel. A profile of "Prominent Tacomans" on November 30, 1890, included Charles as a director of the Union Home Building and Loan association, and a shareholder in the Pacific Navigation company.

Belle was also busy. In addition to her travels and entertaining, in 1890 Belle helped incorporate the interfaith Lend-a-Hand League, and the Tacoma Exchange for Women's Work. She was one of the initial members of the Judith Montefiore Society, participated in the Entre Nous club, and the couple attended Harmony Club events. In December of 1892 she assumed the responsibility of treasurer for the Temple Aid Society fair.

However, the empire was built on a foundation of mortgages that collapsed in January of 1892. The business was quickly reorganized in Oscar's name, then sold to Hyams, Pauson and Company. Oscar stayed on as manager, and eventually moved to San Francisco. After a year of huge creditor lawsuits, Charles moved to Seattle. There he operated the U.S. Clothing Company on Front Street, with his son Walter as manager, and later tried Spokane for a brief period.

Like many other high-risk adventurers, Charles and his son Walter tried their luck in the Klondike, even venturing unsuccessfully into politics in Dawson. Belle operated a boarding house in San Francisco. Eventually Charles settled into semi-retirement, selling insurance. He died in San Francisco in 1922, followed by Belle in 1932.

Oscar Reichenbach with parents and family, San Francisco
Courtesy of Bill Tivol

Charles' eldest son, Oscar (1871–1929), married Belle's niece, Ivy Rosenfeld (1873–1964), in 1902, and had a son O. Robert Reichenbach in 1905. Edwin (1874–1922), did not marry. Walter (1878–1919) married Alice Kaufman, but had no children. Belle's daughter, Eda (1883–1949), married Francis Bloch and had four children between 1908 and 1917. Belle's youngest daughter, Tessie, ran the family insurance business and died in 1981.

Saul and Yetta Robinson

Saul Robinson (1856–1932) and his wife Yetta Kauffman (1851–1914) married around 1887. Saul worked in Tacoma as a tailor as early as 1889, and lived for several years at 1014 I Street. Their son Herbert Louis Robinson was born in Tacoma in December of 1889. In August of 1891 their two-week-old daughter, Florence Dora, was buried in the Home of Peace Cemetery.

ROBINSON & CO.,
118 10th St., Tacoma, Wash.
Suits Made to Order for $25.00 and Up.
Pants for $5.00 and Upwards.
All Goods Guaranteed in Fit and Workmanship.   Repairing and Cleaning Done on Short Notice
DRESS SUITS A SPECIALTY.

Tacoma City Directory 1893–1894

Saul lived and worked from a variety of locations, specializing in suits, and later cleaning and dyeing. Around 1910 the family moved to Everett, where Herbert ran a dye works and Saul had his own tailor shop. Both Yetta and Saul died in Everett but were buried in Tacoma near their infant daughter. Cemetery records note that Yetta was a relative of Valentine Schreck.

Herbert (1889–1957) married Pauline Bunning (1889–1970) and had a son Philip (1922–1973), who died in California.

Sol and Eva Rogers

Sol Rogers (c.1859–1946) married Eva Belle Abrams (c.1865–1961) in San Francisco in 1886. Eva was the second of eight children born to Isaac and Esther Abrams. (See Abrams biography.) Two Rogers children, Florence/Flossie and Harold, were born there in 1887 and 1888. Then the family moved to Tacoma, where Sol operated the San Francisco Tailor store at 917-1/2 Pacific, in the heart of Tacoma's best retail block. Over the next four years he moved to a variety of locations just a few blocks farther south. Two more daughters were born in Tacoma – Freda in 1891 and Rose around 1895.

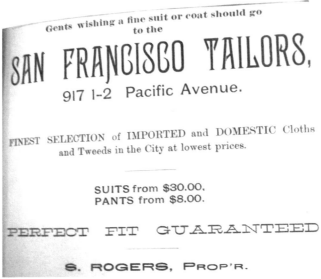

Gents wishing a fine suit or coat should go to the

SAN FRANCISCO TAILORS,

917 1-2 Pacific Avenue.

FINEST SELECTION of IMPORTED and DOMESTIC Cloths and Tweeds in the City at lowest prices.

SUITS from $30.00,
PANTS from $8.00.

PERFECT FIT GUARANTEED

S. ROGERS, PROP'R.

Tacoma City Directory 1891

Sol and Eva were active in Tacoma's burgeon-ing Jewish community. They were among the first forty members of the Home of Peace Cemetery. Sol served as one of the first *B'nai B'rith* trustees in 1890 and helped to lead Passover services in 1893. Eva worked in the toy booth at the Temple Aid Society's Fair in December of 1892.

The Rogers family moved to Seattle around 1896, where Sol operated the Rogers Tailoring Company on First Avenue. They remained in Seattle, where Sol died in 1946, followed by Eva in 1961.

Their daughter Florence (1887–1968) married Philip Mendelsohn and had a daughter Irma in 1922. Harold (1888–1949) married twice and had at least nine children. Freda (1891–1935) married Kalman Loeb in 1919 and had four children. Rose (c.1895–1984) married Henry Fisher and had a son Edward.

Martin and Anna Rosenbaum

Martin Rosenbaum was born in Demopolis, Alabama, on December 19, 1846, the second of perhaps seven children born to Fredrick Rosenbaum and Babette Mayer. His older and younger brothers were born in New York around 1842 and 1851. The remainder of Martin's siblings were born in Cincinnati, Ohio, where Martin grew up.

Around 1876 he married Anna Alexandra, born in Winchester, Virginia, on June 4, 1845. Martin worked as a salesman in Cincinnati through at least 1886, then lived briefly in San Francisco before coming to the Northwest.

In May of 1888 Martin partnered with John H. Chapman in opening a grocery store in Tacoma at 746 Pacific. Because their landlord, Mr. Fife, was opposed to the sale of liquor on the premises, the firm rented a warehouse one block away to store and sell their wines and liquors. A few weeks before their arrival twenty local merchants had signed an agreement to sell no cigarettes for less than ten cents per package. In June Chapman and Rosenbaum offered cigarettes at five cents per pack. The firm occasionally donated magazines and groceries to the Fannie Paddock hospital, earning public acknowledgement.

In February of 1889 the firm went out of business, citing debts of approximately $5,800. Albert Weinberg was able to purchase the stock, fixtures, delivery wagon and three horses at auction for just $3,200. The stock alone was valued at nearly $9,000. Martin found sales work representing the wholesale clothing house of Rothschild, Hays & Co., of Rochester, N.Y.

In January of 1890 Mr. and Mrs. Rosenbaum hosted Dr. Julius Wise of Memphis, son of Rabbi Isaac M. Wise, during his visit to Tacoma. They hosted several elaborate dinner parties, and in May Anna joined the Judith Montefiore Society. The following year Anna participated in the interfaith Lend-a-Hand Society and Martin was active in the organization of the Tacoma Relief Committee, protesting persecution of Jews in Russia.

In April of 1891 Martin was granted a patent for a hotel bed that converted for use as a traveling salesman's show table.

The Rosenbaums left Tacoma around 1892, joining Martin's brothers Henry and Louis in Boston. Martin worked as a traveling salesman well into his sixties. Martin and his wife Anna died in Melrose, Massachusetts, in 1912 and 1910.

Frank S. Rosenberg

Frank S. Rosenberg was born in Russia between 1859 and 1862. As early as 1896 he sold fruits and confections from his home at 1514 Jefferson. He attended the 1899 wedding of Julius Friedman and Augusta Stusser, indicating he was part of Tacoma's Orthodox Jewish community. Around 1904 Frank moved to 1022 Tacoma Avenue and continued as a confectioner. Unmarried, he joined the Home of Peace Cemetery in 1912. Around 1921 he moved to 1014 Tacoma Avenue and sold cigars. Frank died in 1926 and was survived by a brother Charles.

Gustav M. Rosengarden

Gustav M. Rosengarden worked as a shoemaker in Tacoma in 1890 and 1891. His wife joined the Judith Montefiore Society in May of 1890.

Ervin and Milton Rosenheim

David Rosenheim (1831–1910) and Pauline Einstein (1842–1923) had five children in Philadelphia between 1865 and 1884. Their two eldest sons, Ervin and Milton, lived in Tacoma in 1890 and 1891, with their aunt Belle Einstein Reichenbach. Milton worked at the London and Liverpool clothing house for Charles Reichenbach. Ervin offered real estate loans and life insurance. Both attended Jewish social events and Harmony Club dances. By 1894 both young men were back with their parents in Philadelphia.

Ervin (1865–1925) married Marguerite Hannach (c.1883–1916) in 1904 and had three daughters – Beatrice, Muriel and Helen, in Philadelphia before moving to Manhattan.

Milton (1867–1935) married Libbie Adell Smith (1866–1930) in 1894 and moved to Providence, Rhode Island, where he operated a jewelry store. The couple had no children.

Leopold and Rose Rosenthal

Leopold P. Rosenthal was born in Germany about June of 1864. He worked in Tacoma from 1888 until 1890 for Charles Reichenbach, living in the Reichenbach household and attending Jewish social events. Then Leopold moved to Portland, where he worked for the Famous clothing house. In August of 1892 he married Rose Sommer (1870–1917), daughter of La Grande, Oregon, pioneers, Aaron Sommer and Bertha Wertheimer. The couple visited Tacoma on their honeymoon, attending a party given in their honor by Colonel Reichenbach.

Their only daughter Carolyn was born in Portland in 1901, and shortly after the family moved to Spokane, along with Rose's sisters, Mary and Fanny. In 1908 Leopold and Rose made a trip to the Orient, returning via Yokohama, Japan. However, by 1916 Rose was listed in the Spokane directory as a widow. Rose died in Spokane in June of 1917, and her sisters and daughters returned to Oregon. Mary Sommer died in La Grande in 1927 and Fanny and Carolyn moved to San Francisco. There Carolyn (1901–1962) married Allyn Wexel (1901–1950) in April of 1930.

Julius G. and Pauline Salhinger

Unlike many others, Julius G. Salhinger left a clear early paper trail. His name appeared on a list of aliens arriving in London, England, from Prussia on November 2, 1850. From there Julius sailed to New York aboard the *Mechanics Own*, arriving on September 15, 1851. He filed a petition for naturalization in New York on April 3, 1853. And by June of 1855 Julius was included on the New York State census with his wife Pauline and their infant son, Henry. At least nine more children would be born to the couple in New York over the next fifteen years.

Julius worked as a tailor in New York through at least 1874, and in 1875 lived in Chicago. His wife Pauline Fox Salhinger died in Chicago in June of 1885.

At least two of their children stayed in Chicago. Rachel (1863–1920) graduated from high school in 1881 and was a teacher. Moses (1865–1952) worked as a newsboy as a child and as an adult continued operating a newsstand. In 1898 he married Georgiana Wooten (1867–1940) and the couple had one child – Pauline (1898–1982.)

Israel, born about 1859, was likely the first to leave Chicago. He worked in Helena, Montana as early as 1878, and was active in mining. Later he organized several banks, including the First National Bank of Port Angeles in 1890, and became a stockbroker. In 1902 Israel married Jeanette Gensler (c.1880–1920) in Oakland, California. They also had one daughter Pauline (1911–1976). Israel's unmarried sister, Annie (1861–1958), later lived with him in San Francisco.

After Pauline's death Julius moved to the West Coast, bringing five of his children with him. He worked as a tailor in Portland in 1888 and 1889, then moved to Tacoma, where he lived through at least 1901.

His eldest son Henry (1855–1922) married Sarah Rosenberg (1862–1937) in 1880. Their daughter Nettella was born in Chicago in 1882. By 1890 Henry and his brother Samuel were operating a shoe and boot store in Tacoma and Sarah joined the Ladies' Judith Montefiore Society. Another daughter, also Pauline (1892–1970), was born in Tacoma shortly before the family moved to Everett. Their first daughter Nettella died in Everett in 1902.

Samuel (1857–1934) worked in Tacoma and Everett with Henry, then moved to San Francisco, where he married Sarah Wallach (1863–1944) in 1895. Their son Joseph D. was born in 1896 and died in 1970. The San Francisco branch of the family used the more common "Salinger" spelling. (Not to be confused with the author Jerome David Salinger, born in New York in 1919, son of Sol Salinger.)

Louis (1866–1937) moved to Everett with Henry, where they operated the Chicago Clothing House, later the Riverside Clothing Store. Louis married Jennie and had two children, Louis Jr. and Cleo. For many years Louis Jr. (1911–2003) operated a bicycle shop in Everett.

Julius' youngest surviving daughter, Mollie (c.1868–1936), married Walter Cleveland (c.1858–1937) in Tacoma in October of 1891. (Walter's mother, Mathilda, and brother, James, operated the Cleveland House.) The couple had three children in Tacoma in the 1890s – William, Mathilda, and Nancy, and later moved to Centralia, Spokane and Seattle.

Julius' youngest son, Robert (1873–1957) lived in San Francisco in 1896 and 1897, then spent a few years in Everett before returning to San Francisco. He married Nellie Keva (1878–1959).

Wolf and Mina Schafer

Mina (1816–1871) had three children – Sophia, Joseph and Rosa Greenhut – in Austria in the 1840s before her first husband died. She then married Wolf Schafer and came to Chicago around 1852. Their daughter Anna was born a few years later.

In 1860 Sophia married Edward Selig Salomon, who soon joined the Union Army. Her sister, Rosa, married another soldier, Leopold Hirsch, in 1865. Their brother, Joseph Greenhut, also a veteran, married Clara Wolfner in Chicago in 1866. As a reward for his distinguished service in the Union Army, President Grant appointed Salomon Governor of Territorial Washington in

1869. All three couples and the Schafer parents came to Olympia. On May 5, probably 1871, Mina died in Olympia and was buried in Portland. (Olympia's Jewish cemetery was organized the following year.)

Wolf moved to Steilacoom, where he operated the Northern Pacific Railroad Brewery until his death in 1889. His daughter Anna Schafer died just two years later.

Wolf Schafer house
Courtesy of Steilacoom Historical Museum Association

Sophia (1841–1893) and Edward Salomon moved to San Francisco, where he worked as an attorney until his death in 1913. The couple had three children in Chicago in the 1860s – Benjamin, Max and Carrie (Stern). Their daughter Minnie (1873–1898) was born in Olympia and named for her grandmother.

Joseph (1843–1918) and Clara (1850–1927) had two children in Chicago in 1868 and 1870 – Fannie and Benedict. After their sojourn in Olympia they returned to Chicago for the birth of their son Walter in 1878, and lived in Peoria in 1891 when their son Nelson was born. Joseph invented a twine-binder that he sold to McCormick for their harvesting machines, then operated a major distillery and helped build the town of Peoria. He lived the last decade of his life in Manhattan.

Rosa (1846–1915) and Leopold Hirsch (1835–1915) had three children in Chicago in the 1860s – Benedict, William and Edward. Two more were born in Olympia – Herman and Arthur, before the family returned to Peoria. Most of the family stayed in Peoria. The youngest, Arthur, worked for the U.S. Census Bureau in Washington, D.C., eventually becoming the chief clerk.

Jacob and Sadie Schapeero

Jacob Joseph Schapeero (1862–1931) and Sadie Reznik (1867–1900) were married in Germany about 1887, where their daughter Mary was born in June of 1888. They had three more children in Pennsylvania – Rose, Elias and David – between 1891 and 1895. Their fifth child, Ezra, was born in New Jersey in 1897.

The family moved to Tacoma the following year, where Harry was born late in 1898. The Judith Montefiore Society assisted them by hiring a nurse and purchasing groceries. Jacob worked as an expressman, driving a delivery wagon. They were able to attend the wedding of Julius Friedman and Augusta Stusser in December of 1899. A year later Sadie died as a result of childbirth, the day after her thirty-third birthday. Her toddler daughter Anna died in Tacoma's Woolsey home for orphans in 1903. The Judith Montefiore Society again provided assistance, arranging for the younger boys' transportation to the Hebrew Orphan Asylum in San Francisco. They also hired Jacob for small driving jobs.

Jacob wrote to Sadie's family in Europe and received help in the form of her sister, Rebecca. They were married in January of 1907 and her son Leonard was born seven months later. Over the next five years the Judith Montefiore Society repeatedly corresponded with the orphanage in San Francisco, trying to get the boys returned to their father.

Another son, Frank, was born in 1911, but the couple divorced in 1914. Jacob died in Tacoma in 1931. Rebecca married Frank T. Hale and had a son Nathan in 1919. Her Schapeero sons used the name Hale.

David and Celia Shafer

David Shafer (1863–1942) was the eldest son of Abraham Schofowitch and Sarah Jacobs. His brothers Julius and Isador used the name Schofowitch in Seattle from 1892 until about 1901, when they anglicized to Shafer. Beginning as pawnbrokers, they moved up to jewelry, auctioneering, and then land development. Julius was able to purchase Sam Loeb's home in Seattle, now the Shafer-Baillie Mansion bed and breakfast.

David sold fruit and candy from 1332 Pacific in Tacoma in the 1890s, using the spelling Schafowich. He later operated the Red Front clothing store. David married Celia Abrams (1879–1963) in 1901, the youngest of eight Abrams siblings. (See Abrams biography.) The couple had two children in Tacoma – Herbert (1902–1988) and Hortense (1907–1999).

Sichel Siblings – Rose, Emma and Leo

Max Sichel was born in Heldenbergen, Hesse-Darmstadt in 1822 and immigrated to the U.S. in 1848. He and his wife Fannie had three children in New York in the 1850s, followed by six more in San Francisco. Max was noted as a pioneer dentist and a member of the first American Dental Association. Several of his children had Tacoma connections. Simon Kullman married Max's daughter Rose Sichel in San Francisco in 1877. Jacob Kullman married her sister Emma in 1888. (See Kullman biography.)

Max's youngest son Leo (1874–1963) lived in Tacoma in 1892, working as a bookkeeper for Jacob Kullman and living in the Kullman home. In April of 1892 he was one of seven young bachelors in the Stag Seven club. Leo went back to San Francisco and joined his father and brother Henry in the dentistry field. In 1907 Leo married Isabel (1883–1976) but the couple had no children.

Simon Silverman

Simon Silverman was born on December 14, 1855 in Poland/Russia, and arrived in New York in September of 1877. He first declared his intention to become a U.S. citizen in Boston in 1884. A jeweler by trade, Simon typically worked as a wandering peddler.

Around 1892 Simon settled in Tacoma. He boarded with others, often living at a different address each year. In 1898 he received financial aid from the Judith Montefiore Society, after he lost $600 in an illegal dice game. By 1900 he had found lodging with the Martin family on E Street (now Fawcett). In 1905 Simon attempted to remove a large cottonwood tree from the front yard, but was stopped by concerned neighbors. The *Tacoma Daily News'* headline on August 11, 1905, read "OH, SIMON SILVERMAN, SPARE THAT TREE," a play on the poem "Woodman, spare that tree."

Simon filed for citizenship in Pierce County on November 19, 1906. He lived in Tacoma through at least 1919. Home of Peace Cemetery records list a death date of December 12, 1927.

Petition for Naturalization November 19, 1906

Abraham Simon Family

Abraham Simon was likely born in Izbic, Poland, in 1846. He and his first wife Esther had four children in England between 1864 and 1869. Then the family came to New York, where two more children were born in the 1870s. It's likely that at some point – either in England or in New York, Abraham's first wife died. He then married Sarah Lewis, sister of D.P. Lewis. (See Lewis biography.) The family then moved to California, where three more children were born between 1876 and 1882. Another three children were born in Tacoma between 1884 and 1889. The thirteenth was born in Denver, Colorado in 1893, before the family returned to Tacoma in 1894.

Important Announcement!

IN ORDER TO MAKE ROOM FOR A LARGE and carefully selected stock of Men's and Boys'

BOOTS AND SHOES,

Just received and to arrive from the East, I am compelled to dispose of my stock on hand at very **Low Figures.**

All who desire bargains will do well to call at the

IXL BOOT AND SHOE STORE,

PACIFIC AVENUE, two doors south of Central Drug Store, New Tacoma, W. T.

This is not the IXL Dry Goods Store.
☞ CUSTOM WORK done to order in the latest and best style.
Don't forget the place.
1y1   A. SIMON, Proprietor.

Tacoma Daily Ledger April 10, 1883

In the spring of 1883 Abraham opened the IXL boot and shoe store in Tacoma. Possibly to avoid confusion with the IXL clothing store, Abraham changed the name of his business to the Terminal Shoe Store, around the time his son Sam opened the Terminal cigar store. Within a few weeks both gained the more accurate and appealing name of Terminus. That fall Abraham operated a combination cigar and shoe business in Puyallup during hop-picking season.

Abraham struggled to find a permanent location, moving up and down Pacific every few months. He also struggled financially, and in April of 1885 sold his house and two lots on 11th and Tacoma Avenue for $2500. That fall he began construction of a new home on the corner of 24th and Pacific. The following year he briefly opened a dairy business from his new home, then moved to a ranch near Orting.

Sam's cigar store also went through troubles. In July of 1885 Charles Langert apparently bought the stock and fixtures at auction, then kept Sam on as manager. That fall Sam was arrested for gambling when the police raided a game in the back room of the store. He chose to forfeit his $20 bail.

Abraham was also arrested, indicted by a grand jury in September of 1886 for perjury, after testifying under oath that he had not received a $700 check from a prominent attorney. Good news came due to a change in the laws of the territory. *Ledger,* February 28, 1887, "Comes now the prosecuting attorney and moves the court to quash the indictment in the above entitled cause on the ground that the same was returned by both women and men, and under the decision of the Supreme Court of Washington Territory women are not qualified Grand Jurors. And the Court being fully advised in the premises grants said motion, and it is ordered that the defendant be discharged."

In December of 1887 Abraham returned to the shoe business, opening a store at 713 Pacific. He lived at the store for about a year, then built a large home on 21st and Jefferson for his growing family. Abraham wisely joined the cemetery association, and some of his older children attended Harmony Club events – perhaps with weddings as a result. Rachel married John Hussey and had a daughter, Etta, in October of 1893. Rebecca married William Eckstein and had a son Alfred in November of 1893. The couple later ran a secondhand store from 713 Pacific. (See Eckstein biography.)

Abraham and Sarah moved briefly to Denver, Colorado, where their son Ernest was born in December of 1893 – a month after the birth of their second grandchild. They immediately returned to Tacoma, appearing in court in January of 1894 when their twelve-year-old son Murray was sent to the reform school in Chehalis for truancy.

Abraham was last included in Tacoma's city directories in February of 1895. In March he was mentioned as the father of the bride when his daughter Sarah married Harry Hirschfield, but did not sign as a witness. He is likely the Abraham Simon buried in Portland's *Ahavai Shalom* Cemetery, who died May 28, 1895. Mrs. Sarah Simon was listed in Portland's 1895 city directory as the widow of Abraham. She lived in Portland through 1900, then returned to Tacoma where she died in 1904.

The Simon family epitomizes the pattern of leaving few descendants.

Children of Abraham Simon: (nc means no children)

1. Samuel, born about 1864 in England. Married Rose Blumenthal. Died Tacoma 1919. nc
2. George, born about 1865 in England. Married Celia and then Mildred. Died Tacoma 1924. nc
3. Sarah, born Sept. 30, 1866 in London. Married Harry Hirschfield. Died Tacoma 1938. 4 ch
    a. Florence married 3 times, nc
    b. Alfred married Sybil Sidelsky, nc
    c. Beno married Lucille Florsheim, son David Harry b Chicago 1930, m2 Rita Hofbauer
    d. Harriet married George Paiser, Harry Jacobs, and maybe White, nc.
4. Rebecca, born about 1869 in England. Married William Eckstein. Died Tacoma 1929.
    a. Alfred married Dora Powers, nc
    b. Carl married Gladys Huffman, nc, 1 step-daughter
5. Rachel, born about 1873 in New York. Married John Hussey & Thomas Ryan.
    a. Etta married Walter Thomassen, nc
    b. Edward married Clara Schindler, nc
6. Rose, born December 11, 1875 in New York. Married W.W.Ellsworth M Bloom. Died San Francisco 1940. nc
7. Louis, born about 1876 in San Francisco. Married Clara. Died Portland 1952. nc
8. Dave, born about 1879 in California. Lost after 1903
9. Murray, born August 28, 1881 in San Francisco. Married Dora. Died Spokane 1946. nc
10. Fanny, born Dec 1884 in Tacoma. Married Alfred Spelger 1909. Died Seattle 1954. nc
11. Etta, born 1887 in Tacoma. Married Milo Ellsworth. Died Bellevue 1976.
    a. Lucille Viola married Fred P. Bottenberg, nc
    b. Virginia married Louis A. Secord, son Louis JR born 1947
12. Levin, born 1889 in Tacoma. Not in 1904 obit, lost after 1900
13. Ernest, born 1893 in Denver. Married Harriet Verstandig. Died Spokane 1953.
    a. Geraldine married Gerald Wright and Frank Carter, nc

Samuel and Bertha Sondheim

Samuel Sondheim was born in the Bromskirchen, in the Hesse area of Germany, around 1860. He immigrated as a teen and became a naturalized citizen around 1880. Samuel's older brothers Henry, Jonas, and Meyer lived in Pennsylvania. His younger brother, Joseph, lived in Salt Lake City.

In Tacoma Samuel partnered with Abraham Goldenson, opening the Golden Eagle Clothing House about 1890. Unlike others who went bankrupt in the 1890s, Goldenson and Sondheim prospered. By 1895 they were able to open a second location in Seattle, known as the Rochester Clothing Company, with Abraham living in Seattle. (See Goldenson biography.)

Around 1896 Samuel married Bertha Frank, daughter of Emily Ballin Frank. Two years later his partner married her sister Rose. (See Frank biography.) Bertha immediately joined the Judith Montefiore Society, teaching in the religious school and occasionally serving as an officer. Their son, Leonard, was born in 1897.

After the Jacoby-Ash company failed, Samuel's firm moved into their previous location, knocking out a wall and combining 1348 and 1350 Pacific. Store ads often tied in to local events, offering "golden opportunities" during the Klondike rush, and "spreading out" as Hawaii was annexed. In 1903 the partners briefly opened a second Rochester Clothing in Aberdeen.

Tacoma Daily Ledger May 3, 1900

Around 1908 Sam's partner moved to Los Angeles, and Sam brought his nephew, Albert Sondheim, to help. Their store was located at 1308 Pacific. In the teens Bertha again became active in the Judith Montefiore Society. Albert married Celia Levitt in 1916 and she also became a member. After the death of their infant son in 1919, Albert (1887–1944) and Celia (1896–1977) moved to Seattle, where they raised three more children – Harold, Helen, and Marion.

In 1923 Sam's son Leonard (1897–1960) married Bessie Sidelsky (1901–1989). (Her sister Sybil had married Alfred Hirschfield just six months before.) Leonard and Bessie lived in Tacoma through the twenties, then moved to California. Sam and Bertha stayed in Tacoma a few more years, then joined their relatives in Los Angeles. Sam died there in 1933, followed by Bertha in 1946. Leonard and Bessie had two daughters – Marilyn and Elaine.

Soulal Family

Moise Cohen-Soulal, from Tunisia, and his wife Mathilde Debreuil, from France, likely had a jewelry and art stand at the Columbian World Exhibit in Chicago in 1893. Then they traveled to San Francisco and participated in a smaller Midwinter Fair. Their son Louis was born in San Francisco in June of 1894. At the urging of Abe Gross and several others, many of the San Francisco exhibitors came to Tacoma for an even smaller Interstate Fair, which opened that fall. Intended to boost the failed economy, the fair was itself a dismal failure. Within a few weeks the unpaid musicians quit. The fair struggled on, offering reduced ticket prices, then closed several weeks early. Three-month-old Louis died in October and was buried in the Home of Peace Cemetery. His parents returned to Europe, settling in England. Louis' grave was among those that were unmarked until 1999.

Charles and Catharina Stein

Charles Stein was the eldest of four brothers and at least two sisters born in Steele, Germany, in the 1830s and 1840s. In April of 1860 he opened Chas. Stein and Bros. in Waukesha, Wisconsin, and a year later married Catharina Hirschberg in Milwaukee. The couple had seven children over the next fifteen years – Israel, Sophie, Fanny, Max, Albert, Frank and Oswald. Catharina died in Milwaukee on October 15, 1885.

In May of 1870 his sister, Julia Stein, married Charles Reichenbach, who had worked for his brothers, Louis and Marcus, in Milwaukee. (See Reichenbach biography.)

Charles Stein visited his brother-in-law, Charles Reichenbach, in Tacoma in 1889, and shortly after several of his sons moved to Tacoma, living with the Reichenbach family. Reichenbach opened a second location, the Star Clothing House, with his nephew Max Stein as manager and Albert and Oswald as clerks. Oswald gave musical performances with his cousin, Oscar Reichenbach. Albert attended Jewish social events and joined the Stag Seven.

In January of 1893 Charles Stein moved to Everett, Washington, but after the banking panic returned to Chicago and sold insurance. When Reichenbach's business failed, he was indebted to Louis Stein for $6,000. Emma Stein had invested in Reichenbach's real estate development, also a failure.

Charles Stein died in Chicago in May of 1912. Of his seven children, only five were alive at the time of his death, and four of them apparently never married. Oswald married Beatrice Malter Rosenfeld in Chicago in March of 1900. They had two sons – Charles and Philip, in 1914 and 1916. The following year Beatrice published a book about infant care and hygiene.

Virginia Donau Steinman Stedman

Virginia Donau Steinman Stedman
Courtesy of Bettina Lyons

Virginia Donau was born in New York in 1864, the fourth of seven children born to liquor merchant Simon Donau and Amelia Sanger. (See Donau biography.) Around 1888 Virginia married Adolph J. Steinman (1857–1925), the eldest of seven children born to John and Adelaide

Steinman. Adolph worked for his uncle Herman Steinman as a pawnbroker in Sacramento. Their daughter, Adelaide (Adele) was born on May 12, 1890.

In the summer of 1890 Virginia joined her parents in Tacoma, her marriage ending in divorce. She attended Harmony Club dances and other Jewish social events. In December of 1892 Virginia served as secretary of the Temple Aid Society, writing and publishing a daily newspaper from a library booth at the fair. Her sister Florence was president. In May of 1893 Virginia was elected vice president of the Judith Montefiore Society, and in 1896 became president.

In 1897 the entire family moved to San Francisco. In December of 1900 their home was burglarized, and ten-year-old Adele encountered the burglar. According to newspaper accounts she stayed calm and was able to provide a description to the police and later identify the burglar.

Virginia and her sisters joined the Christian Science church. After her mother's death in 1913, Virginia and her daughter, Adelaide, moved to New York. They changed their last name to Stedman. Virginia's literary aspirations were realized through her daughter, who at a young age became a writer and prominent lecturer, a speaker on women's issues and politics, and was active in the National Woman's Party. Adelaide later traveled throughout Europe as a news analyst and political commentator. Virginia died in 1938 and was buried in Tucson, as was Adelaide in 1974.

Cecelia Stenger Family

Cecelia Stenger (1843–1905) and her husband Aaron had five children in Kempen, Prussia, between 1866 and 1875. Their eldest son, George, immigrated to the U.S. around 1884. Widowed Cecelia and her four remaining children immigrated together in 1887. They likely came directly to Spokane, where George was already working as a clerk for the Great Eastern Company, a branch of the Toklas and Singerman store. (Toklas was also from Kempen.)

A year later Cecelia's two eldest daughters were married in Spokane in a double wedding. Their grooms traveled from Tacoma for the wedding. Mollie married D.P. Lewis and Regina married Henry Berliner. Both brides moved to Tacoma with their husbands. (See Lewis and Berliner biographies.) Cecelia and her younger daughter Olga stayed in Spokane.

George moved to Tacoma with Mollie, and worked in her husband's barber supply compa-

ny. Another brother, Albert, found work with the Prager brothers. However, in the spring of 1893 he was one of four clerks arrested for stealing clothing from the store. The goods were returned, the charges were dropped, and Albert continued his employment.

Around 1894 the extended Lewis, Berliner and Stenger families all moved to Portland. George worked as a commercial traveler for the barber supply company, and in 1903 became a partner in Lewis-Stenger. Albert worked for the Prager Brothers in Portland, then clerked for his brother in the barber supply business, eventually becoming secretary/treasurer of the company.

In July of 1897 Olga Stenger (c.1872–1950) married Sigmund Freudenstein (c.1863–1936). The couple made their home in Everett, in Snohomish, Washington, where Sigmund worked as a butcher. The Freudensteins had three daughters – Hannah, Lillian and Helen. Cecelia Stenger died in Portland in 1905. George (1867–1936) married Lema "Georgie" Hahn (1868–1948) in 1904. The couple had a son, Arthur (1906–1980). In 1908 Henry Berliner left Portland to open a Seattle branch of the company.

Around 1913 Albert Stenger (1875–1956) married Alice Rosenthal (1890–1943). They had two sons – Robert (1914–1984) and Howard (1920–1989).

Hugo and Jennie Stusser

Hugo Stusser
University of Washington Special Collections

Jacob Stusser (1831–1917) and his wife Hoda Loev (1832–1914) had a son Hugo (1856–1929). Jacob's brother Abraham, and his wife Mollie Friedman, had a daughter Jennie (1861–1928). These first cousins married around 1880 and had seven children in the next ten years. Hugo and Jennie's siblings, children, cousins, and their spouses would form the core of Tacoma's Orthodox population. Nearly all were from the Courland province of what is now Latvia.

Hugo Stusser immigrated to Tacoma in 1891 and was joined by his wife and children the following year. Early records listed him as Herman, a variation of his Hebrew name Hirsch. He worked as a tailor, starting out as a secondhand merchant. He also did dyeing and cleaning from his shop at 11th and Railroad (now Commerce). Mascha Stusser, Jennie's younger sister (and future wife of Adolph Friedman) lived with the family at 1131-1/2 E Street (now Fawcett), as did Jennie's youngest brother, Julius. (See Adolph Friedman and Julius Stusser biography.)

In December of 1899 Hugo's eldest daughter, Augusta, married Julius Friedman, further grafting the family tree. The sixty-five guests who attended the wedding likely made up nearly all that was left of Tacoma's Jewish population. However, that tide was about to turn. As conditions worsened in what was then Russia, Hugo and others scrambled to bring additional family members to safety. *Ledger*, March 7, 1900, "Tickets were sold for twenty-one farmers, who will shortly make the trip from Libau, Russia, to Tacoma. The money was all paid in Tacoma and the tickets bought here will be sent to … Russia."

In order to support his efforts, Hugo needed to work long days. Yet each spring Tacoma's retail merchants typically agreed to set shorter summer hours. In 1900 he was one of thirteen merchants who signed a petition that was printed in the *Ledger* on May 18.

> "The undersigned retail merchants, finding that the closing of our stores at 6 p.m. will work against the interest of our business, and being in sympathy with the retail clerks for shorter hours, have decided that we will not ask any of our employees to work more than eight hours a day except Saturdays, but reserve the right as Americans to know what hours of the day are for the best interests of our business to keep open. Therefore on and after this date our stores will be found open on all legal working days until 8 p.m. except Saturday, which will be 10 p.m."

A program from the June 27, 1900, Confirmation Ceremony at Congregation Beth Israel included H. Stusser as a trustee. Hugo received his U.S. citizenship in 1902. He moved his clothing store to Pacific Avenue and his home to 1134

E. Jennie's older brother, Herman Stusser, arrived about that time, opening a clothing store on Fifteenth and Commerce. Herman's wife, Betty, and their eight children soon joined him, as did Jennie's sister, Bluma, her husband P.J. Yudelson, and their children. (See Yudelson biography.) Around 1906 Jennie's younger brother, Solomon, his wife Jennie, and their children joined the exodus.

Tacoma now had enough Orthodox Jews to form their own congregation. The Secretary of State's incorporation certificate for Chevra Talmud Torah, dated January 21, 1909, includes the names of Chas. Stusser and H. Stusser among the eleven original members. They met daily for prayer services and commissioned a Torah, now in the collection of Temple Beth El.

Jennie Stusser died in Tacoma in December of 1928. She was survived by four sons – Charles, Julius, Sam and Ben; and three daughters – Mrs. Augusta Friedman, Mrs. Bessie Caplan, and Mrs. Lena Pearl. Hugo then moved to Hoquiam where he lived for a short time with his son Julius. Hugo died in August of 1929, at the age of 74. Both Hugo and Jennie were buried in Tacoma's Home of Peace Cemetery.

Children of Julius and Jennie Stusser:
1. Augusta (1880–1942) married Julius Friedman (1872–1937). (See Friedman biography.)
2. Charles (1881–1968) married Ida Friedman (1889–1980). They had two children – Samuel Millard (Molly Rosen) and Tibe Hode (Joel Reibstein and Alex Greenberg).
3. Bessie (1883–1934) married Isidor Kaplan (1880–1972). They had three children – Marjorie, Theodore (Frieda Janison), and Albert (Mabel Neshafer).
4. Samuel (1884–1966) married Alberta Hecht.
5. Benjamin (1886–1967).
6. Julius Jay (1888–1974) married Hazel Frankford (1889–1968), daughter Jeanette (Homer Gage).
7. Lena Ella (1890–1974) married Louis Pearl (1883–1951). They had four children – Lydia (Victor Offman), Irwin (Lillian Aronin), Milton (Helen Fisher), and Wesley (Alice August).

Jacob Julius and Edith Stusser

Jacob Julius Stusser (1868–1941) was the youngest son of Abraham Stusser and Mollie Friedman, and the youngest brother of Jennie

Stusser (Mrs. Hugo Stusser). He lived with Jennie's family in Tacoma in 1892 and worked as a shoemaker, selling leather and findings and manufacturing "uppers." In January of 1897 he married Edith Hirschfeld (1869–1951), daughter of Sigmund and Leah Hirschfeld. He signed his marriage license as Jacob but was sometimes known as Julius. Their daughter Bernice was born in Tacoma in June of 1898.

During 1898 Jacob suffered some financial troubles, then reorganized with several others as the Washington Leather Company, doing business from 1405 Pacific. Around 1900 he moved to Spokane, where he sold shoe materials and later clothing. In the mid-twenties Jacob and Edith moved to Seattle for a decade, then joined their daughter in California. They died there in 1941 and 1951.

Bernice (1898–1983) married Leopold Wolff (1897–1946) in Spokane in 1923. He was the youngest child of optician Sigfried Wolff and Bertha Jacobs (not to be confused with Tacoma's Leopold Henry Wolff, who also moved to Spokane). Bernice and Leopold had one daughter, Janice Wolff Williams (1929–1985).

Morris and Rebecca Summerfield

Morris Summerfield (c.1859–1932) was the fifth of six children born to Simon and Caroline Summerfield in Massachusetts between 1852 and 1867. In 1879 the family lived in Portland, Oregon, where Simon worked as a merchant tailor. Their eldest daughter, Anna DeFries, was widowed and had four small children. Morris learned the clothing trade, working as a clerk for several years before coming to Tacoma to work for the Gross Brothers. He would become one of their most trusted employees.

Also in Portland lived Hannah Davies, whose husband Lewis had died in 1878. In 1882 her son George Davies married Anna DeFries. Five years later Morris traveled from Tacoma to Portland to marry George's sister, Rebecca (1861–1945). She returned to Portland for the birth of her son Louis in 1888. The following year the couple built a cottage at 418 North K.

418 North K
Tacoma Public Library, BU-785

Rebecca belonged to the Judith Montefiore Society and in 1892 participated in the Temple Aid Society fair. Morris became a skilled player of the card game whist, often earning high scores in city tournaments. Over the next decade he regularly played for the Tacoma Whist Club.

After the suicide of Abe Gross in 1895 Morris had the responsibility of serving as one of the administrators of Abe's estate. When the Gross Brothers closed their business and went their separate ways in 1897, Ellis chose Morris Summerfield to manage his gents' clothing store.

Morris and Rebecca had a daughter, Carol, in 1897. Several years later they moved into a larger home just up the street at 407 North K. In 1903 Rebecca was one of four trustees of the new Council of Jewish Women. Her unmarried sister Jane lived with her and also joined the Judith Montefiore Society.

After nearly twenty years, Morris lost his job in February of 1904 when Ellis Gross moved to Seattle. He used the opportunity to open his own firm, the Summerfield Company, at 1119 1/2 Pacific, selling men's furnishings. Several years later Rebecca's brother, Philip, helped run the store and lived with the family.

Around 1909 Morris moved his clothing store to 948 Pacific. (Originally Kaufman & Berliner, then Hirsch & Frank, and eventually Rhodes Brothers.) However, in May of 1911 the firm was closed in bankruptcy, having bought too much stock in the spring. They tried again for a year or so at 1340 Pacific, then moved to Portland.

Morris, now in his late fifties, took a job selling wholesale notions. He continued working as a traveling salesman for another fifteen years. He died in Portland in 1932, as did Rebecca in 1945. In 1917 their son Louis (1888–1960) married Vesta Senders (1897–1968), whose uncle Albert Senders had married Alma Basinski. Louis and Vesta had five children in Alameda County, California – Morris, Gertrude, Carol, Vesta and Esther. Louis's sister died in Portland in 1968, apparently unmarried.

Nathan Todtman

Nathan Todtman (1856–1919) was the youngest of four children born to Julia and Isaac Todtman in Elmira, New York. After the death of his father, Nathan worked as a clerk in Elmira when he was just a teen. He lived in Tacoma from 1889 until 1891, attending Harmony Club events and prominent Jewish weddings. While in Tacoma he and Jackson Hunt incorporated the North Pacific Live Stock Insurance Company, with a stock of $50,000. Later Nathan sold cigars in Seattle, where he lived until his death in 1919. He was buried in his hometown of Elmira, next to his mother, who died there on October 26, 1894.

Toklas Family

The Toklas family in America was made up of six siblings – Max, Louisa, Jacob W, Ferdinand, Hulda and Nathan. (A seventh child died in infancy.) All were born in Kempen, in the Silesia area of Germany, which is now Kepno, Poland. Their father was Simon Wolf Toklas, son of Marcus Toklas. Their mother was Amalie (Malchen) Gnadenfeld, daughter of Nathan Schapsi Gnadenfeld. Simon and Malchen were married in Kempen on March 17, 1835.

The eldest, Marcus, (known in the U.S. as Max) was born on December 26, 1835. He immigrated as a teen and in 1860 lived in Salt Lake City, Utah. Five years later he registered to vote in California, where he ran a wholesale clothing and importing business known as Toklas, Wise and Company, with Morris Wise (also from Kempen). Max married his partner's daughter, Mary Wise (1846–1935) in 1870 and moved to New York, where he later served as a buyer for his brothers. The couple had at least nine children. Max died in New York in 1917.

Liebe Toklas (known in the U.S. as Louise) was born on May 14, 1839. Around 1865 she married Moses Kaufman Gallewski, born in December of 1838. They had six children in Kempen between 1866 and 1877 before coming to Olympia, Washington. There the entire Gallewski family used the surname Kaufman. Their sons, Nat (c.1866–1943), Leo (c.1868–1933), Samuel (1870–1960), Isidore (1871–1961) and Adolph (1874–1948), lived in Olympia, Spokane,

and later Alaska and Bellingham. Their daugthter Nina (1877–1962) married Max Rosenshine (c.1870–1925). In 1904 the boys purchased their uncle's interest in the Aberdeen store.

Louise and Moses died within a few days of each other in San Francisco in 1923.

Jacob W. Toklas, born on May 25, 1844, was likely the first Toklas sibling to immigrate. Arriving in the U.S. in 1861, Jacob served in Company "K" of the California Infantry during the Civil War. He lived for many years in Yuba, California, and then in Texas, where in 1881 he served as the first postmaster of Benavides. He joined his sister in Olympia in 1887, and opened a store in Aberdeen in 1889, before moving to Spokane to work with his younger brother. There he filed a military pension as an invalid in 1897. Jacob died unmarried in San Francisco in 1925.

Feibel Toklas, born October 5, 1845, was known in the U.S. as Ferdinand. He immigrated around 1863 and was naturalized in San Francisco in 1868. Ferdinand partnered with Paul Singerman in opening the firm of Toklas and Singerman in Seattle as early as 1876. Ferdinand returned to San Francisco and married Amelia Levinsky (1856–1897), daughter of San Francisco developer Louis Levinsky. Their daughter Alice Babette Toklas was born in 1877, followed by a son Clarence in 1888.

Toklas and Singerman opened a Tacoma branch, known first as Peritz and Company, in November of 1884. Later known as Kaufman and Berliner, the store was closed after Meyer Kaufman's death in 1891. (See Kaufman biography.) During the great Seattle fire in 1889, the firm of Toklas and Singerman suffered the greatest losses, totaling over $200,000. In 1892 Ferdinand moved his family to Seattle, where his daughter Alice attended the University of Washington, performing on piano during the 1894 commencement exercises. Several years later the family returned to San Francisco, where Amelia died in 1897. Alice ran the household full of men until after the 1906 earthquake, when she traveled to Paris and met her soulmate, Gertrude Stein. Her father Ferdinand lived in San Francisco until his death in 1924.

Hulda Toklas (c.1848–1905), married Moses Gallewski's younger brother Nathan, known in the U.S. as N. G. Kaufman (1847–1914). A Hebrew prayer book belonging to Hulda Toklas Gallewski Kaufman was inscribed in Kempen on November 23, 1886, as a parting gift from her dear father. Hulda and Nathan (now N.G.) opened a store in Puyallup soon after, and often attended weddings and other Jewish social events in Tacoma. In the spring of 1888 they moved to Aberdeen, building the first brick building there on Heron Street, although they occasionally returned to Tacoma to attend High Holiday services. Hulda died childless in 1905 and was buried in Seattle. N.G. started over, briefly operating the Kaufman and Berliner clothing store in Aberdeen with Henry Berliner, formerly of Tacoma. By 1908 N.G. was out of the clothing business and selling real estate. N.G. spent the last year of his life in a sanitarium near Tacoma, where he died in 1914. The couple had no children.

The youngest Toklas sibling, Nathaniel, was born about 1857, after a gap of nearly nine years. In 1879 he was part of Olympia's firm of Toklas and Goldstein. A few years later Nathaniel operated N. Toklas and Company with his uncle, Gallewski Kaufman, then ran the Great Eastern with his cousin Leo. Working his way around the state, Nathaniel opened a branch store in Puyallup in 1884, and within a few years lived in Spokane, operating the Great Eastern with his brother Jacob. Around 1887 Nathaniel married Laura Levinsky (c.1865–1917), younger sister of Ferdinand's wife, Amelia. During the great Spokane fire in August of 1889, the largest loss of property was the Great Eastern, at about $100,000. Another tragic fire in 1898 killed nine people who lived on the upper floors of the Great Eastern Block, owned by his father-in-law, Louis Levinsky, of San Francisco. Nathaniel and Laura had three children, two of whom died in childhood. The eldest, Vera (1888–1942) married Harry Broh, son of Max Broh. (See Broh biography.) Nathan died in San Francisco in 1926.

Solomon Voloshin (See page 35.)

Solomon Voloshin was born in Russia around 1857 or 1861. He immigrated around 1882 and arrived in Tacoma via Winnipeg about 1896. In Tacoma he worked as a secondhand or junk peddler. Solomon died in Tacoma on March 3, 1902, and was buried in the Home of Peace Cemetery – his only known affiliation with Tacoma's Jewish community.

Louis and Carrie Wallerstein

Louis Wallerstein was born in Thalmessing, Bavaria, on March 5, 1849, and immigrated to the U.S. in 1870. In 1876 he lived in San Francisco, where he was naturalized in April of 1879.

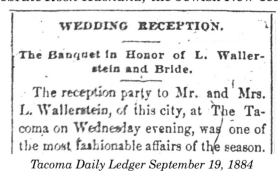

Tacoma Daily Ledger April 8, 1883

In 1883 Louis operated a candy business in Tacoma called McLaren and Wallerstein, which he dissolved in July of 1884. Then he partnered with his future brother-in-law, Isaac N. Cohen in the firm of L. Wallerstein and Company.

In August Louis traveled to San Francisco to stock up for the fall trade. He also returned with a bride. Carrie Cohen, born in 1855, was the eldest daughter of David and Amelia Cohen. (See Cohen biography.) Louis and Carrie were married on September 7 in San Francisco, and ten days later their wedding was celebrated again with a large reception held at the new Tacoma Hotel. A brief description was printed in the *Ledger* on September 18, followed by a complete guest list of 45 people on the nineteenth. That day Tacoma's Jewish merchants closed their stores at 6 p.m. to celebrate *Rosh Hashana,* the Jewish New Year.

> ### WEDDING RECEPTION.
>
> #### The Banquet in Honor of L. Wallerstein and Bride.
>
> The reception party to Mr. and Mrs. L. Wallerstein, of this city, at The Tacoma on Wednesday evening, was one of the most fashionable affairs of the season.

Tacoma Daily Ledger September 19, 1884

The following year Louis and Isaac added a soda fountain to their business, now rightfully dubbed the Pioneer Candy Factory. Carrie gave birth to her first son, Herman, on August 31, 1885. Two months later the couple rented out their home and moved briefly to Butte, Montana. They were back in Tacoma by Thanksgiving. Louis ran a cigar and tobacco store for a year, then partnered with George Brown in another candy store, this time on the corner of Eighth and Pacific. *Ledger,* April 12, 1887, "L. Wallerstein & Co., the candy manufacturers, have just received the largest block of marble that was ever brought to the territory. It is eight feet long, four feet wide and four inches thick and will be used for rolling candy upon it."

In August of 1887 Wallerstein and Brown moved to 946 Pacific, expanding their business to two floors. Carrie added a son Henry to the family in September of 1887, and in the spring of 1888 Louis added offerings of ice cream, coffee, and soda water. That fall Louis helped organize the Hebrew Benevolent association and served as an officer for many years. A third son, David, was born in November of 1889. In 1890 Louis operated the candy factory at 714 Pacific, with retail on the first floor, wholesale on the second, and raw materials on the third.

A LONG AND STORMY VOYAGE.

It Works a Heavy Loss to a Tacoma Importer.

TACOMA, April 15.—Nearly two years ago Louis Wallerstein, a candy manufacturer, ordered 1578 pounds of chocolate of a York, England, manufacturer. It cost 17 cents, and the net cost was 21 cents delivered in Tacoma. The chocolate was shipped June 29, 1889, from Androsan, Scotland, and has since been in transit on the British bark Embleton. The Embleton had one of the stormiest passages in the history of the seas, being 641 days out when she arrived here. She had to put into Rio Janeiro, Valparaiso and other ports for repairs. Once her crew deserted her, claiming that the vessel was bewitched and would never reach the port of destination. The passage is usually made from England to Tacoma in five months by a sailing vessel. Since the chocolate was shipped the passage of the McKinley bill has raised the duty on chocolate to a figure which makes it a most expensive confection. Wallerstein has applied to the Government through the United States District Attorney here for relief. The case is considered a peculiar

San Francisco Chronicle April 16, 1891

During the summer of 1891 many of the proprietors of Tacoma's liquor establishments were arrested for staying open on Sunday. In turn, they filed complaints about other businesses. Wallerstein was found guilty of violating the Sunday ordinance and ordered to pay a $25 fine, after Judge Parker ruled that selling ice cream, soda water and confectionery was not an essential business. The decision was overturned in the superior court that fall, after Wallerstein's attorney explained that no manufacturing was done on Sundays. Also that fall, Carrie gave birth to a daughter, Alma. In January of 1892 the *Ledger* noted that Wallerstein employed 17 people, had done $46,000 worth of business in the prior year, and had made 160,000 pounds of candy.

After the banking panic of 1893 stifled Tacoma's economy, Louis transferred his candy machinery, stock of candies, and accounts to his brother-in-law, Aaron Cohen, but eventually re-opened. The following year the Wallersteins buried their second son, Henry, and their fifth child, Irving.

Louis stayed in the candy business in Tacoma through 1895, then briefly tried operating a restaurant in Butte, Montana. He returned and found employment with Isaac Pincus selling liquor, one of the few stable industries left. He also returned for the birth of his daughter Emily, in June of 1896.

In 1897 they moved back to San Francisco, where a daughter Bernyce was born in the spring of 1898 and a son Monroe in the fall of 1900. Louis died there in 1928, followed by Carrie in 1942. Carrie taught many years in the San Francisco public schools.

Children of Louis Wallerstein and Carrie Cohen:
1. Herman Mendel (1885–1929)
2. Henry Leon (1887–1894)
3. David Cohen (1889–1965) married Bertha, three children – Carol, Jerome and Selina
4. Alma (1891–1892) married Irving Davis, then William Abrams, daughter Jeanne Abrams
5. Irving (1894–1894)
6. Emily (1896–1958) married Gerson Rummelsburg, children Charles and Helen
7. Bernyce (1898–1999)
8. Monroe (1900–1985) married Barbara Goldstone

Albert Weinberg

Albert Weinberg was born on March 9, 1857 in Jonasdorf, Thorne, Germany, son of Julius Weinberg and Caroline Cohn. He immigrated to the U.S. as a teen and in 1880 worked as a fruit dealer in Oakland, California. Albert came to Tacoma in June of 1883 to manage Leon Hershberg's wholesale liquor firm. He sang in the German choir and attended Jewish social events.

In October of 1885 Albert married Esther Levy in Portland, daughter of Isaac Levy and sister of Mrs. William Wolff. (See Levy biography.) However, Esther died just six weeks later, drowning early on the morning of Thanksgiving Day. Albert ended his partnership with Hershberg, and in 1888 opened the Monogram Sample Rooms at 1009 Pacific. The following year he built an entire block of very large houses on D Street, which later became the center of Tacoma's prostitution district, causing Weinberg much grief.

Albert traveled to Ligonier, Indiana, in June of 1890 to marry Mattie Loeb, sister of Tacoma's Sam Loeb. She immediately joined the Judith Montefiore Society. That fall Sam married Blanche Moses and the two couples lived side-by-side on Eighth and G Street. The men also partnered in forming the Milwaukee Brewing Company, with Albert as secretary-treasurer. The ladies frequently entertained and took leadership roles in the 1892 Temple Aid Society.

As the banking panic of 1893 resulted in business failures and sheriff's auctions, Albert frequently was able to purchase merchandise at a fraction of its value, then quickly liquidate the stock for a quick return on his investment. He also diversified, forming the Tampa Cigar Company with Ben Moyses in 1895. The following year he moved to 406 North Tacoma Avenue.

The 1897 beer war with Seattle put pressure on the Milwaukee Brewery, small by comparison. In August Sam and Albert transferred the Milwaukee to the Puget Sound Brewing Company, combining to form the new Pacific Brewing and Malting Company. Over the next several years Albert formed the Great Western Box Company, the Pacific Pulley Manufacturing Company, and served on the board of Congregation Beth Israel.

Eventually the couple moved to Seattle, where Albert died in 1935. His wife Mattie died in Los Angeles in 1958. The couple had no children.

Albert Werther

Albert Werther was born in Prussia about 1840. In March of 1879 he opened a store in Leavenworth, Kansas, selling cigars, wines, and liquors, then worked as a bartender. After a shooting incident in February of 1880 he suddenly moved to the mining town of Breckenridge, Colorado, where he operated a saloon for two years. From there he went on to Butte, Montana, where his partnership with Watkins ended in a scuffle in August of 1884, even though by then he had earned the nickname of Smiling Albert.

Tacoma's *Daily Ledger* on November 12, 1890, reported that Smiling Albert had slipped on an icy porch floor the night before and fallen into a cellar stairway. "Mr. Werther is an educated young man and has many friends in the city, especially among the Jewish people. He is called 'Smiling Albert' by his friends on account of his pleasant manners. The wounds he received by his fall about the body are very painful and will necessitate his confinement in the hospital several weeks."

Tacoma's 1892 directory included Albert Werther working as a bartender at the California Wine House. His name was not listed again.

Henry and Lottie Winkleman

Henry Philip Winkleman was born in 1855 in Jeleniewo, in the Suwalki region of what is now Poland. He was the eldest son of Jacob (Jankiel) Winkleman and Sophia (Dumblanska) Diamond. The family immigrated to Philadelphia in the 1870s.

On March 30, 1879, Henry married Lottie (Zlata) Raphael in New York City. Born in 1858 in Punsk, also in the Suwalki region, Lottie was the daughter of Simon (Scharya) and Rose (Rayza) Rafalin. Lottie gave birth to a daughter, Ella, in New York in February of 1880, followed by a son, Raphael, in January of 1881. Then the family moved to Philadelphia and had three more children – Julia, Minnie and Gabriel – in 1884, 1885 and 1887, before heading west.

Henry sold clothing in Seattle in 1890, but moved to Tacoma in time for the birth of his daughter Rose in June of 1891. He operated a junk business at Nineteenth and D Street, and for many years employed Isaac Moses. A year later he moved a few blocks north to Seventeenth and D Street. A son Isadore was born in 1893, followed by Meyer in 1895. *Ledger*, Tuesday, March 26, 1895:

> "CIRCUMCISED A CHILD. The Ancient Hebrew Ceremony Performed in Tacoma. The impressive ceremony of the Jewish rite of circumcision took place at 10 o'clock yesterday morning at the residence of Mr. H Winkleman, at 1738 D Street.
>
> The subject of the ancient Jewish orthodox custom was the eight days old infant of Mr. Winkleman. The ceremony was performed by Rabbi M. Lincezer, pastor of the local synagogue. Mr. M.S. Jacobs, a wealthy citizen of St. Louis, assisted in the ceremony. The child was brought into the rabbi's presence by Mr. and Mrs. D.L. Coffman.
>
> The services preceding and following the act of circumcision were very beautiful and the large attendance of Tacoma's most prominent Hebrew citizens attested the fact that the members of the Jewish faith still honor and venerate all of the old and beautiful rites of their very ancient creed."

Winkleman Family circa 1905. Back row left-to-right: Minnie, Julia, Raphael, Ella, and Gabriel. Front row left-to-right: Henry, Meyer, Isadore, Lottie and Rose.

Courtesy of Judith Parker Hindin

Around 1896 Henry moved his business to a prominent corner at 1902 Pacific. The family lived just a few streets below, at 1931 South E. (Now Fawcett.) In June of 1898 Ella was one of 54 students who graduated from Tacoma High School. Her obituary later noted that she was the "first Jewish girl graduate from a West Coast high school." That fall Lottie joined the Judith Montefiore Society. In 1900 Julia also graduated from high school, and Minnie was confirmed at Congregation Beth Israel, where Henry served as vice president.

The Winkleman ladies stayed active. Julia went to college to be a teacher, Minnie went to business school, and Ella was shipped off to relatives in the East to find a husband. Around 1905 Ella married Solomon Hyman, eldest of five sons born to Kopel and Golda Hyman. The family ran a dry goods store in Keystone, West Virginia. Ella was the only Winkleman sibling who married.

Gabriel Winkleman died of a heart condition in 1906 while in Denver, Colorado. He was just 19. His remaining siblings organized Winkleman Lumber Company, with Raphael as president and treasurer and Julia as secretary. Later Minnie worked as bookkeeper and Isadore as a clerk.

Winkleman Lumber logo 1910
From the collection of the author

Henry worked as a junk dealer in Tacoma until his death in July of 1911, following an operation. Raphael (Ray) died five years later, in a warehouse fire in Seattle. He had purchased 5000 bales of water-damaged hemp fiber for use in his Portland burlap bag factory. He rented a five-floor warehouse to dry the hemp, but a stove backfired and fire flashed through the building, killing all of the workers, including Raphael.

Lottie and her remaining children moved to Portland. Isidore, Meyer, and Minnie ran the Winkleman Bag and Burlap Company. Julia and Rose worked as teachers. Both Isidore and Meyer served in World War I. Lottie died in 1932 and was buried in Tacoma, as were her sons Isidore (1893–1963) and Meyer (1895–1964). Julia (1884–1975), Minnie (1885–1969), and Rose (1891–1987) were buried in Portland.

Ella (1880–1968) and her husband Sol Hyman (1878–1952) had two children in West Virginia before moving to Columbus, Ohio. Harriet (1910–2001) married Milton Parker and had three children. Philip Ephraim (1912–1949) did not marry.

Witenberg Family

Bernard and Charlotte Witenberg
Courtesy of Toby Witenberg Israel and Bruce Witenberg

Samuel (Saul) Nathan Witenberg (c.1870–1941) was the eldest of four children born to Ezra and Shayna in what is now Mariampol, Lithuania. He immigrated to the U.S. as a teen and in 1894 worked in Seattle as a fruit vendor. He then sold secondhand goods and later clothing.

Samuel married Anne Friedman (1874–1929), daughter of Jacob Friedman and Jenny Kaplan. Her siblings reported their birthplaces as Scholen, Russia; Dorpat, Estonia; and just Lithuania. Two of her younger siblings were born in North Dakota in 1886 and 1888, and two more in Seattle in 1893 and 1896. Anne's sister Lena married in Seattle in 1891, likely around the time of the family's arrival in the Northwest.

Samuel and Anne had two sons in Seattle – Leon in 1895 and Abraham in 1897 – before moving to Tacoma. A daughter, Tillie, was born in 1900, followed by Lena in 1901. Samuel operated a clothing store for many years at 1534 Pacific. More children came – Philip in 1904 and Florence in 1906. A seventh, Lesser, died in infancy in 1907.

Samuel's nephew shared that around 1907 a young man walked into Samuel's store and asked to buy a suit. The elder Witenberg replied, "You don't want to buy a suit – you're my brother!" Samuel's young brother Bernard (1887–1967) had been just a baby when Samuel had immigrated. They were joined in Tacoma by their sister, Mildred (1881–1954), and her husband Abraham Lyon. (Uncle of Vic Lyon and "Babe" Lyon Lehrer.) Together the Witenberg siblings formed the Witenberg Manufacturing Company, making cotton gloves from 2526 South E, (now Fawcett) although Samuel continued his clothing store on Pacific. Another sister, Lillian, married Isaac Raban and lived in Seattle.

Bernard married Charlotte Endelman (1886–1953), daughter of Taube and Philip Endelman. Their daughter, Ruth (1917–1980) married Saul Levy (1913–2003). Their son Favius (1915–2008) married Lillian Smilovitz (1916–1995). Bernard and his son "Fav" both in turn served for decades as dedicated officers of the Home of Peace Cemetery Association. Together they formed Liberty Finance Company on South Tacoma Way in 1953, which operated for sixty years.

Edward and Minna Wolf

Edward Wolf was born in Germany about 1856 and immigrated to the U.S. around 1875. In 1880 he lived in San Francisco with his aunt and uncle, Bernard Heringhi and Minnie Weilheimer. After several years working as a clerk for others, Edward came to Tacoma in the spring of 1888 to open a branch of Arthur Lewin's Seattle wholesale cigar and tobacco store. He arrived just in time to sign an agreement with other merchants, fixing a minimum price for cigarettes – no less than ten cents per package. His store, located at 813 Pacific, had a back room where friends could play an occasional game of cards. Unfortunately his neighbor, Harry Morgan, ran a less reputable place next door and Edward was often caught in the negative publicity.

In March of 1889 Edward traveled to Columbus, Georgia, to marry Minna Lewin, younger sister of Arthur Lewin. Born in 1864, she, too, lived with an aunt and uncle, Mr. and Mrs. M.M. Hirsch. A few months later her brother's store was destroyed in Seattle's great fire. Minna immediately joined the Judith Montefiore Society and the couple attended several Jewish social events. She give birth to a daughter, Claire, in Tacoma in January of 1890.

Edward then partnered briefly with Max Broh in running the wholesale cigar firm of Wolf and Broh, on South Ninth, then moved to Seattle and went back to work for Arthur Lewin. The following fall their son, James, was born in Seattle and died a month later. A daughter, Rose, was born in Seattle in November of 1892. Edward clerked for Schwabacher Brothers in their large hardware store through 1894, then moved to Sacramento, where their son Lester was born in September of 1896.

In 1900 the Wolf family lived in San Francisco, where Edward continued selling wholesale cigars. Edward died there in 1924, followed by Minna in 1927. Their eldest child, Claire (1890–1962) married Alfred Zobel (1873–1949) and had a daughter Claire Ann Modica (1932–1993). Their daughter Rose (1892–1979) married Carl Foorman (1882–1974) and had a son Carl Jr. (1919–2014). Their youngest son, Lester (1896–1970), apparently never married.

Minna's younger brother Edwin died in Seattle in 1921 at the age of 51. Her older brother Arthur Lewin (1861–1924) invested in mining and became quite prosperous. He married Sarah Bauman (1878–1920) in Seattle in 1902 and their daughter Felice was born in San Francisco in 1907. In 1924 Felice married John V. Farrow and had a daughter Felice Patricia in 1926. After her divorce from Farrow, Felice (1907–1993) married writer Edward Paramore. John Farrow remarried and had a daughter, Mia.

Louis and Sarah Wolff

Louis Wolff was born in Germany about 1826, his wife Sarah about 1835. Their daughter, Anna, was born in California in December of 1857. Then the family moved to Victoria, British Columbia. Another daughter, Rosa, was born in October of 1859, followed by a son, William, in September of 1861, Rachel in 1863, and Gustave in August of 1865.

Louis purchased front-page ads in Victoria's newspaper, the *British Colonist,* to promote his clothing store on Yates Street. His name was frequently mentioned on tax lists, among those receiving merchandise and letters, and as a participant in local hook and ladder activities. Louis was able to travel to pure goods and stay abreast of conditions, arriving from Honolulu in 1862, from Portland in 1869, and from San Francisco in 1871. He likely invested in Victoria's real estate, returning in 1885 to check on his "large property interests."

In 1872 Louis closed his Victoria store and moved to Tacoma, where he operated a general store for over twenty years. Louis lived in Old Tacoma, but invested in New Tacoma properties, quickly becoming one of the city's heaviest taxpayers. He owned a lot on the west side of Pacific that housed the Elite photography gallery, destroyed by a block-wide fire in July of 1884 (later 716 Pacific). Residents of Old Tacoma responded by forming their own fire department, with Louis' son Gus as one of the twenty volunteers. Rosa and Rachel Wolff often decorated for holiday dances sponsored by the Eagle Hose Company, including Christmas.

In the spring of 1888 Louis Wolff and Meyer Kaufman built twin buildings on their lots on Pacific Avenue, known for the past four years as the "burnt district." That fall his youngest son Gustave died and was buried in the Jewish cemetery in Olympia. A year later Louis accompanied his eldest daughter, Anna, to California for her marriage. Now in her thirties, Anna married Leopold Lefebvre, a language teacher in Oakland. (A decade later she was widowed and childless.)

Louis continued to operate his general store in Old Tacoma until a few weeks before his death in December of 1896, while visiting his daughter in Oakland. Rachel joined her sister in California, but Rose stayed in Tacoma a few more years – teaching music and joining the Judith Montefiore Society. Eventually the entire family moved to Oakland, where they lived together unmarried until their deaths. Rachel died in 1908, mother Sarah in 1912, Anna in 1914, Rose in 1935, and William in 1938.

Henry and Ernestine Wolff Family

Henry Irwin Wolff and his wife, Ernestine Cohn, had nine children in Lautenburg, Germany, (now Poland). Most of them eventually lived in Tacoma. Their eldest daughter, Adeline, born January 29, 1856, married Amil Zelinsky (see Zelinsky biography). Paula, born February 24, 1858, married Julius Mamlok (see Mamlock biography). Fanny, born January 1, 1864, married Max Cohn (see Cohn biography). Another daughter, Fredricka, married Heymann Salomon and lived in California, but her sons later lived in Tacoma.

The Wolff brothers included Samuel, born October 14, 1848; Leopold Henry, born April 21,

1854; Abraham Jacob, born October 2, 1865; and Herman, born August 6, 1867. Several operated the New York Bakery in Tacoma in 1883 and the California Bakery in 1884, adding a restaurant in 1885. In the summer of 1886 their family picnic included more than twenty-five people. The names of the Wolff brothers were frequently mentioned in the local press in connection with runaway delivery wagons, an occasional small fire, and numerous family squabbles.

They also purchased land in the Hillhurst area south of Tacoma, now a housing develop-ment within Fort Lewis. *Ledger,* December 18, 1884, Hillhurst Notes, "Quite a laughable incident occurred here some days ago. As some children were playing outside of the gate near a neighbor's house, they saw a gentleman coming towards the place. They immediately ran inside exclaiming, "Wolf! Wolf!" The father, supposing it to be a four-legged animal, at once reached for his shotgun to go for him, but just then a transformation scene took place in the person-al appearance of Sam Wolff, who could not help laughing at the joke."

In December of 1887 Sam opened a wholesale grocery store at 728 Pacific. A few years later his brother Leopold sold his bakery and purchased the Popular Restaurant at 717 Pacific, and later ran a restaurant on E Street. In 1889 Samuel be-came a trustee of the new Jewish congregation.

After the 1893 banking panic the brothers went their various ways.

Samuel moved to Butte, Montana, with his sister Fannie and sold cigars. He returned to Ta-coma and ran the German bakery with his Salo-mon nephews. Around 1919 he moved to Seattle, again joining his sister Fannie. Samuel died in Seattle in 1925.

Leopold went to Spokane, where he operated Wolff's Café, a bakery and restaurant. He died there in 1921, his wife in 1919.

A.J. worked in the liquor business for David Hoffman, then sold cigars in Alaska and ran a grocery store in Walla Walla. He married Rose Sternberg, had a son in Albany, Oregon, in 1902, then returned to Tacoma, again selling groceries and liquor. His wife died in 1934, A.J. in 1939.

Herman lived briefly in Tacoma, working for his brother Leopold. He moved with him to Spo-kane, where he died in 1934.

William and Hannah Wolff

William Wolff was born about 1839 in Prus-sia and immigrated to the U.S. as a teen. In Oc-tober of 1872 he married Hannah Levy, eldest daughter of Isaac and Henriette Levy, at her parents' home in Portland, Oregon. (See Isaac Levy biography.) The couple had three children in Oregon – Celia, Libbie and Isaac – before mov-ing to Tacoma in the early 1880s. William and his family lived in Old Tacoma, taking over the management of the Pacific Hotel from Meyer Kaufman.

In the fall of 1885 William led Tacoma's first publicized *Rosh Hashana* services, setting a pat-tern for the next decade. A month later Hannah's sister, Esther Levy, married Albert Weinberg. After Esther's sudden death William and Han-nah named their next child Esther. As the girls grew they participated in Jewish weddings and attended Harmony Club events.

William held office in the new congregation for several years, helped organize the Hebrew Benevolent Society, and in 1890 served as the first president of the Judith Montefiore Society. He also began leading Passover services, assist-ed by Morris Bloom.

After the 1893 banking panic the Wolff fami-ly moved to Oakland, California, where William died in 1903. Hannah died in San Francisco in 1923. Their eldest daughter, Celia (1875–1926) married Joseph Levy in 1898 and had three chil-dren: Bertha, Walter, and Ellis. Libbie (1881–1946) married Max F. Goldsmith in 1901 and also had three children: Beatrice, William and Her-bert. Isaac (1881–1919) married Birdie Moses in 1906 and had two sons: William and Herbert. Esther (1884–1948) married William J. Brown about 1910 and apparently had no children.

Aaron and Lena Yehl

Aaron Yehl (c.1864–1925) was the third of nine children born in San Francisco to Abraham Yehl and Fannie Lowell. In 1887 Aaron married Lena Isaacs, daughter of Michael and Johanna Isaacs. (See Isaacs biography.) The following year Arthur Lewin opened a cigar store in Taco-ma, and Aaron and his brother Samuel came to work in the store. When Lena's brother Alex got married in the summer of 1889, the newlyweds lived with the Yehl family until their home was completed. Aaron's siblings, Charles and Myrtle, also lived in Tacoma in 1890, working as clerks for various Jewish merchants.

On June 1, 1890, Aaron and Lena's daughter Hilda died at the age of ten months. Her grave in the Home of Peace Cemetery was unmarked until 1999. In the fall of 1890 Samuel Yehl sued his partner, Harry Baldwin, as their partnership in a cigar business crumbled. In 1891 Aaron briefly worked as manager of the California Provision Company, then returned to California. Aaron died in San Francisco in 1925, followed by Lena in 1945. They apparently had no more children.

Yudelson/Judelsohn Family

Bernhard Judelsohn (1862–1902) worked as a tailor in Tacoma beginning about 1896, employed by Latvian *landsmen* Julius Friedman and Hugo Stusser. Early directories listed his name as Birman Yudelson. He died unmarried in December of 1902 from consumption. His older brother, Peter Julius (Pesach Jehuda), joined him in Tacoma about a year before his death.

P.J. Yudelson was born April 7, 1860 in Libau, Russia – now Liepaja, Latvia. His parents were Hyman Judelsohn and Chane Jaffe. In the early 1880s P.J. married Bluma Stusser, daughter of Abe Stusser and Malla Friedman, and sister of Jennie and Mascha Stusser. (See Stusser biography.) Descendants relate that Bluma, born December 1, 1854, was attacked as a teenager and suffered a severe back injury. During her marriage Bluma gave birth to seven sons and five daughters, but only the daughters survived.

P.J. arrived in New York in November of 1901, accompanied by his 14-year-old daughter, Augusta (listed as "Gutta, aged 11) and his son Shlome, aged 10. (No further record has been found of his son.) P.J. reported that he possessed $12 and was going directly to Tacoma. In Tacoma P.J. worked as a tailor and later sold secondhand goods.

Bluma joined her husband in August of 1902, after being detained in New York for a week of special medical inquiry. She traveled with her four younger daughters – Betty (Beilah), Ida, Hazel (Hansa) and Emma (Esther.) All five daughters would find husbands in Washington, contributing to the next generation of Tacoma's Orthodox congregation. Bluma died in Tacoma on October 14, 1920. Over the next decade many little girls were given variations of "B" names in her memory.

PJ Yudelson Family c.1907, includes Augusta's husband Henry Molin
Courtesy of Jim Friedman

Augusta (1887–1983) married Henry Leo Molin (1880–1939) in 1907. The couple had six children – Morris, Abraham, H Edward, Burnett, Samuel, and Bea.

Betty (1891–1978) married Nathan Friedman (1880–1947) in 1909 and had three children – Cecil, Margaret, and Philip B.

Ida (1892–1969) married Frank Sussman (1880–1964) in 1910 and had three children – Philip, Molly, and Lorraine.

Hazel (1893–1982) married Abraham Saperstein (1887–1971) in 1921 and had two children – Harold, and Bea.

Emma (1894–1986) married Max Novikoff in 1918 and had four children – Mollie, Bea, Melvin and Harold.

Four days after the fifth wedding, P.J. married again, to Bessie Fisher. The couple lived in Tacoma through at least 1934. P.J. died in Seattle in 1939 and was buried next to Bluma in Tacoma.

Hyman and Rosalie Zelinsky

Hyman Zelinsky was born about 1830 in Prussia. He became a naturalized citizen in Douglas County, Oregon, in 1868. Around that time he married Rosalie Hirschfeld, born in Germany in 1839, sister of Emil Hirschfeld. The couple lived in Oakland, north of Rosebend, along with Hyman's nephew, Amil Zelinsky, in 1870. At least four children were born in Oregon in the 1870s – Jennie, Meta, Annie and Leo. The family returned to Germany for the birth of their son Louis (Ludy) in 1880.

Rosalie came back to the U.S. via Hamburg in June of 1881, traveling alone with five children under the age of 10. Hyman had likely come ahead. The family lived in Tacoma from 1883 until at least 1887 during which time Hyman operated a saloon in Old Tacoma. In November of 1883 Hyman voted for himself for school board. He was defeated by D.B. Hannah's two votes, and Howard Carr's three. The couple invested in real estate, as evidenced by multiple printed notices of deed transfers between the various Zelinsky and Wolff families.

Hyman registered to vote in San Francisco in 1890, claiming a height of five feet and one and a half inches. He died in San Francisco in October of 1897, followed by Rosalie in 1913. Their eldest daughter, Jennie (1875–1942), married Daniel Markowitz (1877–1953) and had a daughter Helen. Meta (1876–1951) married Sol Charmak (1874–1938) in 1899 and had two daughters – Dorothy and Louise. Louis (1880–1952) had a wife Alice.

Zelinsky Brothers – Amil, Solomon, Herman and Joseph

Hyman's brother, Wolff Zelinsky/Zielinski, and Pauline Selig had four sons in Soldau, Prussia, now Dzialdowo, Poland. Amil was born May 30, 1850; followed by Solomon on April 29, 1852; Herman on February 21, 1859; and Joseph on March 29, 1861. Wolff died in Soldau in 1888.

Amil immigrated first, living with his uncle Hyman in Oregon in the early 1870s. Both returned to Germany, where Amil married Adeline Wolff (1856–1898). Their son Henry was born in Germany in the fall of 1878. The young family returned to the U.S., leaving Hamburg in January of 1879. Daughters Meta and Ida were born in Oakland, California, in January of 1880 and in August of 1882. Adeline's sister, Paula/Pauline, traveled and lived with the couple. (See Wolff biography.)

Amil and family moved to Tacoma, where he operated the Mount Tacoma Grocery Store. During the summer of 1883 the framing of his new building blew over in a wind, but most of the lumber was salvaged. The store sold more than groceries. Newspaper ads in 1887 offered "Groceries, Feed, Crockery, glassware and general merchandise."

The family continued to grow, with the birth of Morris in August of 1884 and Frances in October of 1892. The family moved to Spanaway for about five years, then returned to Tacoma and reopened the grocery store. Adeline died in October of 1898, several weeks before the sixth birthday of her daughter, Frances. Two years later Amil filed a petition of voluntary bankruptcy, showing assets of $2,075 and liabilities of $6,414. His brother-in-law, A.J. Wolff, served as president of the grocery for the next few years. In 1906 Amil built a large warehouse.

On September 24, 1916, Amil's store was featured in an article in the *Tacoma Sunday News Ledger* as the oldest grocery store building in Tacoma. "Zelinsky began business in Old Town before there was any Tacoma, and has been in business ever since, 34 years. For many years his store, which is still called the Mount Tacoma grocery, was on the Old Town dock. Zelinsky knew every fisherman and waterfront character in Old Town." Amil died on November 6, 1925.

His son, Henry (1878–1930), lived his adult life in San Francisco. Meta (1880–1949), married Joseph Quintal (1882–1959) in Tacoma in 1919. Ida (1882–1931) did not marry. Morris (1884–1962) married Josephine and then Gertrude and had a daughter Maxine. The youngest, Frances (1892–1970), married George Washburn (1890–1958) in 1915 and had two children – Dolores and Robert.

Henrietta (Jette) Ascher and Solomon Zelinsky
Courtesy of Stanley Mamlock

Solomon Zelinsky joined his brother, Amil, in Tacoma in 1885, leaving his wife, Ida, in an asylum in New York. The couple had married in Germany in 1878 and had four children, who died while en route to New York. Solomon was granted a divorce in 1888, after months of negative newspaper publicity.

Solomon lived with Amil for several years and clerked for him in the grocery store. On July 26, 1890, Solomon married Henrietta (Jetta) Ascher, sister of Jennie Ascher Rammelsberg. The pair operated the Berlin Grocery after Amil moved to Spanaway, with Henrietta as president. Around 1912 they moved their grocery business from North 30th to the foot of McCarver Street. Henrietta died in 1916, followed by Solomon in 1922.

Only two of the couple's children survived – Hugo and Gertrude. Both had vision problems. Newspaper mentions of their childhood birthday parties typically included twenty-five or more family members. In June of 1916 Hugo (1892–1975) married Leah Rose Hirsch (1896–1971). The couple had four children – Adrian, Marcella, Marvin and Gerald. In 1921 Hugo legally changed his surname to Eidinger.

Gertrude (1894–1947) married Henry Mamlock (1884–1954) in 1919. They had four children – Henry, Stanley, Stella and Virginia. Stanley spent many years researching and recording the family's history. (See Mamlock biography.)

Joseph Zelinsky married Sophie Maretsky (1863–1937) in Germany about 1882. The couple had three children in Neidenberg – Benno, Leo and Fred, between 1884 and 1887. The following year Joseph moved to Tacoma, where he worked for his brother Herman, and later operated a poultry business at 23rd and Jefferson. Sophie joined him around 1892.

In 1895 Joseph was involved in a court case over the legal ownership of four chickens, valued at less than two dollars. Eventually the judge gave each party two of the chickens, along with a bill for $20 each in court costs and attorney fees. In 1900 Joseph was evicted from his business property.

Sophie and Joseph then sold secondhand goods, and the boys took jobs as delivery and elevator boys. Joseph died December 20, 1909, leaving Sophie to manage a rooming house. She moved to Butte, Montana, and then to Portland, Oregon, where she died in 1937. All three of her sons died in Portland – Ben in 1930, Leo in 1945, and Fred in 1949. None had any children.

Rosa Gutfeld and Herman Zelinsky,
with their son Walter, born 1889
Courtesy of Stanley Mamlock

Herman Zelinsky was the most colorful of the brothers. In 1885 he assisted as a teacher in Tacoma's German Turn Verein gymnasium and operated a grocery store on G Street with Fred Bogatz. The following year he won prizes for his Spanish and Hungarian costumes. On April 19, 1887, the *Ledger* reported that Herman had returned from Germany with a bride. (Perhaps a fiancée?) That fall he opened a grocery store at 501 Puyallup Avenue and was thereafter dubbed the "east side grocer" (later 311 East Twenty-fifth and 402 East Twenty-sixth). In February of 1888 Herman married Rosa Gutfeld, daughter of Morris and Rebecca Gutfeld. Their son Walter was born in July of 1889. A cluster of Gutfeld relatives soon lived in the neighborhood of his store. (See Gutfeld biography.)

In 1889 Herman joined the Hebrew Benevolent Society and in 1890 became an officer in Tacoma's new *B'nai B'rith* lodge. Rosa sporadically joined and rejoined the Judith Montefiore Society. Herman's name was occasionally published in conjunction with court cases, typically as plaintiff collecting accounts. He was known for his command of multiple languages, including the local Native American jargon.

In 1907 Herman's store building was moved to make way for rail yards. He took the opportunity to move to North Tacoma, building two homes on North Tacoma Avenue.

Rosa died in 1923 and was buried next to her mother in the Home of Peace Cemetery. When Herman died in 1943 he was buried in the Tacoma Mausoleum. Herman's son Walter (1889–1944) married Hannah Floberg (1890–1941) and had three children – Walter, Donald and Robert.

On July 4, 1911, Tacoma celebrated the nation's independence by hosting a "Parade of Nations." Several ethnic groups assembled and marched in one of the parades. The following poem, written by Harry H. Johnston and published in "The Scots Abroad the Nicht," indicated that Herman still enjoyed wearing costumes.

ZELINSKY

The Scotch parade was at its height,
The pipers blew with a' their might
As though to drown the noisy drums,
When lo a shout: "Great Scot, here comes
                              Zelinsky!"

'Midway adown the long parade
Of Scots, clad in a tartan plaid,
Oblivious how the people talked,
Or stared at him amazed, there walked
                              Zelinsky.

No turkey gobbler in its pride,
With wings outstretched on either side,
No pea-cock in its plumage hid
Could strut more gracefully than did
                              Zelinsky.

A group of Hebrew gentlemen
Had closed their shops to rubber when,
At sight of him they up and died,
But ere they rose they gasped and cried:
                              "Zelinsky!"

But one of them survived the shock;
Sam Andrews' heart was made of rock,
And yet Sam cried: "Mein Gott, mein Gott!
How could our Herman be a Scot?
                              Zelinsky!"

It may be that he heard their cries,
It may be tears bedimmed his eyes
To see his Jewish friends throw fits—
Said he: "They'll long remember it's
                              Zelinsky."

Scots wha hae wi' Wallace bled!
There's few dare go where you would tread,
And yet you will concede this much,
It takes some nerve to beat the Dutch
                              Zelinsky.

(Parade of Nations, Tacoma, Wash., July 4, 1911)

Courtesy of Tacoma Public Library

Bibliography

Blackwell, Ruby Chapin. *A Girl in Washington Territory*. Tacoma: Washington State Historical Society, 1972.

Bonney, W. P. *History of Pierce County, Washington*. Chicago: Pioneer Historical Publishing Company, 1927.

Calvert, Frank. *The Cartoon: A Reference Book of Seattle's Successful Men*. Seattle: Metropolitan Press, 1911.

Cartoons and Caricatures of Seattle Citizens. Seattle: Associated Cartoon Service, 1906.

Choir, Melody. *Choir's Pioneer Directory of the City of Seattle and King County, History, Business Directory, and Immigrant's Guide to and Throughout Washington Territory and Vicinity*. Pottsville, Pennsylvania: Miners' Journal Book and Job Rooms, 1878.

Cone, Molly, Howard Droker and Jacqueline Williams. *Family of Strangers: Building a Jewish Community in Washington State*. Seattle: Washington State Jewish Historical Society, 2003.

Curtis, Joan, Alice Watson, Bette Bradley and Steilacoom Historical Museum Association. *Town on the Sound: Stories of Steilacoom*. Steilacoom, Washington: Steilacoom Historical Museum Association, 1988.

Edmonson, Barbara. *Historic Shotglasses: The Pre-Prohibition Era*. Chico, California: B. Edmonson, 1992.

Eidsmoe, W. Burton. *The Keystone of Tacoma: A Guide to Selected Homes and Prominent Buildings in the Stadium-Annie Wright Historical District, 1887–1906*. Tacoma: W. B. Eidsmoe, 1990.

Eker, Glen. *Jewish Residents of Western Canada in the 1870–1901 Censuses of Canada*. Guelph, Ontario: G. Eker, 1994.

Emanu-El Congregation, San Francisco. *Papers and Documents, 1854–1900*. Berkeley: Judah L. Magnes Museum.

Eulenberg, Julia Niebuhr. "Jewish Enterprise in the American West: Washington, 1853–1909." PhD diss., University of Washington, 1996.

Faulkinbury, Jim W. "The San Francisco Call Database – Index." *Jim W. Faulkinbury, CG^SM: Genealogical Research Services*. Accessed May 22, 2016. http://www.jwfgenresearch.com/sfcallindex.htm.

Freedman, Deb. *Beginnings and Endings – Home of Peace Cemetery Inscriptions*. Tacoma: Genfreed Press, 1998.

Frontier Justice Records Project (Washington). *Frontier Justice: Guide to the Court Records of Washington Territory, 1853–1889*. Olympia, Washington: National Historical Publications and Records Commission, 1987.

Gates, Charles M. *Readings in Pacific Northwest History: Washington, 1790–1895*. Seattle: University Bookstore, 1941.

Hildebrand, Lorraine. *Straw Hats, Sandals, and Steel: The Chinese in Washington State*. Tacoma: Washington State American Revolution Bicentennial Commission, 1977.

Hunt, Herbert. *Tacoma, its History and its Builders: A Half Century of Activity*. 3 vols. Chicago: S. J. Clarke Publishing Company, 1916.

Janton, Moses N. *The History of the Jews in Spokane, Washington: From the Early Days Until the Present Time*. Spokane, Washington: M N. Janton, 1926.

Leonoff, Cyril Edel. *Pioneers, Pedlars, and Prayer Shawls: The Jewish Communities in British Columbia and the Yukon*. Victoria: Sono Nis Press, 1978.

Libo, Kenneth and Irving Howe. *We Lived There, Too: In Their Own Words and Pictures – Pioneer Jews and the Westward Movement of America, 1630–1930*. New York: St. Martin's/Marek, 1984.

Lowenstein, Steven. *The Jews of Oregon, 1850–1950*. Portland, Oregon: Jewish Historical Society of Oregon, 1987.

Lyons, Bettina. *Zeckendorfs and Steinfelds: Merchant Princes of the American Southwest*. Tucson: Arizona Historical Society, 2008.

Mallandaine, Edwd. *First Victoria Directory, Second Issue, and British Columbia Guide: Comprising a General Directory of Business-men and Householders in Victoria and the Districts: Including a Large Portion of the Mainland of British Columbia: Also, an Official List of Postal Arrangements, Custom House Tariff and Municipal Bye-Laws, With Prefatory Remarks on the Commerical and Political Prospects of the Colony*. Victoria, British Columbia: E. Mallandaine, 1868.

- *First Victoria Directory, Fifth Issue, and British Columbia Guide: Comprising a General Directory of Businessmen and Householders in Victoria: With Full Lists of Every Important District in the Province: With Preface and Statistics, 1874.* Victoria, British Columbia: E. Mallandaine, 1874.

Mamlock, Stanley M. "The Henry M. Mamlock Family History." Tacoma, 1989.

Mason, Jesse D. *History of Amador County, California, With Illustrations and Biographical Sketches of its Prominent Men and Pioneers.* Oakland, California: Thompson & West, 1881.

McKenney, L. M. *Business Directory of San Francisco and Principal Towns of California and Nevada, 1877.* San Francisco: L. M. McKenney, 1877.

Meier, Gary and Gloria Meier. *Brewed in the Pacific Northwest: A History of Beer-Making in Oregon and Washington.* Seattle: Fjord Press, 1991.

Murphy & Harned. *Puget Sound Business Directory, and Guide to Washington Territory, 1872 Comprising a Correct History of Washington Territory, and a Condensed But Comprehensive Account of Her Agricultural, Commericial and Manufacturing Interests, Climatology, Mineralogy, Inhabitants, Natural Advantages and Industries, Together With a Complete and Thorough Directory of Olympia, Steilacoom, Seattle, Port Madison, Port Gamble, Port Ludlow, Port Townsend, and Every Town and Hamlet on Puget Sound.* Olympia: Murphy & Harned, 1872.

Narell, Irena. *Our City: The Jews of San Francisco.* San Diego: Howell-North Books, 1981.

Newell, Gordon R. *Rogues, Buffoons & Statesmen: The Inside Story of Washington's Capital City and the Hilarious History of 120 Years of State Politics.* Seattle: Superior Publishing Company, 1975.

Notable Men of Washington. Tacoma: Perkins Press, 1912.

Portland Blue Book and Pacific Coast Elite Directory. San Francisco: Bancroft Company, 1890.

Prosser, William Farrand. *A History of the Puget Sound Country, Its Resources, Its Commerce and Its People: With Some Reference to Discoveries and Explorations in North America from the Time of Christopher Columbus Down to that of George Vancouver in 1792.* New York: Lewis Publishing Company, 1903.

R.L. Polk & Co., Publishers. *R.L. Polk & Co.'s Tacoma City Directory.* 1885–1920.

Ripley, Thomas Emerson. *Green Timber: On the Flood Tide to Fortune in the Great Northwest.* New York: Ballentine, 1972.

Rochlin, Harriet and Fred Rochlin. *Pioneer Jews: A New Life in the Far West.* Boston: Houghton Mifflin, 1984.

Rosenbaum, Fred. *Visions of Reform: Congregation Emanuel and the Jews of San Francisco, 1849–1999.* Berkeley: Judah L. Magnes Museum, 2000.

Schwartz, Lois Fields. *The Jews of Ligonier: An American Experience.* Fort Wayne: Indiana Jewish Historical Society, 1978.

Sketches of Washingtonians: Containing Brief Histories of Men of the State of Washington Engaged in Professional and Political Life, in Manufacture, Commerce, Finance and Religion: With a Summary of the Cities of the State Containing Upwards of 5,000 Population. Seattle: W. C. Wolfe & Company, 1907.

Speelman, Mary Jane. "Pioneers Who Settled on Fort Lewis, March 1982." Assignment for Dr. Margaret Gribskov, Evergreen State College. Washington State Library, 1982.

Tacoma Daily News. Tacoma, Washington, 1883–1886.

Tacoma Daily Ledger. Tacoma, Washington, 1883–1937.

Ward, Kirk C. *Business Directory of the City of Seattle for the Year 1876. Comprising a History of the First Settlement, After Development, and Present Population and Business of the City.* Seattle: B. L. Northup, Printer, 1876.

Wirsing, Dale R. *Builders, Brewers, and Burghers: Germans of Washington State.* Olympia: Washington State American Revolution Bicentennial Commission, 1977.

Index

~ Notes~